Discovering India Anew

Discovering India Anew

Out of Africa to its Early History

Alan Machado (Prabhu)

Orient BlackSwan

DISCOVERING INDIA ANEW: OUT OF AFRICA TO ITS EARLY HISTORY

ORIENT BLACKSWAN PRIVATE LIMITED

Registered Office
3-6-752 Himayatnagar, Hyderabad 500 029, Telangana, India
e-mail: centraloffice@orientblackswan.com

Other Offices
Bengaluru, Chennai, Guwahati, Hyderabad,
Kolkata, Mumbai, New Delhi, Noida, Patna

First published by Orient Blackswan Private Limited 2024
This paperback edition 2024

ISBN 978-93-5442-837-1

Typeset in
Adobe Caslon Pro 11.5/13.25
by Manmohan Kumar, Delhi

Printed in India at
Replika Press Pvt. Ltd.

Published by
Orient Blackswan Private Limited
3-6-752 Himayatnagar, Hyderabad 500 029, Telangana, India
e-mail: info@orientblackswan.com

Contents

List of Tables and Figures	vii
List of Abbreviations	ix
Glossary	xi
Timeline	xiii
A Few Words Before We Begin	xv
1. India's First Humans	1
2. Climate Change – Shaping Hominid Evolution	11
3. Populating the Earth – The Story Told by Bones and Stones	18
4. Populating the Earth – The Genetic Story	28
5. South Asia – The Genetic Story	39
6. Tales Languages Tell	63
7. Foraging to Farming	77
8. Foragers – The Retreat	94
9. Discovering a Buried Past	110
10. Timelines and the Elam Connection	120
11. Harappa – An Overview	131
12. The Beginnings	143
13. The Maturing	149
14. The Mechanisms of Control	170
15. The Decline and Dispersal	182
16. Bronze Age Eurasia	191
17. Expansion of Indo-European Speakers	205
18. The Indo-Iranian Speakers	214
19. The Early *Arya* in South Asia	231
20. Fashioning a New Order	251
21. A Forgotten History and a Lost River	269
Notes	291
Bibliography	296
Index	326

Tables and Figures

Tables

1.1:	Stone tool evolutionary stages	2
1.2:	Marine Isotope Stages (MIS)	4
5.1:	South Asian mtDNA Hgs percentages	41
5.2:	Percentage of C-M130 in Tamil tribal groups	48
5.3:	A summing-up	62
7.1:	Domestication of plants and animals globally	82
7.2:	Chronology of domestication of plants and animals in South Asia	85
10.1:	Harappa – Mesopotamia – Elam timeline	128
13.1:	Harappan sites and areas	158
15.1:	Harappan site counts	185
15.2:	Site counts in Cholistan	185
15.3:	Growth and decline of Harappan settlement sizes	186
21.1:	Comparison of Sutlej, Yamuna, and Ghaggar rivers	278

Figures

3.1:	Oldowan pebble tool	21
3.2:	Acheulian handaxe	21
3.3:	Mousterian	21
3.4:	Core and flake	21
3.5:	Routes out of Africa	24
4.1:	Simplified mtDNA tree and main regional presence	29
4.2:	Spread of mtDNA haplogroups M, N, R	29
4.3:	Simplified Y-chromosome tree	30
4.4:	Spread of Y-chromosomes	30

5.1:	AASI-ASI-ANE admixture diagram	43
5.2:	South Asian Y-chromosome haplogroups	46
5.3:	Out-of-Africa – the Middle Palaeolithic	47
5.4:	The Upper Palaeolithic: The Microlithic revolution	50
5.5:	Neolithic migrations from the east	53
5.6:	Immigrations from the west-Iranian farmers	55
5.7:	The expansion of the Yamnaya and their descendants	57
6.1:	Probable pre-Indo-Aryan language map of South Asia	67
7.1:	South Asian macro regions of primary domestication and encounter with secondary domesticates	84
11.1:	Early Harappan site concentration	133
11.2:	Mature Harappan site concentration	134
11.3:	Late Harappan site concentration	135
13.1:	Overland and sea trading routes connecting Harappa with Mesopotania	157
17.1:	Expansion of Yamnaya Steppe pastoralists into Europe and Asia	207
17.2:	Expansion of Indo-European languages	209

Abbreviations

AAA	Ancestral Austro-Asiatic
AASI	Ancient Ancestral South Indian
aDNA	ancient DNA
ANI	Ancestral North Indian
ASI	Ancestral South Indian
ATB	Ancestral Tibeto-Burman
BCE	Before the Common Era
BMAC	Bactria-Margiana Archaeological Complex
BP	Before the Present
EBA	Early Bronze Age (c3500–2300 BCE)
MBA	Middle Bronze Age (c2300–1500 BCE)
LBA	Late Bronze Age (c1500–1200 BCE)
CE	Common Era
Hg	haplogroup
ka	thousand years ago
LGM	Last Glacial Maximum
Ma	million years ago
MIS	Marine Isotope Stage(s)
mtDNA	mitochondrial DNA
OIA	Old Indo-Aryan
SNAC	Southern Neolithic Archaeological Complex
SRTM	Space Shuttle Radar Topography Mission

Glossary

arya	the identifying term used by Indo-Iranians to describe their elite/noble status
aryavarta	land of aryas
dakshinapatha	southern route/s leading from north and west to peninsular India
dasas/ dasyus	inhabitants of the northwest before the arrival of Indo-Aryan speakers
devayajana/ mahavedi	sacred spaces of the soma sacrificial ritual area
haoma/ soma	a mildly intoxicating drink used in Vedic/ Avestan rituals
jana	tribal in modern terminology
jati	caste
mleccha	people who did not speak Aryan languages or practise Vedic rituals
mleccha-desa	lands where non-Aryan languages were spoken and Vedic rituals not observed
mannerbunde	roving war-band of young unmarried elite males in Indo-European society
nisada	'tribal' in modern terminology
purohit	priest
rakshasa	demonised forest dweller; from *raksha* – protect (forest); synonym of *asura*
rta/ arta	natural law governing the regular operation of the universe
sattras	mid-winter sacrificial rituals held in forests
sur	activity to produce; synonym of *deva*, opposite of *asur*
uttarapatha	northern route leading to/through the Ganges basin
vajra	mace, thunderbolt
yajnas/yasnas	sacrifice ritual (Vedic, Avestan)
yupa	post to which the sacrificial animal was tied in the Vedic soma sacrifice

Timeline

195–160 ka	Omo Kibish/Herto humans in Ethiopia
130–120 ka	Skhul-Qafzeh humans in the Levant
125–108 ka	Early humans in Thar Desert
85–74 ka	Early humans in Jurreru Valley
74 ka	Toba super eruption
70–50 ka	Out-of-Africa event – Hg C and D in South Asia
47 ka	Hg F exits Arabia and reaches Europe, eastern Asia, South Asia
47–30 ka	Hgs H, L-M20, and R2 in South Asia
35 ka	Microlithic technology extensively used in Jurreru Valley
9 ka onwards	Hgs O, J, L-M11in South Asia
8.2 ka	Onset of global mega drought
7000–5500 BCE	Early Food Producing Era – Mehrgarh
5500–2600 BCE	Early Harappan
3000–2700 BCE	Yamnaya (Pit Grave) culture – Pontic-Caspian steppe
2600–2500 BCE	Transition from Early to Mature Harappan
2500–1900 BCE	Mature Harappan
2200–1900 BCE	onset of global mega drought – 4.2 ka event
1900–1300 BCE	Late Harappan
Post-2000 BCE	Hg R1a in South Asia
2050–1750 BCE	Sintashta (Timber Grave) culture – Southern Urals
1900–1200 BCE	Andronovo culture – Central Asia
1500 BCE	Rgveda

A Few Words Before We Begin

Where does one begin to tell a story that spans many thousands of years, a story whose origins are obscured by stubborn mists that will not lift and enduring myths that will not shift under the weight of ages of telling? Where does one begin unravelling the history of India and its peoples?

There have been many beginnings in the telling of the story depending on who told it, when and why. Different yardsticks have been used: myth, bias, selective readings and interpretations. Stripped of all this, there is and can be only one beginning. Today, a host of disciplines and technologies, many of them recent developments, are being applied to uncover and write the history of India and Indians. The story they tell begins in Africa. Indian history, or to be more precise, the history of Indians begins in Africa about 200,000 years ago.

That, however, was not what I was taught in school. The history of India that I was taught, some fifty-odd years ago, was based on Rawlinson's *A Concise History of the Indian People*. India had just emerged from Britain's colonial shadow, and that long shadow stretched over the version of history Britain wished Indians to learn. Rawlinson's book is far more enlightening on Britain's purpose than on India's history. It is 400 pages long, of which a little short of half is devoted to 'Modern India', the age of European colonialism. A hundred pages are devoted to 'Medieval India', the period of Indo-Muslim rule and the rest to 'Ancient India'. Except for a passing reference to the Portuguese, the European period is devoted solely to Britain's activities. It covers 350 years, from 1600 to 1947, and the 'Medieval' period a little over 600 years. Rawlinson dismisses all of India's history until the Vedic age in just six pages. Today we know that *that* history begins at least 70,000, perhaps 130,000 years, ago. How many pages would be required to cover that?

I found Rawlinson's narrative of the colonial period, even in those tender years, sad, boring and dispiriting, the medieval period a little more interesting. The ancient period was so remote, sketchy and vague that there was no doubt in my young mind that there was very much more, and that intrigued and impelled me to find out more. At that time, I did not know how far back India's history stretched, but the moment I stepped out of the classroom, tantalising hints of its antiquity emerged in the faces, languages, names and diversity of the people you met on the street and every corner of the cities, towns and villages. Besides temples to a host of gods and goddesses were ancient stones sculpted with entwined serpents daubed in vermilion and saffron, giant banyan and peepal trees encircled with strings, little unrecognisable idols honoured in house and shop corners for a few moments every morning then neglected until the following day, and messages sculpted on ancient granite by some forgotten Indian many, many years ago, weathered and lying by the wayside. The great curtain, heavy and opaque, which obscured those early formative years of India's past remained tightly drawn, fluttering a little here and there to reveal a fleeting glimpse of what might lie beyond. It was termed proto- or pre-history, and it did not cease to beckon.

Britain's version of ancient Indian history depended to a large extent on literary sources. It began with the 'Aryans', a 'tall, fair people, with long, straight, noses, and regular features … who came from the colder climates of the north and were therefore more hardy and vigorous', qualities that soon enabled them to gain dominance over the local dark-skinned, flat-nosed *dasyu*s (inhabitants of the northwest before the arrival of Indo-Aryan speakers) (Rawlinson 1938: 12–13). The 'Aryans', like the British, brought civilisation to India, or so Britain wanted us to believe. The colonial administration adapted laws laid down in Vedic texts in framing laws for all Indians other than Muslims, Christians, Buddhists, Jains and Sikhs. It then clubbed the numerous castes, tribals and others together as one religious community, Hindus. By doing so, and projecting themselves as inheritors of 'Aryan' elitism, Britain sought another way of legitimising its own elite rule over India.

Ironically, it struck a chord in some Indians who saw in the 'Aryans' an identity that could place them on par with their colonial rulers. They vociferously supported the theory of 'Aryan' origin of Indian civilisation and sought to benefit from it by claiming to be their inheritors. And in distant Germany, Indologists discovered long-lost roots in 'Aryan' traditions and used it to construct a national character, ancient and superior. A century or so later, it led to disastrous consequences for Europe and large parts of the world.

Then, in the 1920s, archaeologists unearthed Harappa. Its discovery extended Indian history a few thousand years into the past and undermined the perception of the Vedic age as the fount of Indian civilisation. Harappa in turn takes us to the beginning of the Neolithic and the food-producing economy in northwest South Asia. It marks the beginning of the time when Indians began to adopt a sedentary lifestyle with increasing numbers living in close proximity. It required them to evolve and accept a very different social code from that of their hunter-gatherer forefathers to prevent conflict and work together.

Humans co-operate and work together in groups of up to about 150. Beyond this number, it becomes difficult to maintain cohesion and unity. To make this possible, humans have developed something unique that no other species have, something called 'imagined reality'. It belongs to the realm of myth and a world beyond the natural, of unseen forces, ideologies and symbolisms. It is a key development in human behaviour that allows the formation of large cohesive groups to bond and work together. It is fed by another vital trait of human evolution, the capability of absorbing and transmitting large quantities of information about the world they live in. These developments have allowed humans to colonise vast and varied habitats that have resulted in an immense diversity of elaborate behavioural patterns which are the main components of cultures. Cultures evolve and adapt to changing situations; these developments make history (Harari 2011: 41).

The first evidence of the large-scale and effective use of this human creation of the mind is found at Gobekli Tepe. Here hunter-gatherer groups, not sedentary farmer populations, came together to build what have been considered as the first temples. The gathering of hitherto mobile hunter-gatherer groups was made possible by the localised growth of a new and abundant food source with the onset of the benign climate of the Holocene, einkorn wheat. The construction of Gobekli Tepe required vision and purpose, many years of dedicated labour, the close co-operation of groups of hunter-gatherers and the transmission of large bodies of technical information.

Harappa too was built, though a few millennia later, by local hunter-gatherer populations with some influence from Iran and Mesopotamia. For 700 years, a time span ten times greater than that covering the period of independent India, an elite culture unified a vast territory that was inhabited by a large and diverse population with many regional traits. Populations develop close affinity to the geographical space they inhabit, to its food sources, micro-climate and other unique features to evolve regional ethnic identities. In the age of hunter-gatherers with each group inhabiting a limited territorial range, the number of such identities in the greater Harappan region would have been very many. Many regional languages would have been spoken. Yet, there was one script and one set of commercial practices utilising standard weights, stamp seals and iconography that introduced an overall uniformity over regional and local diversity. For instance, while urban centres were built with a recognisably similar architecture throughout, bricks were predominantly used in Sindh and the Punjab, while Gujarat relied on stones. Haryana grew wheat and barley, Gujarat adapted to its drier climate with millets and pastoralism.

What kept these diversified peoples together for over 700 years despite their many regional features? There is no credible evidence for the use of military force or other forms of coercion.

Could these diversified regions, spread over an area greater than that of Egypt and Mesopotamia combined, have developed a multi-level working relationship that allowed free expressions of multi-regional diversity within an overall unified framework for mutual benefit? If so, there are many lessons that modern India can learn from ancient Harappa.

In the last few decades, the secrets of India's past are being unearthed at an astonishing pace, and the focus has shifted from the earlier chronological narratives to thematic explorations. It involves a large number of researchers who apply a range of the latest scientific advances to generate a wealth of information that needs to be integrated with archaeological and literary sources to get a more complete picture. The horizons of Indian history have shifted from the 5,000-year time frame of the urban Harappan to beyond the 10,000 years of sedentary agro-pastoralism to perhaps 130,000 years of a mobile foraging hunter-gatherer culture. They have all influenced to various extents our present lifestyles and belief systems. They are all part of our history.

How does one write it? We are but individuals exploring a vast darkness with tiny torches. The poem 'The Blind Men and the Elephant' composed by John Godfrey Saxe in 1872, a poem I learnt in school along with Rawlinson's history, comes to mind. To each blind man, touching a different part of the animal, unable to see the whole, the elephant appeared very different: a wall, a spear, a snake, a tree, a fan, a rope. The poet concludes:

> And so these men of Indostan
> Disputed loud and long,
> Each in his own opinion
> Exceeding stiff and strong,
> Though each was partly in the right,
> And all were in the wrong!

India has been 'discovered' numberless times. From the very first humans who traversed the Thar to reach its richly forested heartland to the dreamy-eyed hippies listening to gentle waves lapping the sun-washed beaches of Goa, many have travelled from different parts of the globe in search of its soul: Persians, Greeks, Romans, Chinese, Arabs, Europeans. They all discovered and recorded a small part of an immensely diverse history. This 'rediscovery', therefore, is just one of many; India's history offers scope for many more.

Finally, in writing this book, I must acknowledge the unstinted encouragement and active cooperation of my family, Alpa, Zara, Akil and Zina, and Roopa, my channel to Orient BlackSwan. Alpa's expertise has been invaluable in the design and technical execution of the maps and graphics. Thank you.

1

India's First Humans

Seventy-four thousand years ago, a resident of the Jurreru River Valley (henceforth Jurreru Valley, in Jwalapuram, Andhra Pradesh) stood on a hillock and stared with awe and trepidation at the enveloping darkness approaching from the east. Little did he know that it originated 2,700 kms away from the eruption of the super volcano Toba in Sumatra, or that his world would soon change dramatically, that his very survival was in jeopardy.

We do not know if that man survived the cataclysm; we do know that some of his compatriots did. They left their story for us to decipher in the form of stone tools. Some were excavated below Toba's primary ash layer that smothered the Jurreru Valley, some above. Both used the same technology, evidence that their makers had survived the catastrophe. Over 50,000 stone tools (scrapers, flakes, cores, burins and blades) designed for various applications have been recovered (Clarkson 2009, 2011). They tell us that they were manufactured with Middle Stone Age technology used by contemporary Middle Palaeolithic humans living in Africa and Arabia (Palaeolithic: old stone age; Neolithic: new stone age).

Stone tools tell remarkable stories of the evolutionary history of our hominid and hominin[1] ancestors and of the world they inhabited. Buried in the earth of India's deep south, in Tamil Nadu, is one such story sculpted in hard stone many millennia ago.

On 28 September 1863, Robert Foote discovered a hoard of Palaeolithic artefacts in a gully at Attirampakkam, near present-day Chennai. This cache, he wrote, was a testimony to the skills of ancient Indians in producing 'weapons and tools only by chipping hard stones of convenient size and shape with strikers made of other stones, so as to produce sharp edges and points that fitted them for many useful purposes' (Foote 1916: 1). Foote was not entirely correct in describing their makers as Indians and, therefore, modern humans. The earliest artefacts belonged to the Early Acheulean tradition fashioned 1.7–1.07 Ma by unindentified hominins, probably *Homo erectus*.

Attirampakkam's Middle Palaeolithic tools date to c385 ka, which is much earlier than the dissemination of this technology out of Africa by modern humans c125 ka (Akhilesh 2018). Whether this was a local development or an earlier dispersal out of Africa is not known. Microlithic artefacts on the surface mean the site continued to be occupied for many millennia, well into the time of modern humans.

Table 1.1: Stone tool evolutionary stages

Type	Era	Period	Maker
Oldowan choppers	Lower Palaeolithic	3 Ma–300 ka	*Ergaster, Erectus*
Acheulean handaxes	Lower Palaeolithic	3 Ma–300 ka	*Heidelbergensis*
Flakes, cores	Middle Palaeolithic	300 ka–40 ka	*Neanderthal, Sapiens*
Blades	Upper Palaeolithic	40 ka–10 ka	*Sapiens*
Microliths	Neolithic	Post–10 ka	*Sapiens*

Source: Compiled by author, based on various sources mentioned in-text.

Without conclusive fossil evidence, the identity of Attirampakkam's stone tool makers may never be known. Its stone tool legacy, though, does suggest a succession of dispersals across South Asia. The earliest hominin footprints on Indian soil were left in the northwest, a critical entry corridor from North Africa, Arabia and Central Asia. It is here that the oldest stone tools made by humans in South Asia have been found, in the Thar Desert, 2,000 kms to the north of Attirampakkam.

The Thar (Blinkhorn 2013a, 2013b, 2015, 2017; Petraglia 2011)

The Thar Desert forms the eastern edge of an arid belt that stretches from the Sahara to South Asia. It is located at the meeting point of two different climatic regions, the dry climate to its west and the tropical climate to its east. It covers an area of approximately 300,000 sq. kms of Rajasthan, Gujarat, and Sindh. Its western boundary is largely defined by the Indus and Ghaggar-Hakra (now seasonal) river systems. Upstream, they open wet corridors to the Gangetic basin, and downstream the path to Saurashtra and Gujarat, the west coast and the Deccan. In the past, the Thar underwent cyclical changes from intense aridity to enhanced humidity. During arid times, its deserts formed a near impenetrable barrier, but in wetter periods a dense network of rivers and lakes transformed the Thar into a hospitable environment that hominins used as a corridor into interior South Asia. Such a transformation occurred between 130–74 ka.

Core samples from the ocean floor provide a chronology of these alternating global cold and warm periods for over 2.6 million years. Called Marine Isotope Stages (MIS), these periods acted as triggers for human migrations.

More than 900 sites in the Thar have yielded stone tools from the Lower Palaeolithic (axes, choppers), Middle Palaeolithic (prepared cores, retouched small tools, refined heavy tools) and Late Palaeolithic (blades, microliths). Of interest here is the large number of Middle Palaeolithic sites, the most studied being 16R Dune in Rajasthan. Stone tools from here date to 125–108 ka. Katoati, 50 kms away, was repeatedly occupied by hominins from c96 ka.

Artefacts from both sites were made using technologies contemporary to those in North Africa and Arabia. It means that early *Homo sapiens* populations from those regions had reached South Asia at a time when they were also present in west Eurasia (Skhul-Qafzeh), Arabia (Dhofar, 107 ka; Jebel Faya, 123–95 ka), and China (Daoxian, Zhirendong). And, as similarly crafted stone tools beneath the Toba ash layer in the

Table 1.2: Marine Isotope Stages (MIS)

Stage	ka	Climate	Events
MIS 1	11.7–24	warmer	
MIS 2	24–60	cooler	last glacial maximum; Americas colonised
MIS 3	60–74	warmer	Upper Palaeolithic; out-of-Africa; Australia colonised
MIS 4	74–85	cooler	humans in Jurerru Valley; Mt Toba eruption
MIS 5a	85–93	warmer	
MIS 5b	93–106	cooler	
MIS 5c	106–115	warmer	humans at Skhul/Qafzeh; Katoati, Thar
MIS 5d	115–130	cooler	
MIS 5e	130–190	warmer	early modern humans leave Africa
MIS 6	190–243	cooler	Middle Palaeolithic; Omo Kibish, Herto humans

Source: Compiled by author, based on various sources.

Jurreru River Valley show, they had penetrated, via a series of habitable networks, deep into the heart of the Indian peninsula by MIS 5a (Clarkson 2011).

Dispersal Routes

The Indus, Ganges and Brahmaputra, with their sources in the Himalayas, form South Asia's largest river basins. The Aravallis, Vindhyas and the Western Ghats are source areas for other major rivers such as the Sabarmati, Narmada, Godavari, Krishna, Tungabhadra and Kaveri. Their basins, offering hospitable habitats with raw materials, water, plant and animal resources, became the key hominin dispersal routes into the interior (Korisettar 2011).

These habitats fall into a distinctive pattern of core, peripheral and isolated areas. Named the Purana-Gondwana basins, the core areas contain perennial fresh water sources, high floral and faunal biomass, and hard rocks used for stone tool manufacture. Their caves, rock-shelters and stream beds contain evidence of long-term hominin occupation. In wetter seasons, peripheral areas connected core areas. Isolated areas, characterised by a seasonal grass and scrubland ecosystem with poor water, food and raw material resources, were used to transit between favourable habitats.

There are seven Purana Basins and seven Gondwana Basins of diverse shapes and extent that connect the Aravallis in the west to the southeast coast of peninsular India. The largest Purana Basins are the Vindhyachal (60,000 sq. kms) and Cuddapah (45,000 sq. kms) basins. Others are the Chhattisgarh, Bastar, Pranhita-Godavari, Bhima and Kaladgi basins. The Gondwana basins are smaller and located mainly in the eastern part of the peninsula.

These habitable basins connect the northwest to the Jurreru Valley where stone tools preserve evidence of human occupation before the Toba super-eruption.

The Toba Super-eruption

The 74 ka super-eruption of the Toba volcano in north Sumatra is estimated to have blasted 2,800 cu kms of magma from its core, of which 800 cu kms comprised ash-fall deposits (Jones 2007: 173–200). Toba's ash blanketed large areas of India and Malaysia. It has been found in a number of river valleys throughout India, and in marine cores from the Indian Ocean, Bay of Bengal and Arabian and South China Seas. Ash deposits in Madhya Pradesh, Maharashtra, Odisha, Bihar, Andhra Pradesh and Uttar Pradesh range in thickness from 0.2 to 6 m.

The injection of such a vast amount of volcanic gas and dust into the atmosphere induced a devastating volcanic winter. Ice cores from Greenland identify a six-year-long peak in volcanic sulphate concentration c71 ± 5 ka, followed by a 200-year-long peak in calcium. It means large quantities of wind-blown dust, possibly caused by decreased vegetation cover and/or exposed sea beds, blew across continents and reached Greenland. Sulphuric acid vapours and atmospheric dust blocked sunlight, darkened the skies, and poisoned water bodies. It had damaging repercussions for global climate and environment. For a few years, land temperatures were lowered by 5–15 degrees C. Reduced rainfall caused mega-droughts. The Toba eruption could have caused a bottleneck which greatly reduced modern human diversity and population size.

The Jurreru Valley (Clarkson 2011; Groucutt 2015; Haslam 2010; Petraglia 2011)

The mean thickness of Toba ash across the Jurreru Valley is 1 m, and in low-lying areas up to 2.5 m. Stone tools buried beneath and above this ash tell a story. The earliest tools were Acheulean (axes and choppers) made by *Homo erectus* or *heidelbergensis* populations between 250–130 ka. In the millennia leading to the Toba eruption, they disappeared and were replaced by Middle Palaeolithic tools (blades and microliths), which suggests a gradual replacement of Acheulean hominins. Some of these sites date to MIS 5a. Around 50,000 Middle Palaeolithic artefacts (cores, hammer stones, retouched tools, flakes, blades) have been recovered from above and below the ash layer. An analysis of 867 cores from thirty global sites reveals that the core technology used by the Jurreru Valley hominins was similar to that used by early modern humans in sub-Saharan Africa, Southeast Asia and Australia. This implies that modern humans forming part of an early eastward dispersal from Africa were present in the Jurreru Valley before the Toba eruption.

There was a long period of continuity post-Toba until c35 ka when extensive blade and microlithic artefacts suggest the arrival of modern humans belonging to M and N mtDNA haplogroups. Today there is no genetic evidence of pre-M and N populations which suggests this encounter led to their eventual extinction. It is also possible that admixture between pre- and post-Toba populations resulted in a gradual replacement of pre-Toba genes.

A little after the Toba eruption, ash from the surrounding hill-slopes was re-deposited by wind and rain in the Jurreru valley burying much of its plant life and water bodies. Four major ash re-deposition episodes turned the valley into an inhospitable environment. Minor changes in post-Toba stone tool technology reveal that the valley continued to be inhabited by new groups who exhibited some behavioural differences from the earlier inhabitants. These groups most probably lived in less vulnerable areas nearby, such as hill ranges with running streams, and had not suffered as much. The population as a whole had escaped a major catastrophe.

In fact, there were few technological and behavioural changes immediately after Toba. Instead, there is strong technological continuity before and after the Toba eruption, with differences being less than 1%. The Jurreru Valley continued to be inhabited, and as its occupiers adapted to changing environments caused by climatic variations, there was a gradual evolution of technology until the major transition to microlithic technology c35 ka.

The Middle Son Valley

Toba deposits in India were first found not in the Jurreru Valley but in the Middle Son Valley in Madhya Pradesh. The source of the River Son lies near that of the Narmada. Both basins preserve a rich record of hominin occupation similar to the pre-Toba Jurreru pattern. The earliest artefacts, Acheulean hand axes and cleavers (c130 ka), were probably made by a species related to the oldest hominin fossil found in South Asia. This specimen is known from the fossilised skull cap of a large-bodied robust individual excavated in 1982 near Hathnora in the Narmada basin, *Homo erectus narmadensis*, tentatively identified as *Homo heidelbergensis* (Jones 2012). It lived sometime between 150–250 ka. To date the earliest confirmed human South Asian fossil, dated to c36 ka, comes from Sri Lanka's Batadomba-lena caves (Perera 2011).

Excavated fossils suggest that the Central Narmada valley may have been colonised by at least three other hominin species, two archaic and one early modern (Sankhyan 1997, 2013). Of the two archaic hominins, one was large-bodied and used Acheulean implements. A partial skullcap and a femur fossil (0.2–0.7 Ma) suggest a close relationship with *Homo heidelbergensis*. Two collar bones and a left rib belong to the other, a short, stocky, pygmy-sized hominin who lived c150 ka. A left humerus from the third hominin species is believed to be that of an early modern *Homo sapiens* who used Middle Palaeolithic implements (scrapers, drills, awls, burins, blades). Its location below the Toba ash layer and the age of related archaeological material date it to c80 ka. A skullcap found in sediments dating between 30–50 ka from the banks of the Orsang River in Gujarat, a tributary of the Narmada, may be the oldest *Homo sapiens* fossil recovered in South Asia. Its features suggest a close relation to the robust, large-brained *Homo erectus narmadensis* (Dambricourt-Malasse 2013). The age of the fossil, however, has been questioned as it may not be as old as the sediments it was found in (Clarkson 2011).[2]

Post-Toba, there was a notable shift in the technology and behaviour of Middle Son hominins which suggests the arrival of new hominins. Toba may have had a profoundly deleterious impact on the local environment. The pre-Toba climate appears to have been relatively wet and humid in a region with an active river network having a large catchment area. Toba ash deposits may have choked these waterways, shrank viable habitats, increased aridity and decreased temperatures. This would have severely impacted Middle Son populations. The evidence lies in the technology of stone tools above the ash layer. Unlike in the Jurreru Valley, there is no continuity. They were made by different populations who came from a different region, perhaps from outside India (Jones 2009).

The First Indians – What Happened to Them?

South Asia's modern population, like all global regions beyond Africa, bears the genetic signature of mtDNA haplogroups M and N, daughter clades of the African L3 haplogroup. They descend from a small population that left Africa not long after the Toba super-eruption, during a time of mega-drought and lowered sea levels. It is still unclear if the Toba super-eruption acted as the trigger. It is believed an extended Indian Ocean coast facilitated their fast eastward dispersal. Genetically, these humans belong to what has been termed the out-of-Africa dispersal (c70 ka). Their genetic codes persist in Indian populations today; those of pre-Toba humans do not.

South Asians harbour Denisovan [named after a cave in the Altai Mountains in southern Siberia where the first fossils of this species were found] ancestry. The result of this admixture was a reduction of male fertility (Sankararaman 2016).[3] Did something similar happen to the pre-Toba gene pool?

Archaeology confirms that modern humans were present in South Asia before the Toba eruption. The uniformity of stone tool technology from the Thar, Middle Son and Jurreru Valleys reveals they had colonised much of South Asia for thousands of years (Blinkhorn 2015; Haslam 2010; Mark 2013; Petraglia 2012b). This technology belonged to the Middle Palaeolithic era and had close similarities with that used by *Homo sapiens* in Africa and the Levant. As the evidence in the Jurreru Valley shows, they had survived the effects of the cataclysmic Toba super-eruption. The Jurreru Valley evidence also reveals a gradual, not abrupt, change to Late Palaeolithic technology. There was continuity in populations even if the change took place with the arrival of new influences.

2

Climate Change – Shaping Hominid Evolution

What has climate change got to do with Indian history? A lot, if not everything.

If Earth had not undergone extreme climate fluctuations in the past, humans would not have evolved as they did, and India would not have been populated in the manner it has been. Earth's climate depends on events that take place in the heavens. Many factors are involved, some with short-duration effects, some with long; some predictable, some not; some repeating to a pattern, some not. Perhaps the most regular pattern that has affected hominids over an extended period is that of alternating cold (glacial) and warm (interglacial) periods. For our distant ancestors, such changes posed both extreme challenges and great opportunities. Our history is a result of their responses. Today, we live in the benign Holocene interglacial period [the current geological epoch; *Holocene* from two Greek words meaning 'whole' and 'new'], which began 11.7 ka. Apart from being kind to mankind, the Holocene triggered the beginnings of farming and sedentary life, secure food surpluses and widespread population expansions. It irreversibly changed the way humans had lived since their first tentative footsteps close to 200 ka.

During glacial periods, gigantic ice sheets form and spread over large parts of the northern and southern hemispheres. With Earth's water locked in these ice sheets, ocean levels drop dramatically, sometimes by over 200 metres, causing reduced rainfall and changes in precipitation patterns. Long periods of severe drought ensue; forests turn to grasslands, grasslands to deserts. The pattern reverses in warm, wetter climates. Ice sheets melt and retreat, ocean levels rise, and increased rainfall turns deserts into grasslands and forests. One of the most well known of these patterns is known as the Milankovitch Cycles. They result from inherent cyclical variations in Earth's rotation about its axis and orbit around the sun. The Milankovitch Cycles repeat every 23,000, 41,000 and 100,000 years.

Earth rotates every twenty-four hours about an axis that is tilted 23.5 degrees to the plane of its orbit around the sun. This tilt causes the annual alternating pattern of summer and winter as Earth completes one revolution around the sun. This tilt is not constant but wobbles in a circular path that takes 23,000 years to complete. Further, every 41,000 years, this tilt varies from 22.5 to 24.5 degrees. Earth's orbit around the sun also undergoes changes. Every 100,000 years, it becomes slightly more and then less elliptical. These periodically varying cycles cause long-term changes in the amount of the sun's energy that reaches Earth. Intense hot and cold spells result.

The Milankovitch Cycles are just one of the heavenly forces at play. Earth is subjected to gravitational pulls and tugs from the planets as it orbits the sun. Every 400,000 years these effects get amplified, particularly in the East African Rift Valley which extends southward from the junction of the Red Sea with the Gulf of Aden. In a process that has been going on for millions of years, Africa is being ripped apart along the Rift, slowly, surely, inexorably. Massive geological forces beneath Earth's crust have been pulling a gigantic slice of Africa's eastern edge, from Ethiopia to Mozambique, away from the rest of the continent. Over the past ten million years, it has turned a relatively flat land into one of mountains and valleys. This geography has caused rapid and extreme fluctuations in climate. When Earth's orbit was most elliptical, intense rainfall formed deep lakes, extensive river networks, cool, moist forests and humid savannahs. At other times, the Rift Valley has turned dry and arid. Species that had adapted to the abundance of a green land had to adapt to dry, sere severity or perish. The instinct for survival triggered bodily responses. In hominids, it appears to have somehow led to a dramatic increase in brain size, and the evolution of modern humans (Maslin 2014).

The Rift Valley's thorny scrub is the repository of our very earliest forefathers's secrets, strewn across the Valley floor in places rarely frequented by humans today. This region is grudgingly yielding a treasure trove of hominid fossils to the painstaking pickaxe and brush of archaeologists bent under the hot sun. An ever-increasing number of dots on a map record the location of a bewildering range of hominid fossil finds: a fractured skull or thigh bone, an arm or rib or toe, and in rare cases, a skeleton of a biped who lay down millions of years ago to rest its tired muscles. From these, modern science is uncovering secrets of the history of our origins. As these fossils, bleached by the African sun for millennia, find new homes in museums and research institutes all over the world, the hominid tree grows taller and bushier.

Perhaps the find that generated the most excitement was the skeletal remains of a small chimpanzee-sized female who walked upright in East Africa about 3.5 Ma. Named Lucy, she belongs to the hominid species *Australopithecus afarensis*. As the momentous implications of the discovery in 1974 at the site of her death in Hadar, Ethiopia, sank in, the camp site erupted in celebration. The evening turned to night, the soft hues of twilight to a sparkling canopy above the primeval African bush. Adding to the chorus of crickets and frogs was a new tune played over and over again – the strains of the Beatles's hit song *Lucy in the Sky with Diamonds*. As in the song, Lucy had reappeared after an exhausting and mostly frustrating search: 'Lucy in the sky with diamonds ... Suddenly someone is there ... The girl with kaleidoscope eyes.' She remained for a little over two decades the most significant link to our hominid past.

Then the finds came fast and furious; they still come at regular intervals. They suggest four main stages in hominid evolution. The earliest position on the hominid tree belongs to the *Sahelanthropus* and *Ardipithecus* groups which lived 7–4 Ma. As they disappeared, the *Australopithecus* group emerged and continued for another two million years. About 2.7 Ma, the *Paranthropus* family appeared and walked on the African soil for another two million years. Our own species, *Homo*, emerged between 1.8 and 2.5 Ma. It includes *Homo habilis*, *rudolfensis*, *ergaster*, *erectus*, *heidelbergensis*, *neanderthalensis*, *floresiensis* and *sapiens*, which emerged just 200 ka.

Homo ergaster appeared in our evolutionary tree 1.8 Ma in East Africa when it was under the grip of an extended dry spell. The land was arid and sere, yellow and brown under arching blue, with withering savannah and scrub clinging to the boundaries of depleting water bodies. Representing a fundamental turning point in hominin evolution, *Homo ergaster* possessed an upright-walking, gracile anatomy similar to that of modern humans, a body that suggests life on the plains rather than trees. The best-known skeletal remains of this species belonged to a boy who lived on the shores of Lake Turkana in East Africa. The skeleton suggests marked life-style and body changes that shortened intervals between births, allowed the throwing of projectiles, improved locomotion and facilitated long-distance running.

The most important change was a progressive evolution towards an increased brain size. Lucy had a brain size of 400 cc, ergaster 800 cc and heidelbergensis 1200 cc. The brain size of modern humans is 1600 cc. Such a transformation involved complex developments and adaptation to new ecological conditions. A principal factor in this metamorphosis involved a change to a high-quality diet, and the evolution of complex social interactions and behaviour. Lucy's pot-belly was a result of a predominantly vegetarian diet: edible grasses, leaves, fruits. Such diets require large stomachs to extract nutrition and much of the body's energy is diverted to the stomach to complete the process of digestion. The severe depletion of plant food resources caused by prolonged drought turned *Homo ergaster* into an opportunistic hunter-gatherer, or perhaps scavenger, who expanded their diet to include meat and shellfish. Both are easier to digest than plant resources, and provide high energy from small quantities. Excess energy can be used elsewhere. In the case of *Homo ergaster/erectus*, this energy was used for brain enlargement. The modern human brain consumes a considerable portion of the body's energy intake.

The adoption of a meat and sea-food supplementary diet played a fundamental and crucial role in human evolution. It laid the foundation of much of modern human interactions. In hunting and scavenging migratory herds, humans were forced to traverse large distances. This influenced body growth and strength. The legs and arms strengthened, the gut grew smaller and energy was released for a growing brain. Greater complexity in social behaviour and adaptability to different environments allowed migrations and colonisation of new worlds. Life expectancy increased, group male-bonding, communication skills, mother-child bonds and the protection of territorial and food resources assumed priority and stone tool technology evolved to harvest meat and skins (Foley 2001, n.d.).

The increase in brain size has a remarkable link to the 400,000-year cycle of warmer periods. There were dramatic increases 1.9 Ma and 200 ka when transitory deep-water lakes formed in the Rift Valley (Maslin 2014). Wet spells assured food security; populations grew and expanded into new territories. During dry spells, food grew scarce; populations declined and ventured into new areas in search of food. Alternating wet and dry spells acted as a pump, pushing populations further and further afield from the Rift Valley, the birthplace of modern humans.

Archaeological evidence indicates at least three pre-sapiens migratory waves out of Africa between 1.8–0.7 Ma (Bar-Yosef 2001). The earliest made Oldowan stone tools and crossed into Eurasia around 1.7–1.6 Ma. They were followed by *Homo ergaster*, Acheulean stone tool makers who colonised parts of Eurasia, around 1.4 Ma. In west Asia, ergaster evolved into *Homo georgicus*, and in east Asia, into *Homo erectus*, a species that reached Java and China (Java/Peking Man) and south India. The numerous samples of bifacial cleavers found at Attirampakkam in Tamil Nadu record the presence of *Homo erectus* there 1.5-1.4 Ma (Pappu 2011, n.d; Bar-Yosef 2013). The third wave involved more advanced Acheulean tool makers. Around 800 ka, *Homo heidelbergensis*, probably descending from *Homo ergaster*, appeared in Asia and Europe. In west Asia and Europe, it evolved into the Neanderthal lineage some 500 ka, and in Africa, into early *Homo sapiens*.

The earliest *Homo sapiens* fossils come from Omo Kibish (c195 ka) and Herto (c160 ka) in Ethiopia. These humans lived around fresh water lakes and butchered large mammal carcasses, especially hippopotami, with stone axes and flakes. The region lies about 200 kms north of Lake Turkana into which the Omo River flows from the Ethiopian highlands. This, the birthplace of human culture, was no Garden of Eden. Predatory animals, insects and inimical bacteria preyed on human flesh. It was a place for foraging and scavenging at day, always on the look-out for danger, and a place of hiding from hungry beasts and unseen terrors at night. It was a place of shattering injuries and short lives, of precarious existence without any dreams for the morrow. It was the home of our forefathers.

From here, humans made multiple dispersals into Asia (Beyin 2011, 2015). Between 150–130 ka, early modern humans crossed the Red Sea at the Bab al-Mandab Strait into Arabia with Middle Stone Age technology. Jebel Faya in the UAE preserves evidence of their presence from c127 ka. Only stone tools have been found here, no fossils. Thousands of kilometres away, separated from Jebel Faya by desert, mountain and forest, the caves of Zhirendong in south China preserve a few ancient human teeth. They date to over 100 ka.

A branch of this or another dispersal took humans across the Sinai to the Levant in southwest Asia between 130–90 ka. Their skulls and bones along with the stone tools they made have been found in the Skhul-Qafzeh caves in Israel. No genetic material that can identify these groups has been recovered. The earliest genetic material comes from a later dispersal (80–60 ka) that is believed to have colonised a vast territory stretching through South and Southeast Asia to Australia. It is thought to have been a rapid dispersal that crossed the Bab al-Mandab Strait into Arabia and journeyed along an extended Indian Ocean coastline caused by reduced sea levels during the glacial period. These humans belonged to M and N mtDNA haplogroups to which all non-Africans belong. Around 47 ka, Earth was freed from the grip of freezing ice sheets. Routes to the north were opened and humans moved out again, via Sinai into the Levant, and from the Arabian Peninsula into Asia. It wasn't long before they had reached all regions of Earth.

3

Populating the Earth – The Story Told by Bones and Stones

Bones, stones, and genes mark the human journey out of Africa.

Bones

The Skhul-Qafzeh caves in the Levant, a crossroads to three continents, Europe, Africa and Asia, are the repository of the earliest human fossils and stone tool kits outside Africa. They date to 130–120 ka. The skeletal remains found here suggest that these humans had evolved in a warmer African climate. Alongside them were Neanderthal fossils. Humans and Neanderthals co-existed in the Levant until 75–70 ka, competing for food and shelter, admixing and exchanging ideas. Then, possibly as a result of the Toba super-eruption, the climate turned colder. The cold-adapted Neanderthals continued to occupy the Levant; the Skhul-Qafzeh humans either abandoned it or became extinct. Humans re-appeared in the Levant only c47 ka (Kramer 2001; Petraglia 2010).

From the eastern end of Eurasia, forty-seven human teeth (120,000–80,000 years old) excavated in the Fuyan Cave in Daoxian, South China, reveal that these early humans travelled far. Also in China, two molars and a jawbone (100,000 years old) were found in the Zhirendong Cave (Liu 2010, 2015). There is a long gap in the age of the few other ancient fossils discovered: a human foot bone (67,000 years old) from Callao,

Philippines; a skullcap (50,000–30,000 years old?) from the banks of the Orsang River, India; fossils from Laos (c46,000 years old), Sunda (c46,000 years old), Australia (c40,000 years old), Sri Lanka (c38,000 years old), and India (c20,000 years old) (Boivin 2013; Bae 2017).

Bones disintegrate with time; the stories they tell are lost.

Stones

Stone tools remain intact over millennia. Buried by earth or exposed to the sun, the vast and varied store of stone tool artefacts made by hominids and humans affords fascinating glimpses into their early history. A trail of stone tools marks the hominid/human journeys out of Africa.

Lithic technology (the range of techniques used to produce tools from stones) is possibly the oldest hominid technical and cultural accomplishment. It requires the capability to conceive, plan and execute the transformation of raw stone into a tool that can be used for a particular purpose. It requires skill, patience and informed decision-making in finding and selecting quality raw material and then selectively removing flakes to achieve a desired shape. Generally, it involves a process known as knapping, hitting a stone core with varying force and at varying angles. The core fractures into sharp-edged flakes which can be used to make different tools for chopping, cutting, scraping, inscribing and other applications. The technology evolved into increasing levels of complexity through successive cultural phases during the Palaeolithic (old) and Neolithic (new) stone ages. The Palaeolithic is further divided into the Lower Palaeolithic (3 Ma–300 ka), Middle Palaeolithic (300–40 ka) and Upper Palaeolithic (40–10 ka); the Neolithic follows.

Cut-marked fossils discovered at Dikka in Ethiopia suggest that the earliest use of stone tools by hominids could have been before 3.39 Ma, around the time of *Australopithecus afarensis*,

Lucy's species (De la Torre 2011). The oldest artefacts (c2.6 Ma), however, come from Gona in Ethiopia in the northern part of the East African Rift Valley, a region that played a critical role in hominin evolution.

The earliest type of stone tool, the Oldowan or pebble tool named after Olduvai Gorge in Tanzania, is a simple tool formed by roughly knapping one side of a pebble to produce a jagged cutting edge that can be used for chopping. It marked a major event in hominid evolution by enabling them to enhance their biological ability. It triggered changes in body shape, brain size and cognitive ability.

Homo ergaster arrived in the evolutionary record shortly after Oldowan tools appeared, and developed the technology to the next stage, the Acheulian (1.7 Ma–200 ka), named after the French town of Saint-Acheul. The manufacture of Acheulian tools (bi-facial handaxes and cleavers) required a leap forward in cognitive ability, planning capability and knowledge of materials and processes. It opened hominin diet to a variety of new food items, including meat and bone marrow. This in turn introduced numerous behavioural adaptations in lifestyle and foraging strategies like hunting, and the use of fire. It led to more complex social behaviour.

Mousterian tools (200–40 ka), named after Le Moustier in France, mark the next stage in the evolution of lithic technology. They were smaller than Acheulian, and were made by a knapping method that struck flakes from a prepared core giving it a distinctive tortoise-shell appearance. The flakes were used as saws, knives, scrapers, borers, hand axes, choppers and cleavers. This technology is associated with Neanderthals and anatomically modern humans in North Africa. A further development was the Aterian tradition [Middle Palaeolithic stone tool industry named after the site of Bir el Ater, Algeria] in which a tang was added to sharpened points so that they could be attached to a shaft to form spears. It provides evidence of early hunting behaviour and increased social complexity.

Figure 3.1: Oldowan pebble tool

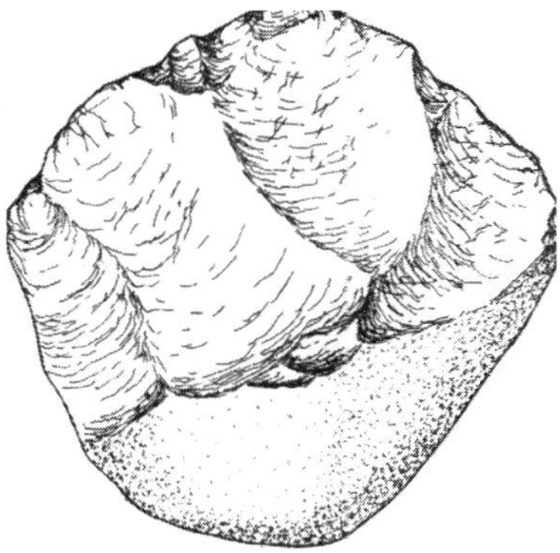

Source: https://commons.wikimedia.org/wiki/Category:Oldowan_choppers#/media/File:Basalt_chopper_sketch.jpg (accessed April 2024).

Figure 3.2: Acheulian handaxe

Source: https://commons.wikimedia.org/wiki/File:Acheulian_bifacial_tools_(hand-axes)_Wellcome_M0015373.jpg (accessed April 2024).

Figure 3.3: Mousterian

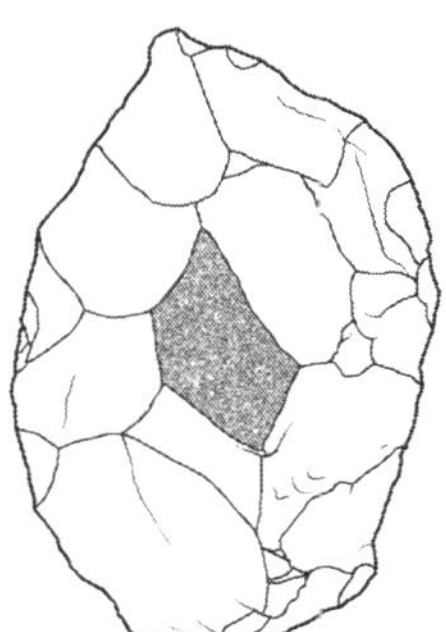

Source:https://commons.wikimedia.org/wiki/File:Mousterian_scrapers_and_points_Wellcome_M0015181.jpg (accessed April 2024).

Figure 3.4: Core and flake

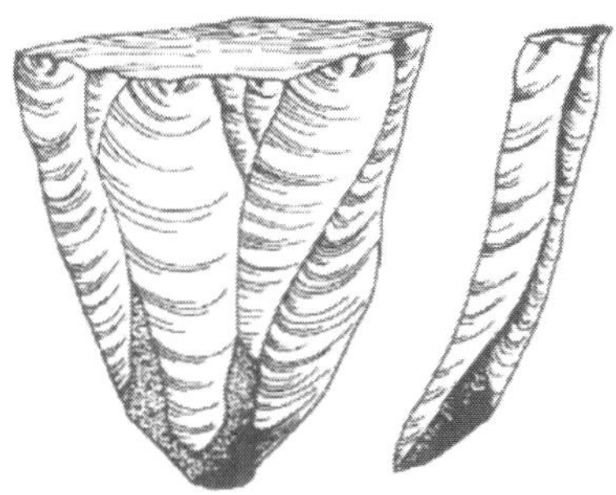

Source: https://commons.wikimedia.org/w/index.php?search=core+and+flake&title=Special:MediaSearch&go=Go&type=image (accessed April 2024).

The Upper Palaeolithic was dominated by microliths or small stone tools. Long, narrow-flaked blades with parallel sides were struck from prepared cores and modified into specialised tools for a variety of applications like making bone and ivory fish hooks, harpoons, possibly bows and arrows, and the atlatl or throwing spear. These tools opened human minds to new imaginative worlds that took them beyond the routine of humdrum existence. Cave and rock paintings of long extinct animals dominating the canvas and tiny humans alongside with spears reveal an outpouring of a new creative expression, of an attempt to understand, capture and record facets of the great world of nature humans were part of. Remnants of body ornamentation reveals status consciousness, and elaborate ritual burials belief in an after-life. Exquisite bone, clay, ivory and stone carvings, of mother goddess figurines, graceful flying swans and a lion-man are the first surviving material expressions of religious belief.

During the Neolithic, humans adopted farming. Microliths underwent a further refinement towards developing farming tools. Small geometric flakes were hafted into wood for harvesting crops while larger implements, querns and mullers were developed for processing grain.

Multiple Dispersals

From the oldest Middle Palaeolithic sites centred around Omo Kibish in Ethiopia, humans spread outward into other parts of Africa and beyond. The dispersals out of Africa fall broadly into two periods, pre- and post-Toba. Two routes appear to have been used, one via Sinai and the other via Bab al-Mandab (Groucutt 2014).

The pre-Toba dispersals, between 130–75 ka, appear to have used both routes. The Skhul-Qafzeh fossils represent those humans who entered the Levant via Sinai. Others crossed the

Bab al-Mandab into Arabia by MIS 5e and South Asia by MIS 5a [Table 1.2, Chapter 1]. No genetic material that can establish the identity of these humans has been recovered as yet. There is, however, a close physical affinity between the Skhul-Qafzeh fossils and Australians and Papuans. The fossils recovered from Lake Mungo in Australia support the possibility of multiple dispersals at different times. One of these has a robust anatomy suggestive of an earlier dispersal. The other has a gracile structure more similar to modern humans.

Pre-Toba stone tools are associated with African Middle Stone Age technology. They exhibit significant regional differences between each other which suggests independent development and repeated re-invention over a long time period. In contrast, post-Toba tools were uniformly made using MIS 5 technology from East Africa to Australia. It suggests a rapid colonisation by related groups of populations.

Estimated divergence of dates between Africans and others suggests a first dispersal c130 ka and a second c50 ka (Reyes-Centeno 2014, 2015). It is possible that the first expansion colonised Australia, Papua New Guinea, Melanesia and in-between regions including South and Southeast Asia. These 'relict' populations remained relatively isolated, but admixed with Denisovan and other hominin populations. In Australia, their descendants may have survived among Aboriginals, and in Southeast Asia among the Orang Asli, short in stature, dark skinned and with tufted hair.

Cyclical climate changes opened and closed the two dispersal corridors out of Africa. The only land route, via Sinai, led to the Levant. During wet periods, the Nile provided a food resource highway from Ethiopia to Sinai. Palaeo-environmental studies reveal that wet corridors connected Sinai, the Levant, and Arabia for a brief period c130 ka, but not for millennia before (Breeze 2016). From Sinai, the southward corridor into Arabia faced a formidable barrier in the arid Nefud Desert of central Arabia. But further eastward, a corridor opened out along the River

Figure 3.5: Routes out of Africa

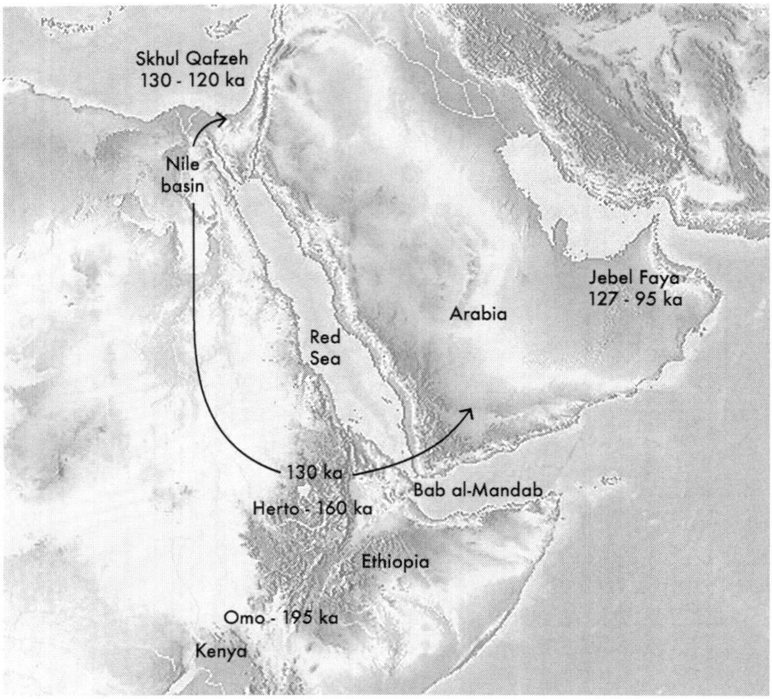

Note: All maps in this book have been created by the author, which means jointly designed by Alan Machado (Prabhu) (content) and Alpa Machado (technical).
Source: Created by author.

Euphrates. It split at its mouth to follow both coasts of the Persian Gulf. The eastern route followed the Iranian coastline towards South Asia, the western, the Arabian coastline.

The other route crossed a short stretch of water at the Bab al-Mandab Strait. Circa 130 ka, the width of the sea crossing was at a minimum (Armitage 2011). On the Eritrean coast, mounds of seashells interspersed with stone tools reveal that humans exploited this shore during a mega drought that afflicted East

Africa through MIS 5 (Macaulay 2005). This trail passed along the southern Arabian coastline via Dhofar (Oman) to Jebel Faya (Sharjah). Both sites are littered with stone tools, as are numerous other sites in the Arabian peninsula.

At Abdur on the Red Sea coast of Eritrea, Middle Stone Age tools and discarded marine shells dated to c125 ka reveal it was occupied by humans at a time when *Homo sapiens* groups inhabited interior east Africa. It is possible that hyper-arid conditions had pushed some groups to exploit marine resources on the Red Sea, and the Haycock Islands provided a transit to Arabia.

Arabia played the crucial role of an incubator for the first human populations outside Africa. Humans once thrived there in a green land now turned brown. MIS 5, particularly MIS 5e (130–115 ka), was a wet period in Arabia with heavy rains forming great lakes, like the 2,000 sq. kms Mudawwara palaeolake between Saudi Arabia and Jordan. The Mundafan palaeolake once filled a 300 sq. kms area to a depth of 30 m in Arabia's Empty Quarter, Rub' al Khali, the largest continuous sandy desert in the world today. At Mundafan Al-Buhayrah, located on its now dried-out shores, excavated stone tools date to 100-80 ka (Groucutt 2015b).

Further south at Dhofar in Oman, stone tools dated to 106 ka have been found (Blinkhorn 2013a). They were made by technologies similar to that used in east Africa, the Levant and Jwalapuram during MIS 5. South of the Arabian coastline, geologists have discovered fresh water streams flowing under the seabed, streams that once flowed on land.

Encounter with Earlier Hominins

Genetic data of non-Africans suggests a single successful dispersal between 70-50 ka via the Bab al-Mandab into Arabia. Following the Southern Coastal Route, this dispersal journeyed through South Asia to Australia. The genetic trail is paralleled by a trail of stone tools made using microlithic technologies. This 70–50 ka dispersal was followed by another c47 ka that spread many new 'modern' cultural traits (blade technology, symbolism, long-distance trade).

By correlating genetic data from different tribes of modern hunter-gatherers worldwide with cultural behaviour, it has been proposed that the 70–50 ka out-of-Africa migrants were belligerent warriors who resorted to ritualised fights, warfare, murder and suicide in resolving conflicts. Such behaviour patterns were limited only to the descendants of mtDNA Hg L3 which had left Africa, but not to Hgs L0, L1, and L2 who remained behind [Chapter 4]. These traits have been found to be common to all global groups, in Asia, Australia, the Arctic and the Americas.

Before this dispersal from Africa, humans were already hunting with bows and arrows, stone axes and spears. However, c80 ka, a transition occurred with the invention of protective armour such as shields, the appearance of ritual fighting as socially accepted behaviour and the construction of war canoes for fast transport. In other words, foraging hunters became warriors who used canoes to traverse sea coasts and rivers. This warfare culture may have given the out-of-Africa migrants a competitive advantage that enabled them to neutralise other hominin species like the Neanderthals, and perhaps the earlier human colonisers. Further, their belligerent behaviour may have also prevented subsequent human emigrations from Africa (Moreno 2011, 2013).

This human journey out of Africa followed in the footsteps of earlier hominins, some of whom still inhabited the lands they had colonised when humans arrived there. *Homo neanderthalensis* populations lived in the Middle East and Europe, the Denisovans from the deciduous forests of Siberia to the tropics of Southeast Asia, also home to *Homo floresiensis*. *Homo neanderthalensis* is believed to have evolved from *Homo heidelbergensis*, the Denisovans and *Homo floresiensis* from *Homo erectus*. The

Neanderthals, a robust species that had adapted to extreme ice-age European climatic conditions, were pushed out of the Levant by humans c47 ka. Intense rivalry continued as humans pushed westwards into Europe. The final encounters occurred in Iberia. Circa 30 ka, Neanderthals were extinct. It was not long before *Homo sapiens* remained as the only surviving member of the *Homo* family.

Modern genetics adds an interesting twist to the Neanderthal and Denisovan story. Analyses of Neanderthal and Denisovan genomes reveal their admixture with humans. Between 1–3% of the genome of all Eurasians and native Amerindians is of Neanderthal origin. Inter-breeding may have taken place between 47–65 ka (Sankararaman 2012). New Guineans and Aboriginal Australians have 4–6% of the Denisovan genome (Reich 2011). Indians, including Andamanese, Papuans, and Aboriginal Australians carry genomic contributions of between 2–3% from an extinct hominin population (Mondal 2016). In the case of the Andamanese, it came from a new and still unknown hominin population which separated early in the hominin tree.

Into Eurasia

Jebel Faya was occupied by humans by 127–95 ka (Armitage 2011). Just beyond, the Arabian coast juts out into the Strait of Hormuz and is separated from Iran by a short stretch of water. It offered a path out of Arabia to the Asian landmass. Jebel Faya is 1,500 kms away from the Thar Desert in India (stone tool dates: between 125–108 ka) and 2,000 kms further to the south is Jwalapuram (stone tool dates: 85–74 ka).

4

Populating the Earth – The Genetic Story

We humans are all of African origin. Africa has the highest diversity of human genetic material. Genetic diversity is evidence of the place of origin of a species or group.

Our genetic inheritance, contained in our DNA, is passed on in almost equal proportion from each parent to their children through a process by which most of it is broken down and recombined to form new persons. There exist, however, two small portions that are passed on without recombination: mitochondrial DNA (mtDNA) from the maternal line, and the non-recombining part of the Y-chromosome from the paternal. Every thousand generations or so, though, these undergo a slight, random mutation as they are passed on. Individuals sharing identical combinations of mutations are grouped under the same haplotype (Greek *haplo* = single).[1] A group of haplotypes that can be traced back to a common ancestor is called a haplogroup. The origin of these mutations can be traced to a time and a place. By mapping these mutations, we can create family trees of our maternal and paternal lineages, and trace their migratory history.

In the mid-1990s, alphabetic labels were given to mtDNA haplogroups from different regions. Ironically, Africa, the region with the maximum diversity, was assigned just one letter, L (Kivisild 2015). Mitochondrial DNA traces our origins to an African woman who lived between 200–150 ka. Sometime between 80–65 ka, an effective female breeding population of just a few hundred defined by the genetically distinct mtDNA haplotype L3 (originated c85 ka) left Africa. Known as the out-of-Africa event, all non-Africans descend from this small group of humans. Outside Africa c63 ka, L3 split into M and N. R,

Figure 4.1: Simplified mtDNA tree and main regional presence

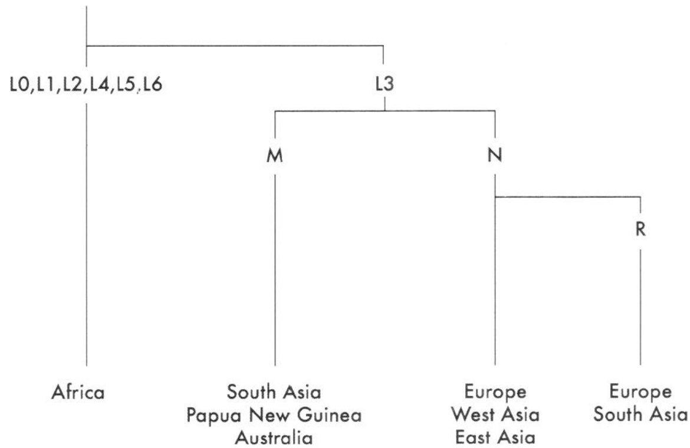

Source: Created by author.

Figure 4.2: Spread of mtDNA haplogroups M, N, R

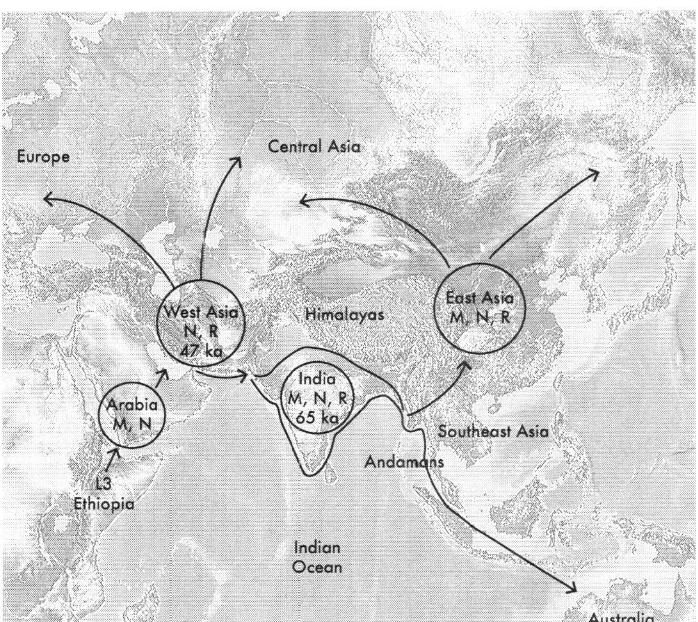

Source: Created by author.

Figure 4.3: Simplified Y-chromosome tree

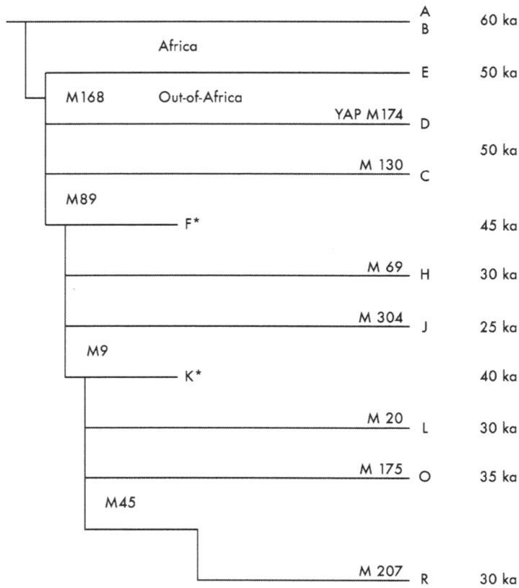

Source: Created by author.

Figure 4.4: Spread of Y-chromosomes

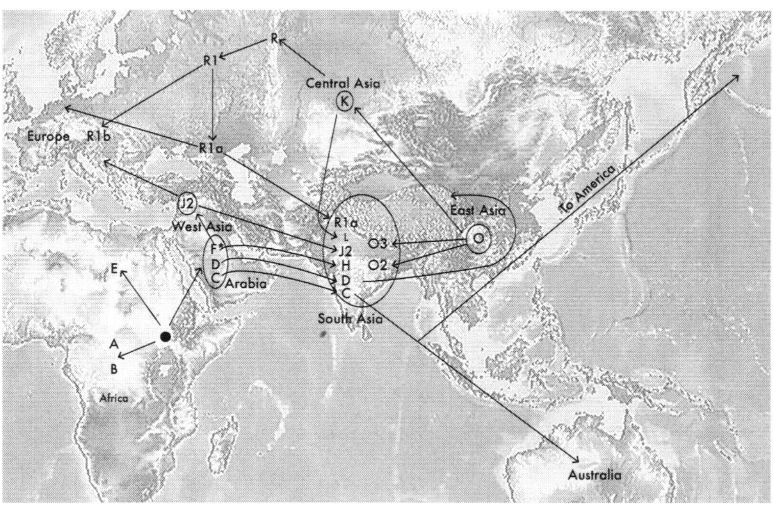

Source: Created by author.

a derivative of N, emerged c60 ka. These, M, N and R, are the founder lineages of all non-Africans.

The paternal Y-chromosome tree has roots, A and B. The out-of-Africa migrants belong to a branch of B identified by the marker M168 which split c70–50 ka. This marker split further into three others: M130, Yap, and M89, associated with haplogroups C, D/E and F respectively.

While the timing and manner of dispersal is still being debated, the similarity of founder ages of mtDNA Hgs M and N and their global spread suggest a rapid dispersal along the Southern Coastal Route that reached India c65 ka and Australia c63 ka (Macaulay 2005; Groucutt 2015). Severe climatic conditions blocked the way northward and locked humans within Africa and Arabia, which is why mtDNA Hg M and the Y-chromosomes Hgs C and D/E are absent in the Levant and Europe. It was only when the climate warmed up once again that humans with mtDNA Hgs N and R, and Y-chromosomes Hg F re-appeared in the Levant, c47 ka.

Here is that story.

The Bab al-Mandab (The Gate of Tears) (Beyin 2006; Erlandson 2015; Lambeck 2011; Walter 2000; Tassi 2015)

Around 80 ka, a prolonged ice age caused widespread aridification of Africa and pushed humans to coastal regions in search of food. It was at that time, about 1,500 kms from Omo Kibish, the repository of the bones of our earliest known ancestor, that a man stood on a bleak African shoreline of the Bab al-Mandab Strait separating Djibouti from Yemen peering intently at the soaring flights of gulls and other birds. He was the leader of the out-of-Africa group. The birds told our peripatetic ancestor that there was land across the water, land that could feed his people. Lowered sea levels had narrowed the gap between Africa and Arabia and made the crossing feasible, though still risky. Of that man, Spencer Wells, the man behind the Genographic Project conducted by the National Geographic Society, writes: 'the picture that emerges is of a dark-skinned–reasonably tall, thin person who wouldn't look that out of place today dressed in a suit and sitting opposite you on a train' (Wells 2002: 59). That man took one of the most difficult decisions ever taken. He led his small tribe, perhaps 1,000 in all, men, women and children, across the water to the then wet and fertile Arabian Peninsula.

The Bab al-Mandab Strait separates Africa from Arabia at the southern tip of the Red Sea. During glacial periods, between 61–68 ka and 94–96 ka for instance, lowered sea levels exposed considerable tracts of the Red Sea bed. Approximately 200 kms north of the Bab al-Mandab Strait, narrow, shallow channels dotted by small islands, the Haycock Islands, formed. This created a series of short crossings, approximately 1–3 kms wide with land being visible on both sides of the channel at all times. The mouth of the Red Sea itself, 29 kms wide at Bab al-Mandab today, was only a few kilometres wide, and simple to cross with rudimentary rafts or boats. With possible evidence that humans were experimenting with boats as early as c125 ka, this crossing opened a gateway out of Africa and made passage to Arabia feasible.

The genome of all non-Africans, white, brown and yellow, can be traced back to that small group who made that crossing c70 ka. It derives from just three mtDNA haplogroups (M, N, R), and three Y-chromosome lineages (C, D, F) identified by the marker M168. While M, N and R lineages are found in populations to the east, from South Asia to Australia, only later derivatives of N and R lineages are present in west Eurasian and European populations. The initial migration out of Arabia was, therefore, eastward along the Iranian coast.

Arabia (Abu-Amero 2008; Armitage 2011; Fernandes 2012; Groucutt 2012, 2015; Jennings 2015; Petraglia 2015; Rose 2007)

Arabia for the most part is starkly dry desert, undulating brown sand dunes interspersed with rocky outcrops:

> In the deserts of southern Arabia there is no rhythm of the seasons, no rise and fall of sap, but empty wastes where only the changing temperature marks the passage of the year. It is a bitter, desiccated land which knows nothing of gentleness or ease. Yet men have lived there since earliest times (Thesiger 1959).

It was not always so in the past when the monsoon shifted northward. Arabia was transformed into a land of rivers and fresh-water lakes, of marshes, grasslands, and forests where plant, animal and aquatic life thrived. The bones of oryx, elephant, horse, fox, leopard, grebe, fish and reptiles from sites in the Nafud Desert attest to this. A greened ecosystem opened viable routes through the interior, and fresh water streams flowed to the sea along the coastline. This happened every 23,000 years during MIS 5.

Many Middle Palaeolithic sites provide evidence of past human occupation. During MIS 5e (128–115 ka), 5c (105–95 ka) and 5a (85–75 ka), increased monsoon rainfall created large lakes in the Empty Quarter. The Arabian Peninsula became the centre for human population growth in the initial period outside Africa. Alternating climatic spells acted like a pump, drawing in settlers during wet times, pushing them out again when it was drier. Modern Arabian populations harbour only a small percentage of the founder M and N lineages; they have been swamped by more recent migrations from the Levant and from along the coast.

Arabia provided a key corridor for the movement of humans from Africa into continental Asia. The Persian Gulf today averages forty metres in depth. During MIS 5d and 5b, and between 75–14 ka, lowered sea levels exposed much of the Strait of Hormuz and created a land corridor between Arabia and Iran. As the repeated occupation of Jebel Faya between 125–40 ka suggests, this was a major route used by humans.

The Southern Coastal Route (Buck 2007; Erlandson 2015; Reyes-Centeno 2014, 2015; Stringer 2000; Wells 2002)

The Southern Coastal Route was made feasible by an ice age that locked large amounts of ocean water in polar ice sheets c74–60 ka. Sea levels were about eighty metres below what they are today. The southern Arabian coast extended far into the sea, the islands in the Persian Gulf and Sri Lanka were connected to the mainland, and the Andaman Islands were just thirty kms across a shallow sea from mainland Asia. This extended coastline was formed all along the Indian Ocean rim from Arabia to Indonesia. Genetic data points to a rapid dispersal along this rim. Known as the Southern Coastal Route, it took out-of-Africa humans, via South and Southeast Asia, to Papua New Guinea and Australia.

Much of South Asia's then coastline extended into a continental shelf 100–250 kms wide, an even and relatively easy route marked by extensive mangrove – covered river deltas. By bridging land and sea environments, mangroves provided a wealth of highly nutritious food resources like birds, animals, fish, crabs, shrimp and molluscs, as well as wood for shelter, fuel and boat-building These resources turned the Southern Coastal Route into a veritable 'mangrove highway' with South Asian river basins shortening coast-to-coast distances.

'Relict' populations in south and central India and Southeast Asia harbouring mtDNA macro-haplogroup M (Malaysia-M21, M22; Andamans-M31) form a link between South Asia and Papua New Guinea/Australia.[2] Craniofacial diversity around the Indian Ocean rim provide explicit support for the Southern Coastal Route migration. So too the Y-chromosome Hg C with the marker M130 which is considered the signature of the

Southern Coastal Route colonisers. Hg C-M130 constitutes 5% of Y-chromosome types in India (C5), 10% in Malaysia (C1, C2), 15% in Papua New Guinea (C2) and 60% in Australia (C4). Each group is identified by different sub-markers. It suggests a long period of isolation after the initial exodus.

Asia: South, Southeast and East Asia (Aghakhanian 2015; Boivin 2013; Endicott 2007; Shi 2008; Wang 2013; Zhang 2007; Zhong 2010)

South Asia harbours a genetic diversity second only to Africa's, strong evidence that it was settled soon after humans left Africa and became a secondary centre for early human dispersals. Coalescence dates for mtDNA Hg M provide a possible entry date of at least 60 ka. Archaeological evidence supports genetic findings that by 50 ka much of South Asia had been colonised. The present geographical distribution of Y-chromosome Hgs C and D/E suggests two major eastward routes taken by these first colonisers: a coastal route through South Asia to Southeast Asia by the C lineage and a sub-Himalayan route to Tibet, East Asia and the Andamans by the D lineage. From Southeast Asia, a northward expansion to East Asia started c40 ka along the Chinese coastline, reached Siberia c15 ka and finally the Americas. A southward expansion reached Australia and Oceania.

Living in Malaysia's jungles are 'relict' populations known as the *Orang Asli* (Original People): the Semang, Senoi and aboriginal Malays. They comprise just 0.6% of the population today. The Semang have 'Negrito' characteristics like small body size, dark skin pigmentation, cranio-facial morphology and frizzy hair. They are phenotypically and genetically different from the other groups and believed to represent the first human settlers in peninsular Malaysia. They have a genetic link to the Andamanese and divergence from African populations c67 ka.

The M1 (YAP+) lineage and its sub-haplogroup D-M174 have their highest diversity among Tibetans, the Ainu of Japan, and the Daic and Hmong Mien of eastern Asia. It is also found in the Andaman islanders (56.25%) who have lived in isolation for millennia. It is rare in other populations. The origin of the Tibetan D-M174 sub-lineage dates to 52 ka, suggesting an initial colonisation date around 60 ka.

East Asian populations harbour all three Y-chromosome markers, YAP, M89 and M130. There is a distinct north-south divide in both mtDNA and Y-chromosome lineages. The Y-chromosome macro-haplogroup O predominates among Han Chinese. It derives from M89 which originated in west Eurasia. Hg O greatly expanded during the Neolithic age and pushed C-M130 and D-M174 populations to the outer regions beyond the fertile Yellow River basin.

Australia (Bergstrom 2016; Hudjashov 2007; Ingman 2003; Pugach 2012; Redd 2002)

Australia, separated from Africa by 15,000 kms of ocean, was colonised by modern humans before Europe, a detail which contains the key pieces of the jigsaw puzzle of how and when humans settled the world. Aboriginal Australian lineages indicate a small founding population size and subsequent isolation for a long period of time. There is a broad agreement between archaeological and genetic data on the time of colonisation. Archaeological evidence confirms the presence of humans in Australia 50–60 ka; genetic studies give a time period between 70–40 ka. This was a time when lowered sea levels connected Malaysia and Indonesia into a single landmass, Sunda. Australia, Tasmania and New Guinea were similarly joined together to form Sahul. Islands between these land masses were separated by distances of 30–90 kms of shallow seas, a distance traversed by simple boats. The presence of out-of-Africa mtDNA and Y chromosome haplogroups (mtDNA: M, N, R, and Y-chromosome: C, F) suggests a relatively rapid migration from southwest Asia to Australia, estimated to have taken 5,200 years.

There could also be a more recent genetic link between Australians and south Indian Dravidian speakers (Chenchu, Kurumba). This gene flow is dated to between 5–3 ka when a number of changes also appear in the Australian archaeological record: the first appearance of the dingo and microlithic stone tools, new food plant-processing technologies, the expansion of the Pama-Nyungan language, which appears to have some similarities with south Indian Dravidian languages, over seven-eighths of Australia. The dingo is not native to Australia. Although its mtDNA suggests a Southeast Asian origin, morphologically it most closely resembles Indian dogs. They may have accompanied a human migration originating in south India. These inferences, though, have been disputed by researchers.

Eurasia: From the Levant to Central Asia (Brandt 2013; Haak 2015; Richards 2000)

Of the three out-of-Africa paternal lineages, Hg F and its derivatives have the widest global presence today. The marker M89 identifies its place of origin as west Asia where humans reappeared, either via Sinai or Arabia, after a warmer climate c47 ka opened northward land routes.

The period 50–30 ka saw major cultural and demographic changes in the human story. From Eurasia, humans spread to Europe and Asia again (mtDNA Hgs N and R). The eastward branch moved into South and Central Asia. Central Asia became an important reservoir of genetic diversity and the source of at least three later major outward migrations leading into Europe, America and India.

The advances in agriculture and domestication of animals in west Eurasia c9 ka generated a renewed movement of populations the world over. Circa 4.5 ka, Yamnaya herders made a massive migration from the Pontic-Caspian steppes into the heartland of Europe spreading Indo-European languages. Others moved eastward to form the Sintashta and Andronovo cultures, and eventually southward to Iran and South Asia.

Between 1500–2000 CE, Europeans colonised lands they had newly discovered, the Americas, Australia and New Zealand, and acquired political domination over a large part of the world. It resulted in a global spread of European haplogroups. South Asia provided a cheap and competent work force to run their colonies; the South Asian gene pool followed. The most disruptive result of the colonial era was the decimation of an enormous and diverse gene pool of native populations, many of whom had lived in isolation for millennia and developed unique traits. Another defining event of the early phase of the colonial era was an extensive slave trade in Africans, particularly to the Americas. In effect, it created a second out-of-Africa exodus.

South Asia became a major staging point in that incredible journey that took humans out of Africa to all corners of Earth. That is where our story now takes us.

5

South Asia – The Genetic Story

About one-fifth of the world's population, around 1.5 billion people, live in South Asia, a region comprising less than 3% of the global land mass. South Asia, 4.4 million sq. kms in area, covers Bangladesh, Bhutan, India, Nepal, Pakistan, Sri Lanka and the Maldives. Of this, India comprises 3.3 million sq. kms. It is a land of a vast cultural, linguistic and ethnic diversity. 'The truth.' writes Reich, 'is that India is composed of a large number of small populations' (Reich 2018: 165). Modern India has 4,635 anthropologically well-defined human populations, 532 of whom are designated as tribes, some still employing a hunter-gatherer lifestyle. Indians speak 850 languages and dialects categorised into four major families (Indo-European, Dravidian, Austro-Asiatic and Tibeto-Burman) and a number of isolates spoken by small populations (Endicott 2007; Tamang 2012).

South Asia's diverse geographic features, large river basins and annual monsoon rainfall make it a fertile and hospitable land. The nearly impenetrable snow-bound Himalayas deter entry from the north, and an extensive ocean coastline separates it from other land masses. The northwest and northeast offer feasible land routes into South Asia, and it is from these two directions that the ancestors of current populations came.

The northeastern terrain is one of mountains covered in thick jungle. For a considerable part of the year, monsoon rains make the passage hazardous and difficult. The northwest too is bounded by high mountain ridges, though bare and brown which the monsoons do not reach. Their valleys lead to the plains of the Indus basin. To its east, the Thar Desert offers a barren barrier to further eastward movement. To its north and south, however, pathways open out into the Indian heartland. The *uttarapatha* (northern route) leads to the Ganges basin, and the *dakshinapatha* (southern route) to the Deccan.

A five-stage process best fits South Asia's colonisation history (Chandrasekar 2007; Gayden 2009; Arunkumar 2015a; Singh 2016; Gangal 2014; Underhill 2014; Basu 2003, 2016; Chaubey 2010). The archaeological record takes us back to perhaps c130 ka; the genetic record begins only at c65 ka when Y-chromosome Hgs C and D appeared. The third stage, between 47–30 ka, records the arrival of Y-chromosome Hgs H, L, and R2. These three stages of colonisation were all made by hunter-gatherer populations. The fourth represents the movements of pastoral and farming cultures during the Neolithic from the east (Hgs O2 and O3) and west (Hgs J2, L, and R1a). It is associated with the arrival and spread of Austro-Asiatic, Dravidian and Indo-Aryan languages. The final stage brought small groups in recent times from different regions largely due to trade and conflicts, among them Jews, Africans (Siddis), Europeans, Armenians, Chinese and Muslims of various ethnic origins (Arab, Persian, Turk). The genetic profile of the majority of the 400 million Muslims in India, Pakistan and Bangladesh today is largely South Asian (Eaaswarkhanth 2009).

The mtDNA profile (Chandrasekar 2009; Kivisild 1999, 2002; Metspalu 2005)

The oft-repeated phrase 'unity in diversity' most aptly describes South Asia's modern population, the unity coming from its maternal heritage, the diversity from its paternal.

An estimated 88% South Asian mtDNA derives from the out-of-Africa dispersal. There has been very little fresh infusion and very limited gene outflow since then. The defining South Asian mtDNA Hg M is present in about 66% of its population. It has a high diversity within South Asia, and its frequency drops abruptly to about 5% beyond its borders. The rest belong to Hg N which came in three stages: 22% with the earliest settlers; 4% with the Y-chromosome Hgs H and L; 8% during the Neolithic.

Table 5.1: South Asian mtDNA Hgs percentages

From	Origin	Total	M	N/U2i	N/R	N/W	N/U7
c65 ka	Out-of-Africa	88%	66%	8%	14%		
c47 ka	West Asia	4%				1–2%	2–3%
c10 ka	West Asia	8%					

Source: Adapted from Kivisild (2002).

South Asia played a key role in the expansion of humans beyond Africa. South Asian mtDNA lineages expanded dramatically after the initial colonisation with a five-fold increase in population by c52 ka, the earliest and most pronounced outside Africa. Between 45–20 ka, over half the global population lived in a region stretching from South Asia to Malaysia with a peak estimate of 60% c38 ka. By 35 ka, this growth began to slow down (Atkinson 2008).

Migratory Influences and the Y-chromosome Profile

(Arunkumar 2012, 2015b; Harcourt 2017; Kivisild 2003; Mahal 2018; Sengupta 2006; Silva 2017; Tumonggor 2013)

In contrast to the maternal heritage, roughly two-thirds of South Asia's Y-chromosome genotypes derive from male-dominated migrations of farming and pastoral cultures from east, west and Central Asia during the Neolithic. While South Asia's women preserved and spread the initial gene pool in a hunter-gatherer economy, male immigrants brought new genetic material from farming and herding cultures originating beyond its borders. The admixture, therefore, involved a considerable degree of cultural, linguistic and lifestyle adoptions and adaptations. It has had a deep and lasting impact on many aspects of South Asian history.

Migratory populations in the past have had a tendency to be male-dominated with a male-female ratio of around 3:1. In the case of the Bronze Age migrations of Indo-European-speaking populations into Europe, this ratio has been calculated to have been even more dramatic with 5–14 males for every female. This deficit was compensated for by resident female populations resulting in additional Y-chromosome but negligible mtDNA types.

Trading communities also spread Y-chromosome diversity in a far greater proportion than that of mtDNA. In the past, mobile trading classes were almost exclusively male-dominated, spending many months, even years, away from home. For instance, in the case of the Moplas of Malabar, an exclusively male Arab trading community was stuck annually in Malabar for many months by the monsoon. Islam sanctioned marriages with local women; an infusion of Y-chromosome genetic material from Yemen resulted.

The situation is different in resident farming cultures where the land is generally owned and worked by males. They, therefore, become the resident sex. Females, in contrast, move to the lands of their husbands. This means that Y-chromosome types tended to have a regional bias, while mtDNA types became more widespread. It also means the adoption of the husband's language, so that regional languages became identified with the Y-chromosome, not mtDNA, types of a population. The mother tongue should be more aptly termed the father tongue.

Until the Neolithic, all South Asian populations were hunter-gatherers. They cherished their mobility and travelled light with minimal possessions. Groups met periodically to exchange information, technology and marriage partners, thereby spreading genetic material, both maternal and paternal.

This pattern changed with the arrival of farming, pastoral and trading cultures during the Neolithic. This male-driven genetic influx was complemented by the expansion of several South Asian mtDNA lineages, primarily from the south. This means that the new male immigrants admixed with local women partners. A similar expansion of M lineages had occurred earlier, between 45–35 ka, coinciding with the spread of microlithic technology.

Shaping the Modern South Asian Gene Pool (Basu 2016; Chaubey 2015; Gangal 2014; Moorjani 2013; Narasimhan et al. 2018; Quintana-Murci 2001, 2004; Reich 2009; Vahia 2017; Watkins 2008)

The modern South Asian gene pool reveals five distinct ancestries: Ancient Ancestral South Indian (AASI), Ancestral

Figure 5.1: AASI-ASI-ANE admixture diagram

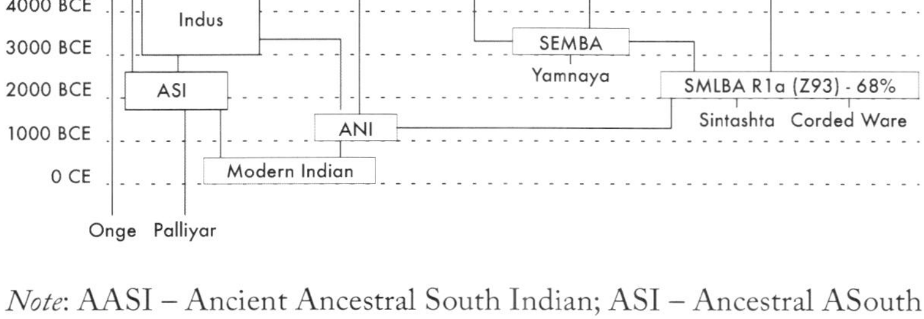

Note: AASI – Ancient Ancestral South Indian; ASI – Ancestral ASouth Indian; ANI – Ancestral North Indian; WEHG – West European Hunter-Gatherer; WSHG – West Siberiaqn Hunter-Gatherer; EEHG – East European Hunter-Gatherer; SEMBA – Steppe Early-Middle Bronze Age; SMLBA – Steppe Middle-Late Bronze Age
Source: Adapted from Narasimhan et al. (2018).

South Indian (ASI), Ancestral Austro-Asiatic (AAA), Ancestral Tibeto-Burman (ATB) and Ancestral North Indian (ANI).

The AASI is comprised of pre-Neolithic hunter-gatherer lineages. Today, only the Andaman islanders possess the AASI component in near unadulterated form. Their remote and isolated existence for millennia is good evidence that it was widespread throughout South Asia before the Neolithic.

During the Neolithic, westward moving AAA populations met and admixed with AASI populations. Hindered by mountainous jungles, their movement into central India was characterised by small groups penetrating valleys and then spreading out in more open land. Linguistic evidence suggests that AAA populations were present much further to the west of their present locations, perhaps as far west as the Punjab by the time of the Harappan Civilisation.

The Harappan region lay directly on the route from both West Asia (via Iran) and Central Asia (via the BMAC) into South Asia. It was the single most important source in the formation of South Asia's modern gene pool. From about 9 ka, Iranian farmer-herder groups trickling into South Asia via Mehrgarh admixed with local AASI hunter-gatherer populations. The greater part of this admixture occurred between c4700–3000 BCE. Iranian farmer-herders harboured a distinctive type of ancestry associated with the Zagros Mountains, shaped between the 7th–6th millennia BCE when Anatolian farmers brought wheat and barley to the region. Iranian farmer-herder groups spread this economy based on domesticated wheat, barley, goats and sheep to South Asia. Their admixture with AASI varied. Three sampled individuals showed a range of 14–42% AASI.

By 1900 BCE, most Harappan urban sites had been substantially depopulated. Southern populations moved southward and admixed further with AASI groups to form the ASI population. Four south Indian tribal groups (Palliyar, Ulladan, Malayan, Adiyan) show this ancestry in nearly unmixed form. In the Palliyar, admixture between AASI and Indus populations occurred between 1700–400 BCE. This implies that these tribes, now resident in Tamil Nadu, once lived on the southeastern fringes of the Indus basin. These dispersals most probably spread Dravidian languages to the Peninsula.

Harappan populations underwent further admixture when the southward expansion of Eurasian steppe pastoral populations reached South Asia during the period of decline of the Harappan Civilisation. Around 3000 BCE, an Early-Middle Bronze Age (EMBA) steppe population had been formed by admixture between East European hunter-gatherers and Iranian farmer/herder populations. By the Middle-Late Bronze Age (MLBA, c2300–1500 BCE), it had spread across the Eurasian plain from Europe to Siberia. About 68% of its Y-chromosome DNA belonged to Hg R1a. A branch reached the Indus Valley bringing the Indo-Aryan language with them. The admixture of Steppe MLBA with Indus populations post-1500 BCE formed the ANI population, sometimes re-designated as ANE (Ancestral North Eurasian) to emphasise its relation to west Eurasia (Central Asia, west Asia, Caucasus, east Europe).

South Asia's modern population has been formed largely by admixture between ASI and ANE populations. ANE is significantly higher in Indo-Aryan than Dravidian speakers, suggesting that ASI populations spoke Dravidian languages before this admixture. The admixture was thorough and pervasive and left its mark on nearly every group in India. Significantly, the admixture date estimates are older in Dravidians (108 generations) than in Indo-Aryans (72 generations).

This period was a time of profound change in India, characterised by the de-urbanisation of the Indus Valley, its population shift to the Ganges basin and Gujarat, and the appearance of Indo-Aryan languages and the Vedic religion. The subsequent genetic record shows a shift from major and common population admixture to strict endogamy. This can also be inferred in the Rgveda whose older parts suggest a substantial social movement across groups. People with non-Indo-Aryan names were accepted as chieftains and poets. The caste (*jati*) system of endogamous groups having specific social or occupational roles is not mentioned; it appears only in texts composed centuries later, for instance in Manu's law code which forbids intermarriage between castes. By the the time of the Gupta Empire (319–550 CE), new social values and strictures were laid down and strictly imposed. Its effects are visible in India's complex matrix of over 2,000 caste populations today.

South Asia's Hunter-Gatherer heritage: Hgs C and D; Hgs H, L and R2

All non-Africans belong to one of three Y-chromosome lineages (C, D, F) and carry the marker M168. South Asia's oldest Y-chromosome lineages derive from Hgs C and D.

Figure 5.2: South Asian Y-chromosome haplogroups[7]

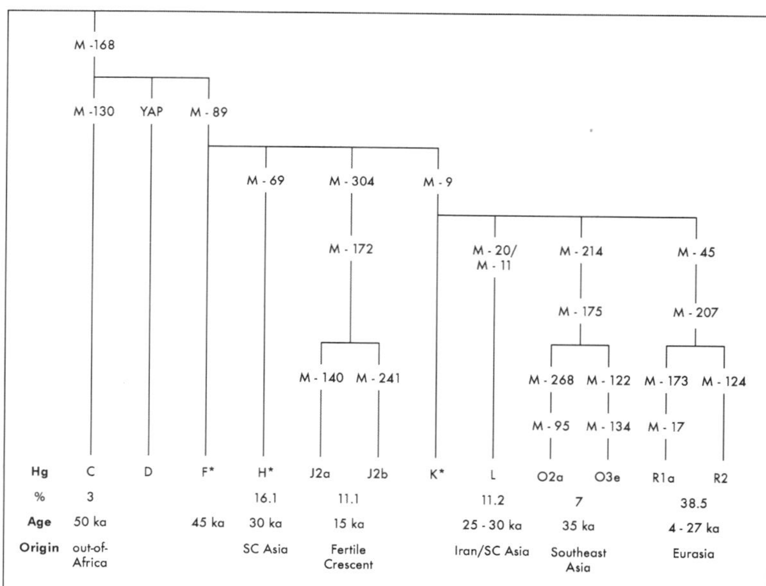

Source: Created by author.

Hg C, the signature of the Southern Coastal Route colonisers who reached South Asia c65 ka, is found all along the route to Australia. Aboriginal Australians share a genetic link to certain South Indian populations with whom they also share a close physical likeness.[1] Their Y-chromosomes belong to Hg C, and Australian-specific mtDNA Hg M42 has been linked to Dravidian and Austro-Asiatic populations in central India. This suggests the route to Australia passed swiftly through South Asia, spreading the same founder haplogroups along the entire trail before they mutated. In South Asia, Hg C has been swamped by later arrivals and survives only among tribal communities.[2]

India's tribals, traditionally known as *jana* as opposed to jati, comprise hunter-gatherers, pastoralists, shifting cultivators

Figure 5.3: Out-of-Africa – The Middle Palaeolithic

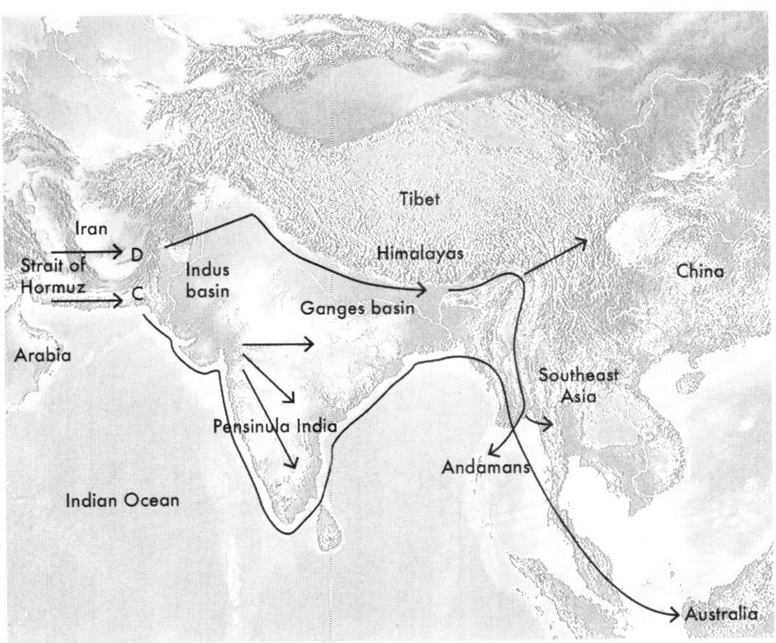

Source: Modified from Wang (2013).

and settled agriculturists. According to the 2011 census, they constitute 8.6% of India's population, numbering 104.5 million. They are defined as exhibiting primitive traits, distinctive cultures, geographical isolation, shyness of contact with the larger community at large and backwardness (Ministry of Tribal Affairs, Govt. of India, Lok Sabha, question no. †221, 17 July 2017). They speak about 750 dialects and inhabit predominantly hilly tracts in five geographic regions of the northeast, north and north-west, east and central, west and south. Their highest concentrations are in the northeast, central and south, as well as Rajasthan and Gujarat.

Table 5.2: Percentage of C-M130 in Tamil tribal groups

Paniya	15.28
Kadar	10.71
Paliyan	10.53
Piramalai Kallar	9.43
Parayar NTN	7.69
Thoda	7.69
Vanniyar NTN	7.29
Irula	6.25
Parayar	4.17

Source: Adapted from Arunkumar et al. (2012).

Hg D-M174 has high frequencies in the Andaman and Tibeto-Burman populations and the Ainu of Japan. Its distribution suggests a sub-Himalayan route until a branching off to Tibet and east Asia, and Southeast Asia and the Andamans.

The Andaman archipelago consists of about 200 islands rising above a sea depth of 200 m. Its inhabitants, small foraging communities, have lived in isolation for millennia until Britain colonised the islands in the mid-nineteenth century. The years since have been harsh. Large numbers of islanders have been decimated by disease and pushed out of their land by settlers. Today, only the Jarawa, Sentinelese, Great Andamanese and

Onge survive. Their numbers are small, and their unique heritage may soon be lost.

The Andamanese harbour mtDNA Hgs M2 and M4, (coalescence dates 63 ka and 32 ka), which are common especially in south India, and the unique Hgs M31 and M32 not found anywhere else. Their paternal DNA contains a high frequency of Y-chromosome Hg D-M174 (56.25%). So while the maternal DNA suggests that the islanders are descendants of the original out-of-Africa migrants with a close affinity to south Indians, their paternal DNA suggests Southeast Asian relationship and a settlement date of c26 ka (Thangaraj 2005a 2006; Endicott 2003; Chaubey 2013; Barik 2008).

The predominant Y-chromosome lineage outside Africa belongs to Hg F with the marker M-89. It expanded rapidly when global warming ushered in the Upper Palaeolithic and opened land routes out of Arabia c47 ka (Petraglia 2015). Its derivatives arrived in South Asia in two broad time periods: Hgs H, L-M20 and R2 in the Upper Palaeolithic c47–30 ka; Hgs O, J, L-M11 and R1a1 in the Neolithic from c10 ka.

Hg H arrived in South Asia from the Iranian plateau. Its marker M-69 originated in west India c30 ka. Hgs L-M20 and R2 arrived separately a little later from Central Asia. Hg L-M20 is found all along India's west coast till south India where it has a high frequency (Wells 2002). These demographic movements added a small addition to the South Asian maternal gene pool with west Eurasian mtDNA Hgs W and U7.

The Upper Palaeolithic in South Asia has been associated with a strong technological signature. The archaeological record shows clear signs of new and complex developments in which the construction of structures and manufacture of symbolic items suggest group identities were formed. Four cranial vault fragments and an isolated tooth dated to twenty and twelve ka are the earliest securely dated human remains in India. They show signs of having been cremated. A number of stone and bone beads used as personal ornaments indicate the performance of a wide range of domestic, artistic and ritualistic activities. A

Figure 5.4: The Upper Palaeolithic: The Microlithic revolution

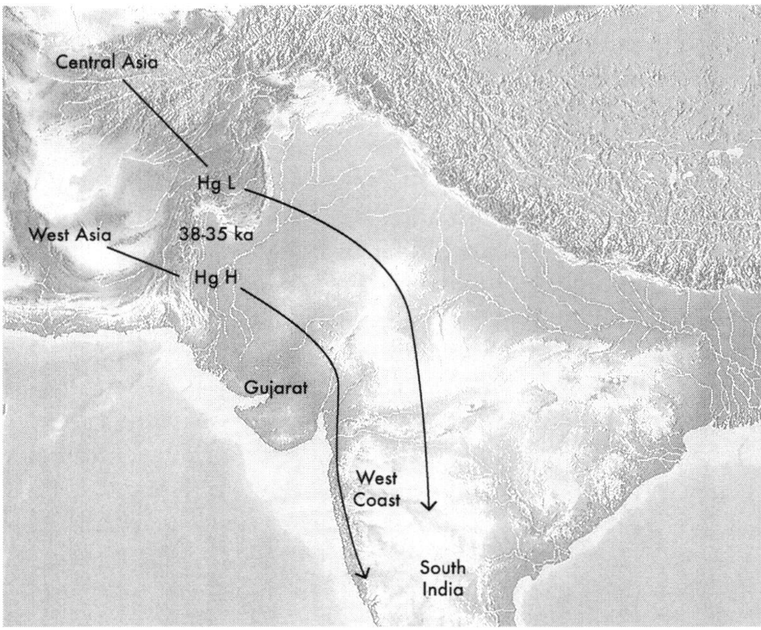

Source: Created by author.

34,000–20,000-year-old sharpened bone may have been used as an awl to manufacture these beads.

Excavated fossil bones include those of deer, boar, antelope, hare, buffalo and dog as well as fresh-water mollusc shells. Faded red ochre outlines on rock faces depict wild animals including elephants, many since disappeared from the valley, and humans in an ancient landscape. Only these elusive artefacts and art, weathered by climatic vagaries of thousands of years, remain of a cultural site preserving a long evolutionary history of a complex range of human behaviour and social interaction in a small part of South Asia (Haslam 2012; Clarkson 2009; Petraglia 2009; Tacon 2010).

Around c35 ka, Jurreru Valley inhabitants began manufacturing micro blade tool kits from high quality stone material shaped from prepared cores. Flakes were re-sharpened and re-shaped to extend the supply of raw material or to transform them for different applications (blades, scrapers, burins, arrowheads with tangs). The emphasis was on reliability, standardisation, multi-functional use, the possibility of reuse and utility. The range of tools reveals continuous development to meet the need for more efficient and reliable hunting strategies. Hunting kits were designed for different prey species, mainly small to medium-sized ungulates.

Two possibilities have been put forward for the appearance of these microlithic tools. The first suggests it was a gradual cultural change, a result of local technological response to increasing aridity and population pressure. Circa 36 ka, there was a rapid deterioration in South Asia's climate which led to the Last Glacial Maximum (ice age) and a severe reduction in rainfall. Food resources diminished. The adoption of more reliable and hafted (arrows and spears) tool kits suggests a situation that required greater mobility as larger game disappeared (Clarkson 2013).

The other possibility comes from the analysis of a 100-year-old lock of hair of an aboriginal from Western Australia. It suggests that Australia was subject to two colonising waves, an earlier mtDNA M lineage c62–74 ka and a later N lineage c25–38 ka (Rasmussen 2011). Both groups passed via South Asia where admixture occurred between the two groups. The time period fits in neatly with the arrival of Hgs H, L-M20, R2 in South Asia. Perhaps they brought these new technologies with them.

The Farmer-Herder heritage – Hgs O2a, O3e, J2, L-M11, and R1a

Circa 11.7 ka, the onset of a mild and hospitable climate brought the dawn of the Holocene. It continues till today. A benign climate encouraged plant and animal growth and led to the domestication of some varieties in certain parts of the world: wheat and barley in the Fertile Crescent, rice in China and India; maize in South America; goats in the Zagros region; and buffaloes and cattle in India. Humans developed new types of stone tools to harvest them: sickles, mortars and pestles for plants, hunting tools, scrapers and knives for animals. As a farming and pastoral economy emerged, populations expanded and appropriated forest and grassland. Hunter-gatherers were forced to adapt to this new economy and adjust to a sedentary life, or, in pursuance of the lifestyle and culture bequeathed by their forefathers, move further into the interior.

An incipient South Asian farming economy received a substantial boost with population movements, primarily male-dominated, from East and Southeast Asia (Austro-Asiatic and Tibeto-Burman speakers), and from West and Central Asia.

The Immigrants from the East – Austro-Asiatics and Tibeto-Burmans

Spoken by 104 million people worldwide today, Austro-Asiatic is the eighth largest language family. There are two major branches: Munda, spoken in east, northeast, and central India, and Mon-Khmer, spoken from northeast India to the Nicobar Islands, Malaysia and the Mekong basin (Burma, Thailand, Laos, Cambodia, Vietnam). While the absence of shared mtDNA haplogroups makes a clear distinction between Munda and Mon-Khmer speakers, the presence of the Y-chromosome O2a1-M95 in both populations (India 66.44%, Southeast Asia 56.55%) reveals a shared paternal ancestry.

Various proposals have been put forward for the origin of India's Austro-Asiatic populations: (i) an Indian origin c65 ka, and subsequent spread to east and Southeast Asia; (ii) considering coalescence times for the O2a1-M95 lineage (22.4 ka versus 15.9 ka), a Southeast Asian origin c20 ka, migration to India, and extensive admixture with local populations; (iii) an origin among the Daic-speaking populations (in southern China, northeast

Figure 5.5: Neolithic migrations from the east

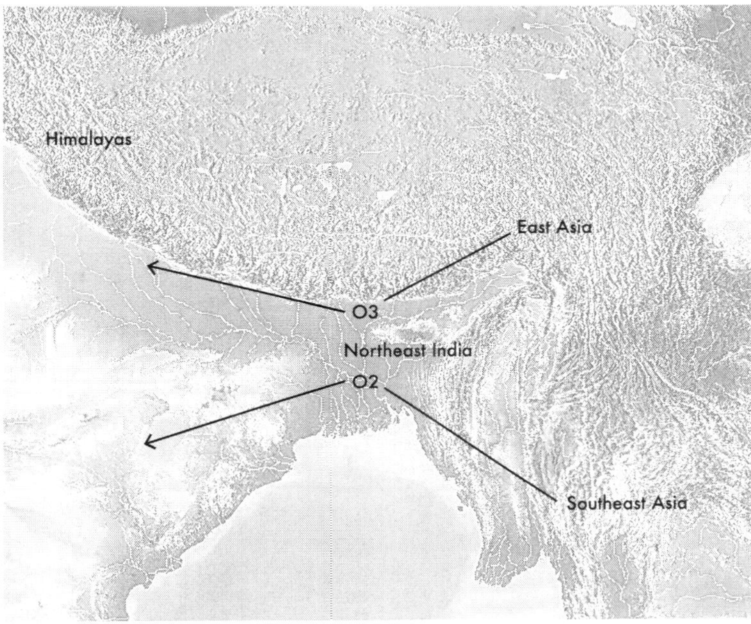

Source: Wang et al. (2013).

India, and Southeast Asia) c40–20 ka, a southward dispersal to the heartland of Southeast Asia c16 ka, and a westward migration to India c10 ka; and (iv) an origin in Laos with a late Neolithic expansion to India in multiple migratory events. This westward movement into South Asia followed large infusions of Hg O into Southeast Asia from the Yellow River basin in China as a result of the domestication of rice (Chaubey 2011; Kumar 2007; Zhang 2015; Thangaraj 2005b; Su 2000).

Tibeto-Burman populations exhibit both maternal and paternal gene flow from east Asia via Burma and Tibet. Their Y-chromosome reveals a high percentage of Hg O3. Their migration has been linked to the population expansion from the upper and middle Yellow River basin in China consequent to the domestication of millet.

The Immigrants from the West – Iranian Farmers and Steppe Pastoralists

The Neolithic peopling of South Asia from the west has a remarkable parallel with that of Europe. Both regions received major genetic inputs from regions lying between them: west Asia and the Pontic-Caspian-Ural steppes.

Genetic data from Europeans who lived between 8–3 ka reveals that two major migrations contributed to modern European populations. The beginning of the Neolithic in Europe, 8–7 ka, saw the arrival of the first farmers from west Asia. The second migration brought Yamnaya pastoralists, of east European hunter-gatherers and west Asian ancestry, from the steppe c4.5 ka. This migration replaced about three-quarters of Central European ancestry and brought the proto-Indo-European language to Europe (Haak 2015).

Like Europe, South Asia underwent immigration from populations related to both Iranian farmers and steppe pastoralists about the same time. The first encounters took place in the Indus Valley.

Overall, west Asian mtDNA haplogroups form 12% of the South Asian gene pool, 8% having arrived during the Neolithic. They range in frequency from a high of 40 % in the Punjab to 16 % in the south and 7 % in the east. The presence of mtDNA Hgs HV14 and U1a1 in Iranian and south India's Dravidian populations suggests a shared ancestry. Their coalescence time of 10.5–17.9 ka is consistent with the proto-Elamo-Dravidian language diffusion hypothesis which proposes that the proto-Dravidian language evolved over 15 ka in west Asia and was introduced into South Asia by Neolithic pastoralists. Proto-Dravidian has no words for agriculture but is familiar with words associated with pastoralism. The Zagros Mountains border Elam whose language Elamite was Dravidian. It makes a strong case that Iranian herders were proto-Dravidian speakers and they brought it to South Asia along with the west Asian gene pool.

The present distribution of Dravidian and Indo-Aryan speakers suggests this occurred before the arrival of the latter.

Iranian herders introduced Y-chromosome Hgs L1a and J-M172 into the South Asian gene pool. Hg L1a is present among both Dravidian speakers of south India and Iranian populations, but virtually absent in Indo-Aryan speakers. Its coalescence time of 9.1 ka suggests a migration of Dravidian-speaking pastoralists from Iran that eventually reached south India during the Neolithic (Palanichamy 2015; Grugni 2012). Hg L-M11 has a frequency of about 28% in west Pakistan and Baluchistan and is believed to be associated with the Harappan Civilisation (McElreavey 2005; Qamar 2002; Sengupta 2006).

This Neolithic connection with Iran is further strengthened by Hg J-M172. In Iran it is the main Y-chromosome haplogroup

Figure 5.6: Immigrations from the west-Iranian farmers

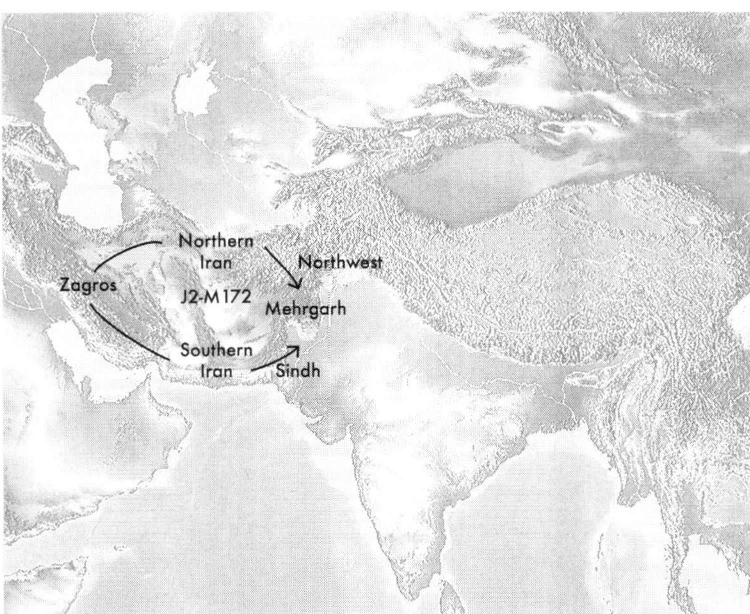

Source: Created by author.

(22.5%), being almost entirely (92.9%) represented by J2a-M410 sub-clades [a clade is a grouping that includes a common ancestor and all the descendants (living and extinct) of that ancestor] (Grugni 2012; Singh 2016). In South Asia, Hg J-M172, is present in both caste and tribal populations in two sub-lineages, J2a-M410 and J2b-M102, to the extent of about 13% (Singh 2016; Sahoo 2006). Both have genealogical ages correlating with the appearance of agriculture in the Indus Valley. Except in the northwest where Indo-Aryan languages are now dominant, the main concentrations of J2 populations today are where Dravidian languages are spoken: south, parts of central India and Baluchistan (Brahui) (Palanichamy 2015; Metspalu 2004; Grugni 2012; Sahoo 2006; Sengupta 2006; Pagel 2013). Hg J2a-M410 peaks in northwest South Asia, declines towards the centre and east, but again rises in the south.

Hg J2a-M410 spread from the northwest to the south via the Deccan. It is absent in central and eastern India, but present along the west coast indicating that Hg J2a-M410 populations were pushed into their present locations by later inroads made by populations from other gene pools via central India. Both archaeobotanical and linguistic evidence support this hypothesis.

The distribution of Iranian haplogroups in South Asia suggests a complex pattern of westward migration. The substantial presence of J2a-M410 and J2b-M102 haplogroups in tribal populations suggests their presence in the northwest during the period when this gene pool arrived, and their later dispersal into other parts of India after a period of admixture. Hg J2a-M410 has a frequency of 17–50% among pastoral and hunter-gatherer groups (Toda, Chenchu, Banjara, Kamboj, Lohana, Kashmiri Muslims) (Singh 2016; Cordaux 2004). J2b-M102 occurs in significant levels (15–35%) in central and east India among Austro-Asiatic populations and south Indian pastoral nomads. It implies significant transfer of west Asian Y-chromosomes to hunter-gatherer women before they moved to south, central and eastern India. Like the Chenchus, Austro-Asiatic populations have a high presence of mtDNA Hg M2 (frequency 32%).

Major climatic and cultural changes triggered large-scale migrations and population replacements in Bronze Age Eurasia. From the Early Bronze Age, over a period of a few centuries, the Yamnaya gene pool had expanded from the Pontic-Caspian steppes and spread across a vast distance from Europe to Siberia (Allentoft et al. 2015). The expansion of the Yamnaya people played a primary role in the formation of the Ancestral North Eurasian (ANE) gene pool. It is closely identified with Y-chromosome Hg R1a (coalescence age 10–15 ka) which has its highest density in southern Russia and Ukraine.

Between c2500–1600 BCE, the climate in the steppes of southwest Siberia and Kazakhstan underwent a rapid change to severe aridity and caused nomadic pastoralists to push

Figure 5.7: The expansion of the Yamnaya and their descendants

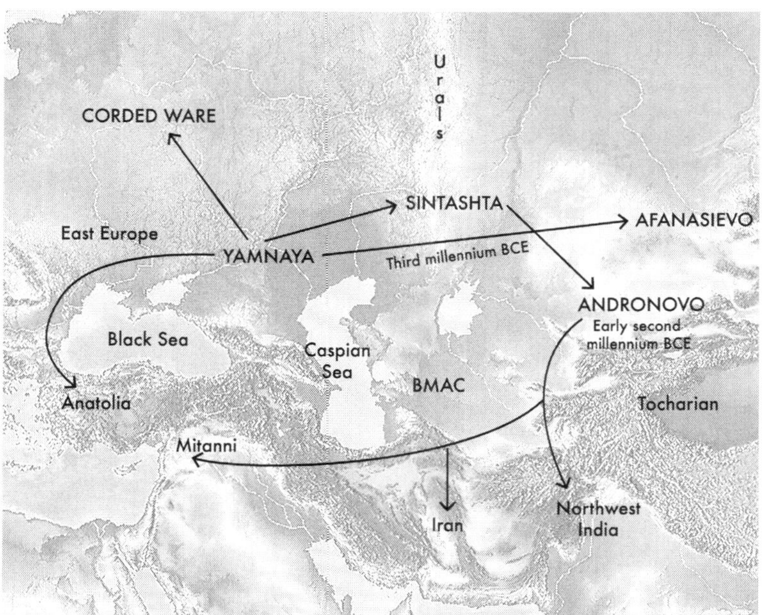

Source: Adapted from Allentoft et al. (2015).

southwards into the Iranian plateau via the BMAC. By c2000 BCE the vanguard had reached northwest South Asia, just as the decline of the Harappan Civilisation intensified. The trickle of steppe pastoralists continued until, some six centuries later, a major movement of Indo-Aryan speakers brought Vedic culture to South Asia (Allchin 1996: 301).

The male-dominated migratory nature of this last influx is strongly suggested by latest genetic findings on the genetic structure of the Ror community (Haryana) which has occupied regions of the northwest since Vedic times (Pathak 2018). Among South Asians, the Ror have the highest proportion of west Eurasian and steppe paternal ancestry (between 20%–55% of J-M172 and R1a1-M17) though 58% of their maternal lineages are South Asian (M18, M2, M3, M4, M5, M6, R5, U2). The contact with Central Asian/Steppe peoples took place earlier than 1,500 years ago. The Ror have a light skin colour and a high degree of lactose tolerance.

Lactose Tolerance – A Legacy of the Migrations from the West

A critical development that led to the expansion of the Yamnaya from the Pontic-Caspian steppes was a genetic mutation that gave Yamnaya adults the ability to digest milk and benefit from its full nutritional value. Lactose tolerance arises from a condition known as lactase persistence. Lactase's only function is the digestion of lactose, a sugar found in milk. The activity of the enzyme reduces dramatically after weaning so that many populations lack lactose tolerance in adulthood. Consuming milk or its products can cause in them severe flatulence, bloating, nausea, stomach cramps and pains and diarrhoea, besides depriving them of their nutritional value. Lactase persistence is most common in northwest Europe, decreases towards the east and south, and is virtually absent east of South Asia.

Lactose tolerance added a valuable food resource to the diet of steppe pastoralists. It resulted in population increases and the consequent need for more pasture lands. It acted as a powerful stimulus for territorial expansion, which together with the domestication of the horse and invention of the wagon allowed Indo-European speakers to move far and wide. This brought them into confrontation with sedentary farmers spread out in small holdings over whom their mobility and other advantages allowed them to establish themselves as the ruling elite (Garnier 2017).

India is the world's largest milk producer today, with a history that goes back to the domestication of zebu cattle (*bos indicus*) and the water buffalo (*bubalus bubalis*) in the Indus Valley. A substantial proportion of lactase persistence in India is due to the -13910*T gene variant. It is more common among pastoralist groups and those that traditionally practise a dairying economy, and is identical to that found in Europe and west Asia.[3] Indo-European speakers, like the Ror, from north and west India have, in general, substantially higher frequencies of the -13910*T allele [the alternative form or versions of a gene] than Dravidian speakers from the south. Its distribution in India follows a general northwest-to-southeast declining pattern. It is almost absent among speakers of Tibeto-Burman and Austro-Asiatic languages who have no known histories of pastoralism. All this suggests lactose tolerance was introduced into India via the west and northwest over a long time period (Romero 2012).

CE Immigrants

Adding to South Asia's population diversity are small ethnic communities who reached its shores at different times. They include Jews, Siddis, Parsis and Muslims of different ethnic groups like Turks, Afghans, Arabs and Iranians.

Muslims form India's largest minority religious group, comprising 14.23% of its population (172 million) according to the 2011 census. They belong to both the major Islamic sects, Sunni and Shia, and form many distinct communities with different ethnic and historic origins, like Dawoodi Bohras, Navayats, Khojas, etc.

The majority of present-day Indian Muslims have a close genetic affinity with indigenous Indian non-Muslim populations together with a small frequency of paternal ancestry especially from Iran and Arabia. There is a significant correlation between genetics and geography but not religion. In other words, Muslim communities are generally closer to non-Muslim geographical neighbours than to other Muslims in India. For instance, the major genetic contribution to Mappla Muslims of Kerala comes from the local gene pool (77%) and the rest comes from Iran (15%) and Arabia (8%). The spread of Islam was predominantly a cultural change and was not accompanied by significant gene flow (Eaaswarkhanth 2009; Gutala 2006).

The Jewish community living in India has four distinct origins centred in different regions. The oldest, the Jews of Kochi, Kerala, settled in India during the fifth–sixth centuries. The Bene Israel Jews of Mumbai, the largest group, are supposed to have migrated roughly 1,000 years ago. During the nineteenth century, Baghdadi Jews settled in Kolkata. The fourth group, the Paradesi Jews, migrated from Portugal and Spain during the fifteenth–sixteenth centuries and integrated into the Kochi Jewish community. Their genetic profile reveals ancestries inherited from both Middle Eastern and Indian populations with some degree of relative isolation (Chaubey 2016).

Siddis are of African origin, descendants of the Bantu-speakers of sub-Saharan Africa. They live in Karnataka, Gujarat and Andhra Pradesh. Their ancestors were brought mainly from Mozambique by the Portuguese about 300–500 years ago, and sold as slaves and soldiers. Studies have shown that the modern Siddi population has a combined ancestry with 70% being African and 30% Indian and European. African haplogroups, however, have not been observed in neighbouring Indian populations which suggests that gene flow between the Siddis and Indian populations has been unidirectional (Shah 2011; Gauniyal 2010).

Parsis are Zoroastrians who migrated to India after Iran was conquered by Arabs between 633–654 CE. Their religion was founded by Zarathustra who is believed to have lived c1200 BCE. Zoroastrianism became the state religion of three great Iranian empires: Achaemenid (559–330 BCE), Parthian (247 BCE–224 CE) and Sasanian (224–651 CE). Parsi tradition remembers how a group of Zoroastrians escaping persecution by the Muslim majority in Iran settled in Gujarat. Genetic research confirms the arrival of a founding group of Parsi males, belonging largely to Y-chromosome Hgs R1a1a and L, from Iran to India where they married local women. The admixture dates to between 785–936 CE which matches that of traditional dates (Lopez 2017).

A summing-up

Table 5.3 lists the major inward migratory pattern that populated South Asia, and the current distribution of mtDNA and Y-chromosome haplogroups. These percentages are for current sampled populations only. They cannot be extrapolated to infer the numbers of original immigrants with any degree of accuracy. For instance, no genetic evidence of pre-Toba populations has been found in modern populations, but archaeology gives irrefutable evidence of their presence before and after Toba. Similarly, Y-chromosome Hg C once dominated the South Asian genetic profile for thousands of years following the out-of-Africa event, but constitutes just 5% of the modern population. In contrast, R1a is present in 33% of modern populations. It does not imply large-scale migrations from Central Asia; rather they reflect on the immense influence such migrants acquired over South Asian society over time, an influence that extends to the cultural and religious spheres as well. Perhaps it also reflects on natural gene selection in succeeding generations that helps improve survival chances, for instance lactose tolerance.

Table 5.3: A summing-up

ka	mtDNA (%)	Y-chromosome (%)	Region	Anthropological	Language	Traits	Triggers
125–74	?	?	Africa	Negrito	Isolates	H-G: Middle Palaeolithic	?
65	M (66), U2i (8), R (14)	C-M130 (5), D	Out-of-Africa	Pro-Australoid	Isolates	H-G: Middle Palaeolithic	East African drought
47–30	W (1-2), U7 (2-3)	H, L, R2 (33 combined)	West/ Central Asia	Mediterranean	Isolates	H-G: Microliths	End of Ice Age
10		O2, O3 (12 combined)	Southeast/ East Asia	Austric, Mongoloid	Austro-Asiatic/ Sino-Tibetan	Farming – rice, yams, millets	Farming diffusion
10–4	H, V, K, U5, J, T (8)	J2 (13)	West Asia	Mediterranean	Dravidian	Farming – wheat, barley, goats	Farming, trade, mega droughts (west Asia)
4–3.2		R1a (33)	Central Asia	Nordic	Indo-Aryan	Pastoral	Mega drought (Central Asia)

Note: CE: Jews, Muslims (Turks, Afghans, Arabs, Navayats), Siddis, Europeans, Armenians

Source: Compiled by author; various sources.

6

Tales Languages Tell

Languages tell tales.

Languages have words and grammatical structures that provide information on their origins, speakers and their movements and interactions with others. Linguistics, the study of languages, provides insights into a population's history by studying these features and unravelling where, why and how these contacts occurred. For instance, Sanskrit while exhibiting features of early Indo-European languages spoken in Eurasia, also exhibits features found in South Asian languages. These shared structural features and their distribution suggest a major linguistic influence from Eurasia followed by a considerable period of close interaction within South Asia, which, despite its vastness and diversity, forms its own linguistic area in which several language families share a number of structural features that influence each other (Hock 2016; Southworth 2005: 40).

Modern South Asian languages belong mainly to four families: Indo-Aryan, Dravidian, Austro-Asiatic and Tibeto-Burman. All appeared during the Neolithic with the spread of the farming and pastoral economy. Before that, South Asia was populated by small mobile hunter-gatherer communities leading relatively isolated lives, each with their own local language. Hunter-gatherer languages do not have vocabularies relevant to the farming or pastoral economy; they have no need for them. Instead, their vocabularies have relevance to their world of flora and fauna, spirits and natural features. Today, swamped by the four major language families, only a few of them survive, together with some words and identifiable traits like prefixing in the vocabulary of dominant families.

Of the four dominant language families, Indo-Aryan, the largest group, is widespread in north India, Dravidian in the south and in pockets of central and north India, Austro-Asiatic in central and eastern India and Tibeto-Burman in the northeast nd Himalayan foothills.

Indo-Aryan (Burrow 1995; Masica 1991)

Indo-Aryan belongs to the Indo-Iranian branch of the Indo-European language family which today contains 144 languages divided among eleven distinct branches. South Asia has 221 variants spoken by about 650 million people (Simons 2018; Southworth 2005). These variants spread in a roughly northwest-southeast gradient leaving other language pockets in central, eastern and southern India. Indo-Aryan languages contain numerous terms relating to agriculture which cannot be traced to any known linguistic families of South Asia. This implies that many previously spoken languages have now vanished (Erdosy 1995).

A distinguishing feature of Proto-Indo-European is its strong bias toward domesticated animals rather than crops. It suggests an original pastoral rather than agricultural society. Words relating to wheels and wheeled vehicles date their origin to c6 ka, around the time the wheel was invented. The entry of the verb 'to milk' in early Indo-European vocabulary indicates the appearance of the gene mutation that gave Indo-European speakers lactose tolerance (Garnier 2017).

The earliest traces of Indo-Aryan are found neither in India nor Iran but, surprisingly, in northern Syria, in a treaty (c1380 BCE) between the Mitanni [northern Syria] and Hittites [Anatolia]. The language used was not that of the region but of a select elite aristocracy. It contains features that pre-date the language of the Rgveda (Hock 2016: 17). The distance between

Syria and South Asia is great; Indo-Aryan communities of this period were highly mobile.

The modern distribution of Indo-Iranian daughter languages suggests that around 2000 BCE a north/south split occurred between Indo-Aryan and Iranian-speakers. Proto-Indo-Aryans moved south to northeastern Iran, Afghanistan and Bactria, and eventually northwestern Iran. It was this pre-Vedic variant of Indo-Aryan that reached Syria. Between 1700–1200 BCE, in a gradual, continuing movement, Proto-Indo-Aryans moved into northwest South Asia in several phases. Here the Vedic language and religion struck roots. Around the fourteenth century BCE, Proto-Iranians reached northeastern Iran and Bactria. Here Zarathustra introduced his religious reforms and composed the Gathas. His followers converted or drove out remaining pockets of Proto-Indo-Aryans who adhered to the old Indo-Iranian religion. They eventually occupied southwestern Iran and founded their great empires together with the earlier inhabitants (Elamites and others). The movement of a few Proto-Indo-Aryans into inaccessible valleys of the Hindu Kush brought the Indo-Aryan languages Dardic and Nuristani to parts of northern Pakistan, northwestern India and northeastern Afghanistan. Alternatively, these may have been one of the earlier migrant groups. This chronology best explains the archaeological and toponymic evidence, the relationship between the Avestan and Vedic languages and religion, the distribution of Iranian peoples, Mitanni and Hittite records and the existence of the Nuristani languages.

Dravidian

South Asian Dravidian languages comprise eighty-six variants spoken by an estimated 220 million people (Simons 2018). Spoken mainly in southern India, Dravidian-speaking pockets also exist in central and north India, Nepal and Baluchistan. The term Dravidian, first used by Robert Caldwell in 1856, derives from *dravida*, the Sanskrit word for Tamil. Dravidian languages are first mentioned in the Sanskrit epics around the middle of the first millennium BCE.

Modern Dravidian languages have been classified under four groups: South I, South II, Central and North (Krishnamurti 2013: 19). The diversification into the North, Central and South branches has been placed between 4500–4000 BCE, coinciding with the beginnings of the Southern Neolithic Archaeological Complex (SNAC; Chapter 7, Figure 7.1). As it expanded, the South branch split into South I and South II between 3800–3200 BCE.

There is a strong possibility that Dravidian languages were once widespread in west and northwest South Asia and that Dravidian and Elamite have a common origin (Southworth 2005: 48; Blench 2008: 159–78; McAlpin 1981: 129, 1975). Interestingly, the Tamil word for homeland is *eelam*, similar to Elam, the homeland of Elamite.

While Proto-Dravidian, the ancestor of all Dravidian languages, may have been spoken around 4500 BCE, the root of the Dravidian language family may be as old as 6000–6500 BCE, and may have a connection not just with Elamite but also Uralic (Tyler 1968). A statistical model proposes that both Dravidian and Indo-European belong to a Eurasiatic super-family (Altaic, Chukchi-Kamchatkan, Dravidian, Eskimo, Indo-European, Kartvelian and Uralic) whose roots go back to c 14.5 ka, to the Eurasian heartland (Pagel 2013).[1] Within this super-family tree, Proto-Dravidian is older than Proto-Indo-European. This language super-family spread as the global climate warmed up and the glaciers of the last ice age began to retreat c15 ka. The initial separation of these families occurred before the development of agriculture (before c11 ka). It supports genetic data that Dravidian populations represent an early expansion into South Asia, before that of the Indo-Europeans.

Figure 6.1: Probable pre-Indo-Aryan language map of South Asia

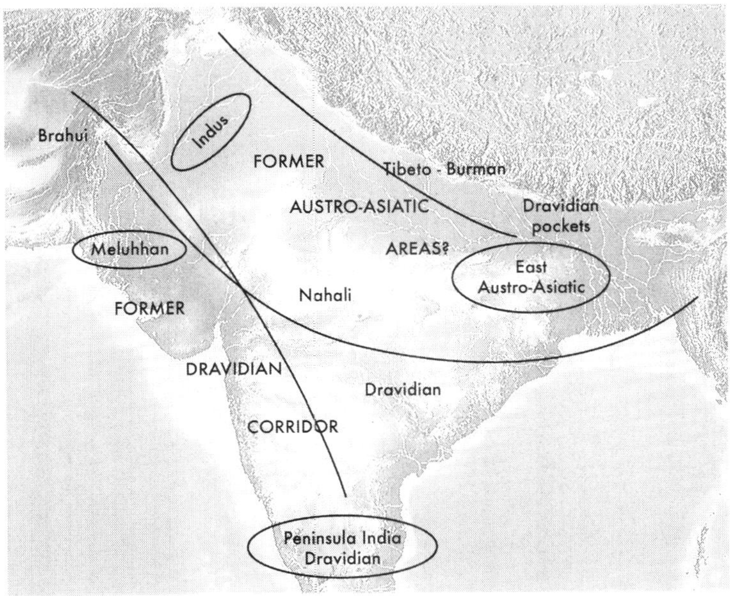

Source: Southworth (2005).

Austro-Asiatic

Southeast Asia is considered the homeland of Austro-Asiatic languages. The Munda languages spoken in central and eastern India by perhaps ten million people constitute its westernmost branch (Anderson 2008). Numerous terms referring to the cultivation of rice and agriculture (ox, pig, taro, millets) connect Munda with languages to the east. It suggests Austro-Asiatic speakers expanded westwards into South Asia with farming cultures connected with Southeast Asia which would explain the significant presence of Y-chromosome O2 among them. Munda's linguistic features point to long-term bi-lingualism with non-Austro-Asiatic languages. Its present geography and the presence of Munda speakers in remote pockets of Madhya

Pradesh, Chhattisgarh, Odisha, West Bengal, Uttar Pradesh, Andhra Pradesh and Maharashtra suggest that they once inhabited a much larger region before being marginalised into the relatively remote forested hill country by Indo-Aryan and Dravidian speakers.

Munda is less internally diverse than Mon-Khmer, the Southeast Asian branch, suggesting its lower age. Apart from Munda (twenty-two sub-families), Austro-Asiatic has two other branches in South Asia, Khasian (three), spoken in the northeast, and Nicobarese (six) (Blench 2007). The genetic structure of South Asia's Austro-Asiatic speakers confirms a westward migration from Southeast Asia.

Tibeto-Burman

Tibeto-Burman is one branch of the Sino-Tibetan family, the other being Chinese (Thurgood 2003). Tibeto-Burman-speaking hunter-gatherers may have settled the Tibetan Plateau c7000–6000 BP with the domestication of the yak and expansion of millet cultivation. In South Asia, they inhabit the northeast and speak about fifty to sixty languages with the highest linguistic diversity being in Arunachal Pradesh, Manipur and Nagaland. Tibeto-Burman is also spoken along the Himalayan foothills. While little is known about their earlier history, traces of the language family are found in Indo-Aryan. For instance, the names Kosala and Kosi may be of Tibeto-Burman origin.

Isolates

South Asia has small populations who speak languages, known as *isolates*, that show no identifiable relationship with any language families: Burushaski (Kashmir), Nahali (central India), Kusunda (central Nepal), Vedda (Sri Lanka), Tharu (south Nepal and UP) and Shom Pen (Nicobar) (Kuiper n.d.). Burushaski has almost no native crop or livestock vocabulary which suggests that its speakers were originally hunter-gatherers who adopted agriculture. Nahali is spoken by an agricultural people with close cultural connections to Munda. However, its agricultural vocabulary seems to derive from Marathi and not Munda, pointing to a hunter-gatherer group that adopted agriculture under the influence of Indo-Aryan populations. Kusunda is spoken by semi-nomadic hunter-gatherers living in the jungles of central Nepal. It has no similarities to neighbouriing languages, but has a distinctive agricultural vocabulary that suggests an agricultural community that returned to foraging.

Isolates were once widespread. They belong to the oldest surviving linguistic strata in South Asia and could have been contemporary to languages that are now extinct. Some of these inferred languages have been identified: the Indus language(s), the source of numerous words, mainly plant names, found in OIA (Old Indo-Aryan) and early Dravidian; Meluhhan; Proto-Bhili, a substrate (underlying language layer) language(s) of which little is known, in the region where Gujarat, Rajasthan, Madhya Pradesh and Maharashtra adjoin each other; Proto-Nilgiri, a pre-Dravidian substrate in the Nilgiris in south India; the Vedda substrate in Sri Lanka; Central Asian substrate(s) which may be the source of a number of words in early OIA and Iranian languages; and an extinct Language X proposed to account for some 30% of Hindi agricultural vocabulary.

Nahali's vocabulary contains clues of what may have happened to these extinct languages and the future of isolates. Today, it is spoken by a few thousand people on the banks of the Tapti River in Madhya Pradesh. Roughly 24% of Nahali words, having no cognates with any other languages, might belong to the oldest languages traceable in India. Beneath its Indo-Aryan appearance, Nahali reveals, at successively lower levels, traces of Dravidian (Kurukh) (9%) and Munda (Korku) (36%). This implies successive levels of immigration by speakers of Austro-

Asiatic, Dravidian and Indo-Aryan, and a gradual retreat of Nahali speakers from a larger region into remote, inaccessible areas before advancing newcomers.

On a linguistic map of South Asia, isolates appear as ever-decreasing islands on the road to eventual extinction.

What the Earliest Texts Reveal

The earliest evidence for Indo-Aryan languages in South Asia appears only around 3.5 ka, after that of the other language families. Unlike the other families, however, they have a considerable body of texts dating to this early period, the oldest in South Asia. They contain important information on the diffusion of the Indo-Aryan speakers into South Asia, and of the people who were already living there. The texts, however, being mainly related to priestly functions, are preserved in the language of an elite section of society and provide only a limited view of the larger world. For instance, we learn of the *dasas* and dasyus only from the few references made to them, and of contemporary Indus languages from the words borrowed from them. It is from this small window that we have to infer much of the rest.

Rgvedic scriptures have been classified into three periods: the early period (1700–1450 BCE) which contains hymns referring to the Yadu-Turvasa and Anu-Druhyu tribes; the middle period (1450–1300 BCE) which focuses on the Bharata chieftain Sudas and his rivals the Trasadasyu and Puru tribes; and the late period (1300–1200 BCE) which focuses on the emergence of the Kuru super tribe (Masica 1991; Witzel 1999a, 1999b, 2000). Later OIA literary tradition reflects a movement of Indo-Aryan speakers from the Punjab eastward to the Ganga-Yamuna *doab*, while the archaeological record reveals a southward expansion from the north Indus into Sindh by the middle Rgvedic period, followed by eastward movements into central India and the Deccan. These migratory routes paralleled each other and eventually met in the fourth century BCE in the central Ganges Valley. Linguistic evidence indicates that by then differences had arisen in the dialects, classified as the inner and outer Indo-Aryan, spoken in the two regions. The OIA literary tradition considers outer Indo-Aryan as an aberrant form, and its speakers as beyond the pale of Vedic society. The *Satapatha Brahmana* terms the regions they inhabited as *mleccha* (non-Vedic, barbarian), possibly derived from Meluhha (south Sindh). Mleccha regions included Sindh, Saurashtra, Gujarat, Maharashtra, Bihar, Bengal and Odisha. This regional division represented by the north-central and southwest-east languages corresponds to a long-standing historical division between the Aryavarta, or land of Vedic orthodoxy, and the *mleccha-desa*, lands where non-Aryan languages were spoken and Vedic rituals not observed.

The Rgveda is composed in Vedic Sanskrit, an Indo-European language belonging to the Indo-Iranian branch (Indo-Aryan, Iranian, Nuristani). Some 383 words, 4% of this text, are of non-Indo-Aryan origin, borrowed from languages spoken c1450 BCE in the Punjab (Witzel 2000). Relating mostly to agriculture, animals, plants, music and names of persons, clans/tribes, places and rivers, these loanwords are suggestive of a people moving into a new and unfamiliar environment, and interacting with populations who already have agriculture. The names of things peculiar to South Asia (Munda: banana-*kadali*, cotton-*karpasa*, pepper-*marica*, mongoose-*nakula*; Dravidian: palm-*tala*, lotus-*kamala*, *kumuda*, *kuvalaya*, *nalina*, sandalwood-*candana*, peacock-*mayura*) are either borrowed or coined and suggest an encounter with something new.

These words were borrowed from Harappan languages. Four have been identified: a pre-Rgvedic Para-Munda substrate in the Punjab; a northern Indus language; a southern Indus language, Meluhhan, the source of some forty words referring to Harappan products traded in Mesopotamia and recorded in its texts; Dravidian words in the middle and late Vedic period (Witzel 1999a).

The earliest foreign elements found in the Rgveda are Austro-Asiatic in appearance (names of individuals, tribes, geographical features) and belong to a prefixing language(s) (Kuiper 1948: 5). Prefixes are common in Munda and other Austro-Asiatic languages, but unknown in Dravidian, Tibeto-Burman and Burushaski. Variously termed Proto-Munda, Para-Munda or Harappan, there is reason to believe that it was once the predominant language family spoken in the Indus Valley in the second millennium BCE. Its influence may have extended to southeast Iran, Baluchistan and Makran. A possible link between Sumerian and Kherwani, a Munda language, has been suggested based on the presence of thirty-four words common to both languages (Diakonoff n.d.; 1997: 56).

River and geographical features mostly remain constant in the forever-changing flux of population movements. Their names can open windows into the early linguistic history of a region and are often ancient and contain clues on the identities of the earlier inhabitants of a territory. River names may be adopted directly from the local language (Kausiki, Kosi), or transformed from a local name (Ganga, Kubha, Sutudri). They may be translations (Sadanira), or new but related to the old name (Vitasta). Some reflect transfers from an older place of migration (Sarasvati, Gomati, Sarayu). Many of the names of rivers listed in the Rgveda are Vedic, but as their modern names show these were probably not their pre-Vedic names: Sutudri (Sutlej), Vipas (Beas), Parushni (Ravi), Asikni (Chenab), Vitasta (Jhelum), Sarasvati (Ghaggar), Drishadvati (Chautang), Kubha (Kabul), Gomati (Gomal), Krumu (Kurram). Sutudri, possibly of Munda origin, became Satadru ('flowing in a hundred channels') before being renamed Sutlej. The visambal/pal (*vaisambhalya/phalya*) was Sankritised to *saras-vati*. A number of river names (Ganga, Gandak, Narmada, Godavari, Alakananda, Mandakini) contain elements that can be reconstructed from Munda words related to water and river (*da, dak, gandak*) (Witzel n.d.).

Dravidian place names locate Dravidian speakers at the very crossroads of ancient population movements into and through

South Asia. They trace a route from the Iranian plateau to Sindh, suggesting they were in Iran before Indo-Aryan speakers. Dravidian loanwords appear in Rgvedic texts from c1450 BCE. They have no association with agriculture, a clear indication that the language of the northern Indus people was not Dravidian. The main contact between Dravidian and Indo-Aryan speakers appears to have taken place in the mleccha-desa lands of Sindh, the southwest, and the Deccan where Dravidian speakers appear to have once formed a significant part of the population before the arrival of the outer Indo-Aryan groups. These areas are now occupied by the speakers of Marathi, Konkani, Gujarati and Sindhi. These languages contain traits that suggest an early Dravidian influence in the form of lexical and structural borrowings, and place and river names. Marathi, for instance, has a substantial Dravidian substrate with about 5 % of its basic vocabulary being of Dravidian origin. Further, place and river names reveal that one or more Dravidian languages were spoken earlier in Maharashtra (Southworth n.d.a). It has been suggested that the first agricultural settlers who formed the chalcolithic (Copper Age; transition between Neolithic and Bronze Age) Jorwe culture in Maharashtra between mid-second and early first millennium BCE were Dravidian-speaking, and the culture underwent changes when Indo-Aryan immigrants speaking a precursor of modern Marathi arrived from the north (Allchin 1996: 352).

Together with genetic and linguistic evidence, archaeobotany supports the view that Proto-Dravidian speakers dispersed from the margins of the Thar Desert to south Deccan between 5.5–4.5 ka (Fuller 2011). The current distribution of Dravidian languages and Y-chromosome Hgs J and L suggests its speakers were once widespread over large parts of India and were part of a common gene pool. In the northwest, the Dravidian family was swamped by Indo-Aryan languages; in central and east India, Indo-Aryan languages cut swathes through them isolating Dravidian speakers into pockets; only in the south did Dravidian speakers hold their ground.

As this encounter took place, Proto-Dravidian split into Proto-North-Dravidian (Brahui, Kurukh, Malto), Proto-Central-Dravidian (Gondi, others) and Proto-South-Dravidian (Krishnamurti 2003; Southworth n.d.b). This split was complete by c1500 BCE. The movement of Dravidian speakers from the northwest, therefore, began earlier, with predominantly hunter-gatherer groups moving into central India, and agro-pastoralists moving into the Deccan to form the SNAC. Further south, Proto-South-Dravidian (PSD) split into PSD 1 (Telugu, others) and PSD 2 (Tamil, Kannada, Malayalam, others). This process was completed by 1100 BCE.

Reconstructed vocabularies of Proto-Dravidian and Proto-South Dravidian languages, while demonstrating a steady movement from the Indus Valley to the Deccan, also reveal a steady progress towards increasing complexity in agriculture, material culture, habitation, as well as political, economic and social relations of their speakers (Southworth 2005: 238). Proto-Dravidian depicts an economy based mainly on herding (sheep and cattle), with limited agricultural products acquired through gathering, trade and occasional periods of sedentism. Agriculture appears to have been taken up in South Asia after the adoption of wheat cultivation c3500 BCE (Bellwood 2011). After a period of acculturation, Dravidian farmers adopted rice and millet cultivation in Sindh. Dravidian-derived words relevant to agriculture (fruit, field, threshing ground, joint of plant) and animals (sheep, ass, hoof), suggest a significant role for Dravidian speakers in Harappan agriculture subsequently.

Proto-Dravidian speech knows much of the fauna depicted on Indus seals and a number of trees native to the region. This list gets expanded in Proto-South Dravidian with the inclusion of species more common to the Deccan and the sea coast. Proto-Dravidian reveals that its speakers were part of the agricultural economy of eastern and southern Harappan areas by at least c1800 BCE, and practised pastoralism and hunting. Proto-South Dravidian introduces additional crops adapted to a drier climate, irrigation gains in importance and becomes more sophisticated and words appear for commercial and other transactions involving grain. A more complex society begins to emerge with kings and chiefs, managers, taxes, armies, territorial divisions, customs and debt collection. There are villages, towns, castles, forts, prisons, palaces and streets, and the caste system appears to be present in a well-developed form. There are words for different types of buildings, weapons and ironwork, wheeled vehicles and ships, umbrellas, garments and precious stones. Elaborate religious practices require an expanded vocabulary for priests and temple servants, gods, worship and ritual ceremonies. It does not differentiate between human rulers and deities.

A Summing-up

At the outset, it must be emphasised that the language spoken by an individual or community in no way identifies their genetic group. People adopt languages. For instance, English is spoken by a large number of Indians; in no way does that link them to English haplogroups. Languages spread for various reasons, mainly because they serve a basic need to communicate. The language used for that communication depends on particular circumstances, the relative status of the communicating persons and other factors.

The earliest linguistic scene in South Asia suggests a region in which multiple hunter-gatherer languages were spoken by small populations with some sort of lingua franca at border regions. The Neolithic brought South Asia's four dominant modern language families, Austro-Asiatic and Tibeto-Burman from the east, and Dravidian and Indo-Aryan from the west with the inward migration of farming/herding communities. While Tibeto-Burman speakers were confined to the northeastern hills and Himalayan foothills, Austro-Asiatic speakers may have moved as far west as the Harappan region.

Farmer/herder groups began moving in from the Iranian plateau from c8000 BCE. The movement of Dravidian-speaking pastoralists intensified by c4500 BCE into the lower Indus basin, in Sindh, from where they moved on to the Peninsula via Saurashtra, Gujarat and Maharashtra. As the appearance of the first Dravidian words in the Rgveda c1450–1300 BCE reveals, some contact was established with Indo-Aryan speakers here, and in the Greater Punjab as well.

Considering both archaeological and linguistic evidence, it appears that the migrations of Indo-Aryan speakers into the northwest occurred over a few centuries. The earlier groups made contact with Dravidian speakers in Sindh and eventually developed the Outer Indo-Aryan group of languages. OIA speakers, the composers of the Rgveda, arrived in the Punjab a little later and expanded into the Gangetic basin where the Inner Indo-Aryan languages began evolving.

This pattern of regional settlement is suggested by the names for wheat and rice in Dravidian and Indo-Aryan dialects. The Rgveda is unfamiliar with wheat; barley (*yava*) is more important. Rice is not known (Witzel n.d.). The Avestan name for wheat, *gantuma*, becomes *godhuma* (from the northern Indus dialect) in Sanskrit and *godi* (from the southern Dravidian dialect) in Kannada. Similarly, Indo-Aryan derives the name for rice from the northern Indus dialect (*vrihi*), while Dravidian acquires it from the southern (*varinci*, *[v]ariki*).

As these language families pushed further into India, earlier languages retreated and disappeared. Most of South Asia's early languages are now extinct. Just a few isolates spoken by small and, as the term implies, isolated populations remain. As isolates disappear, a rich historical record is being increasingly lost.

7

Foraging to Farming

Until about 10 ka, for over 95% of their history, humans lived exclusively as foragers, a way of life inherited from their hominid ancestors. Hunting and gathering, one of the most successful survival strategies adopted, helped humans survive some of the harshest fluctuations in earth's climatic history experienced by hominids. Some of the most important behavioural changes in social evolution occurred during this phase of human history.

The foraging or hunter-gatherer economy depends on food collection. The farming economy is based on food production. Foragers collect fruits, honey, nuts, plants, seeds and tubers, and scavenge or hunt animals, birds, fish and insects. They allow the land to re-generate and leave the environment in which they live largely untouched. Having no direct control over their food sources, they adapt to a wide range of habitats and diets. The objective of foragers is to maximise value at minimum cost and effort. The focus is on harvesting foods of higher nutritional value.

Foraging technology developed diverse capabilities in different regions. For instance, nineteenth-century forest-dwelling Gonds lived in communities of fifteen nto twenty persons in five or six poorly constructed huts. Often a single hut separated from the next by a distance of two to three kms constituted a village. Even in open country, the largest village consisted of no more than thirty to thirty-five huts, each housing five to eight persons (Rowney 1882: 10).

Required to scour large areas for food, foragers live in small, highly mobile groups. They do not accumulate property. Population growth rates are low with a typical gap of four years between children. This enhances mobility as it allows children to travel at the pace of the group. Groups meet at places that can support larger populations at particular times. They communicate and exchange goods and ideas, share stories and songs and seek marriage partners. Such networks are crucial for collective learning. Their society is egalitarian. It values individual autonomy, diffused authority, mobility, sharing of resources, skills, tools and immediate consumption of food. Foragers influence others through persuasion rather than physical force; oral rhetoric replaces the authority of elders, religious edicts or legal systems. They adopt kinship-based social systems, ideologies and subsistence strategies which differ from those of food cultivators. Forager identities are largely based on territory, sartorial choice, language variation or clan group. They worship spirits and deities, and their relation with animals and nature is governed by how these entities affect them (Fortier 2009).

In South Asia, forty contemporary societies still adopt a hunter-gatherer lifestyle as their primary subsistence strategy, despite being pushed by an ever – expanding agricultural and urban culture into marginal areas. They speak a language belonging to one of six families: Andamanese, Austro-Asiatic, Dravidian, Indo-European, Isolate or Tibeto-Burman (Fortier 2009). Their numbers vary from about 20,000 (Hill Kharias and Yanadis) to less than 350 members (Aranadan, Jarawa, Jeru, Kusunda, Onge, Shompen, Vedda, and Yerukula). Of the languages spoken, Dravidian numbers the most speakers.

These 'tribals' are often seen as being beyond the pale of 'civilised' society, living as they do in hills and forests rather than in plains and villages, not conforming to caste-based and hierarchical society, speaking their own languages and following different religious and economic practices. Today, in the strict understanding of the term, forager numbers are limited to a few thousands. From colonial times many have been forced out of the forests to live in economic backwardness as landless agricultural labourers or employed in fishing, hunting, mining, quarrying and construction (Pluciennik 2004: 21–23).

The Middle to Upper Palaeolithic Transition

The Middle to Upper Palaeolithic transition saw a quantum change in the way South Asian foragers perceived and interacted with their world. Their cultural innovations suggest it was a time of environmental deterioration and habitat fragmentation along with population expansions that overtaxed the carrying capacity of fragile ecosystems. Foragers were forced to hunt smaller game which offered low dietary returns at relatively high hunting costs. At this stressful stage, mass-produced microliths appeared. Light, portable and replaceable, they enhanced tool reliability, and as barbed projectiles, hunting technology. Bead manufacture, the use of ochre and the adoption of symbolic practices suggest an early phase of formalising ritual and religion.

Throughout South Asia, foragers adapted lifestyles to exploit depleting local resources. The best-studied site that documents forager adaptation to changing environments over a long time-span is Jwalapuram. Its landscape, ranging from open grassland to woodland, experienced increasing aridity and environmental degradation from 35 ka. A proliferation of microlithic tools, beads, worked bone and fragments of a human cranium recovered here reveal much about how humans responded to this changing situation and developed modern capacities for complex behaviour and symbolic thought (Clarkson 2009; Chapter 5).

Batadomba-lena in Sri Lanka preserves evidence of a foraging culture from at least c36 ka (Perera 2011). People lived in rock shelters located in evergreen forests traversed by streams. They hunted small and agile animals, largely arboreal like monkeys and squirrels, fish and snails and gathered fruits and nuts. They used projectiles, snares and traps and developed a complex toolkit made from bones and stones. Batadomba-lena's inhabitants practised symbolic behaviour and made artefacts from objects brought from the sea shore 80 kms away.

Farmers

The Holocene brought about a fundamental change in the way humans saw their world and exploited it. Plants and animals began to thrive in a warmer climate, and in some parts of the world edible plants grew in profusion. It was no longer necessary to be constantly mobile in the search for food. It led to sedentism and the beginnings of agriculture. Food-producers were soon confronted by entirely new situations never faced by foragers.

The first and most important site where food-gatherers became food-producers was Gobekli Tepe in Turkey (Schmidt 2010). Here, c10 ka, hunter-gatherer groups from surrounding regions began to build permanent settlements and form larger communities. It required the creation of a symbolic dimension to culture to hold them together.

Gobekli Tepe consisted of circular megalithic enclosures built on an elevated spot. It was a sacred site, a regional centre where communities met to engage in complex rites, possibly humanity's first temple. There were no residential buildings. Gobekli Tepe was built not by a sedentary agricultural population but by large groups of hunter-gatherers working together. Its monuments reveal a crucial innovation humans evolved to unite and motivate disparate groups without physical coercion.

When human groups grow beyond 150 individuals, significant differences appear among them which makes productive cooperation difficult (Harari 2011: 101). This is one reason why hunter-gatherer groups remain small. At Gobekli Tepe, large hunter-gatherer groups with their own individual mini-cultures worked together to build the first large expressions of monumental and extraordinarily rich symbolic culture over a long period of time. Motivating these groups and holding them together required, apart from a dependable source of food, a broader, common ideology with shared identities. It required the creation of shared myths and symbolic culture to unite them to achieve a common objective: the building of a gateway to tap the powers of a divine realm.

Gobekli Tepe was located in a region where wild wheat and barley grew in abundance within the Fertile Crescent, a region extending from Jordan, Israel, Lebanon and Syria through southeast Turkey and along the Tigris and Euphrates rivers through Iraq and west Iran. Here, c12,000 years ago, hunter-gatherers began intensive gathering, processing and storage of wild wheat and barley. The ancestors of two wheat variants found here, einkorn and emmer, constitute most of the world's domesticated wheat crops today. Over the years, selective gathering and dispersal of larger seeds led to denser concentrations of harvestable plants and their eventual domestication. By 9000 BCE, the region was dotted with farming sites and permanent settlements with stone granaries. New stone implements, scythes, pestles and mortars, were devised to feed a growing population that relied increasingly on domesticated food sources.

This farming technology, together with the culture required to hold larger populations that it generated together, spread westward to Europe and eastward to South Asia. Domesticated einkorn and emmer wheat appeared in south Levant and southeast Turkey c7500 BCE. About 6000 BCE, they spread south to Mesopotamia and west to Anatolia, the Mediterranean basin, and Europe (Faris 2014).

Global Plant and Animal Domestication Centres

Of the very many wild plants that grow all over the globe, only a few can be domesticated for human consumption. It is in these regions that the first domestications of wild grains occurred. Domestication is the process by which humans gain a measure of control over the propagation of plants and animals and modify them for their use. It allows cultivation on a large scale.

Plants and animals were domesticated independently in different regions of the globe at different times.

Table 7.1: Domestication of plants and animals globally

Time	Region	Domesticated crop/animal
c9000 BCE	Fertile Crescent	barley, flax, wheat, chickpeas, lentils, peas, cows, dogs, goats, sheep
c6500 BCE	Yellow/Yangtze River Valleys	millet, rice, wheat, soya beans, chickens, goats, sheep
c6500 BCE	Papua New Guinea	sugarcane, bananas, sago, taro, yams, dogs, pigs
c6000 BCE	Indus Valley	barley, rice, rye, wheat, cotton, lentils, peas, chickens, dogs, pigs
c3500 BCE	Mesoamerica	amaranth, maize, beans, cocoa, chillies, papaya, squash, tomatoes, dogs, ducks, turkeys
c3000 BCE	Andes	quinoa, beans, cocoa, potatoes, alpacas, guinea pigs, llamas

Source: Adapted from https://www.khanacademy.org/humanities/big-history-project/agriculture-civilization/first-cities-states/a/activity-comparing-crops (accessed April 2024).

The Beginnings of the South Asian Farming Economy

The South Asian farming economy evolved through both primary and secondary domestication. The former relates to independent domestication of local wild flora and fauna, the latter to the adoption of crops domesticated in other regions. The most important secondary domesticated crop was einkorn wheat which first appeared around Mehrgarh along with other varieties of wheat, barley, lentils, chickpeas/gram, peas, grass pea and flax/

linseed as part of the west Asian Neolithic founder crop package. Einkorn wheat's current geographical distribution suggests four possible diffusion routes out of the Fertile Crescent. Of these, two eventually reached South Asia, one via trade routes through Iran and the other via Ethiopia (introduced there via Egypt and Sudan) and Oman via maritime trade (Badaeva 2015).

At Mehrgarh, this triggered a primary domestication of zebu cattle (*Bos indicus*), sheep, cotton, sesame and water buffalo. Over the centuries, a range of secondary domesticates reached South Asia from other regions: China (citrus, japonica rice, millets); Southeast Asia (yams); Africa (millets, pulses); America (potato, tomato, chilli, cashew, cocoa); and Europe (vegetables, fruits).

The Spread of Farming in South Asia (Blench 2008; Fuller 2003; Kingwell-Banham 2015)

The four major South Asian language families contain information about the association of their speakers with agriculture.

Austro-Asiatic speakers appear to have arrived from Southeast Asia via river valleys with fully established agriculture that encompassed cattle, pig, taro, millets and rice. Southeast Asian farmers may have adopted farming as early as 8000 BCE. Tibeto-Burman hunter-gatherers in Nepal and Bhutan appear to have become sedentary around 5000–4000 BCE with the domestication of the yak and cultivation of millets.

Dravidian in its earliest phase, that is before Brahui split from the rest, shows no sign of agriculture. Instead, there are references to animal herding and wild food processing. By the time Kurux and Malto split, the cultivation of taro had begun but not of cereals. The final phases, South and Central Dravidian, reveal a full range of agricultural production associated with the SNAC (2300–1800 BCE). Proto-Indo-European knows only horses and other livestock indicating their world centred around the horse and that they adopted agriculture from their neighbours later.

Figure 7.1 : South Asian macro regions of primary domestication and encounter with secondary domesticates

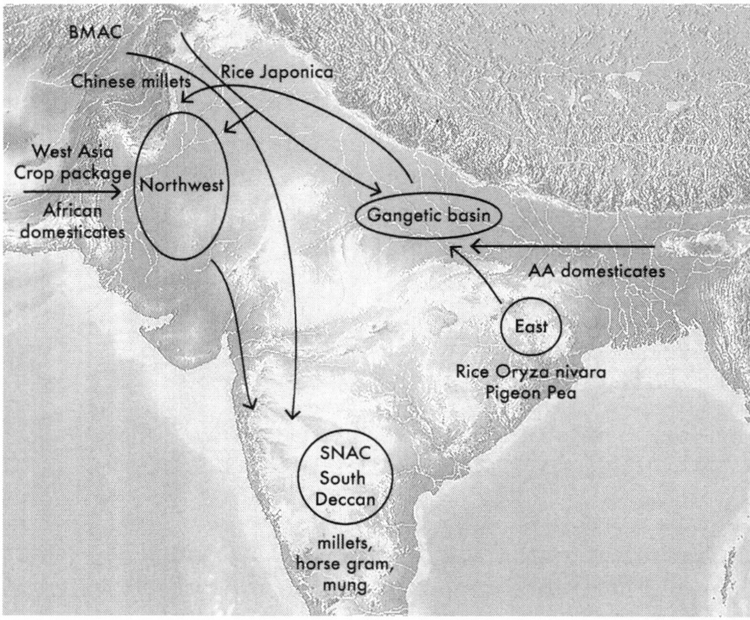

Source: Kingwell-Banham (2015).

The South Asian archaeological record identifies four macro regions where primary domestication occurred: the greater Indus valley in the northwest; the Gangetic plains; east India; and south Deccan (Karnataka).

The Northwest (Indus Basin)

The transition from foraging to settled agriculture spread from c8500 BCE from Mehrgarh to Punjab, Uttar Pradesh and Gujarat. It took another 4,000 years before it eventually reached southern Peninsular India (Kivisild 2002). These first farmers were either

Table 7.2: Chronology of domestication of plants and animals in South Asia

	7000 BCE	6500 BCE	6000 BCE	3500 BCE	2500 BCE	2000 BCE	1500 BCE
Northwest	wheat, zebu barley (WA)	goats, cattle			millets, pulses (SA); ragi (A)	Rice (*japonica*) (C)	cow pea, sorghum (A)
Ganges basin			rice (SA)		goats, zebu cattle	millets, pulses (SA)	p. millet, sorghum (A); citrus, millet (C)
SNAC				zebu cattle	millets, pulses (SA); goats	ragi (A)	cow pea, hyacinth bean, p. millet, sorghum (A)
East					rice, pulses (SA)	zebu cattle	

Note: WA- West Asia; SA- South Asia; A- Africa; C- China
Source: Compiled by author; various sources.

local foragers who had adopted farming technology (cultural diffusion) or immigrants (demic diffusion).

The early farming phase at Mehrgarh had several similarities with sites to the west: pottery types, circular fire pits filled with burnt pebbles, large granaries. Burials bore strong resemblance to those in the Zagros and clay figurines to those found in Iran and Central Asia. Genetically, the worldwide spread of farmers from the Fertile Crescent is associated with the Y-chromosome J2-M172 and its sub-lineages. Mehrgarh is connected to Iran and Afghanistan by semi-arid plateaus, ridges and deserts. Rainfall is low and agriculture possible only in the foothills and valleys. Neolithic settlements were small and widely separated, and populations mobile and dependent on pastoralism. Ancient trade routes passing through these lands are littered with artefacts, figurines, pottery, mud-bricks of striking similarity and association with agriculture. It suggests a common incipient culture and continuity across this extensive region, and a systematic eastward spread at a speed of about 0.65 km/yr, not by large population movements but rather through diffused admixture and trade contacts at border regions still inhabited by hunter-gatherer groups (Gangal 2014; Singh 2016).

Between 2400–1500 BCE, domesticated African crops, finger millet (ragi), hyacinth bean, varieties of sorghum, pearl millet and cow pea appeared in the Indus Valley. Unlike west Asian crops which spread in a coherent pattern suggestive of demic diffusion, African crops came in an irregular pattern through the medium of trade. Being drought resistant, they were a welcome supplement as monsoon rainfall entered a declining trend. Double cropping intensified food production during the Mature Harappan (2500–2000 BCE).

Agriculture led to major socio-cultural transitions, technological developments and population expansions in the Indus basin. Huge granaries made the founding of South Asia's first cities possible. Harappan crops and livestock dispersed eastwards, into the Ganges basin and the Deccan via trading channels. Wheat and barley, rice, pearl millet, sorghum, finger millet and pigeon pea reached south India, especially after 1700 BCE.

The Middle Ganges Basin and the East

Rice (*Oryza sativa*) is the pre-eminent crop of the Ganges basin. Charred rice grains dated to c6400 BCE recovered at Lahuradewan in the Middle Ganges Basin may represent the earliest use of wild rice by hunter-gatherers (Bates 2016; Gross 2014; Huang 2012; Tewari 2006).

The two most important wild progenitors of Asian rice come from China (*Oryza rufipogon*) and India (*Oryza nivara*). Both underwent a domestication process that finished around 4500 BCE in China with Yangtze *japonica* and about two millennia later in India when *proto-indica* hybridised with japonica. In the Yangtze basin, farmers used irrigation to induce higher grain productivity from wild rufipogon. In contrast, early rice cultivation in India essentially depended on monsoon rains. Monsoon-fed Oryza nivara was collected from the wild after probably burning off competing vegetation to induce higher harvests (Fuller 2012).

The plains of the Mahanadi River basin and the surrounding hills of Odisha in east India, being home to diverse and widespread wild rice species, are the most likely regions for the origin of rice domestication. The foothills, uplands and coastal plains were seasonally cultivated by planting rice, pulses (horse gram, pigeon pea) and millets (brown top millet, Setaria sp.). Pigeon pea is native to Odisha. Pockets of Dravidian-speaking groups in Jharkhand, west Odisha and Chhattisgarh indicate early migrations of agro-pastoral communities and the establishment of agriculture by the mid-second millennium BCE with primary and secondary domesticates, cattle and buffalo.

South Asian rice was fully domesticated only after a genetic input from japonica. As the introduction of western domesticates (taurine cattle, sheep, wheat, barley) into China during this period demonstrates, the stimulus came from an intensification of east-west trade. The BMAC region played a significant role in this trade and is the most likely route for the introduction of japonica into South Asia. At Pirak in Baluchistan, there is the first clear evidence of the presence of Bactrian camels and horses used for transport in this trade c1700 BCE (McIntosh 2008: 98). Hybridised genes and irrigation created larger-grained *indica* rice varieties which spread throughout South Asia. The earliest evidence for fully domesticated rice appears c1800 BCE at Mahagara in the Indus Valley. A progressive increase in the proportion of domesticated to wild types suggests a steady rise in rice cultivation from the Early Harappan (3200–2600 BCE) to the Late Harappan (1900–1300 BCE).

From c2500 BCE, rice became more common in the Ganges basin, a meeting point for agriculture spreading from the east and west. Wheat and barley arrived c2400 BCE and goats, sheep and domestic cattle by c2000 BCE. Shortly after, south Indian crops (brown top millet, horse gram, mung bean) were cultivated with a double-cropping system, clear evidence of trade contacts with peninsular India (Fuller 2011, 2012). Chinese crops (citrus, peach, apricot, millets, cannabis sativa) and hand harvest knives reached c1400 BCE.

Peninsular India

Unlike the rest of India where agriculture began with cereal farming, in the south pastoralism developed into a well-integrated agro-pastoral system (Blench 2001).

Pastoralism arose from a need for increased pasture for surplus farm animals and mobility to prevent the spread of diseases. Pastoralists usually inhabit marginalised lands where crop cultivation is limited. Their territories often overlap with that of foragers with whom they maintain a complex relationship. Pastoralists follow seasonal changes in resources, like water and grazing lands, required to feed their flocks. They can be nomadic (resorting to highly mobile, irregular patterns), transhumant (moving in regular seasonal patterns between relatively fixed locations) or sedentary. Their mobility and knowledge of difficult terrain have involved them in trade and warfare from the earliest times.

Pastoral societies herd domesticated livestock for their livelihood, exploiting them for milk, meat, hides and wool. The most common in South Asia are buffalo, cattle, goats and sheep, and in some areas, ducks and geese. Such societies are mostly patrilineal and male-dominated, with genealogies, actual or fictitious, stretching back many generations. Group sizes are typically limited to between fifty and 200 persons with men usually taking care of herding. Herd size often determines wealth and status. Women are responsible for less strenuous work like handicraft, food processing and milking of livestock.

The ashmounds of the Deccan are an enduring legacy of its pastoral past (Fuller 2001). Accumulations of burnt animal dung at ancient corrals, they preserve fossilised cattle hoof-prints, stone tools, pottery fragments and animal bones, predominantly of cattle but also of sheep and goats. Located in uncultivated sandy soils, they reflect on the relative unimportance of crops at least initially. The economic importance of cattle is recorded in the peninsula's rock art depicting long-horned cattle. Zebu bulls with accentuated humps and horns overwhelmingly dominate these ancient images.

Ashmounds developed into monumental structures. The mound at Kupgal (in the Deccan), for example, is approximately fifty metres long and 5.5 m high. When set alight, these large burning mounds of dung would have been visible from afar. It served to attract large seasonal gatherings that facilitated trade in cattle and goods (beads, copper objects, axes and other implements), cultural and knowledge exchanges, and establishing ties through marriage. There is evidence of ritual activities and feasting with cattle butchering sites located nearby.

After ashmound formation ceased, the sites became villages. Ashmounds, therefore, played a significant role in identifying places for long-term human habitation.

In south India, the first settlements, with ceramics but no ashmounds, date to 3000 BCE. There is no clear evidence of either animal herding or plant cultivation. The first ashmounds appeared c2500 BCE. They contain bones of cattle, sheep and goats, and suggest the beginnings of cultivation. Three centuries later, villages appeared on hilltops. Their earliest agricultural sites leave evidence of domesticated native species, pulses (mung bean, horse gram), and millets (brown top, bristly foxtail). By c2000 BCE, hilltop ashmounds-turned-villages were abundant, and cultivated crops included wheat and barley. The first African crops appeared c1800 BCE. A century later, ashmounds were no more formed, and by c800 BCE, hilltop villages were abandoned. There is clear evidence of iron working, horses and the earliest cultivation of rice after c1000 BCE. By c300 BCE, settlements moved to the plains and rice was cultivated more widely.

Ironically, South Asia preserves the earliest archaeobotanical evidence for African crops. At least four varieties were cultivated in the Peninsula from 2500–1500 BCE. The earliest dates for cow pea come from the Harappan site of Hulas (2200 BCE) and from Diamabad (c1700 BCE) in Maharashtra. Pearl millet was grown in Hallur, Karnataka c2200 BCE. Hyacinth bean shows a high diversity either due to an early arrival or multiple introductions. The earliest (c2000 BCE) samples come from the Harappan site of Mahorana. Finger millet (ragi) originated in the East African highlands, and sorghum was introduced from southeast Africa on multiple occasions. Linguistically, sorghum and pearl millet can be reconstructed in Proto-South-Central Dravidian (c1500 BCE). Ragi is dated slightly later to Proto-South-Dravidian.

As the South Asian climate became more arid c4 ka and people abandoned the Indus Valley, sedentary agriculture took hold in central and south India (Ponton 2012a, 2012b). Between 2300–1900 BCE, Rajasthan experienced particularly unstable climate with frequent and long-lasting droughts. Transhumant forager-herders who habitually used the Thar-Deccan savannah corridor began settling down in the Deccan with their domesticated sheep, goats and perhaps cattle. Most likely they were Proto-Dravidian speakers who had knowledge of livestock, seed gathering and processing, and the flora of the Deccan. The Thar-Deccan corridor, a semi-arid zone with 400–890 mm annual rainfall, became increasingly populated by sedentary farmers who grew winter crops (wheat, barley, lentil, pea, grass pea).

Settlements in peninsular India increased markedly after 2000 BCE. By c1200 BCE, about 60% of these sites were located in areas with less than 1000 mm of rainfall. This was made possible by the development of a unique system of water storage tanks constructed for irrigation and to tide over the dry summer months.

South India receives most of its rainfall from an unpredictable northeast monsoon which, however, sometimes brings heavy cyclonic precipitation. Prior to c1200 BCE, semi-nomadism remained the solution to monsoon variability. The tank system of irrigation probably started with the use of small ponds as watering holes for cattle. The tank (Portuguese: *tangue* – lake) is a man-made reservoir designed to collect and store run-off water during the rainy season made by constructing an earthen bund or embankment across the slope of a valley. Collected water is released to fields by a network of small canals during the subsequent dry season. Tanks vary in size and can irrigate land from three to 3000 acres or more. They are often interlinked and can store water for more than a year. The construction and maintenance of tanks involves collective community action, and in the past this was sponsored by local rulers and dominant groups (Gunnell 2007).

The Forager Response

Globally, populations adopted agriculture in different ways. In some regions, agriculture was established rapidly with large-scale displacement of hunter-gathering communities. In others, there was prolonged interaction between farmers and foragers before the adoption of agriculture. In still others, there was a transfer of crops, livestock and technology. South Asia, in addition to local domestication of plants and animals, adopted all these processes along with pastoralism.

Food production gave farmers enormous advantages over hunter-gatherers. It triggered population expansions, migration and the spread of new language families. In contrast to traditional low birth rates among hunter-gatherers with typical child spacing 3–4 years, higher food yields supported higher farmer population densities with a skewed male-female growth rate, a possible outcome of reduced hunting-related mortality rates among males. In certain regions, especially between 6.5–2 ka, there was a ten- to 100-fold increase in male populations with the advent of agriculture. Sedentary food-producing societies accumulated and stored food surpluses. It precipitated fundamental changes in social organisations, human perception of the environment and relationship to plants and animals. It led to the development of complex technology, social stratification, centralised states and professional armies (Diamond 2003).

The contact between farmers and hunter-gatherers was complex. Some intermarriage, rather gene transfer from farmer men to hunter-gatherer women, occurred. Farming societies, exposed to infectious diseases such as smallpox and measles from domesticated animals, developed some resistance to them. Hunter-gatherers, having none, succumbed when they came in contact with expanding farming societies.

South Asia's foragers countered the relentless pressure from the farming economy by adopting a range of economic and social strategies. They added animal husbandry, small-scale agriculture and trading to their core hunter-gatherer subsistence strategy. This economic flexibility enabled them to maintain a certain distance from other sections of the population, and to retain their values, beliefs and lifestyles. It required a finely-tuned balancing act, with different regional approaches, as their lands were appropriated for agriculture and pasture.

An example of this interaction comes from sites 100–300 kms distant from Lothal, an important commercial and manufacturing centre of the Late Harappan period located at its southeastern border in Gujarat (Possehl 1979). Here, a variety of raw materials and finished products (stone and bronze tools, copper and gold, marine shells, elephant tusks, steatite, semi-precious stones) have been excavated. At Langhnaj, 100 kms to the north, black-and-red pottery, steatite beads and a copper knife, all typical of Harappan manufacture dating to c2040, show that the site was seasonally occupied by hunter-gatherers. Excavated skeletons reveal regular gene flow between them and Harappans.

The aversion to assimilation and persistence in preserving their cultural heritage and traditional lifestyles pushed foragers further into forests and marginal lands. Today, they face a new threat from economic and political forces that eye the minerals and other resources that these lands possess. Many have become landless tenants, suffered declining birth rates and have been absorbed into complex societies in the lower rungs of society with little chance of advancement. The very survival of the history, culture and life-styles of these earliest colonisers of South Asia is at stake. Global statistical estimates irrefutably support this conclusion. From c9500 BCE, forager numbers have declined from roughly 99% of the world's population to about 1% by 1800 CE (Macedo 2015: 47).

8

Foragers – The Retreat

In 1694, the Moghul Prince Muhammad Masum, passing by Kurnool (in present-day Andhra Pradesh), encountered a group of 'wild men', dark-skinned and hairy, wearing caps made of leaves. They spoke a language that was not understood even by nearby village folk and they subsisted on honey, tubers and the flesh of animals they hunted with bows and arrows. Living in caves or sheltering under trees, they harmed no one. They did not care for the gold and silver presented to them by the prince and when a small gun was fired, they ran up the mountains with surprising speed (Scott 1794: 83).

These 'wild men' were the Chenchus, a proto-Australoid tribe living in the jungles of Andhra. The Chenchus are described as distinct from other tribal groups, with, surprisingly, considerable levels of external gene flow. Their DNA happens to cluster with caste populations of Uttar Pradesh and not with their south Indian geographical neighbours.

The most frequent mtDNA M sub-cluster in Chenchus, M2 with a coalescence time of about 73,000 years, suggests their early settlement of South Asia, from about the time of the Toba super eruption (Sirajuddin 1994; Laybourn 2016; Oppenheimer n.d.). In contrast, their Y-chromosome gene pool contains significant levels of Hgs J-M172 (17–50%) and R1a1 (27%) (Cordaux 2004; Singh 2016).

Hg R1a1 has a frequency of 20%–40% in Central Asia, and up to 40% in north Indian caste groups (Kivisild 2003; Klyosov 2011). The average frequency of R1a1 in fifteen tribal groups from south India is 9% (6% if Chenchus are excluded). The unusually high frequency in Chenchus is not representative of other tribal groups. Associated with Indo-Aryan speakers, the highest frequency of Hg R1a1 is found in the Punjab, about 2,500 kms from where the Chenchus presently live, a distance covered by forests, hills and ravines. The Chenchu R1a1 haplotypes represent two lineages, one about 3,200 years old and the other 350. The earlier date is closely linked to the migrations of Indo-Aryan speakers; the other to the time of the Moghul campaign in Andhra.

This genetic data suggests that the Chenchus inhabited the northwest when farming and pastoral groups from west and Central Asia arrived. The largely one-way transfer of paternal haplotypes tells the story of a losing encounter. Their retreat southwards may have been due to the growing aridity that affected the region from the third millennium and the destruction of forests under the relentless advance of the food-producing economy. It was a period when agro-pastoral communities from the region trekked to the Deccan and triggered the SNAC. Chenchus speak a language belonging to the Dravidian family.

This story of the displacement of the Chenchus is replicated throughout history; the interaction between farmers and foragers has been mainly one of conflict and eventual expropriation of traditional foraging lands for agriculture and pasture. Until the beginnings of pastoralism and sedentary agriculture, foragers freely roamed the entire length and breadth of South Asia. Its forest resources, numerous river basins, extensive coastline, hills and mountains and broad plains were solely theirs to exploit. Today, they live on the margins of society, in isolated pockets of forest and desert, clinging on to the last vestiges of an ancient lifestyle, resisting assimilation into a new one to which they are ill-adapted and in which they will be forced into the lowest rungs of society.

Their stories of resistance repeatedly appear in the traditions of the victors as victories of good over evil. But when the righteous veneer of the story-makers is stripped away, they appear as innumerable records of deprivation and subjugation, sometimes assimilation, of hunter-gatherer communities under a relentlessly advancing alien culture. An alien ideology is used to justify an otherwise plain and simple act of conquest that is one-sided.

Kuruvas (Murty 1993)

Kuruvas (Kurumas/Kurabas) and Gollas, pastoralists of south Deccan, tend sheep, goats and cattle. They live in villages, in permanent dwelling places and lead sedentary or semi-sedentary lives. Early village farming settlements appeared in this region around 3000 BCE. The archaeological evidence in this semi-arid landscape suggests colonisation by food-producing groups growing millet, with pastoralism branching off as a distinct economic activity. This expropriation of hunter-gatherer land by pastoralists is preserved in the oral traditions of their gods – Birappa of the Kuruvas and Mallanna of the Gollas – both deified ancestors.

Birappa, the seventh son of a pastoral family, is believed to have been born with supernatural qualities. This made his elder brothers jealous. Scheming his downfall, they asked Birappa to cultivate a distant patch of forest and move his bullocks there. Beneath a tree growing on this land was a termite mound which was protected at Shiva's bidding by a demoness. Birappa's brothers hoped he, unaware of this, would cut the tree and provoke the demoness into killing him. When Birappa approached the tree with an axe, he was challenged by the children of the demoness. Birappa killed them. The demoness sought justice from Shiva, but was told that Birappa was his son, and henceforth the land belonged to him.

Meanwhile in heaven, Shiva's wife Parvati asked him for a sheep. Shiva obliged her with two. They multiplied and began to damage the heavenly gardens. Shiva buried the sheep in a pit on Birappa's land and covered its entrance with a stone slab. Hearing them bleat while ploughing his land, Birappa lifted the stone slab. At this point, Shiva appeared and told him to release the sheep, rear them and take them to a nearby town. The townsfolk prevented him from entering the town as they considered sheep-rearing a lowly profession. Birappa spent the next twelve years in the forest tending his flock until Shiva schemed to end his exile.

He caused the simultaneous death of one of Birappa's rams and Nandi (Shiva's *vahana*, mount), worshipped in the town, and told Birappa to sell the ram's wool and meat in the town. But the townsfolk still refused him entry.

So, Birappa placed his dead ram on a pyre. The smoke drifted into the town and enraged its folk who believed their prayers to revive Nandi had been negated. Birappa challenged them: if they could not revive Nandi, they should let him revive his ram and then buy his wool and meat. The townsfolk failed to revive Nandi. Birappa invoked Shiva with prayer, music and drumbeats. The ram came back to life and ran amok in the town causing destruction. Seeing this, many of the townsfolk converted to Birappa's religion and way of life.

A similar tradition concerning the god Mallanna exists among the Gollas. Birappa and Mallanna are ancestral decision-makers who emerged later as gods.

There is much that this tradition tells us. Certain trees are considered sacred by hunter-gatherer groups. Guardian spirits are believed to dwell in their branches as well as in termite mounds. Foragers give them due respect, honour and space in their way of life. Cutting down the tree and destroying the termite mound is a clear appropriation of forager lands by force. The traditions concerning Birappa and Mallana are seen as attempts at legitimising, by invoking divine sanction, this appropriation by different pastoralist groups migrating from north and west India. Among them are eighteen Yadava clans who are believed to have migrated from the north to the Deccan in 800 BCE, and pastoral Abhiras from north India around 400 CE.

The Story Etched on Rocks

Dotting South Asia's landscape are numerous rocky outcrops, many remote and hidden in jungle and scrub, that tell the other side of the encounter. They preserve some of South Asia's earliest rock art in drawings, paintings and sculptures. Some of their creators left their signatures on the rock surface as an outline of their palm. Their stories talk of forager lands, rich in fruit, fish and animal resources, being progressively encroached upon and denuded by newcomers, of conflict, resistance and eviction.

South Asia's rock art has been divided into three major groups belonging to central India, south Deccan and the western Himalayas (Allchin 1987). Immensely diverse with a range of drawing and painting styles, and a variety of methods of imprinting them on rock surfaces, they yet reveal a remarkable continuity from the earliest times.

Central India, largely corresponding to Madhya Pradesh and Chhattisgarh, is rugged, relatively inaccessible and infertile. More isolated than neighbouring regions, it has developed a complementary relationship with them as a supplier of labour and natural resources and a market for cereals and manufactured goods. The commonest subjects of central India's rock art are animals, people in different situations, abstract designs and inscriptions. Red is the commonest colour; white, green and purple are also used. Painting styles use simple outlines or outlines filled by cross-hatching or colour. Birds, reptiles, fish, animals and people are full of life and movement; there is hunting, dancing and fighting.

Central India's premier rock paintings in Bhimbetka, near Bhopal, date to between 18–8 ka (Archaeological Survey of India 2003; Dubey-Pathak 2014; Malla n.d.). The earliest phase coincides with a find of ostrich shells in burial sites. Fishing and hunting with microlithic arrowheads are themes in the next phase. The third reveals contact with Chalcolithic cultures whose weapons, carts, chariots and potsherds have been recovered here. The style of these paintings, with rows of stylised animal-headed dancers, birds and animals, is similar to pottery painting from second and third millennia BCE Chalcolithic sites in north India. The final phases reveal contact with Iron Age cultures, of advancing warriors, armed horsemen and war elephants; little is left to the imagination.

The people whose ancestors made these paintings still live in the area (Chaubey 2015). Their lifestyles, however, have changed radically in response to increasing contact with an ever-closing-in world. Among them are the Dravidian-speaking Gonds, Munda-speaking Murias in the east and Indo-European-speaking Bhils in the west. Bhils, Kols and Gonds are conspicuous by their presence in the *Ramayana*.

The Deccan's rock art, dating from the Neolithic, is found in caves and rock shelters. Mostly red in colour, they have a wide range of styles and a distinctive character. The predominant motif throughout is the humped bull (*Bos indicus*). Antelope, tiger, sheep and other animals are also depicted. But the motifs that record the story most eloquently are of men, dancing, hunting or armed, on foot, horseback or riding elephants. The earliest show them dancing among wild and domesticated animals, mainly humped bulls. Hunters and armed men on horseback appear in the later paintings.

The ancient routes leading through South Asia's northwest to the Silk Road preserve the art of the indigenous people and of travellers. The first consists of pictures of ibex, makhor, wild sheep and goat, men hunting them with bows and arrows, and hand and footprints. Travellers' art is more recent and includes inscriptions in many scripts and symbols of cultural and religious traditions, predominantly Buddhist.

Bhimbetka

Bhimbetka's caves preserve the world's oldest known rock art. They represent very specific hominin cultural behaviour and some of the earliest examples of Indian artistic and religious expression. Considered together with other evidence, like some of the earliest recorded use of pigments in the world, this art projects South Asia as a hub of cognitive development in hominins (Bednarik 2001, 2008, 2010, 2013; Bednarik et al. 2005).

Bhimbetka's rock art includes cupules, cup-like depressions painstakingly hammered out of hard rock. The shaping of cupules requires specially designed stone tools and many hammer blows, precisely placed, and of correct force. Bhimbetka's cupules date to between 400–200 ka. This means their makers were not modern humans, but most likely *Homo erectus*. India's earliest hominin fossil, *Homo erectus narmadensis*, comes from Hathnora, about sixty kms away.

Below nine cupules on a large vertical boulder at Bhimbetka lies a tenth with a meandering groove wrapping around part of its periphery. Measuring between seventy-eight and eighty mm in diameter and 14.1 mm in depth, the cupule is almost perfectly hemispherical. The meander is around nine mm wide, four mm deep, and 295 mm long. Said to date to 290 ka, the cupule-meander took a long time and much effort to shape and get right at the first attempt. There is no rework. It had an important message.

The petroglyph was prised out of hard stone, a symbol of indestructibility, stability and our earthen roots. A stone that is so shaped by human hands is believed to assume the power and presence of a primordial being. It speaks to us. The reward of long hours of hard, concentrated work lies in a message that can be communicated and understood. The undulating meander approaches the cupule, follows its circumference ever so gently without disturbing its integrity, and then turns away and fades into the rock. Its core meaning, as interpreted by a modern scholar, is startlingly direct:

> This place is eternity and brief
> Undulation, a double movement,
> Evolving, even in stone, touch it
> (Harrod 2007: 317–30).

Transported back to a time when life was fragile, short and often brutally sudden in its end to a place of rock shelters in the midst of predator-infested jungle, one pictures a lone form within a darkening cave hunched over the rock. The tapping of rock on rock broadcasts a muffled repetitive rhythm into the enveloping silence. It conveys the passion of an all too vulnerable human reaching beyond his world for a brief moment to convey his message to those who follow, of our fleeting existence in an eternal universe.

A weathered rock painting at Morhana Pagar in central India records that world falling apart as two war chariots, one drawn by four horses, the other by two, advance. Their riders are armed and primed for battle. On the ground, two bare-footed men, one wielding a spear, the other aiming his bow and arrow, attempt a futile resistance. There are other paintings of more men armed with swords, spears and shields advancing on war elephants and on foot. They outnumber the odd defender with his bow and arrow.

It was an unequal battle.

The Narratives Preserved in the Rgveda (Jamison 2014)

The first South Asian text, the 1,028 hymns of the Rgveda (RV), records that unequal struggle from the lens of the victors who made their gods active allies. There is no ambiguity that the battle is directed against the Dasyus of 'non-deeds, of non-thought, the non-man' (RV 10.22). Showered by praise and suffused in *soma* (a mildly intoxicating drink used in Vedic rituals), Indra is roused and urged to lead the charge against every demon (RV 1.133). Indra complied and razed the fortresses of Dasas and Dasyus (RV 2.20).

Wielding his *vajra* (mace, thunderbolt) and accompanied by his comrades-in-arms, the boisterous troop of male gods, the Maruts, wildly leading the charge on their chariots, terrorising all and sundry, Indra won for the Arya the sun and the waters, cows, horses, plants and trees (Jamison 2014: 100; 103). He tamed the Dasyus and made them the lowest of all. The Dasa he deprived of glory and made the earth his pillow (Jamison 2014: RV 1.130; RV 4.18; RV 4.28).

The dasyus and dasas were inhabitants of the northwest before the arrival of Indo-Aryan speakers (Jamison 2014: 56–57; Witzel n.d.). Some succumbed to the onslaught, some were incorporated into the new order. Of the number of Vedic tribal and clan names compiled, twenty-two are identified as of non-Indo-Aryan origin. The dasas and dasyus were people who did not become part of the *arya* (elite/noble) community. The Rgveda differentiates between them. The dasyus were constantly hostile, and the gods were constantly urged to strike them down and drive them away. Dasyus were still human but well on the way to being demonised. They were not given the arya name (Jamison 2014: RV 10.9).

The dasas possessed wealth and had 'forts'. Some had ties to the aryas. Balbutha Taruska, a wealthy dasa, donated 100 camels to the arya cause (Jamison 2014: RV 8.46). Balbutha was not an Indo-Aryan name. That he could donate 100 camels means he was a wealthy man and part of the food-producing economy. The dasyus, in contrast, classified in the 'non' category, were most likely foragers, well beyond the pale of arya society.

It was against them that the main thrust of the strengthening agro-pastoral food-producing economy was directed as it battled to acquire more land:

> There was continuous war between the Indo-Aryans and the dark-skinned aborigines during this age. The aborigines retreated before … the Aryans, but hung around in fastnesses and forests, plundered the peaceful villages of the Aryans and stole their cattle. With that tenacity which is peculiar to barbarians, they fought for centuries as they retreated; they interrupted the religious sacrifices of the conquerors, despised their 'bright gods' and plundered their wealth. But the Aryans conquered in the end; the area of civilisation widened, waste and jungle lands were reclaimed and dotted with villages and towns, and the barbarians either submitted to the conquerors or retreated to those hills and mountains where their descendants still live … the banks of the Indus were cleared of their non-Aryan races eighteen hundred years before Christ … (Dutt 1900: 3).

Agni Burned …

Agni, the god of fire, burned the forests, deprived foragers of sustenance, and forced them to migrate. Forests were replaced by farms and pastures. The *Mahabharata* tells one such story (Van Buitenen 1973: 415–22).

Tasked to burn the Khandava Forest, Agni was repeatedly foiled by Indra who doused the flames with rain. Finally, he approached Arjuna and Krishna in the guise of a brahman, "tall like a huge sala tree, fair like molten gold, orange-colored, with a reddish beard, of well-proportioned limbs, radiant like the morning sun, black-garbed, hair braided, eyes like lotus leaves, and fairly blazing with glory, the red man …" He asked them to feed him saying he was "a voracious Brahmin … I always eat boundlessly … This forest is the food I have chosen."

As Agni burned the forest, Arjuna and Krishna stood guard in their chariots. They kept the clouds away with an incessant shower of arrows, and forced terrified forest creatures back into the flames. Arjuna pierced one with a hundred arrows or a hundred with one, and lifeless they fell into the fire. Khandava's forest-dwelling foragers (*danava*s, *rakshasa*s, *pisaca*s, *asura*s, *yaksha*s, *naga*s), snakes, hyenas, bears, elephants, tigers, lions, deer, buffalo and birds were cut down by the thousands. They scattered, burned, scorched and shattered. Some embraced their sons, others their fathers and mothers unable to abandon them. They all succumbed to the agony of the fire, even the turtles and fish as forest streams and ponds boiled and evaporated. The massacre was truly great, relentless, and unforgiving. Only six forest creatures escaped: the serpent Asvasena, Maya, an Asura, and four Sarngaka birds.

Feasted on an abundance of blood, flesh and fat, Agni became happy, sated and supremely blissful.

Agni journeyed eastward across the Ganges plain:

> Mathava, the Videgha, was at that time on the (river) Sarasvati. He (Agni) thence went burning along this earth towards the east;

> and Gotama Rahugana and the Videgha Mathava followed after him as he was burning along. He burnt over (dried up) all these rivers. Now that (river), which is called Sadanira, flows from the northern (Himalaya) mountain: that one he did not burn over. That one the Brahmans did not cross in former times, thinking, 'it has not been burnt over by Agni Vaisvanara.' Nowadays, however, there are many Brahmans to the east of it. At that time, it (the land east of the Sadanira) was very uncultivated, very marshy, because it had not been tasted by Agni Vaisvanara. Now-a-days, however, it is very cultivated, for the Brahmans have caused (Agni) to taste it through sacrifices ... Mathava, the Videgha, then said (to Agni), 'Where am I to abide?' 'To the east of this (river) be thy abode!' said he (*Satapatha Brahmana* 1.4.1.14–17).

Agni, the deified fire of the sacrifice, is invoked in the first hymn of the Rgveda. He moves between the divine and human realms, visible and accessible as fire ascending, an intermediary between humans and other gods. He brings wealth and prosperity: 'Like a father for a son, be of easy approach for us, O Agni. Accompany us for our well-being' (Jamison 2014: RV 1.1).

After being father to son in life, Agni becomes son to father at the funeral pyre. The Rgveda pictures a touching scene of him conducting the deceased warrior to the afterlife with dignity through his cremation: 'Don't burn him through, Agni; don't scorch him; don't singe his skin, nor his body ... deliver him to the forefathers.' Death is not an end, but a return: 'Let your eye go to the sun, your life-breath to the wind. Go to heaven and to earth as is fitting. Or go to the waters, if it has been fixed for you there.' Some were buried: 'Arch up, Earth; do not press down. Become easy to approach for him, easy to curl up in. Like a mother her son with her hem, cover him, Earth.' In either case, the warrior's legacy lived on. His bow was taken gently from his body, the bow which had won many a battle, and passed on to his successor: 'Taking the bow from the hand of the dead for our dominion, lustre, and strength, you there and we here – may we with good heroes win all contests and hostile engagements'

(Jamison 2014: RV 10.16, 18). A warrior had fallen, his purpose served, and Agni continued burning.

An ancient memory survives in the traditions of some of the expelled, scattered and displaced, a memory that cannot be erased. The Dravidian-speaking Oraons (Kurukhs) of Jharkhand believe they came to India from the west, probably via Baluchistan and settled in Karnataka for some time before migrating north along the banks of the Narmada river (Hahn 1911: xii). Modern linguistic and genetic research supports such a narrative of migration of nomadic pastoral Dravidian speakers from Iran to Harappa and from there to the SNAC followed by an expansion from there.

Forest to Farmland

The destruction of north India's extensive forest wealth is recorded by ancient texts.

The *Markandeya Purana* talks of the primeval human race as initially respecting the earth and its different environments (Pargiter 1904: canto 49; Bailey 1983: 161–63). People lived without habitations and were neither troubled by pisacas, nagas and rakshasas, nor by excess heat or cold. It was a time of full and contented lives. When they ultimately died out and were replaced by modern men, things changed.

Initially, *kalpa* trees were common and provided shelter, clothing, fruits, honey and ornaments. But then people grew covetous and selfish. They used force to acquire private property; they fenced trees and destroyed them; they built houses, villages, towns and fortresses; they fought against each other. Earth retaliated. The kalpa trees disappeared; people became confused and despondent and experienced cold, heat, thirst and hunger.

In desperation, they approached Brahma for relief. Brahma taught them how to cultivate seventeen cereals (rice, barley, wheat, millets, pulses) and fourteen sacrificial plants as a means of livelihood. The food-gathering economy had been replaced by the food-producing economy and the extensive kalpa forests became agricultural fields.

Texts in Jainism refer nostalgically to *kalpavriksha*s, dense polyculture forests, which provided shelter, fruits and nuts, liquids and materials for building, clothing, utensils, musical instruments, ornaments and decoration (Jain 2003). With the clearing of kalpavrikshas for agriculture, the concept of individual property evolved, and the domestication of animals reduced the dependency on wild animals being hunted for food and other produce. This new source of food, largely under human control, led to dramatic population growth, resulting in further inroads into virgin forests. It deprived hunter-gatherers of their resources and led to bitter and unrelenting conflict.

Early Vedic literature depicts this conflict as one between *sur* and *asur* or *deva* and rakshasa. Sur denotes activity to produce; asur is its opposite. Sur and asur are synonyms of deva and rakshasa respectively. Rakshasa is derived from raksha, or protection. Suras (devas) adopted agriculture, destroying forests in the process, while asuras (rakshasas) defended the forests which provided them their livelihood. As devas cut, burned and cleared forests for agriculture, the rakshasas fought back. Ultimately, they were vanquished, not by superior valour or power, but because devas burnt the forests and deprived them of their livelihood.

Agni had triumphed.

The Demonisation of the Forager

The expulsion of hunter-gatherers was justified by a relentless propaganda campaign that demonised them and depicted them as sub-human creatures fit only for contempt and revulsion, for enslavement and exile. Vedic literature uses the term *pancajanah*, the five classes of men consisting of the four *varnas* and the *nisada* (tribal), to describe contemporary society (Chanda 1976: 4–6 quoting from *Mahabharata* xii. 59.94–97). The term nisada[1] first appears in the Yajurveda:

> Vena, a slave of wrath and malice, became unrighteous in his conduct towards all creatures. The Rsis, those utterers of Brahma, slew him with kusa blades inspired with mantras. Uttering mantras the while, those Rsis pierced the right thigh of Vena. Thereupon, from that thigh, came out a short-limbed person on earth, resembling a charred brand, with blood-red eyes and black hair. Those utterers of Brahma then said unto him, *Nisada, sit here*. From him have sprung the Nisadas, viz. those wicked tribes that have the hills and the forests for their abode, as also those hundreds and thousands of others, called Mlecchas, residing on the Vindhya mountains.

The nisadas were placed beyond the pale of the *jati*: 'His (Nisada's) descendants are settled in the hills and forests; the Nisadas, Kiratas, Bhillas, Nahalkas, Bhramaras, Pulindas, and other Mlechha tribes addicted to vices are all sprung from his body' (*Padma Purana* II.27.42–43).

Other texts reinforced this vilification: nisadas had a dwarfish stature with short arms, a flattened nose and features, high cheekbones, thick lips, low chin with full jaws, red eyes and a dark projecting forehead with copper-coloured hair; they were black like a crow, with the complexion of a charred stake, 'like night that always accompanied him in his wild exploits' (*Visnu Purana* I.13; *Bhagavata Purana* iv.14.44; *Harsacarita*, sixth century).

Such descriptions continued into recent times: 'The typical Bhil is ... ugly...' (Chanda 1908: 6–7 quoting *Rajputana Gazetteer*, Calcutta 1908: 87). 'The Gonds are ... ugly ...' (Chanda ibid. quoting *Central Provinces Gazetteer*, Calcutta 1908: 163). Today, Bhils have a presence primarily in central India, and the Gonds are spread over Madhya Pradesh, Maharashtra, Chhattisgarh, Uttar Pradesh and Telangana. Numbering over four million, they speak Gondi, which belongs to the Dravidian family.

The presence of significant levels of Y-chromosome Hgs R1a1 and J-M172 among tribal populations tells another side of this story:

> The asymmetry of admixture, with ANI populations providing genomic inputs to tribal populations (AA, Dravidian tribe, and TB) but not vice versa, is consistent with elite dominance and patriarchy. Males from dominant populations, possibly upper castes, with high ANI component, mated outside of their caste, but their offspring were not allowed to be inducted into the caste. This phenomenon has been previously observed as asymmetry in homogeneity of mtDNA and heterogeneity of Y-chromosomal haplotypes in tribal populations of India (Basu 2016).

The processes through which this occurred are complex and varied. The *Panchavimsha Brahmana* xvi.6.7 relates that the performer of the *visvajit* sacrifice was required to live for three days among the nisadas whose chiefs were the only ones authorised to perform certain sacrifices. Among the Koravas, it was a practice to mortgage unmarried daughters who become the absolute property of the mortgagee till the debt was discharged. In times of stress, wives were sold or pawned. If she had children by the creditor, the boys remained with him and worked on his fields, the girls were sent back along with the wife when the debt was discharged (Thurston 1909: 487–88). Though most Chenchus exhibit characteristics of 'unadulterated jungle tribes' like short stature and high nasal index, there is a marked diversity among them in their physical traits. Many individuals are tall with long narrow noses (Thurston 1909, vol. 1, page xlvii).

We can visualise the following scenarios in times of drought when lakes dry and trees don't bear fruit, when grasses wither and herbivores migrate to other pastures. We can visualise a hunter-gatherer lead his women to a neighbouring farm and offer their labour and whatever else went along with it to the farmer for a little food and shelter until the hard times passed. We can visualise Chenchus living in the wilds of the northwest 3,200 years ago doing just that as a mega drought depleted their food resource base; we follow them trekking south to the Deccan and its forests, perhaps in the company of pastoralists.

The centuries between c2200 BCE–100 CE were eras of intense re-structuring of South Asian society resulting from the de-urbanisation of the Harappan Civilisation and migration of Harappans to other parts of the country, and appearance of Indo-Aryan speakers in the northwest. The earliest sections of the Rgveda reflect substantial interaction and social movement across groups. Inter-marriages took place, languages were enriched by loanwords, chieftains and poets from other groups were accepted.

South Asia's second urbanisation in the Gangetic plains, with its vigorous churning of ideas relating to kingship, religion and scientific and social concepts had a profound effect on its genetic composition. By the time the *Manusmriti* (*The Laws of Manu*) was composed (200 BCE–200 CE – Kane 1941 vol. 2–1: xi), the free admixture of ANE-ASI groups [Chapter 5] had transformed into one of strict endogamy and a rigidly stratified society composed of four castes (Moorjani 2013). The brahman stood at its apex, the shudra at the bottom. The *Manusmriti* is emphatic about the role of the shudra: "One occupation only the lord prescribed to the shudra, to serve meekly even these (other) three castes" (Buhler 1886: 1–91). A shudra was allowed to marry a woman of his caste only, a brahman could have one from each of the four castes. The text, however, warns that marriage to a shudra woman would degrade a brahman and his family to the status of shudras, and on his death would consign him to hell. For the shudra, life on earth had become hell. The place of the nisadas, the earliest colonisers of South Asia, was somewhere beyond.

9

Discovering a Buried Past

A little over a century ago, not much was known about Sargon of Akkad or Meluhha.

In 1887, a French diplomat stationed at Basra learned of the unearthing of ancient artefacts in Mesopotamia, the land between the rivers Tigris and Euphrates. Intrigued, he excavated the site and unearthed a treasure trove of stone statues, bricks, inscribed tablets, jars, cylinders and jewellery. Eventually, a hidden world of palaces and temples, crowded tenements and brick platforms emerged from under desert sands. The door had been opened into the lost civilisation of Sumer and the world's first cities (McIntosh 2005; Michalowski 2008; *Sumer* 1993: 9; Weiss 1993b).

Sumer lay at the southern border of the Fertile Crescent on a featureless plain formed by silt brought down by the two rivers. To its immediate north was Akkad, and farther away, Subir. The three regions experienced relatively independent development initially. In the fourth millennium, Sumer underwent a veritable revolution in social, political and economic organisation. Cities and towns replaced villages. Rival city states were forged into political alliances, and its civilisation began to spread into southwest Iran and Upper Mesopotamia. By c2600 BCE, Sumer, Akkad and Subir were drawn into a greater cultural and economic union with its urban centre in Sumer. Also drawn into this urban culture through overland and sea trade was a distant land known as Meluhha, now identified as the Indus Valley.

Palaces suddenly appeared in Sumer's city states Uruk, Ur, Nippur and Eridu, suggesting radical social, economic and political changes on a grand scale. Until Sargon's conquest, Uruk remained the largest of a number of independent city states.

A similar transformation occurred in Subir. Cities and towns replaced villages (Weiss 1993b; *Sumer*: 54).

Sumer's earliest settlements date to 6000 BCE. Excavations at Uruk have exposed eighteen levels of occupation that reached twenty metres into the soil. Pottery and clay tablets inscribed with symbols used to certify ownership confirm industrial-scale production by 3500–3300 BCE. Short of raw materials, trade was central to Mesopotamia's economy and a critical factor in the development of its urban life. Luxury goods and construction material flowed in through extensive and continual conquests, and through trading networks that spread eastwards across the Iranian plateau. This trade declined sharply c2500 BCE when Sumer turned to the Persian Gulf (hereafter, 'Gulf') and developed close trading links with three regions, Dilmun (Bahrain), Magan (Oman) and Melukkha (Meluhha). Sargon's reign saw a great expansion in foreign contacts and the first textual evidence for direct relations with Meluhha. Subsequent Mesopotamian texts continue to record the import of building materials, precious metals and jewels from Meluhha.

Ur, among the finest of Sumer's cities, was an important trading centre. It was situated on the Euphrates at the head of the Gulf, ideally placed to become the focus of overseas trade. The Royal Graves of Ur (c2600 BCE) reflect Ur's rise in wealth and power. The spectacularly furnished graves contained exquisite jewellery and artefacts ornamented in gold, silver and lapis lazuli. Ur imported a wide range of luxury articles: copper from Anatolia, Oman and Iran, diorite from Oman, chlorite from Iran and turquoise from Central Asia.

Grave goods included a variety of objects from the Indus Valley: seals with Indus style script, carnelian and green beads, cylinder seals made from Indus marine species, and silver disc beads of a style common not in Mesopotamia but in Lothal and Mohenjo-daro. Among them was a lapis lazuli cylinder seal and a copper stamp seal with Harappan inscriptions attached to a dressing-pin. The main source of lapis lazuli was Badakshan in Afghanistan. The copper seal was unusual in Ur and suggests it was manufactured further east, probably made for someone from the Indus cultural sphere with business interests in Mesopotamia. Found together with the cylinder seal, it suggests it belonged to someone active in both regions (Kenoyer 2013; Reade n.d; Parpola 2015: 295; Olijdam 1995).

South and north Mesopotamia followed markedly different political and socio-economic systems. Sumer's city states were clearly demarcated territorial units with a major city surrounded by towns and villages. They were considered the private property of the chief god of an extended divine family. The capital city belonged to him/her exclusively. Lesser gods owned smaller towns and villages. Enlil, chief god of Nippur, was treated as the overlord of the entire south. He arbitrated conflicts between city states, especially border disputes. Borders separating city states were considered permanent and divinely-sanctioned making territorial expansion or unification within the system difficult. Each city state was ruled by an official who functioned as an earthly representative of the city-god. His office combined both secular and religious duties (Steinkeller 1993).

North Mesopotamia, on the other hand, formed a single territorial state with its power centre at the city of Kish. About 2316 BCE, Sargon of Akkad defeated a coalition of Sumerian city states led by Lugalzagesi, and gained control over south Mesopotamia. It was the beginning of the Sargonic Akkadian Empire.

Sargon (reigned c2334–2279 BCE) rose from a lowly social status ('my father I do not know') to become king of Akkad (Franke 1995; Freewalt 2014; Hamblin 2006: 79, 81). Reigning for fifty-six years, he extended his empire to most of modern Iraq and Syria. Sargon created a powerful standing army loyal to his person, boasting that 5,400 men ate daily from his kitchens. His successors continued his aggressive policies. Rimush, his son, won a great victory against a coalition of forces led by neighbouring Elam c2273 BCE. This coalition, the Akkadian record states, included troops from Meluhha, which may also have been subjected to a sea-borne campaign launched by Rimush's brother and successor, Manishtusu.

Sargon's grandson, Naram-Sin (2254–2218 BCE) launched campaigns against Syria to the west, Anatolia to the north, Elam to the east and Magan to the south. Meluhha is mentioned as an ally of some of these countries. The vanquished received no mercy. With the permission of the gods Ishtar, Enlil, Dagan, Ninkursag, Enki, Sin, Shamash and Nergal, Naram-Sin was made god, protective deity and owner of the city of Akkad. Some saw him as the consort of Ishtar, goddess of love and war and the principal deity of Akkad.

Offered safety and trading opportunities in exchange for unconditional loyalty, Akkad's citizens prospered. Sea trade grew exponentially, especially to Dilmun, Magan and Meluhha.

Dilmun (Laursen 2009; Tews 2011)

Bahrain is a small island in the Gulf, about 45 kms in length and 25 kms in width. Its location and abundant reservoirs of underground freshwater made it a strategic sea port. The island's numerous burial mounds testify to this.

Bahrain's history begins c2800 BCE when a simple, kinship-based society which imported vessels and fine wares from Mesopotamia appears to have come into existence. Around 2050 BCE, major socio-economic measures brought about a number of changes in material culture. The small trading post of Qal'at al-Bahrain expanded to become a city of fifteen hectares with a stone wall, a palace, warehouses, religious buildings and large burial mounds. Stamp seals of a distinct local style suggest the emergence of a uniting social elite. In the next couple of centuries, as its population increased by about 34%, Dilmun took over Magan's monopoly in the copper trade with Mesopotamia. This change was accompanied by a dramatic reduction in the supply and capacity of trading vessels, a possible result of organisational changes in Mesopotamia's easterly trade relations in which control passed from public institutions such as temples to private entrepreneurs.

Dilmun continued to maintain trading relations with Harappa where the majority of its cubical weights dating to this period originated. A local weight corresponding exactly to Harappan standards with its distinctive characters and iconography was also introduced. Artefacts found in Bahrain indicate that copper was also imported from sources beyond Oman, probably Rajasthan and Gujarat.

Dilmun's stamp seals were influenced more by Harappan square seals than Mesopotamia's cylinder seals, with similar iconography and script. The context in which Harappan pottery has been recovered from settlements and graves suggests they belonged to natives of Bahrain and not to Harappan merchants.

From c1950 BCE, the influence from the Indus Valley began to decline. Square weights were increasingly replaced by cylinder-shaped Mesopotamian weights. Mesopotamian influence also appeared on seal iconography and temple layouts. Increasing fortifications around villages suggest political unrest. Post-1800 BCE, Bahrain's population declined alarmingly and villages were abandoned, possibly as a result of the breakdown of the urban economies connecting Mesopotamia, southeastern Iran and Harappa.

Magan (Frenez 2016; Lombardi 2105; McIntosh 2008: 175–77; Vidale 2004)

Magan appears in Mesopotamian texts from the Akkad Empire period (2330–2150 BCE) as a supplier of copper, diorite, wood, marine products and specialised workers (miners, metalsmiths, stone cutters and ship builders). In exchange, Magan sourced bitumen, barley, sesame oil, wool, textiles, reeds, palm-fibres and skins from Mesopotamia. Magan's copper was used to manufacture weapons, furniture and statues and its diorite for royal and prestigious sculptures.

Pottery, seals, beads and other third millennium BCE artefacts found in Magan suggest the settlement of a Harappan-related community directly involved in the Harappan trade. Pottery was used for shipping goods, domestic purposes, food preservation and ritual purposes. Luxury items like carnelian beads and inscribed seals used in trade indicate that they were well established and closely linked to powerful trading communities. Excavated terracotta toys suggest that these communities included children.

The peak period of diffusion of Harappan ceramics along the Gulf coasts occurred between 2400–2200 BCE. At Ras al-Jinz on Oman's east coast, Harappan pottery, copper stamp seals, weights, beads, an ivory comb and a copper axe have been unearthed. Bitumen from the second half of the third millennium BCE, an essential raw material for shipbuilding and maintenance, reveals shipping activity. These sites were occupied between September and March, when gentle northeast monsoon winds made sailing from Makran and Gujarat ports feasible in thirty to forty hours. Magan's main attraction was its extensive copper deposits. In return, Magan received grain, carnelian and lapis lazuli beads and ivory combs. South Asian zebu cattle were introduced during the third millennium BCE. The extension of this trade to Yemen, Djibouti and Ethiopia brought African crops to South Asia.

Meluhha

Distinctive artefacts recovered in Mesopotamia and western Iran reveal that a thriving trade existed between these regions and Harappa. Mesopotamian texts refer to the supply of a range of essential, luxury and exotic goods including timber, carnelian beads, agate, lapis lazuli, ivory, gold, figurines of monkeys, shell bangles made of marine species found only in Indus waters and animals from Meluhha (Kenoyer 2013; McIntosh 2008: 151, 182, 185, 190, 195). Harappan stamp seals and cubical stone weights were used in this trade. A Meluhhan multi-coloured *haia* bird (peacock) was highly valued. Its cries echoed within royal palaces, and its dances at the snapping of fingers and clapping of hands entertained royalty. Imported timber, used in construction and to make boats, chariots and furniture, included *mesu* (*Dalbergia sissoo*?), *kusabku* (teak?), the black wood of Meluhha *sulum meluhhi* (ebony or rosewood, *Dalbergia latifolia*) and *ab-ba*, used for special chairs or thrones with ivory inlays. Meluhha came to be associated with such luxury goods. When Harappa was forgotten, some of these products came from Ethiopia which inherited the name Meluhha.

The return trade carried gold, silver, wool, incense and perishable items. Both land and sea routes were used. The overland distance of 2,500 kms to Baluchistan passed through northern Iran. Another route crossed the Zagros Mountains and Elam. Gulf-based middlemen controlled the sea trade along the Persian and Makran coasts. Colonies along these routes facilitated this trade. Marriage contracts may have been used to cement trading relations.[1]

Seals and small personal objects of Harappan origin and references to Meluhhans in various economic contexts reveal the presence of Harappan merchants in major Sumerian cities and their participation in local trade organisations. Most seals were made of square steatite (soapstone) blocks hardened by firing. Each bore the picture of an animal and carried an inscription in the still undeciphered Harappan script. A boss on the other side allowed the seals to be carried by a cord. Seals were used to identify merchandise and ensure they were not tampered with.

The Meluhhan trade was first referred to by Sargon (Parpola 1994: 14). During Naram-Sin's reign, Meluhhans, the men of the 'black country', brought all kinds of exotic wares in their ships to Sumer. Meluhha supplied wood, gold dust, carnelian and other luxury items for the construction of the main temple in the capital of Gudea, king of Lagash (2144–2124 BCE). A village near it was called Meluhha, probably a Meluhhan colony which existed there for at least thirty-five years (2105–2071 BCE).

In the Mesopotamian myth, *Enki and the World Order*, Enki the water-god decreed: 'Let the lands of Meluha, Magan and Dilmun look upon me, upon Enki. Let the Dilmun boats be loaded (?) with timber. Let the Magan boats be loaded sky-high. Let the *magilum* boats of Meluha transport gold and silver and bring them to Nibru for Enlil, king of all the lands' (Black 1998). Crossing the Iranian plateau (*kur*), he reached *kur-gi* (country of dark soil or dark-skinned people) and blessed it:

> Black land, may your trees be great trees, may your forests be forests of highland *mes* trees! Chairs made from them will grace royal palaces! May your reeds be great reeds … ! Heroes shall … [*word lost in the original text*] them on the battlefield as weapons! May your bulls be great bulls, may they be bulls of the mountains! May their bellowing be the bellowing of wild bulls of the mountains! The great powers of the gods shall be made perfect for you! May the francolins of the mountains wear cornelian beards! May your birds all be peacocks! May their cries grace royal palaces! May all your silver be gold! May all your copper be tin-bronze! Land, may all you possess be plentiful! May your people …! May your men go forth like bulls against their fellow men! [*some words missing in the original text*]

Clearly Meluhha was important to the Mesopotamian economy.

The Meluhhan Village in Mesopotamia (Vermaak 2008)

Sumerian and Akkadian texts refer to a Meluhhan community living in Guabba in southern Mesopotamia. Large boats linked this trading colony with Meluhha. Meluhhans paid taxes to the local government and had a leading role in the textile industry. Guabba was a textile hub with many women and children (one text mentions 4,272 women and 1,800 children) working in the weaving sector. They may have been descendants of skilled immigrants from Meluhha. The colony delivered large quantities of barley to the royal treasury, up to three times more than other granaries. It had two temples dedicated to the gods Nanshe and Ninmar, and a temple garden.

Some names of Meluhhan merchants in Sumer are known. Ur-dLamma occurs frequently. Lu-Sunzida paid Urur, son of Amar-Luku, ten shekels of silver as compensation for a broken tooth. A Mesopotamian cylinder seal identifies Su-i-li-su, a Meluhha interpreter, as its owner.

The DNA of skeletal remains of four individuals who lived in the middle Euphrates valley between 2500 BCE and 500 CE (Early Bronze Age to Late Roman period) suggests a genetic link with Indians (Palanichamy 2014; Prasad 2011: 21–26; Witas 2013). Their mtDNA haplotypes are commonly found in South Asian populations, but absent in west Asia today. A male, aged thirty (500–700 AD), belonged to Hg M4b1. The other three belong to haplotypes which probably arose between twenty-five and fifty-eight ka in South Asia. A female aged twenty-five (200–300 CE) and a male aged forty (2650–2450 BCE) belonged to Hg M49. Another male aged twenty-five (2200–1900 BCE) belonged to Hg M49 or M61. Another haplogroup, M65a, has been observed in Tamil populations. The Indian eastern coastline had extensive trade contacts with and via Mesopotamia from 2500 BCE to Roman times.

The Collapse

Akkad controlled an area of about 30,000 sq. kms with a standing army and an administrative network of scribes and specialist craftsmen. It was still expanding when the 2200–1900 BCE mega drought, known as the 4.2 ka event, struck. Global climate change abruptly weakened the Mediterranean westerlies and the Indian monsoon, generating aridity across the Mediterranean, northeast

Africa, west Asia and the Indus. Agriculture collapsed, long-settled towns and villages were abandoned and populations were forced to adapt to survive. Many resorted to nomadic pastoralism and migration (Weiss 2017).

The Akkadian collapse was sudden and swift. The economy shrank and debilitating political unrest set in. Then the Gutians, described as enemies with canine instincts and monkey's features, fell upon the tottering state. Nothing escaped their clutches, none slipped from their grasp. Herds of livestock together with their herdsmen were taken captive to their land. The stark end is graphically described in *The Curse of Akkad.*

> The great agricultural tracts produced no grain,
> The inundated tracts produced no fish,
> The irrigated orchards produced neither syrup nor wine,
> The gathered clouds did not rain, the masgurum did not grow...
> He who slept on the roof, died on the roof,
> He who slept in the house, had no burial,
> People were flailing at themselves from hunger ...

The mega drought extended its deathly shadow over the Indus Valley. Like Mesopotamia, the populous Indus cities were abandoned. In both regions, sands, swept by desert winds, settled over extensive urban sites, century after century. A vibrant history of human achievement and accomplishment remained smothered and forgotten – until recently.

10

Timelines and the Elam Connection

Acutely short of raw material resources, Mesopotamia's merchants travelled in different directions to source products to meet the insatiable demand for luxury and other goods of an expanding economy fuelled by the growth of city states. Among the most important was the route leading eastwards across the Susiana plain, over the Zagros Mountains and beyond the Iranian plateau to Afghanistan and the Indus basin. In the early centuries of this contact, the land known as Elam acted as intermediary between Mesopotamia and Harappa. Traders used two arterial routes to the north and south of the Iranian plateau.

The name Elam (in Sumerian: highlands) first appears in Sumerian texts between 2600–2500 BCE for the highlands of Iran. On the east, the highlands merge into the Indo-Iranian borderlands, known today as Sistan-Baluchistan. Pastoral nomads using a network of routes through mountains and deserts have always been channels for dissemination of technologies, goods, ideologies and genetic material across these lands inhabited by a collection of ethnically and linguistically diverse groups.

The Zagros Mountains mark the border between Mesopotamia and the Iranian plateau to its east. Between the central Zagros Mountains and Mesopotamia proper lies the Susiana plain, an extension of the Tigris-Euphrates valley. Its principal city, Susa, founded c4000 BCE, became the focal point of interaction between the lowland sedentary Mesopotamian civilisation and the highland nomadic Elamite culture (Jarrige, J.-F 2011; Mutin 2012; Potts 2004; The Metropolitan Museum of Art 1992).

The people of Susiana, though under the Mesopotamian orbit, were always in close contact with highland tribal populations to the east, particularly with those in the modern province of Fars in the southeastern Iranian plateau. Around the third millennium BCE, Fars became the centre of a powerful political and cultural entity that encompassed Susiana. The name Elam came to be applied to this political entity which roughly corresponds to modern Khuzistan, Fars and parts of Kerman, Luristan and Kurdistan. Its principal cities were Anshan (Tal-i Malyan) in the highlands and Susa in the plains.

Susa's rise to prominence followed the burning of Chogha Mish, the previous principal settlement in the Susiana plain. It may have been a deliberate act signifying the shifting of the power centre to Susa, a 'kind of purification that attends rededication to fundamental values and beliefs' (Hole 1983). Susa's great architectural feature was a monumental brick platform built in the midst of a sacred grove within the High City, the elite section. It included a ziggurat and temples, and was surrounded by a wall with richly decorated gates.

Through the fifth and fourth millennia BCE, Mesopotamia, the Iranian plateau, the Indo-Iranian borderlands and Central Asia were drawn together to form a region of general interaction. Susa played a key role in this development. Wood, precious stones, metals and craftsmen passed through Susa to Mesopotamia from as far away as Afghanistan. As Mesopotamia's focus shifted to the material resources of highland Iran, concepts related to the development of urbanism and state organisations, materials, technologies, political and economic ideas, art, architecture and town planning flowed eastward. Pottery, potter's marks, seal iconography and language record these cultural developments.

Political History (Carter 1984; Herrenschmidt 1996)

Around 3000 BCE, a sharp drop in Susa's population suggests movements to Sumer, then undergoing an intensive urbanisation phase, and to the central Zagros highlands which experienced an unusually high population growth at this time. A strong political entity took root at Anshan, located roughly halfway between Susa and Tepe Yahya. First occupied around c5500 BCE, Anshan came into prominence during the Proto-Elamite (c3500–2800 BCE) and Old Elamite (c2200–1600 BCE) periods. Tepe Yahya, further east along the southern fringes of the great Iranian desert, became an important town in an otherwise sparsely populated region on the route to Makran. Between 4500–3600 BCE, it underwent a massive urbanisation phase which involved a large labour force.

Proto-Elamite culture was carried east to the Indo-Iran borderlands between 3100–2700 BCE by a small number of powerful emigrants. They established trading relations with Early Harappans and became partners/mediators in the trade with Mesopotamia. These contacts greatly diminished in the beginning of the Mature Harappan, c2600 BCE, when Harappan ships began sailing directly to Mesopotamia with Dilmun acting as an intermediary.

Elam suffered from continual warfare with Mesopotamia especially from Sargon's reign. Rimush destroyed Susa's forts and ruled ruthlessly. Thousands were killed or taken into slavery. Elam's king was taken prisoner, and mounds of corpses rotted in its cities as their walls were razed. The roots of the old order were torn out. Naram-Sin suppressed a general uprising and signed a treaty of alliance with Susa calling on close to forty gods as witnesses. Subdued Elam was reunified with Mesopotamia c2100 BCE. This intensified communication between Sumer and the east and the flow of distinctive ceramics and administrative texts written on tablets in Proto-Elamite.

Pottery (Potts 2004)

The earliest ceramic tradition, the Ubaid, originated in south Mesopotamia in the latter seventh millennium BCE and spread to north Mesopotamia, Anatolia, Iran and the Persian Gulf. Regional and extra-regional interaction, especially trade and seasonal nomadic migrations, spread this pottery technology progressively eastward. By the fifth millennium BCE, there were at least three separate ceramic traditions in the Indo-Iranian highlands: Bakun (Fars), Soghun (Kerman) and Mehrgarh (Baluchistan).

At the eastern boundary of the Iranian highlands, Mehrgarh underwent major changes from around 5000 BCE. Living conditions improved and workshops dealing in semi-precious stones and shells appeared. Pottery production increased with, as qualitative refinements reveal, a degree of specialisation.

To its south, Makran became a dynamic region for demic and cultural interaction not just between east and west but also north and south. Grave sites in Shahr-i Sokhta in Sistan (Helmand civilisation [c3300–2350 BCE]), 1,000 kms to the north contain bowls decorated with swastikas, similar to those excavated in Makran. Marine shells found at Mehrgarh and Fars highlight interactions with the coast.

Potter's Marks (Potts 1981)

Pottery recovered from Tepe Yahya, as also from Baluchistan, was incised by a variety of signs before firing. Some are identical to signs used in the Proto-Elamite script on tablets, cylinder seals and ceramics. They also appear in the Harappan script, and on pottery made in south India c1000 BCE.

The signs of particular interest are those that are common to both the Proto-Elamite and Harappan scripts. The Proto-Elamite script was developed and used in southwest Iran between 3400–2800 BCE; the Harappan script appeared c2600 BCE. Both appear to have developed from potter's marks. Mature Harappan pottery has potter's marks identical to signs in the Harappan script as well as pre-Harappan potter's marks.

The relation between Proto-Elamite and Harappan scripts is still not established. It is possible that the Proto-Elamite script may have been the inspiration for potter's marks in the Indo-Iranian borderlands and may have provided a partial basis for the development of the Harappan script.

Language

The earliest tablets bearing the Proto-Elamite script (c3200 BCE) come from Susa. They have also been found at Tepe Sialk (Kashan), Tepe Yahya (Kerman), Anshan (Fars), and Shahr-i Sokhta (Sistan). Scholars have suggested that the relationship between the Proto-Elamite and Harappan scripts may extend to the languages. In 1932, Hunter, stating that the resemblances between the two languages could not be explained by coincidence, proposed a common origin (Hunter 1932). More recently, McAlpin has tried to establish a shared origin between Elamite and Dravidian, and attempted to reconstruct Proto-Elamo-Dravidian (McAlpin 1975, 1981).

The Elamite script developed as a means of recording transactions related to the transfer of goods. Quantities were counted by *calculi*, small man-made objects fashioned out of soft clay and moulded into various shapes like elongated sticks, balls, discs and cones. These were kept in round, hollow clay vessels called *bullae* identified by impressions made by rolling cylinder seals lengthwise onto their soft clay before firing. The cylinder seal was a personal object which identified its owner, a government official who recorded, stored and redistributed the harvest. It represented social status and testified to a central authority. Here, writing progressed from an economic need to that of maintaining authority in the political and religious realms. From the second millennium most texts of Elamite kings relate to the foundation or dedication of religious buildings, the very visible and powerful messages of the presence of the gods, and the king's role as an intermediary between them and his subjects. Writing became a vital medium of communication with the gods and such messages were used by kings and priests to maintain political and social order. As often happens, when that political order collapsed, the need for writing disappeared (Herrenschmidt 1996).

Seal iconography (Roach 2008; Hole 1983)

A seal is an object, usually of stone, but also of other materials, that has been carved with a particular design which serves the purpose, more or less, of a modern signature. This iconography is transferred by pressing the seal on a soft substance like unfired clay.

Mesopotamia and Elam used two types, the stamp and the cylinder seal. The stamp seal first appeared c7000 BCE, the cylinder seal c3500 BCE. A cylinder seal had a cylindrical shape with the design carved along its face. The image was transferred by rolling it over clay. It served four distinct functions: administrative, amuletic, votive and funerary.

In its administrative function, it served the purpose of a signature for executive orders, and when used on clay that secured jars, bales, sacks, boxes, baskets and doors, as a sort of lock. It was used to control or regulate the economy in functions like taxation, tribute and trade. For seals to be effective, they had to be recognised as symbols of authority with their iconography identifying the individual.

Seals were also used in a symbolic way as amulets to ward off evil or act as a protective charm, or dedicated to a god in a temple. Sometimes seals were buried with the person with whom they were identified.

Elamite iconography used symbols centred more on animals than humans to convey ideas. Some are similar to the Harappan. The 'master of animals' is a motif common to both styles. Elamite seals depict a figure wearing a goat-horn headdress holding snakes in each of its outstretched hands. Similar scenes are depicted in Mesopotamian and Harappan iconography, but with lions and tigers respectively replacing snakes. A much-discussed Harappan seal depicts a seated human in a yoga pose with possibly an erect upturned phallus surrounded by a host of wild animals.

The horned headdress, some with elaborate flowing tresses, is a common motif in Harappan iconography. So too are fantastical animals composed of body parts from different species. An Elamite seal (c3100–2900 BCE) depicts a lion striding forward with its head turned back towards a bull behind it (The Metropolitan Museum of Art 1992: 72). In Harappan seals, the lion is replaced by a tiger looking behind and upwards at a gesturing goddess in a tree.

The swastika appears in Elamite as well as Iranian motifs painted on bowls or fashioned into stamp seals. The symbol has been painted on pottery found in Shahr-i Sokhta and Makran (Jarrige, J.-F. et al. 2011). Elamite sculptures depict kneeling figures seated on their haunches in a pose remarkably similar to stone sculptures of seated men, possibly of men in authority, from Mohenjo-daro and Dholavira. They were all found broken, most likely deliberately (McIntosh 2008: 395; The Metropolitan Museum of Art 1992: 62).

The Direction, Nature, Timing and Nature of the Two Principal Influences on Harappa from across the Iranian Plateau

Two principal routes for the dispersal of populations from across the Iranian plateau into the Indus basin have been proposed (Gangal 2014). The first to arrive set out from north Zagros. It passed through north Iran and reached Mehrgarh at an average dispersal rate of 1.9 km/yr. This would mean an arrival date in South Asia c6000 BCE, around the time when the west Asian crop package appeared in Mehrgarh. The other dispersal originating from south Zagros at about the same time was slower (0.66 km/yr), probably due to the inhospitable terrain. Its route through Fars and Kerman provinces touched the Makran coast, southeastern Baluchistan and Sindh.

Though there is no evidence as yet, it is possible that the northern dispersal passed on Hg J2b-M102 to tribal populations living in central and eastern India today, and J2a-M410 may have been brought mainly by the southern dispersal. The many technological skills and considerable labour required in the urbanisation of Tepe Yahya are proof of its settlement by powerful groups with access to money and resources. This may have resulted from these groups being an intermediary in the trade between Elam and Harappa during the Early Harappan when southern Indus sites like Kot Diji and Amri grew in importance. The burning of Kot Diji c2800 BCE suggests, like Chogha Mish, the arrival of a new and powerful ideology that spread with increasing trade and urbanisation. By then the centre of power in Mesopotamia had shifted to Ur at the mouth of the Gulf. Its growing wealth and thirst for raw materials and luxury goods led to the opening of the sea route via Dilmun, Magan and the Makran coast to Harappa. Together with wealth, it brought in a range of new concepts that initiated the Transition and transformed the Early Harappan to the Mature Harappan within the space of just a century.

Elam's eclipse by the Mesopotamian sun turned to perpetual darkness as another people moved in:

> In the middle or at the end of the second and especially of the first millennium B.C., Iran was gradually invaded by the populations who gave this region the name of Iran, a word that means "land of the Aryans" – who spoke an ancient Iranian language, a first cousin of Vedic Sanskrit, both members of the Indo-European language family. Linguistically, politically, and culturally, the Iranians in the strict sense – whom one ought to call Aryans – overlaid the ancient Elamite civilization (Herrenschmidt 1996).

Harappa underwent a rather similar experience as a branch of the 'Aryans' reached the Indus plains. Before we get to that story, let us visit Harappa.

Table 10.1: Harappa – Mesopotamia – Elam timeline

BCE	Harappa	Mesopotamia	Elam
11500– 8500		hunter-gatherer settlements in Levant and north Zagros	
10000–2000	Foraging Era – hunter-gatherers		
8500– 7000		aceramic rain-fed agriculture; some domestic animals.	
7000–5500	Early Food Producing Era – Mehrgarh	pottery, metallurgy, farming, animal husbandry	
6200–6000		8.2 ka mega drought	
6000–4100		Ubaid: farming with simple irrigation, shrines, economic specialisation	
5500–2600	Early Harappan		
4100–3400		Early Uruk: settlements increase; wheel-made pottery, wheeled transport, wool.	Susa I
3700–3100		severe drought: 3700–3600, 3300–3100	Susa II
3900–2800	Ravi/Hakra: handmade pottery		

3400–3100		Later Uruk – developing writing, economy, administration, urbanism, temples, Elam ties. North: culturally/economically less developed, politically fragmented	
3100–2900		first cities; social and political complexity. Writing more sophisticated; link to highlands	Susa III: Proto-Elamite writing/culture
2900–2750		Early Dynastic I – first city states with kings, warfare, city walls; urbanisation; cuneiform script	
2800–2600	Kot Diji: potter's wheel, heavy transport, writing		Susa IV Old Elamite
2750–2600		Early Dynastic II – prolifcration of city states.	
2600–2334		Early Dynastic III – Ur Royal Cemetery; writing; large political units, military force, economy, standardisation	
2600–2500	Transition: urbanisation, standardisation, social stratification		
2500–1900	Mature Harappan		

2450–2200	Monumental architecture		
2334–2193		Akkadian Empire – Sargon unites Sumer and Akkad; conquers north Levant, east Anatolia, Zagros, Gulf regions	Akkad rule
2200–1900		4.2 ka mega drought	
2193–2154		Collapse of Akkad; Gutian raids	
2153–2113		Revival in Sumer	
2112–2004		Third Dynasty of Ur (Ur III): Sumer and Akkad reunited; close-knit highly bureaucratic state and trade; sack of Ur	
1900–1300	Late Harappan		
1900–1800	over-population, loss of script, weights, habitation pattern		
1800–1300	decline accelerates		

Source: Kenoyer (n.d.a) ; McIntosh (2005).

11

Harappa – An Overview

The first tentative hints that Baluchistan's mountain ranges may have been hiding more than hostile tribesmen came from an Englishman, Charles Masson. On a tour of the region in 1844, he found numerous mounds that suggested ancient villages and towns may have once dotted the bleak landscape. These 'works of infidels', walls and parapets of stones, buried jars full of ashes, even cities, were to be found in many places (Masson 1844: 386–87). It was not, however, until eighty years later, that the *Illustrated London News*, on 20 September 1924, was able to announce to the world the excavation of two sites on the Indus plains, Harappa and Mohenjo-daro. It reported: 'At both these places there is a vast expanse of artificial mounds evidently covering the remains of once flourishing cities, which . . . must have been in existence for many hundreds of years.'

The Indus River basin spans approximately 3,000 kms from the Himalayas to the Arabian Sea, and ranges in width from fifty to 300 kms, from the Baluchistan foothills to the Thar Desert. Once flowing to its east and roughly parallel to its course, was the Ghaggar-Hakra River. Together with their tributaries, these two rivers, over a period of a few thousand years, supported a civilisation, the Harappan or Indus Valley, which included an estimated 2,500 urban sites. Harappa and Mohenjo-daro were just two of them, the largest and most well known.

The term 'Harappan Civilisation' is generally used for the period of integration and urbanism. A more appropriate and all-encompassing term to describe the prolonged cultural developments in the Indo-Iranian borderlands and the greater Indus basin is 'Harappan Tradition' (Kenoyer n.d.a). The coming together of multi-ethnic and multi-language groups that inhabited this geographically diverse region created a network of urban homogeneity supported by extensive agricultural hinterlands in a complex and unique material culture. Exploiting, processing and marketing mineral and marine resources, they added trade to a growing agro-pastoralist economy to create an extensive network that connected Harappan settlements to the coast, southeast Iran, Central Asia and Mesopotamia. It eventually covered an area roughly 1,210,000 sq. kms in extent, 1,100 kms north to south and east to west, nearly twenty times the area of Egypt, and over twelve times the settled area of Egypt and Mesopotamia combined. The distance between the two major Indus cities, Harappa and Mohenjo-daro, is greater than Mesopotamia's north-south extent of about 440 kms.

The Major Eras (Kenoyer 2004)

Around 10,000 BCE, a mobile and semi-sedentary foraging population initiated the local domestication of specific wild animals and plants. A similar transition had already occurred in the Fertile Crescent 1,500 years earlier. Foragers continued to inhabit these regions as they evolved through various stages of agro-pastoralism and urbanisation.

Circa 7000 BCE, around the time of the 8.2 ka mega drought (Nieuwenhuyse 1994), an early food-producing economy based on crops and animals domesticated in west Asia (barley, wheat, sheep, goats) and locally domesticated zebu cattle took root. Some twenty small agriculture-based village settlements and pastoral camps appeared in the Baluchistan hills around Mehrgarh, to the west of the Indus, indicative of an eastward spread of Iranian Neolithic culture. People raised cattle, sheep and goats, cultivated wheat and barley during the winter rains and stored it in granaries. They made pottery by hand, human and bovine figurines as part of fertility cult rituals and ornaments for small-scale local trade. Between 4300–3200 BCE, settlements

Figure 11.1: Early Harappan site concentration

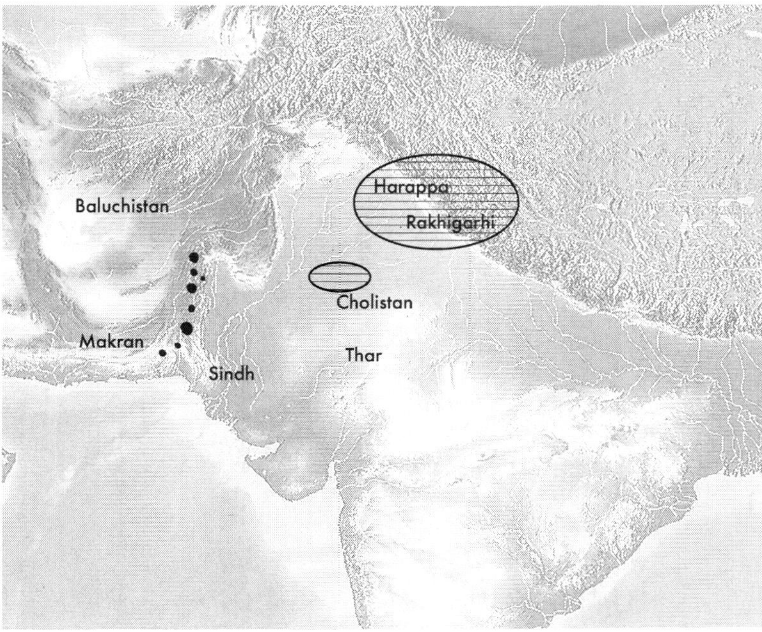

Source: Created by author.

grew in size to a few hectares and spread into the Indus plain and eastwards to the inland Derawar delta of the Ghaggar-Hakra River in Cholistan Desert. Copper tools were made and the potter's wheel was used to make beautifully painted vessels. Their similarity with Central Asian and north Iranian styles suggests mobility and trade. Harappa on the Ravi began to assume importance.

During the Early Harappan (3200–2600 BCE), many new sites appeared in the Indus Valley along the Makran coast, in the upper Ganges basin and Gujarat. Towns like Rahman Dheri were built with walls and a grid pattern of streets in this early phase of urbanism. Stamp seals with geometric motifs suggest administrative control over intensifying trading

Figure 11.2: Mature Harappan site concentration

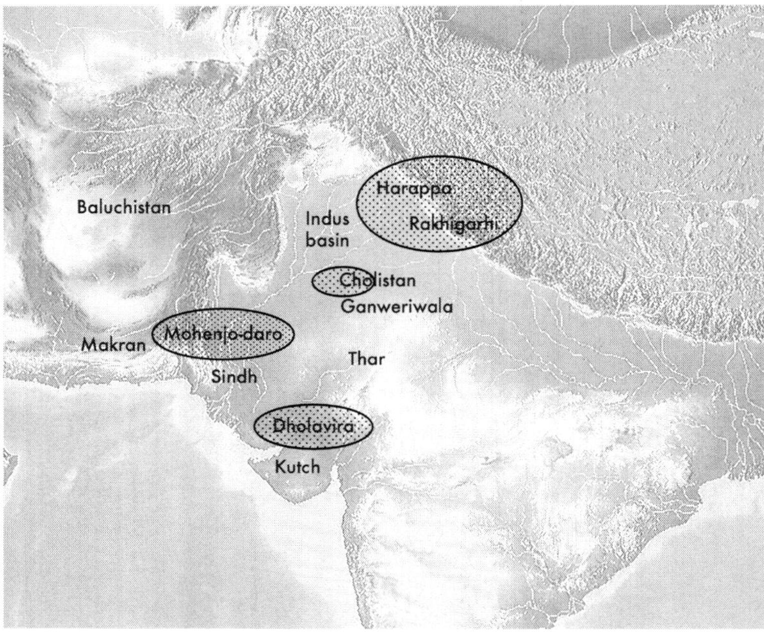

Source: Created by author.

volumes. Terracotta models of bullock carts reveal an improved transportation network that spread cultural uniformity. Ceramics assumed distinct regional styles (Ravi, Kot Diji, Amri, Hakra), and the first traits of the Mature Harappan in jewellery and ornament styles appeared. Large jars with distinctive potter's marks, the earliest stage of a script, were kept in houses for storing grains.

The Transition (2600–2500 BCE) to the Mature Harappan saw a sharp decline in the number of sites, suggestive of major social upheavals.

The Mature Harappan (2500–1900 BCE) showcases the finest traditions of Harappan culture. A number of extraordinarily well-planned, constructed and maintained cities and towns utilising

Figure 11.3: Late Harappan site concentration

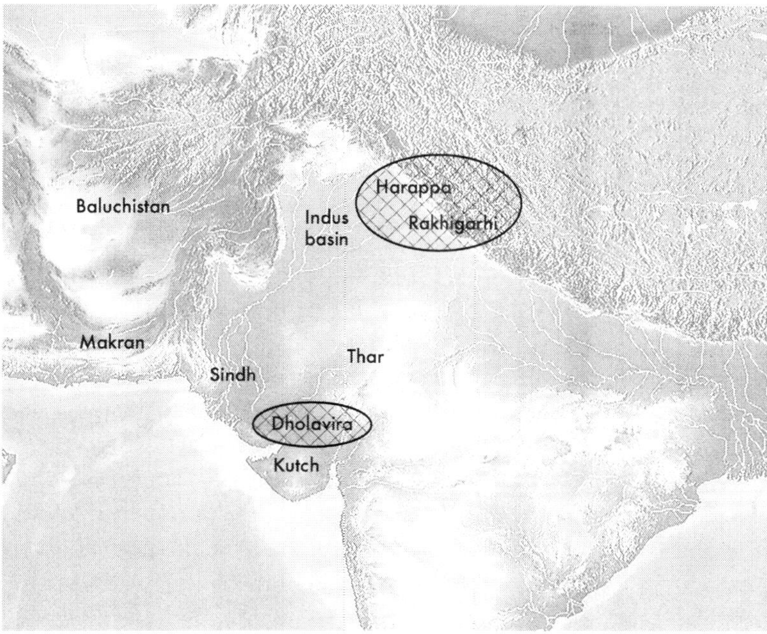

Source: Created by author.

the finest hydraulic engineering of the contemporary world sprung up over the vast territory. Five major cities, Mohenjo-daro, Harappa, Ganweriwala, Rakhigarhi and Dholavira developed into regional centres. Enclosed within monumental walls, they formed a network of industrial and commercial activity which through intense interaction was integrated into a larger economic, political and ideological system.

The Harappans achieved a remarkable level of standardisation and a uniform cultural pattern in the production of artefacts and urban spaces. Relatively uniform pottery styles, material cultures and ritual symbols emerged across the region. Sun-dried and fired bricks were standardised. Streets were laid out in grid patterns with demarcated areas for granaries and other functional requirements. Harappan urban planning and sanitation levels were not reached again globally until 2,000 years later, in Rome. This speaks of a high level of administrative control and an ideological framework to support it. However, unambiguous information on a controlling ideology, religion or political elite is still lacking.

Together with standardised weights and measures, a formalised writing system indicates taxation and trade regulations were in force. Urban layouts and architectural styles reflect a hierarchical and stratified social order, though the absence of elite burials, temples and palaces suggests there was no single dominant political organisation. There is little evidence of warfare. Instead, a well-developed water and land transportation system and a large number of seals with symbolic significance, suggest the presence of a common and powerful ideologically integrating force.

The Harappans maintained an extensive trade network that reached far into other parts of India, Afghanistan, Central Asia, Iran and Mesopotamia. Sea routes followed the Makran coast to Oman, Mesopotamia and Africa. Raw materials flowed in from east and west, north and south; a range of finished products, exquisite jewellery, timber and exotic animals flowed out to Mesopotamia and Central Asia. Steatite seal markings identified their owners. Trading colonies, seasonal and permanent, came up in Mesopotamia, Oman and Afghanistan. The high concentration of urban sites in Gujarat and its port cities of Dholavira and Lothal suggests it played a pivotal role in the west Asian and coastal trade.

Harappan agriculture, which was stimulated by the introduction of domesticated barley, wheat, goats and sheep from west Asia, adapted to a long-term declining trend in the summer monsoon with the domestication of South Asian primaries viz. rice (*Oryza nivara*), cotton, mustard and local millet varieties. As summer precipitation continued to decline, domesticates from Africa (sorghum, jowar, bajra, millets including ragi, cowpea, gram) and China (*japonica* rice, citrus, other millet varieties) were added to the cropping pattern.

The unifying trend of the Mature Harappan disappeared in the Late Harappan (1900–1300 BCE). Populations migrated to the upper Indus-Gangetic basin and Gujarat largely abandoning the middle Indus and Ghaggar-Hakra basins. Settlements grew smaller in size and density but increased in number. Seals, weights and the script disappeared. This phase overlapped with the Regionalisation Phase of Indo-Gangetic Tradition and the emergence of local chiefdoms with limited social and political interaction. It saw the early spread of Indo-Aryan languages and Vedic ideology. Foundations were laid for later brahmanical Hinduism, Buddhism and Jainism. Indus farming techniques and technologies, however, continued to be used.

What Triggered the Beginning and the End?

Two global mega droughts, 4,000 years apart, may have been the triggers for the beginning and end of the Harappan Civilisation. Major changes have been recorded in the pattern of the annual summer monsoon and the Mediterranean westerlies which bring rain to South Asia and west Asia respectively c8.2 ka, 5.2 ka, 4.2 ka. Rainfall decreased by 30–50%. The first two coincide with the beginnings of farming in Mehrgarh, while the 4.2 ka event accelerated the decline of the Harappan Civilisation.

Over large tracts of land, dust storms blew away surface soil and fresh water levels dropped alarmingly. In Mesopotamia, populations migrated from dry farming regions to riverine environments; in the Indus basin, rivers changed courses and disrupted settlement patterns. From Egypt to Greece, from Mesopotamia to the Indus Valley, severe social, economic and political upheaval disrupted long-established societies. Cities and towns were abandoned, agriculture was devastated and severe famines followed.

The 8.2 ka event lasted from 6200–6000 BCE. It caused the eastward migration of farming populations from the Zagros

Mountains. The eastward movement split in two, bypassing the hostile desert terrain of the Iranian plateau. The northern line reached Mehrgarh at the foothills of the Bolan pass c5000 BCE, when a sudden surge in the nascent Neolithic culture of the region occurred. Many west Asian and Zagrosian traits appear together with Y-chromosome genes (Hgs J and L) associated with the spread of Neolithic farmers from west Asia. These new arrivals were primarily nomadic herders of domesticated goats and sheep belonging to the widespread agro-pastoral economy of the Fertile Crescent and the first global urbanised centres. The cultural traits they brought acted as yeast to fertile Harappan talent.

The southern pincer, meeting a more hostile geography of the Iranian plateau, took longer as a trail of pottery reveals. It reached the lower Indus basin in the fourth millennium BCE just as more droughts gripped the region (3700–3600 and 3300–3100 BCE) (Clarke 2016). At the same time, a severe 600-year drought afflicted the Zagros Mountains. South Asia too became drier.

The second global mega drought lasted 300 years from 4200–3900 BCE. By 1900 BCE it had blighted much of Asia. The cataclysmic effect of this mega drought is recorded at the archaeological site of Tell Leilan on Khabur Plains in northeast Syria, once part of the Akkadian Empire. Tell Leilan began as a small farming village c5000 BCE, and by c2600 BCE had grown into an independent city of some 30,000 people. Excavations uncovered an acropolis, large grain-storage rooms, and a crowded residential area serviced by paved roads. The residents of Tell Leilan were ruled by a rigidly organised, state-run economy. They grew barley and varieties of wheat, used carts for transportation and a written script. Tell Leilan was completely abandoned between 2200–1900 BCE. The abandonment began when a thick layer of volcanic ash from Turkey rained down on the town in 2200 BCE. This layer was covered by an even thicker layer of soil containing large amounts of fine wind-blown sand and dust blown in by the mega drought of the 4.2 ka event. This layer had no earthworm holes or insect tracks; the severity of the drought killed them all. Tell Leilan saw a swift and immediate reduction of 87% in settled area and total abandonment within thirty to fifty years. The Akkadian Empire passed into history (Weiss 1993a, 2015; Nieuwenhuyse 1994; Dalfes 1997).

Tell Leilan was just one of many settlements similarly affected. Populations migrated in search of food, water and shelter. Some turned to a pastoral nomadic economy. Some reached the Indus Valley.

Who were the Harappans?

A thousand years later, the *Taittiriya Brahmana*-II 4, 6, 8 refers to 'The people to whom these ruined sites belonged, lacking posts, these many settlements, widely distributed, they O Agni, having been expelled by thee, have migrated to another land' (Allchin 1996: 308).

This text leaves a revealing clue as to the identity of the Harappans, or rather who they were not. They had created an extensive urban landscape which, by the time the Brahmanas were composed c900–700 BCE, lay ruined and abandoned. They had no connection to the composers of Vedic texts for the *yupa* (wooden post used in Vedic soma sacrifice) mentioned in the verse had no place in their religious practices. They did not worship Agni who is credited with expelling them from their lands.

Unfortunately, there are no Harappan texts. A pictographic script that uses about 3,500 characters is yet to be deciphered. Considering that the Harappans were in close contact with Mesopotamia and Elam and adopted some of their cultural traits, it is inconceivable that they did not commit some details of their great civilisation to writing as the other two did. Yet, nothing has been found. Perhaps, like much of later Indian texts, perishable material like palm leaves were used in Harappa. If so, they have succumbed to the passage of time. Only a few samples of the script survive, inscribed on pottery and seals. Sadly, these may just be names, identification marks and invocations to protective deities.

The Harappan gene pool came from its diverse hunter-gatherer populations admixed to a smaller extent with Iranian hunter-gatherers/farmers (Gangal 2014; Narasimhan et al. 2018; Singh 2016). A recent analysis of the genome of a person buried in a Rakhigarhi cemetery reveals insights into the genetic profile of Harappans (Shinde 2019). The DNA matches that of eleven other individuals from Gonur in Turkmenistan and Shahr-i-Sokhta in eastern Iran, sites which were in cultural contact with the Harappan region (Narasimhan et al. 2018). It was a mix of ancient Iranian and AASI genes whose mtDNA belongs to Hg U2b2 which is nearly exclusive to South Asia and derives from the out-of-Africa migrants. The South Asian component is closest to that of Andamanese hunter-gatherers. The Iranian-related ancestry dates to a time before farming originated on the Iranian plateau c7000–6000 BCE, to hunter-gatherers who lived in the Zagros Mountains. The Iranian-related component in early Harappans, therefore, predates the advent of farming.

Multiple lines of evidence lead to the conclusion that this ancestry profile was widespread in the northwest in Harappan times, and also extended to parts of Central Asia. Further, rather than an eastward flow into South Asia, its presence suggests the reverse, that is, gene flow from South Asia. There is no detectable ancestry from Steppe pastoralists or later Iranian farmers. This genetic profile has since been changed by subsequent gene flow spread by Steppe pastoralists via Central Asia from c2000–1500 BCE. Steppe pastoralist ancestry in South Asia matches that in Bronze Age Eastern Europe but not Western Europe which explains distinctive features shared by Balto-Slavic and Indo-Iranian languages.

The Faces of Harappans

Just a few sculptures leave behind faces and forms from which a meagre picture of what they looked like emerges. Of one, just the bust remains. Found in Mohenjo-daro, this steatite sculpture exudes the authority of a middle-aged man commonly referred to as a priest-king. His features hint he or his forebears came from another land, perhaps Mesopotamia or Central Asia. His face is covered by a neatly trimmed beard. His hair, combed back to cover a balding patch, is parted in the centre and held down by a ribbon tied above his broad forehead. The ribbon holds a circular pendant above the bridge of his nose. His head, held upright with the hint of an upward tilt, allows his eyes, partially closed, to gaze down in silent contemplation at, perhaps, a subservient audience. An amulet, similar to the one on his forehead, is tied to his bare right arm. From his left shoulder, a toga-like garment in trefoil design flows smoothly over his front and back. He exudes the unmistakable air of aristocracy. His posture, his garment, his badges leave little doubt that his place is among the elite of his society.

The second sculpture is a small bronze statue of a dancing girl, heavily jewelled, saucily exposing her nude beauty. About 4,500 years old, it too was excavated at Mohenjo-daro, in 1926. All of 10.5 centimetres tall, the girl is perhaps still in her teens. Unlike the fertility goddess figurines in their fleshy feminine fullness, she is thin and supple, a model that would be totally at home in any global fashion show today. Her right hand rests on the small of her back, her left on her left knee pushed challengingly forward. She exposes her pubic region carved by the sculptor's blade, open and inviting, thrusting its mystery and magic at all who look at her. Her hair, thick and luxuriantly curly, has been carefully woven into an elaborate hairdo that seems to draw her head back with its weight, and push her breasts, small, firm and upright, forward. A large necklace hangs provocatively above them. Her arm is covered from wrist to armpit in bangles, a distinctive display of status in Harappan society. Her African-like features, thick pouting lips and broad nostrils, suggest she is dark-skinned and, in Rgvedic terminology, of nisada origins. Yet, her confident poise and ornaments leave no doubt that she is totally at ease with her profession, whatever it may have been, and that she was a valued member of her community and social milieu. She was someone's favourite, perhaps a temple dancer or influential courtesan.

There is a third sculpture, nine centimetres tall, a faceless one, the lithe, muscular torso of a man, carved c2000 BCE in red limestone. His head, arms and legs have been broken, as too his male member. What survives exhibits the skill of the sculptor's wrist, moving smoothly in minute detail, picking out the sensuous curves of broad shoulders, gently protruding belly and firm, narrow buttocks. The man was accustomed to physical exercise, a warrior, perhaps, making an offering, for the remnants of his arms point forward and up.

A head sculpted in stone may give an idea of what he looked like. It is quite different from that of the priest-king and betrays some nisada features. The cheek-bones are high, the cheeks full, the forehead low, and the lips frozen in a petulant pout. The hair is neatly combed back into a double bun and held in place, like that of the priest-king, by a head band; unlike the priest-king's straight hair, it is curly and wavy.

These sculptures took time and skill to make and cost a lot of money. They represent important sections of Harappan elite and their diverse origins. We can recognise in them the priest, the administrator, the warrior, and the dancer of today. They manifest power, authority and confident control of a society founded on the flourishing economy they created. Animals and human figures carved into Harappan seals add more tantalising details. The elephant, the rhinoceros and the tiger have disappeared from the Indus basin, but the pipal tree still remains sacred, and the obscure human figures sheltered within its branches appear teasingly familiar and recognisable in the many gods and goddesses that Indians honour and worship today. Like the Harappan gene pool which played an instrumental role in the formation of modern South Asians, Harappa's culture, religion and traditions form the foundation on which much of modern India's heritage of multiple beliefs and rituals, agro-pastoral practices, artisan skills and languages has been shaped.

12

The Beginnings

The origins of the Harappan Tradition were humble and unspectacular with local developments being primarily responsible for the initial stimulus (Kenoyer 2011). Microliths excavated from the lowest levels of many urban sites confirm foragers were present in the exact locations where settled agro-pastoral communities emerged between 7000–2800 BCE. The centre of these earliest Neolithic sites in northwest South Asia was Mehrgarh, situated in the Kachi Plain at the foothills of the Bolan Pass where the Bolan River flows from Baluchistan into the Indus plains. Sited at the junction of major communication routes between the Iranian Plateau, Central Asia and the Indus Valley, Mehrgarh was the gateway to the Indus Valley from Iran.

A simulation of the Neolithic transition from a foraging to a predominantly agro-pastoralist economy in this region between 6300–3800 BCE reveals a general movement from the Iranian plateau towards the Indus basin (Lemmen 2012). Scattered sites first appeared c5000 BCE on the Baluchistan highlands around Kili Ghul Mohammad and Mehrgarh and extended to the Makran coast. By 4300 BCE, the concentration around these two sites increased as others appeared along the eastern border of the Baluchistan foothills. Handmade pottery, copper, burnt pebbles and bone and stone tools marked this advance. Cultivation of domesticated wheat, barley, cotton and possibly pulses spread. Between 4300–3800 BCE, settlements increased in number and bunched around the Bolan Pass waiting, as it would appear, to burst through into the Kachi Plain and the Indus Valley. It cleared the way eastward towards the Ghaggar-Hakra River. Technological developments in pottery manufacture and the use of seals, beads and possibly gold accompanied this espansion. By 3200 BCE, the concentration of sites along the Indus and Ghaggar-Hakra Rivers and Gujarat grew denser, and at the beginning of the Early Harappan (3200–2600 BCE), several settlements contemporary to the Amri and Kot Diji culture appeared. Wheat largely replaced barley. There is evidence of localised irrigation near Mehrgarh. The distinctive Hakra Ware pottery emerged in Punjab, and microlithic tools become more abundant. Fine pottery was produced on a large scale using the wheel, and workshops made beads from a variety of gem stones and smelted copper. A network of settlements across the Iranian plateau now linked the Indus region to west and Central Asia.

Major cultural developments in north and central Baluchistan c3500–3000 BCE and the emergence of farming settlements at Kili Ghul Mohammad, Anjira, Siah Damb, and Rana Ghundai suggest the arrival of new influences or immigrants from the west, via Mundigak in Afghanistan (Allchin 1968: 105, 132–33; 1996: 131). The proliferation of settlements came together with an improvement in living conditions and a development of material culture. Meat from domesticated cattle, sheep and goats began to replace that of hunted game. Cattle became progressively more important in the economy. Small-scale irrigation and granaries indicate the increasing importance of cereal cultivation and average male (170 cm) and female (160 cm) heights of overall good diet and health. Some skeletons reveal evidence of dentistry. Grave goods (a range of ornaments, beads, necklaces and head bands made of seashells, lapis lazuli, turquoise, steatite and other gem stones, some from far away areas) give an idea of growing trade networks and prosperity. Industrial fireplaces and workshops manufactured jewellery from semi-precious stones and shells, some brought from the Arabian Sea coast. Pottery production increased and became more specialised. Jars were made for storing food. Stone tool technology made progressive advancement. Harvesting sickles were made by setting microliths slantwise in bitumen attached to a wooden handle.

The Zagros Influence (Costantini 2006; Jarrige, Catherine et al. 2006; Jarrige, Jean-Francois et al. 2006)

Mehrgarh's archaeology provides evidence for both an early local background and a strong connection with the Neolithic in west Asia; pottery styles, brick designs, stone tool technologies, red wall paintings, circular fire-pits and large granaries were common to both. Houses commonly consisted of four rooms built with mud-brick walls plastered with clay mortar. Circular fire-pits, some of 400–600 mm diameter and depth of 350 mm, containing heavily burnt cracked pebbles warmed rooms and open spaces between houses. They were also used for cooking. Numerous clay figurines of females and bulls similar to ones found from west Asia to Central Asia have been recovered. The females have beaked noses, large hollows for eyes, elaborate hairstyles and headdresses, wear necklaces and display their bare bulbous breasts and broad thighs. Known as the Zhob type, they date to the seventh millennium BCE and suggest an ideology associated with fecundity, fertility and farming.

Mehrgarh's granaries, similar in design and construction to those in Mesopotamia, provide evidence of efficiency in agricultural production and social organisation (McIntosh 2008). The main crops were barley (90%) and emmer wheat of southwest Asian origin. The presence of wild barley suggests an element of local domestication. People hunted elephants, gazelle, swamp deer, nilgai, blackbuck, onager, chital, water buffaloes and wild pigs.

Burials bear strong resemblance to those in the Zagros Mountains. Young goats buried in the earliest graves hint at the domestication of goats and their importance to the economy. Pastoral activity, limited to goats initially, increasingly focused on sheep and cattle.[1] Lapis lazuli and turquoise beads from Turkmenia and north Afghanistan, and shells from the Arabian Sea 500 kms to the south, reveal a complex pattern of regional trade networks between nomadic pastoralists and sedentary agriculturalists.

Goats were first domesticated in the Zagros Mountains. The earliest Neolithic sites in central Zagros appeared during a global dry and cold spell, the Younger Dryas (c11000–9500 BCE) (Abdi 2003; Darabi 2012). Towards its end, increased temperatures and rainfall brought growth in vegetation and seasonally occupied settlements. Sedentism encouraged population growth and a nascent food-producing economy involving both agriculture and animal husbandry. Permanent settlements appeared during the mid-ninth millennium BCE. By c7500 BCE, crops domesticated in the Fertile Crescent were grown. The rugged terrain is unsuitable for large-scale agriculture but ideal for pastoralism. A sudden increase in sheep and goat populations indicates their domestication. Sometime between 4500–3500 BCE, full-fledged nomadic pastoralism became a part of the economy.

The Iranian Plateau

The relatively wetter landscape of the Zagros Mountains gives way to semi-arid terrain and desert as one proceeds towards eastern Iran. Here, between 6200–6000 BCE, the 8.2 ka mega drought caused major social and economic disruptions in lifestyles with abandonment of settlements and migrations. Reliance on sheep and goats which require less fodder than cattle grew with a shift away from their exploitation for meat to milk and wool production. Further periods of heightened aridity in the fourth millennium caused more disruptions and as archaeological, genetic and linguistic evidence reveal, migrations, particularly of nomadic pastoralists, to Baluchistan and the Indus basin.

Iran is a land of ancient cultures over which newer populations have successively imposed their own. Iran's modern population reflects this. Y-chromosome Hg J, associated with the demic diffusion of farming cultures from the Fertile Crescent during the Neolithic, is predominant in Iran. Its highest frequencies are in the Zagros Mountains and the Caspian Sea shoreline. It dominates the Iranian plateau and is exceptionally high in Sistan Baluchistan (Grugni 2012). This presence spills over into neighbouring northwest South Asia. Another Y-chromosome Hg L1 is also common in Iranian and Dravidian-speaking populations of south India.

Anthropological studies of human remains from Mehrgarh suggest South Asian ancestry. As the Harappan seals reveal, the northwest then was a fertile terrain with abundant aquatic and faunal food resources for hunter-gatherer populations. Iranian immigrants arrived as herders, in small groups over many centuries. By 3500 BCE, the population here is estimated at 2.5 million. Clearly, the food production economy had drawn significant numbers of hunter-gatherer populations into its ambit.

Ceramic artefacts from the fourth millennium BCE reveal an extensive trading network that connected south Iran, Baluchistan, and Central Asia (Mutin 2012). Influences from northeast Baluchistan and south Afghanistan are visible in ceramic artefacts from Mehrgarh (seventh millennium BCE) and Balakot and Amri (fourth millennium BCE). They also preserve distinctive regional traits. The diffusion of populations through migrations and matrimonial exchanges, technologies and political and economic ideas cemented that connection.

Beyond Mehrgarh

Hakra Ware pottery from the Kachi Plain reveals an expanding population which by 4300–3200 BCE spilled over into the greater Indus plains, and intensified towards the Ghaggar-Hakra plains. With the Indus constantly changing its course over a wide flood plain, the control of flood water now became as critical as its conservation. The design of urban spaces required new construction technologies using standardised mud and burnt clay bricks and advanced hydraulic systems for piping of fresh water and disposal of sewage. The Early Harappan (3200–2600 BCE) was characterised by incipient urbanism, growth and expansion of the farming communities. Regional styles evolved (Madella 2006).

The emergence of an early writing system together with a standardised system of weights and stamp seals bearing geometric designs similar to those in Central Asia and Iran reveals a growing trading network and developing social organisation. When Mesopotamia's focus shifted to the Gulf route, goods began to be shipped in bulk via the Indus and Makran coast. Towns like Amri and Kot Diji in Sindh gained importance, and Mohenjo-daro on the right bank of the Indus at the heart of the routes connecting the northern, central and southern regions with Baluchistan began to grow in importance. The entire region underwent a dramatic and drastic overhaul between 2600–2500 BCE during a period known as the Transition. It was a painful process as Kot Diji shows. The town was burnt down at least twice, around 2800 and 2520 BCE (Allchin 1996: 142–46). Amri suffered a similar fate. It has been suggested that the destruction, as in the case of Chogha Mish in Elam, was deliberate, an act of ritual or ideological purification following the adoption of a new ideology underling the unity and uniformity of the Indus civilisation. It may also have had something to do with creating facilities for handling goods in bulk and control of the river trade.

The process of change was widespread. At the end of it all, the Mature Harappan emerged with all its advances in culture, technology and the economy.

13

The Maturing

The Transition (2600–2500 BCE) was a veritable revolution within the Harappan urbanisation process. By the time it ended, a complex and highly organised society, the Mature Harappan (2500–1900 BCE), had emerged. It was significantly different in scale, organisational and social complexity, cultural uniformity and ideology and ethos from that of the Early Harappan.

The Transition took place with the abandonment of more than three-fifths of Early Harappan settlements. In Cholistan, only four out of thirty-seven identified sites continued to be occupied; 130 new towns were built. These were constructed according to a plan with the wide variety of features associated with Harappan town planning: grids with cardinally orientated streets, mud and baked bricks manufactured to a standardised size, new foundations, brick wells and public water supply systems, drains for sewage disposal, garbage collection and disposal systems and massive walls (Possehl 1990; McIntosh 2008: 80–88; Allchin 1968: 146; Kenoyer 2016).

Such an enterprise would have required control of substantial resources in material and labour by elite groups. It would also have required expertise, motivation and the power to accomplish it. The initial means by which such power came to be concentrated in elite sections may have come from controlling the agricultural surpluses generated during the years of good monsoons through the Early Harappan. In an urbanising society, such control would have been critical and decisive.[1]

This developing concentration of power got a boost from Mesopotamia's insatiable demand for Harappan luxury products. Harappan merchants gained direct access to Mesopotamia via the sea route and established strategically placed colonies along the coast. Their wealth, status and influence grew enormously. Mesopotamian ideologies of social control and technologies related to urbanisation in turn influenced Harappan society. It probably included the role of city gods as depositories of power over men and nature and arbitrators of disputes.

Urbanisation was a potent means of concentrating and consolidating an elite power structure. It allowed the securing, storage and tight control of agricultural surpluses and industrial and commercial activity. This concentration of power was reinforced by an ideology that used ritual and material symbols to perpetuate superior status, demonstrated by the possession and wearing of artefacts made out of raw materials brought from great distances and requiring specialised skills and technology to fashion. A widely used system of uniform weights and stamp seals was introduced to register ownership and control the flow of goods. A written script allowed control over technology, administration and commerce. The elite section of the city was sited on mounds within massive protective walls. Set apart from other sections of the city, its high visibility and restricted access enhanced exclusivity and the perception of power. The control of agricultural surpluses became a powerful resource during lean months. It paid for the enormous labour required to construct cities and manufacture a host of artefacts.[2]

Though Mature Harappan influence spanned a diverse region of over 1.5 million sq. kms inhabited by a million people for 700 years, it left little by way of literary texts, palaces, imposing temples or tombs to indicate who ruled or controlled it and whether it functioned under an overall centralised political, religious or military authority (Kenoyer 1994). Instead, there is evidence of different levels of integration, with rival elite groups (merchants, ritual specialists and individuals who controlled resources such as land, livestock and raw materials) exercising different levels of regional control. Trade, shared ideologies and economic systems, reflected in common styles of seals, ornaments, ceramics and other artefacts, seem to have linked these regional elites. Harappan urban populations were organised in a stratified structure, and its rural populations (farmers, pastoralists, fishermen, miners, hunter-gatherers) integrated into it at various levels in different degrees.

Harappa's neighbours belonged to different cultures. In the northwest, Rehman Dheri and Gumla have been identified with the Late Kot Dijian Culture. The Helmand Culture, centred in Mundigak, flourished in the Kandahar Valley. The Kulli Culture (south Baluchistan) was closely integrated with the Harappan and played an important role in its trade by linking the coast with the highlands and the Kachi and Indus plains. Mature Harappan sites dotted the Makran coast further south. Of these, Sutkagen-dor, with its towered walls and fortified gateway, was the westernmost outpost in the Persian Gulf trade.

Hunter-gatherers and pastoralists inhabited neighbouring eastern regions. The people of the Jodhpura-Ganeshwar hunter-gatherer culture, living in the Khetri region of the Aravalli hills to the south of Cholistan, supplied much of Harappa's copper ore requirement. To its southwest, the people of the Ahar-Banas Culture practised farming (millets, wheat, barley, pulses, cattle). North of the Narmada River in Madhya Pradesh, the people of the Kayatha Culture lived in farming settlements.

Lothal in Gujarat formed the southwest limit of Harappan urbanism. Farther away, the Deccan was dominated by the SNAC in which cattle dominated the economy and seasonal pastoralists acted as conduits to Harappa.

The Timing

Contrary to earlier assumptions that the Harappan Civilisation flourished during a period of optimal rainfall, the Mature Harappan coincided with the beginning of a declining trend in summer monsoon precipitation (Madella 2006). Beginning c5200 BCE, the decline intensified from 3900 BCE (Prasad 2014).[3]

The period 7000–5200 BCE was a time of high rainfall with peak winter rains which increased the output of the winter-spring crop package (wheat, barley, peas, lentils, grass pea, linseed), the staples of pre-Harappan agriculture. Small village communities expanded into newer areas and increased grasslands made pastoralism widespread. This was the time when the water buffalo, which was to have such great symbolic value in the Mature Harappan, was domesticated. Surpluses and pastoralism encouraged trade.

The sudden and dramatic Early–Mature Harappan Transition occurred just as the declining trend in the summer monsoon rainfall set in (Possehl 1990; McIntosh 2998: 80–88). River flows became remarkably stable as flood intensity decreased (Giosan 2012; Singh 2017). It stimulated the growth of settlements along river banks, especially along the Ghaggar-Hakra which, being monsoon- and not glacier-fed, was less flood-prone than the Indus. Increased sedimentation due to reduced flows created oxbow lakes on the floodplains which supplied water in drier months. Agricultural activity received a boost with the adoption of a two-season cropping pattern growing African (finger millet 2600 BCE, pearl millet 2400 BCE, sorghum 2400 BCE, cow pea 2200 BCE, hyacinth bean 2200 BCE) (Fuller 2003) and Chinese summer crops. Winter rain contributed between 15–30% of annual rainfall. Winter crops comprised 15–19% and summer crops 48–68% of the total (Giosan 2018; Petrie 2016).[4] Controlling surpluses to counter inter-seasonal shortfalls contributed to urban centralisation.

Trade – A Primary Trigger

The most notable feature of the Transition was the abruptness of the change.

While historical and cultural continuity made the Harappan Civilisation a predominantly South Asian affair, the Mature

Harappan was marked by a range of previously absent cultural innovations and unifying traits that betray foreign influences (Possehl 1990). Regional diversities, though, persisted within an overall uniformity in cultural traits: a common script; a widely used system of weights and measures; the stamp seal (with new styles of human and animal depiction); new ceramic types (dishes-on-stand, jars with beaded rims, perforated vessels) and painted decorations (horned deities, pipal leaves, the lotus motif); the wide range of metal tools and weapons (flat axes, arrow heads); bead types (etched carnelian, micro-beads in steatite, disk beads); town planning (massive brick platforms, wells, drainage systems, grid plans); standard brick dimensions. Harappan society underwent core changes related to the urbanisation process: social stratification; the apparent emergence of the state and political differentiation; craft and career specialisation; new technologies and economic configurations; institutionalised control of ideology, public rituals and the supply of resources. Militarisation may possibly have added another dimension. These distinctive features differ both from the Early Harappan and the material culture of contemporary neighbours.

The stimulus for the Transition may have come from a spurt in overseas trade with Mesopotamia. Newly established trading channels with other developed economies can intensify economic processes and revolutionise socio-cultural systems and technological levels of a society (Possehl 1990). They can lead to the re-evaluation of resources and influence how their ownership, access and distribution are perceived. They bring new opportunities for craftsmen and merchants. Populations tend to agglomerate in order to take advantage of economies of scale and other opportunities. This promotes the development of new forms of social control and ideologies that aim to regulate economic, political and religious processes. It enhances social stratification, competitive forces and social distances between individuals or groups. Eventually, it weaves diverse beliefs and traditions into a complex web of ideology and belief systems that unites and creates a common identity and civilisation.

The intensification of marine trade exposed Harappans directly to the cultures of the Gulf when, in the throes of frenzied urbanisation, they were undergoing radical social, economic and political changes. Carbon dating of Harappan artefacts, motifs and seals found in Mesopotamia indicate that the earliest contact with Ur took place c2500 BCE, just as the Mature Harappan began and its cities grew to monumental proportions. They all adopted administrative tools from southern Mesopotamia (Weiss 1993b).

Mesopotamian ships did not sail beyond the Gulf, possibly because the Harappans had taken the initiative in the sea trade and the development of seaworthy vessels was a Harappan innovation. The transport of animals like water buffaloes to Mesopotamia depicted on Akkadian seals and mentioned in texts implies that these ships were large. Lothal, Dholavira, Sotka Koh and Sutkagen-dor, located along important coastal trade routes, provide indirect evidence for seagoing vessels. Terracotta models of ocean-going ships have been found at Lothal. The export of timber and goods of relatively low value but high bulk is evidence of a well-developed trading network with substantial profits for the Harappans. Similarly, in the lapis lazuli trade, Harappans went to great lengths to import raw stones from Afghanistan and process them for almost exclusive export to Mesopotamia.

Boats were also built for river navigation. Harappan seals depict boats with no mast and sharply upturned prows lashed together at both bow and stern suggesting they were made of reeds. Another seal shows a ship with a rectangular cabin and birds aboard. While waterways connected places all along the Indus and its tributaries, wheeled bullock carts, models of which have been found at Mohenjo-daro, connected river settlements to the interior.

A Meluhhan colony came up in Mesopotamia. It is not known if Mesopotamians lived in Harappa, though burials in Harappa suggest they might have. Rgvedic verses (RV 6.20.12, RV 6.45.1) praise Indra for guiding the Rgvedic Turvasa and Yadu tribes from overseas places. RV 10.62.10 describes them as enslaved dasas required to serve as cowherds. Mentioned along with them are the Purus, Druhyus and Anus who may have also had overseas connections (Chanda 1976: 11–25, 33). It has been suggested that *mlechha* (barbarian) may have originally referred to the inhabitants of Meluhha (coastal Baluchistan, southern Sindh, Kutch, Gujarat).

Harappa's trade with Mesopotamia drew it firmly into the networks passing north and south of the arid regions of central Iran. The northern route, later to become part of the Silk Road, passed through the Khyber Pass to Kabul and Shortugai in Afghanistan. Passing westward, it met another route from the Bolan Pass that passed through Mundigak and Herat. Skirting the Caspian Sea, it touched the northern Mesopotamian city of Kish. Here, it was joined by the southern route which followed the Zagros Mountains to Tepe Yahya and onto the coast at Suktagen-dor. Sumer was located west of the central Zagros Mountains and Elam a little further south. Throughout the third millennium BCE Harappa exported steatite, ivory and carnelian beads shell inlays and bracelets, gaming pieces, pottery seals, terracotta mouse-traps and figurines, wooden articles, beads and bangles to Helmand (Kenoyer n.d.; Cortesi 2008; McIntosh 2008: 162; Frenez 2016). Interaction with this network brought a diverse mix of ideas as well.

Shortugai in north Afghanistan was an important link in the Harappan import of tin, turquoise and lapis lazuli. Harappan carnelian beads and seals have been found there. Monumental structures in Mundigak and Shar-i-Sokhta may have inspired Harappan architecture.

The Indus – A Unifying Channel (Jansen 1985, 1993; Kenoyer 2013; Law 2006)

A major shift from land to water transportation accompanied the urban revolution that ushered in the Mature Harappan. It could have been a reason for the destruction of older settlements and their rebuilding along new planning norms during the Transition so as to accommodate the needs of a more complex trading economy, the collection of food surpluses and the acquisition of natural resources from marginal areas.

The utilisation of the Indus for water transportation was a factor in unifying the Harappan region. The Harappans did not use the river for irrigation; it was too difficult to control. Their reason for siting urban centres close to major waterways was to utilise them for transportation. The Indus, therefore, played a vital role in the integration of the Harappan region by providing a quick and effective means for transportation of people and bulk goods and in spreading unifying technologies and ideology. Without it the Early–Mature Harappan Transition may not have been possible.

The geography of the Himalayan foothills differs considerably from that of the deserts of Cholistan and lower Sindh. Populations speaking various languages and of diverse local cultures had occupied different sections of the course of the Indus and its five major tributaries, Jhelum, Chenab, Ravi, Beas and Sutlej. This diversity prevented any single group from taking control of the whole valley despite its integration into the Mature Harappan.

Urbanisation (Gangal 2010; Possehl 1997a)

Where once maps of South Asia's northwest showed dreary stretches of unmarked sand, today the locations of ancient Harappan sites dot them like the skin of a small pockmarked face. The dots follow the twisting curves of ancient river beds, some dry and forgotten. They mark Sutkagen-dor on the Makran coast in the west to Alamgirpur, near Delhi, in the east, and from beyond Harappa in the north to Malvan, south of the Narmada River in the south. The densest cluster is around Cholistan, and along the dry bed of a river that is no more. The two most well-known cities, Mohenjo-daro and Harappa, do not lie in the regions of maximum density, but at the peripheries of this dense cluster.

The development and growth of Harappan urban sites occurred in three distinct regional centres: Baluchistan, Gujarat and the Ghaggar-Hakra basin. Between 7000–5000 BCE, settlements dotted the Baluchistan uplands from the Bolan Pass to the Makran coast. Around 4000 BCE, along with an increase of Baluchistan sites, a cluster of sites appeared in Gujarat, and 800 kms away, a small site at Binjour on the Ghaggar-Hakra palaeochannel. In the next 300 years, a large cluster of sites stretched downstream from Binjour. These spread northwards to the headwaters of the Ghaggar–Hakra and south to the lower Indus plains over the next 500 years. A dense distribution of sites along the Indus, the Ghaggar-Hakra and in Gujarat ushered in the beginning of the Mature Harappan. This continued for the next 700 years until 1900 BCE, when the number of sites

Figure 13.1: Overland and sea trading routes connecting Harappa with Mesopotamia

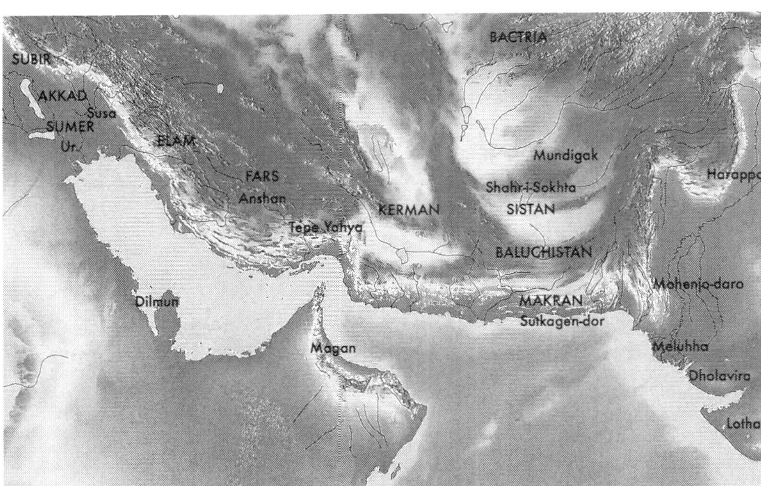

Source: Created by author.

along the mid-Ghaggar-Hakra decreased, but increased along its headwaters. Significantly, these sites were smaller in size, indicating a breakdown in urbanism. The most rapid decline occurred in the lower Indus. In Gujarat, the decline was gradual and spread over 400 years. By 1000 BCE, they too were abandoned. The focus shifted to the Gangetic plain, where the second phase of urbanisation developed from around 600 BCE.

Site-area statistics show that while numbers increased in the Post-Urban phase, there was a dramatic drop in total urban area and average site size. Large urban settlements could no more be supported and smaller settlements needed to be more spread out and evenly distributed in surrounding farmlands as agricultural output fell.

Table 13.1: Harappan sites and areas

	Sites	Total area ha	Average size ha
Kili Ghul Mohammad (c7000–5000 BCE)	20	52	2.6
Early Harappan (c3200–2600 BCE)	477	2146	4.5
Mature Harappan (c2500–1900 BCE)	1022	7358	7.2
Post-Urban phase (c1900–1400 BCE)	1281	4484	3.5

Note: 1 ha (hectare)= 10,000 sq. m.
Source: Possehl (1997a).

Distinguishing Characteristics of Harappan Urban Sites (McIntosh 2008: 223–39)

Harappan urban sites share two principal characteristics. On the one hand, a strong and uniform cultural pattern produced the same range of artefacts, the same types of houses and the same civic arrangement of separate walled mounds in each city and town. On the other hand, there was diversity in urban layouts and other fundamental aspects.

Harappan cities were surrounded by massive walls, sometimes with bastions and towers, constructed of baked or mud bricks, rubble or stone. Imposing gateways monitored the flow of people and goods into and out of the city. Harappa's southern gateway, for instance, had side chambers, probably for gatekeepers, and was wide enough (2.8 metres) to allow only one cart to pass through at a time. Immediately inside the gate was a large open space where vehicles and people entering the city could be detained as required. Gates also controlled movement between walled sections inside the settlement such as the citadel and residential areas. At Dholavira, a gateway flanked by chambers and bastions gave access from the Lower to the Middle Town.

Mohenjo-daro, Harappa, Chanhu-daro, Lothal and Banawali, among other cities, were wholly or partly built on artificial platforms with substantial retaining walls. These required enormous amounts of materials, time and labour to construct and offered some protection against flooding.

Suburbs were a feature of cities, which probably developed gradually as the population grew. They may have accommodated heavy industry, craft activities, fields, orchards and pastures. In Harappa and Dholavira, suburbs were enclosed later by additional walls.

A distinguishing feature of major Harappan cities was the 'citadel', a prominent walled sector constructed on a mound. The citadels of Banawali, Kalibangan, Dholavira, Lothal and to some extent Harappa were constructed over the remains of earlier settlements. At Mohenjo-daro, the citadel was constructed on brick platforms more than six metres high indicating that it was a deliberate policy to elevate it and the buildings it contained. The imposing wall emphasised the distinctiveness, importance and exclusivity of this area from the rest of the settlement. Its structures focused on aspects of its elite nature: religious (the Great Bath at Mohenjo-daro); economic (warehouses, granaries, industrial complexes); political; residential. Entry was controlled and designed to enhance its importance. At Mohenjo-daro, the entrance combined massive brick towers with a narrow gateway. Inside, more gates and stairways restricted access to specific areas. The citadel at Dholavira was divided into two separately walled areas with gates flanked by chambers. One of them contained the remains of a wooden signboard, probably placed above the gateway, with nine characters of the Indus script. An impressive southern gateway, flanked by towers, provided access to Kalibangan's citadel, which was separated into sections by gated internal walls. Access to Harappa's citadel was through gates, stairs, ramps and terraces, all controlled by bastions and guard rooms.

Citadels were most likely the main location of official activity. They also contained residences, possibly for persons involved in such activity. The facilities at the Pillared Hall at Mohenjo-daro included an unusually high proportion of bathrooms and large-scale cooking facilities, suggesting it was a place for public functions.

Beyond the citadel was the lower town, generally walled, and suburbs. The former was built to high standards of civic architecture, with excellent provision of water and sanitation, housing and light industry. Towns were laid out in a grid with broad north-south running straight main streets. Narrow lanes leading off the principal streets provided access to the houses which presented only blank walls to the main roads. Sanitary drains, usually of closely fitted baked bricks, ran along the main streets and discharged sewage outside city walls. Inspection covers allowed maintenance and sump pits collected solids so that water flow remained unimpeded. Some towns (Kalibangan, Lothal) used sunken soak jars along the streets. Rubbish was collected in large jars half sunk into the ground along streets, and rubbish dumps were located outside the city. Some towns (Mohenjo-daro, Kalibangan) had brick platforms outside houses where people could sit and talk.

Most Harappan towns leave evidence of industrial activity, both in individual houses and in designated sectors. Workshops manufactured beads and ceramics, and artefacts of shell, stone, antler, bone, wood, metal and steatite. Polluting industries were located in the suburbs. One of the most impressive workshops, the bead-making factory at Chanhu-daro, included a furnace.

Harappan houses were built of baked and unfired mud bricks of uniform proportions (1:2:4) and standard sizes (70 x 140 x 280 mm). In Gujarat, stone was also used. Traces of plaster suggest colourfully painted walls. Baked bricks were used for wells, drains and bathroom floors. Wood was employed for doors and windows. Houses were built to a rectangular plan with rooms opening into a courtyard and stairs to upper chambers. The main entrance usually opened into a room or passage which functioned as an intermediate zone between the interior and outside. It afforded the occupants privacy while also acting as a barrier to rubbish blowing in from the street. The courtyard was the centre of the household where much of the day-to-day activity took place: preparing grain, fruit and vegetables for storage or immediate consumption; washing and drying clothes; spinning, weaving, sewing; cooking, eating, playing, sleeping. The roof was constructed of wooden beams covered by packed clay or matting and plaster, and the floor of beaten earth or bricks.

The bathroom was an important feature of the Harappan house. Its watertight floor was usually constructed of close-fitting baked bricks. A slight slope allowed water to flow into the city sewerage system. A large jar built into the floor and connected to the sewerage line served as a latrine.

At Kalibangan, Banawali and Lothal, some houses had a room with what appears to have been a domestic shrine, or a small kitchen with a fireplace for cooking food and heating water. Some contained clay-lined grain silos.

Cemeteries were located outside the walled settlement.

The Five Mega-Urban Sites (McIntosh 2008: 211–16; Jansen 1985, 1989, 1993)

Five major regional centres were located on what appears to be a grid with calculated distances separating them: Mohenjo-daro (250 ha, Sindh) on the Indus in the south; Harappa (150 ha, Punjab) on the Ravi in the north; Ganweriwala (80 ha, Cholistan) on the Ghaggar-Hakra; Rakhigarhi (+80 ha, Haryana) on the Chautang in the northeast; Dholavira (100 ha, Kutch/Gujarat) in the southwest. Rakhigarhi and Dholavira were situated towards the outer edges of the Indus region and with Ganweriwala in the centre formed a crescent on the western boundary of the Thar. Ganweriwala was 407 kms from Rakhigarhi, 558 kms from Dholavira, 280 kms from Harappa and 308 kms from Mohenjo-daro. Harappa was 570 kms distant from Mohenjo-daro and 350 kms from Rakhigarhi (Kenoyer n.d.b).

Mohenjo-daro, the largest city, was strategically located on the Indus in central Sindh to control communications along the north-south riverine highway from the Himalayas to the sea and the east-west route from the southern Baluchistan uplands to the Ghaggar-Hakra basin.

In relation to contemporary Harappan settlements, it was a place of gigantic dimensions populated by about 100,000 people. It had two major sections. The western citadel was constructed on an enormous platform of sand and silt measuring 200 by 400 metres within a six-metre-thick mud-brick retaining wall, seven metres high. Each of the citadel's structures had its own additional platform. The Great Bath, a large watertight basin with a capacity to store 160 cubic metres of water, set in the centre of a complex of rooms, may have been a religious structure of state-wide importance. Bathrooms and residential buildings were also built in the citadel.

To its east, the lower city contained two- and three-storey houses built on a grid pattern of north-south streets and east-west lanes. Mohenjo-daro's main street was ten metres wide.

House designs suggest a repetitive, modular pattern comprising individual elements such as specific rooms, staircases and courtyards. Almost every house had a bathing place connected to a drain or soak pit in the street. The city had around 700 wells, an excellent network of drains and a number of cesspits. Some structures were possibly temples and caravanserais. Industrial areas were concentrated in the suburbs. Workshops produced artefacts of every kind manufactured by the Indus people in a manner that hints at well-developed bureaucratic controls.

Due to the high water table, it has never been possible to excavate down to the earliest levels, estimated to be at least seven metres below the present surface. Most of its excavated architecture, therefore, belongs to the latter Mature Harappan.

Harappa is the only major city that enjoyed continuous development from the Kot Diji period into the Mature Harappan. Unlike many Early Harappan settlements, it was not rebuilt to a new plan during the Transition but grew organically. Located on the banks of the Ravi, it began c3700 BCE as a small agro-pastoral settlement with workshops for stone bead making and other crafts. Harappa's location enabled it to control the flow of raw materials from the Himalayas.

By 2600 BCE, it had expanded into an urban centre with two walled sectors, more than twenty-five ha in area with many flourishing industries. The citadel was sited on a high mound on the west. Harappa was heavily plundered for bricks in the nineteenth century, but what remains still tell a tale of massive and impressive brick buildings, public and private, that served various purposes. Within a perimeter wall, fourteen metres thick in places, were impressive buildings including a fifty-by-forty-metre granary and a number of working platforms for craft manufacture. During the Mature Harappan, the population grew to perhaps 60,000 and the city expanded beyond the walled mounds to occupy an area of around 150 ha on four major mounds, each walled and gated. They were settled at different times as the city expanded, and may have been controlled by different elite groups.

Harappa produced a range of artefacts in great quantity, some unique to the city. A network of trading routes brought a variety of raw materials, marine resources, timber, stone and metal from distant regions for processing into various utilitarian and prestige objects for local use, as well as for regional and extra-regional trade. Harappans traded with coastal regions 900 kms to the south, and with Afghanistan, Baluchistan and the Himalayas, some 300–1000 kms to the west and north.

Harappa's cemeteries reveal many local females were buried alongside males who were clearly not local. It suggests male immigration from different regions, mainly motivated by trade; the immigrants married local women and settled down in the city.

Harappa flourished until 1900 BCE. The excavated upper layers document the slow decay to the Late Harappan, with overcrowded housing spilling into streets and former open areas, pot-holed roads and the mixing of residential and industrial areas.

Located in the Ghaggar-Hakra valley, Ganweriwala was divided into two distinct parts, the citadel on a small mound on the west and the lower town to the east. The city is yet to be excavated. What is known comes only from surface materials from the Mature Harappan, like ceramics and clay toys and a tablet with a man seated in the yogi motif.

Rakhigarhi stands on an old bed of the Chautang (Drishadvati), a tributary of the Ghaggar-Hakra. Ongoing excavations have now extended its boundaries to nine mounds covering an area of about 350 ha. Rakhigarhi appears to have been first settled during the Early Harappan. It expanded greatly during the Mature Harappan with flourishing industries, walled residential areas and cardinally oriented streets. Located on a mound in the northwest was the walled citadel with a platform with fire altars, a well and pits containing cattle bones.

Dholavira, built on Khadir Island in the Rann of Kutch, was located on the tri-junction of water routes from Sindh, Rajasthan and Kutch at a time when sea levels were two to six metres higher than at present. It was ideally placed to control navigation between the south and the rest of the Harappan region. Constructed in stone, it was enclosed by successive massive walls eighteen metres wide and six metres high. The city was laid out in a geometric layout consisting of a number of rectangles, each divided into smaller rectangles or squares. At least sixteen massive water storage tanks were constructed along the inner faces of an outer wall that surrounded the whole city. They were filled with water diverted from two seasonal streams that flowed past the settlement. A complex system of catchment areas and drains also collected rainwater from the citadel and channelled it into stone chambers. Two other reservoirs were constructed adjacent to the citadel, one more than five metres deep.

The settlement appears to have been remodelled at the beginning of the Mature Harappan by clearing housing for the construction of a citadel surrounded by double ramparts of stone. Beyond this lay the walled middle town, a residential area with cardinally oriented streets and with jars and sumps instead of drains. Access to the citadel and middle town was through gateways approached by a flight of stone steps. Later, the city expanded to include the lower town, also enclosed by walls.

Signs, Seals and a Script (Parpola 1994, 2005)

The Transition from the Early to the Mature Harappan with the sudden and swift implementation of great technological innovations saw the parallel development of an as yet undeciphered script, an advanced and complex communication system that met the demands of administration and records, transportation, commerce and trade, and the recording and transfer of architectural and engineering elements.

The first published account of this long-lost script appeared as a result of Cunningham's exploration of Harappa in 1875. He included a description of a stamp seal with the image of a bull and strange characters. Today, more than 5,900 objects with specimens from this script have been recovered, 5,500 of them from Mohenjo-daro and Harappa alone. These include inscribed stamp seals, amulets, pottery, various types of tokens or tablets and other artefacts. The total number of signs is generally agreed to be around 400, though it could be as high as 676. Preserved texts are all short, averaging just five discrete symbols. The longest inscription consists of twenty-six characters.

More than 100 published attempts at deciphering the Indus script have been unsuccessful. The brevity of Indus texts, the almost complete lack of knowledge of the languages spoken by the Indus people and the absence of any bilingual document have foiled its decipherment. Not surprisingly, different conclusions have been arrived at. The Indus script has been described as a Hittite, Proto-Elamite or archaic Sumerian import and related to the Brahmi script which appeared about 1,500 years later! The most persistent is a Dravidian connection, a conclusion supported by two independent computer-assisted studies done in Russia and Finland. More recently, citing the large number of variations in symbols and the limited number and repetition of signs used, it has been proposed that the script was never intended to encode detailed messages.

Several key features, however, point to its use for a written language (Rao 2010; Yadav 2011). Indus signs form a standardised system, are written in regular lines and form regularly repeated sequences that follow certain rules. Symbols are modified by the addition of specific sets of marks over, around or inside a symbol. Particular signs or clusters of signs are used in particular positions within texts.

Three kinds of elements were used to compose Indus signs: basic signs, provisional basic signs and modifiers. Basic signs are relatively simple in their design, while composite signs are a combination of two or more elements. About 60% of the signs conform to either vertical or horizontal symmetry and some of them are inspired by familiar entities like fishes and jars.

The signs and sequences of the Indus texts are uniform throughout the Harappan region and also on the square Harappan seals found in Mesopotamia. This demonstrates their versatility. Round Gulf and Elamite seals and cylindrical Mesopotamian seals used by Harappan merchants use common Indus signs but in different sequences which suggests it was used for local languages, Sumerian, Akkadian and Elamite. An Akkadian cylinder seal belonging to Su-i-li-su, an interpreter of Meluhhan, reveals that the language of southern Sindh was different.

The earliest samples of the script come from Early Harappan sites as simple pottery markings during the Ravi (3900–2800 BCE) and Kot Diji (3900–2600 BCE) phases (Kenoyer n.d.a; Sparavigna n.d.). Etched onto jars before firing, perhaps to indicate the contents or ownership of the jar or an association with a deity, these signs evolved into a standardised and uniform script during the Mature Harappan.

Harappan writing has survived as graffiti on pottery and on small stone seals. Being fragile, there are few complete pottery inscriptions. The inscriptions on seals, while complete, are short and accompanied by various iconographic motifs. Their general function would have been to identify the ownership of goods, commercial transactions or record socio-political or ritual events. Writing is also found on ornaments and artefacts, bronze tools and storage containers. Possibly, detailed messages were recorded on perishable media like palm leaves or cotton cloth.

While it appears that a common script was used, it is almost certain that more than one language was spoken (Witzel 2000; Parpola 2005; Southworth 2005: 65). These can only be inferred from the traces they have left behind in existing languages. Broadly, they can be considered as 'Indus' languages in the north, and Meluhhan in southern Sindh and the hilly areas of Baluchistan bordering the Indus Valley where an ancestor of Brahui, a Dravidian language, may also have been spoken.

The Indus script appears to have been used primarily by elites. The most numerous samples appear on inscribed seals and tablets. Seals, used to establish ownership and content of goods, may contain the names of owners, place of origin/destination, and god(s), but no verbs or adjectives. Apart from the text, most seals depict a single animal or mythical composite figure facing either right or left, and an object that has variously been described as an offering stand or a brazier placed in front of the animal. Other seals have complex iconographic scenes depicting mythological or socio-ritual events. Seals were hung from a pierced boss on the back of the seal, and probably worn around the neck or at the waist. Seal impressions have been found on pottery and lumps of clay used for sealing containers or rope-tied bales. It means that traders were familiar with the script.

Deciphering a script requires knowledge of the script type and the underlying language(s). Unfortunately, the Indus script has no clear connection to any other known writing system which could help define the phonetic values of Indus signs. All surviving texts are very short; they may contain only nouns and phrases, no complete sentences.

However, an alternate approach may offer some hope. It uses the principle that each writing system represents its own unique approach to meet the needs of its own cultural and economic situation (Kenoyer 2008). This is best illustrated at the city of Harappa which has been continuously occupied from the Early Harappan. Over 680 inscribed objects such as seals, tablets, and over 1,200 pottery sherds have been recovered here. The sherds contain both pre-firing potter's marks and post-firing graffiti and date to 3300–2600 BCE. Some of these signs are found in the later Indus script which means the script evolved over time. Categorisation of sherds into sub-groups based on chronological and typological features reveals animal (elephant and bull) motifs dating to c2600–2450 BCE that appeared on the earliest seals with writing.

While pre-firing potter's marks are simple and probably identified the customer, post-firing graffiti includes many single and some multiple signs that could represent early forms of the Indus script. They would have been made by the user of the pot with the signs indentifying the owner, vessel contents or something else. Most of these signs became part of the Indus script during the Mature Harappan when the city expanded and was integrated into the larger economic and political sphere of the greater Indus Valley. There is no evidence for the use of inscribed seals or tablets in the Late Harappan which may indicate a breakdown in long-distance trade. Changes in ceramic styles, painted motifs and burial traditions suggest a gradual change in ideology and major social and political restructuring (Parpola 2010).

14

The Mechanisms of Control

The remarkable feature of the Mature Harappan is the overall acceptance for 700 years, despite regional differences, of a unifying culture by over a million people inhabiting a diverse geographical environment spread over a million sq. kms. There are no recorded texts to tell us how this was done. So it is to other sources that we must turn to understand how it was all held together.

Throughout history, four sources of power – economic, military, political, ideological – have been used in various combinations to enforce authority and retain control by elite groups (Butters 1996). An elite group can be considered as a minority that possesses a disproportionate share of resources or power within a group or society. Power, in this context, means might together with the exercise of sovereign authority. In Harappa, economic and ideological factors seem to have been the primary means of elite dominance.

The control of surplus agricultural wealth and its distribution for services from labourers and artisans formed a supporting pillar of this power structure. It helped to build the cities with their public infrastructure and monumental brick platforms and architecture, and finance their maintenance. Sited on mounds, their awe-inspiring visibility would have impressed and intimidated onlookers with the power and capability of their builders and keepers. Trade became a primary source of wealth creation. Silver may have been imported from Mesopotamia to pay for raw materials. Not used before the Early Harappan, it ceased to be used after the Mature Harappan.

Harappa provides little evidence for the exercise of military power (Thompson 2005: 365–84). No memorials to military campaigns have been found nor battle damage reflected in physical structures. Although Harappans possessed sophisticated metalworking techniques, they made extraordinarily few kinds of specialised fighting weapons and no defensive armour. The monumental walls encircling Harappan cities have been explained as protection against flooding or control of industry and trade. Only at Dholavira was a system of concentric walls built as a defence probably from raiding sea pirates. Otherwise, evidence seems to suggest that armed force was not used to manage Harappan cities during the Mature Harappan.

Despite this, the Transition occurred with the burning, rebuilding, and relocation of Early Harappan settlements. It is difficult to conceive that this took place without some degree of resistance. Some degree of force must have been used to suppress it. There is some evidence for expertise in warfare, albeit in Akkadian texts, scarce though it may be. One such text glorifies Rimush's victory over an anti-Akkadian coalition which included troops from Meluhha: 'Rimush, king of the entire world, was victorious in battle over Abalgamash, king of Parahshum. Zahara, Elam, Gupin, and Meluhha had assembled in Parahshum for battle...' (Hamblin 2006: 80). Another text describes Naram-Sin's victory over Meluhha: 'Dilmun, Makkan, Meluhha, in the midst of the sea, as many as they were, they killed' (Studevent-Hickman n.d.: 37). These Meluhhans may have been Gulf residents conscripted by rival kings or mercenaries from Harappa. The point here is that Meluhhans involved themselves in warfare when it mattered, and this expertise could have been used in Harappa as well.

Harappan city planning does suggest some attention to defensive fortifications. The elite sections were always built on mounds enclosed by massive walls. As these elevated locations would have been relatively safe from flooding, the walls most likely served some other purpose. Banawali, Harappa, Kalibangan, Mohenjo-daro, Dholavira, Kuntasi, Lothal and Surkotada reveal many features which can be considered primarily as defensive military fortifications (Petersen 2012). They include bastions from which defenders could fire on attacking enemies, massive defendable gates, V-sectioned ditches alongside the wall, ramparts, embankments, salients, towers, parapets and posterns. All show a regular layout in which the 'citadel' was located, on an elevated mound separate from the lower town. The citadel's 'fortifications' were mostly built during the Transition and Mature phases, often by razing older buildings and replacing them with newer ones. It suggests a purpose.

Banawali, located on the north bank of the Hakra-Ban river, was divided into the citadel and the lower town. The citadel was located on higher ground and surrounded by walls which were doubled in width and bastions incorporated. During the Transition and again during the Mature Harappan, houses throughout the settlement were demolished and replaced by new ones. A moat was dug around the settlement and the citadel became the centre around which a new system of streets was developed. A gateway in the eastern wall provided access to it.

At least four of the mounds in the city of Harappa were fortified during the Mature Harappan, while Kalibangan added bastions and salients to its citadel walls. These structures, while not perhaps reflecting a state at perpetual warfare, do suggest an intention to deter potential rivals and awe them with the imposing and impregnable status of ruling elite groups each occupying a different mound.

It seems unlikely there was any tightly knit political unity. Instead, the mega cities may have been five regional power centres strategically located to exploit and control a fertile and extensive agricultural hinterland. Mohenjo-daro controlled the flow of goods to and from upstream Indus (Rakhigarhi, Harappa, Ganweriwala) as well as from the Kachi plain, making it rich and perhaps the religious, ideological, ceremonial, cultural and economic centre (Maisels 2001: 217). Rakhigarhi controlled and processed the flow of raw materials and labour, and perhaps finished goods, from the Ganges basin to its east. Harappa played a similar role with the territory to the northwest, Afghanistan and Central Asia. Ganweriwala and

Kalibangan had access to the considerable agricultural output of the Ghaggar-Hakra valley and the raw material resources of the Aravallis. Dholavira at the southwest controlled the sea routes to the Gulf from pirates. All these cities gained prominence during the Transition.

These monumental cities were the largest and most well planned of those times, and their construction and maintenance reveal the presence of powerful regional authorities working in a loose alliance possibly with Mohenjo-daro acting as some sort of inspirational centre for a shared ideology that bound the region together. Elite groups most probably included wealthy merchants, powerful landlords and spiritual leaders who built and maintained city infrastructure, enforced their status through control of trade, ritual and religion and ruled by consensus, resorting to economic and ideological means to retain authority (Petersen 2012; Kenoyer 1998: 17, 81).

Ideology

Ideology is central to a culture. When given a material form, it becomes an important source of social power to a controlling dominant group, enabling it to govern and manage populations.

Multiple ideas and beliefs exist in every society. In order to legitimise its position and authority, the ruling elite must promote or create a unique ideology – shared ideas, beliefs and their representations – and control it. Ideology has both a material and a symbolic component. Symbols, icons, rituals, monuments and written texts convey and transmit information and meaning to their viewers (Butters 1996).

The process of giving an ideology a concrete and physical form has been termed 'the materialisation of ideology'. Materialisation is the transformation of ideas, values, stories, myths and the like into physical reality – a ceremonial event, a symbolic object or icon, a monument or a writing system. Materialisation makes it possible to extend an ideology beyond the local group and to communicate the power of a central authority to a broader population. All this comes at a considerable cost and is therefore available only to wealthy elite segments. The Mature Harappan demonstrates the presence of all these material features. It indicates that ideology and control of the economy were central to the mechanisms of dominance.

Seals were probably used to identify elite Harappan groups (Thompson 2005). Most likely, they belonged to the commercial elite who controlled access to and supply of a range of raw material and agricultural resources, manipulating their processing and distribution to their advantage. The animals, real and imagined, depicted on administrative and trade seals may have been the identifying emblems of individuals or clans belonging to this elite. If so, there were at least ten major trading groups operating throughout the Harappan region. They may have belonged to clans or cohesive groups based on real or imagined blood relationships secured through marriage. Family ties and bonds would have been crucial in securing the loyalty of members involved in trading across such distant places with permanent or seasonal settlements. Such risky but profitable enterprises required wealth, holding power, diplomacy, language and negotiating skills which only experienced, large, professional trading clans could muster.

Harappan investment in large seagoing vessels and trading colonies in Mesopotamia and Shortugai in Afghanistan shows this trade was very substantial. It required a competent sourcing and conversion industry with a loyal labour force possessing wide-ranging skills. It also required the construction of factories, warehouses and trading hubs that could be used to enforce some degree of monopoly.

Dholavira shows signs of being one such hub with access to the sea. Built on a scale that could only be handled by a powerful group with access to huge funds and labour, it would have required considerable costs to maintain, defend and sustain. The coast has been known as a haven for sea pirates; Dholavira's imposing walls are testimony to it. The region is dry requiring much effort to store food and water; Dholavira's sixteen massive water tanks attest to that. Its location, providing access to Gujarat's hinterland, though, made the investment worthwhile; Dholavira's continuing trade with west Asia long after the centre had collapsed by 1900 BCE is evidence that Dholavira was a worthwhile investment for Harappa's commercial elite. It was worth razing Early Harappan settlements like Amri and Kot Diji and shifting or rebuilding them to accommodate the needs of a new economy which depended on the exploitation of the Indus for fast transportation of bulk goods. Apart from meeting infrastructural needs for handling bulk trade, the razing and rebuilding of these settlements also served a symbolic purpose, that of stamping the authority of a new order.

Lothal, at the southeastern limits of Harappan territory, was not only a trading hub between Harappan and local populations but also with overseas regions, particularly the Gulf. It provides no evidence of Early Harappan occupation but all the architectural features of the Mature Harappan, and appears to have been built from scratch specifically as a port city. It had a large brick-lined reservoir believed to be a dockyard. The large number of seal impressions found here reveal the intensity and extent of Lothal's trading activity. They indicate the presence of representatives of merchant groups from other cities supervising the shipment of their goods. Many seal impressions at Harappa and Mohenjo-daro display the elephant motif. They are absent in the seals excavated at Lothal in which the unicorn motif appears in the largest number (Ameri 2013).

The greatest number of seals comes from Mohenjo-daro (77%) and Harappa (9%). The unicorn is the subject of about 80% of them, with bovids (bison, zebu, buffalo) constituting the next highest, and rhino, elephant, tiger and other smaller creatures the rest.

These motifs were probably the unique identifying symbols of different merchant groups whose names were given by the inscription running across the top of the seal. If so, the unicorn icon would have belonged to the group with the largest commitment in overseas trade (Thompson 2005). It appears to have had its headquarters in Mohenjo-daro, a major ritual centre, indicating it had strong links to religious authority. This was a common practice in Mesopotamia as well, where pledges made with gods as witnesses carried much weight and reduced the chances of defaulting. Apart from commencing a new enterprise with the blessings of the gods, it also lowered transaction costs. If temple priests were part of the unicorn group, they benefitted greatly from its commercial activities and the promotion of ideology would have got a tremendous boost.

Not all seals were connected directly with commerce. Many had ritual and symbolic significance. Some of their iconography is similar with that of contemporary Sumer and Elam, which suggests a common and widespread shared heritage. A common Mesopotamian-Elamite-Harappan motif is that of a human holding an animal or reptile by its throat in each outstretched hand. In Mesopotamian iconography it is the lion or bull, in Elamite the snake and in Harappan the tiger. A cylinder seal from Kalibangan depicts a goddess standing between two warriors spearing each other. The same deity appears next to this scene with a horned crown merged to the rear of a tiger's body. The hairstyle of the warriors is characteristic of warring Mesopotamian kings. Other seals show sacrificed water buffaloes being offered to a tiger-riding goddess. Some seals depict a man placing one foot on a water buffalo that he has speared, a pose signifying victory in Mesopotamian art. A popular deity appearing in a horned headdress sits in a yogic position, sometimes with a number of animals around him. A seal from Chanhu-daro depicts a bull with an erect penis in the act of penetrating a supine female, a scene that may represent the heavenly father fertilising mother earth. In another seal, reminiscent of the popular *jallikatu* sport held annually in Tamil Nadu today, as also in distant Spain, a wild buffalo is shown attacking and scattering a number of humans in all directions. These highly suggestive depictions of power and fertility emphasise the authority of the possessors and users of the seals.

The Role of Writing, Sealing and Standardised Weights in Exercising Social Control (Rahmstorf 2012)

Harappan elite groups used administrative means – writing, seals, standardised weights – to regulate and control the exploitation of resources and thereby exercise power at many different levels.

Writing was a most efficient control mechanism in early literate societies when used for administrative purposes. By recording information about resources, manpower, rations and commercial activities it became a direct medium of control and verification. Its use involved considerable expenditure as groups of salaried scribes were required to record and maintain details.

In Mesopotamia, writing evolved from this need to record everyday commercial transactions to recording royal deeds and creating a body of literature for controlling cultural memory. Writing extended the boundaries of human memory to texts and public inscriptions and was used to invent the past by creating 'cultural texts'.

The Harappan script, being still undeciphered and with known texts being limited to very short inscriptions averaging only four to five signs, does not tell much on whether it was so used in exercising social power. It is possible larger texts were written on perishable material like palm leaves or wood and therefore did not survive. However, with 80% of surviving texts being used in seals or seal impressions/sealings, it is clear that the Indus script had a predominant role in economic and administrative activity.

Apart from identifying ownership of goods, sealing was used for goods containers and storeroom doors. It stood for the integrity of the package and reduced the risks involved in exchanges between unfamiliar partners. This integrity was emphasised by the image carved on the seal's surface, often bearing religious or supernatural motifs. It created a little field of symbolic protective power around the sealed object that reflected on the authority of its owner. In Lothal, impressions of different seals are found on a single sealing which suggests the involvement of more than one official during the sealing.

Weighing was another effective control mechanism. It most likely appeared with the intensive use of precious metals and jewellery. Being of amorphous shapes, these could only be accurately valued by weighing. Standard weights or units have to be accepted by traders over a large area and verified by an authority. Their manufacture, authentication and distribution must be controlled and knowledge of their use widely accepted. That this was achieved over such a vast and diversified area means the involvement of local independent traders with possibly a limited range of social power and their interaction with others in overlapping territories. This suggests a decentralised political landscape where the major towns/cities pursued their own affairs but cooperated in countering external threats.

Harappan society shows more signs of a heterarchical organisation with distributed authority rather than one with a hierarchical structure It appears to to have been governed collectively by councils and assemblies representative of the broader community who lived in close proximity to each other. Such indications come from evidence of great differences in wealth and status within an overall egalitarian social organisation. While cemeteries do not contain outstanding elaborate graves with rich furnishings and ostentatious displays of power and status, more than two dozen hoards containing objects of gold, silver, copper/bronze, semi-precious stones (lapis lazuli, cornelian, turquoise, jade, onyx, etc.) and chert weights excavated in private houses reveal the presence of wealthy sections of society with controlling powers. These social classes emerged over time on the basis of occupational specialisation, kin relations, religion and ideology which may have developed into the rigidly stratified caste system of later Indian society.

The Iconography of Power – Animals

The 'master of animals' is a recurring theme in Mesopotamian-Elamite-Harappan iconography. At a time when large and powerful wild animals, dangerous to humans, dominated the environment, iconography depicting human dominance over them became a cogent theme in demonstrating the power of an individual or elite group.

Among the most well-known Harappan seals is the so-called *pashupati* seal.[1] In it, the 'master of animals' is surrounded by the four most powerful animals of the Indus plains, an elephant, a tiger, a rhinoceros and a wild buffalo, and by two large-horned caprids beneath his seat. He dominates the seal, seated calmly in the centre in a yogic pose wearing a large horned headdress with a fan-shaped adornment worn by Zhob (Baluchistan) female figurines. His aged, striated face shows total unconcern at being surrounded by the fierce animals, even the tiger springing towards him with open jaws. He is truly the master. His meditative yogic pose may also suggest the secret of his power: religious authority.

Another scene presents a female with flowing hair neatly combed, wearing bangles from wrist to armpit on each hand, seated in the yogic pose and wearing an outsized horned headdress like the 'master of animals'. She, however, is not surrounded by wild animals, but by a number of characters of the Harappan script. Evidently, they conveyed a message we will not know until the script is deciphered.

In the composite animal seal, a human, a tiger, an elephant and a water buffalo merge into one creature. The hindquarters belong to the tiger, the front to the buffalo whose large horns project above the head with a human face; an elephant's trunk drops from the face like a long beard. The seal appears to project the human as having appropriated all the powers and attributes of these powerful animals.

The tiger motif reinforces this dominance and appropriation of the physical power of wild beasts. It recurs in at least eighteen seals and tablets in which a human kneels on the limb of a tree with left hand extended (Possehl 2008). Beneath the tree, a prowling tiger stops to look back at the human gesturing from the safety of his perch. A seal from Chanhu-daro shows a tiger licking the face of a human poised on one knee before it. The tiger with a tumescent penis dominates the seal. The human's left hand is extended in a gesture of appeasement towards the conciliatory feline. Mesopotamian iconography contains a similar motif, that of a chained lion looking back at its captor who is carrying its cub. The scene is replete with the exercise of raw physical force to subdue and dominate. The Harappan seal, in contrast, appears to rely on spiritual power, a potent and pervasive resource if society is convinced of and accepts its related ideology. It avoids the expense of maintaining a strong army.

The Iconography of Power – Divinity

The horn motif is a persistent symbol in the iconography of gods and goddesses in many ancient cultures. Horns are powerful tools used by wild animals in offensive and defensive capacities. Horns became important motifs in the symbolisms of power, being mounted on Elamite temples as signs of strength and authority. Naram-Sin wears a horned crown as a symbol of divinity in a famous stele that depicts the king as a super-human.

Horned headdresses are worn by a number of human figures in Harappan iconography. One appears on the head of a goddess in the 'divinity seal'. She stands among the branches of a pipal tree in the shape of a large U-shaped vessel wearing bangles and sporting a flowing hairdo. Kneeling before her is a horned worshipper and behind, a bovid with a ruffed neck and human face, with huge curly horns stretching horizontally outward from either side of its head. At the bottom of the seal, seven female figures, all bangled and with a flowing hairdo, appear to be queuing to perform the same ritual.

A Final Word

Harappa was held together by economic bonds that tied resources to centres of craft specialisation strategically sited to effect smooth and efficient transactions. Ideology had a central place in the functioning of Harappan society with 'diffuse, diverse and often domestic ritual practices, (being) unified by a set of shared themes ('cardinal tenets') and beliefs' (Maisels 2001: 222). Spread throughout the region by the process termed 'materialisation of ideology', they served as powerful integrative forces that bound regional centres together under a common culture and commercial practices. Elite Harappans exploited agricultural resources and augmented their economic and political power through craft manufacture and trade. As Harappa's widespread iconography of power inscribed and painted on pottery, seals and tablets show, legitimation of their status was achieved through ritualistic practices rather than warfare (Petersen 2012). Monumental Harappan public architecture reaffirmed the connection of an elite group to its territory. Such architecture consumed huge amounts of human energy, mostly of low status individuals, and its very visible and imposing dominance of the landscape enhanced elite status by projecting their authority over those individuals and by instilling a sense of inferiority in them. It intimidated and deterred opposition and reinforced the dominance of one group over another. Defensive fortifications accentuated this. The services rendered in maintaining urban infrastructure and the control of food distribution in urban centres reinforced elite status, as did the wearing of beads and shell jewellery, bangles, fine clothes, use of fine pottery and sponsoring the public practice of rituals. A script used by a few literate groups preserved privileged information that could be used in enforcing their interests.

15

The Decline and Dispersal

The year 1900 BCE is generally recognised as marking the end of the Mature Harappan. The cultural, administrative and economic unity of the Indus region broke down due to a complex combination of inter-linked developments that included environmental change, river relocations, disruption of the subsistence base, social causes and a breakdown in the important integrative factors of trade and a shared ideology (Kenoyer n.d.a). Climatic and environmental factors were among the most crucial with the 4.2 ka event being the most decisive cause. This 300-year-long mega drought (2200–1900 BCE) afflicted an extensive territory and is cited as the prime cause for the collapse of many civilisations, including Mesopotamia.

By 1900 BCE, summer monsoon precipitation in the Harappan region had reached its lowest levels. Most rivers had shrunk, others had dried. Together with lengthening sand dunes, their tortuously winding channels wrinkled the landscape. Cholistan and Sindh were largely abandoned, their crumbling cities, towns and villages eroded by wind-borne sand. Year after year it settled over the empty streets and houses, layer upon layer. No one remained to clear it. The mounds of the dead and abandoned grew and what lay concealed within forgotten.

As people migrated from the stricken centre, some upstream towards the upper Ganges basin and others downstream to Gujarat and the Deccan beyond, the bonds that united diverse Harappan territories fell apart. Mohenjo-daro and Ganweriwala once connected Rakhigarhi and Dholavira. Now there was only desert in between. Harappa's cities suffocated and died; Harappans lived on, carrying their gene pool, their culture and beliefs and their artisan and commercial skills to other parts of India.

The decline was slow and painful.

The Fall of Harappa's Elite

It has been proposed that the accumulation, storage and control of grain surpluses by elite groups enhanced their power and led to the Transition to the Mature Harappan (Menzel 2014; Madella 2006; Sarkar 2016). This source disappeared as aridity increased with continually declining monsoons. Harappans shifted their cropping pattern from large-grained cereals (wheat, barley) to drought-tolerant African species (small millets) and rice. As these crops generally have a lower yield, the organised large storage system of the Mature Harappan was abandoned and replaced by smaller individual household-based crop processing and storage systems. Large agricultural surpluses disappeared. It contributed to the decline of the Harappan economy and the economic power and authority of the elite and led to de-urbanisation and a decentralised society.

The 4.2 ka mega drought devastated Mesopotamia's economy. Its Harappan trade collapsed. Mesopotamian records continue to refer to trade with Meluhha until at least 2028 BCE, but this name now refers exclusively to Gujarat. Dholavira's explosive growth between 2200–2000 BCE suggests this. Trade between the two regions continued through intermediary merchants in Dilmun. Harappa's trade-related towns were gradually abandoned (Weiss 2017). By 1900 BCE, Harappan seals and weights and its script were no more used; there was no more need for them.

This disappearance of the Harappan elite is reflected in the general breakdown of civic standards in the form of poor-quality housing, kilns and industrial waste in former public and residential buildings and corpses abandoned in disused buildings and streets. Buildings encroached onto streets and the spacious courtyards of houses were partitioned to accommodate more people. Residential areas began to be used for industrial activity. Many features that defined the Harappan tradition – writing, shell ornaments, weights and seals, strong social and political organisation, refined craftsmanship, comfortable life styles – disappeared. Ceramic vessel shapes and designs and copper tools and weapons changed.

At Mohenjo-daro, a few stone sculptures may hint at the fate of Harappa's elite. They are of seated men, all decapitated. McIntosh speculates: 'It is tempting to see them as the smashed portraits of a line of hated rulers' (McIntosh 2008: 395).

Population Shift

As the climate continued to become drier, the population shift to Gujarat and the upper Ganges basin intensified. The number of sites increased in the upper Punjab and Haryana where monsoon rains were more consistent. The settlements were of smaller village-type sizes. This decentralisation enabled people to live off their immediate environment without exhausting it. In contrast, in lower Punjab and Sindh, regions with a similarly intense history of human activity, the number of sites decreased over the same interval. Kutch, a coastal region that was never dependent on flood agriculture but instead relied on trade, remained active into the Late Harappan.

Harappa and Mohenjo-daro which had grown to 150 ha and 200 ha by 1900 BCE downsized to 8 ha (1500 BCE) and 20 ha (1300 BCE) respectively. About the same time Rakhigarhi and Ganweriwala (between Mohenjo-daro and Rakhigarhi) had grown to 80 ha. Rakhigarhi on the gateway to the Gangetic basin maintained that size for another 500 years. Gujarat saw a substantial increase in population. Dholavira tripled in size between 2200–1900 BCE. From Gujarat, the road opened out to south India where wheat and barley, ragi and bajra, sheep and goats appeared by 1800 BCE (McIntosh 2008: 193).

Table 15.1: Harappan site counts

		number	size ha
Mature Harappan (2500–2000 BCE)	Punjab, Haryana, North Rajasthan, West UP	217	10.9
Post-urban times (2000–1500 BCE)		854	3.6
Mature Harappan (2500–2000 BCE)	Sindh, Kutch	140	8.7
Post-urban times (2000–1500 BCE)		18	6.6

Source: Possehl (1997b).

Table 15.2: Site counts in Cholistan

	number	size ha
Hakra Ware 3800–3200 BCE	99	643
Early Harappan (Kot Dijian) 3200–2600 BCE	40	256
Mature Harappan 2500–1900 BCE	174	974
Post-urban Harappan 1900–1700 BCE	50	255
Early Iron Age (Painted Gray Ware) 1000–500 BCE	14	36

Source: Possehl (1997a).

What Harappan Bricks Reveal (Khan 2013)

Bricks constitute the largest number of Harappan artefacts and they tell a story. They first drew archaeological attention in the 1850s when they began to appear as construction material at

Table 15.3: Growth and decline of Harappan settlement sizes

Mehrgarh	BCE	7000–5000	5500–4800	4800–3500		3500–3250	3250–3000								
	ha	30	16	9		9	18								
Amri	BCE				4300–3800	3800–3300	3300–3200								
	Ha				10	30	20								
Harappa	BCE					3800–3200		3200–2800	2800–2600	2600–2200	2200 1900			1900–1800	1800–1500
	Ha					1		1.5	32	100	150			100	8
Rakhigarhi	BCE							3200–2600		2600–1800					1800–1300
	ha							2		0					80
Mohenjo-daro	BCE								2900–2600	2600–2250	2250–1900			1900–1700	1700–1300
	ha								5	75	200			100	20
Ganweriwala	BCE									2600–2250	2250–1900			1900–1800	
	ha									79	81.5			80	
Kalibangan	BCE									2600–2250	2250–1900			1900–1300	
	Ha									10	12			5	
Lothal	BCE									2600–2250	2250–1900			1900–1700	1700–1300
	Ha									4.2	25			25	10
Dholavira	BCE									2600–2250	2550–2200	2200–2000	2000–1900	1900–1800	1659–1450
	ha									2	30	80	100	70	15

Source: Compiled by author; various sources.

building sites. Of remarkably consistent dimensions, they were predominantly sun-dried. Early Harappan cities like Mehrgarh, Amri and Kot Diji were built from sun-dried bricks. Baked bricks came to be used in quantity, especially for walls and floors exposed to water, during the Mature Harappan but only until 1900 BCE, a distinct 1,500-year period within the almost 6,000 years of the Harappan Tradition.

Baked brickwork is one of the signature marks of Harappan technologies. A superior technology, it was extensively used where improved strength was important. Baked bricks have greater resistance to long-term water exposure. This became a key factor in the Harappan expansion into the Punjab and Sindh flood plains, as the massive flood protection structures built around Mohenjo-daro, Harappa and the flood-prone city of Chanhu-daro demonstrate. Baked bricks were used for house foundations, encasing sewerage lines, city walls and citadels.

The manufacture of baked bricks required skilled labour, standards and natural resources, all available during the Mature phase. Fine silt, water and firewood were plentiful. Bricks were made to a standardised ratio of 4:2:1 (length: width: height) using moulds. This changed in the Late phase, an indication of changed social norms or lack of skilled craftsmen. Apart from choosing the correct clay and mixing it with the right proportion of water, bricks have to be fired at the right temperature for the optimum time to achieve maximum strength. The stoppage in manufacture could therefore mean that, apart from the absence of demand in the Punjab and Sindh, skilled craftsmen had migrated. The late appearance of bricks in Gujarat sites, predominantly Lothal, after 2200 BCE suggests this may have been so.

Harappa's Cemeteries (Schug 2012, 2013, 2016)

Skeletons from Harappa's cemeteries confirm a serious decline in civic standards and control. They show signs of infection from virulent water-borne diseases, malaria and cholera, a result of the breakdown in water and waste management. Sewage from ill-maintained brick-lined drain-pipes and soak pits seeped into the ground and contaminated well water (McIntosh 2008: 396; Maisels 2001: 233, 238).

Burials also reveal that personal violence increased in the post-urban period with the socially and economically marginalised communities being most vulnerable. Considering Harappa's massive population (30,000–40,000), the small number of burials suggests it was reserved for the elite. To date, remains of only 600 skeletons have been recovered. This mortuary data supports the likelihood of Harappa being governed by elite groups.

The earliest cemetery R-37 (2550–2030 BCE), covering an area of about 50 m x 50 m, was located just beyond the wall surrounding the citadel. The dead were both local and non-local, probably traders, merchants and craftsmen. Some of the males appear to be immigrants, possibly from Mesopotamian cities (Kenoyer 2013). These individuals led relatively healthy lives with relatively low risk of personal violence and had greater access to medical care. Some burials were elaborate and rich. Bodies were usually interred in a supine, extended posture, with the head facing north. They were buried along with steatite bead necklaces, anklets of paste beads, copper earrings, shell bangles, copper rings, mother-of-pearl shells, antimony, shell spoons, amulets of semi-precious stone, gold, copper mirrors and small containers. A number of decorated pots containing water and food were placed near the head. The figure of a bird (peacock?) was the dominant motif; trees (pipal?), leaves, geometric and floral designs were also used.

Between 2200–1900 BCE, Harappa experienced massive population growth possibly due to migration from rural areas reeling under aridity. It led to increasing stress on the city's infrastructure and the beginnings of a breakdown in civic administration. Post-1900 BCE, there was a dramatic drop in population growth and a process of decentralisation began. Mound centres continued to be occupied but peripheral areas were abandoned. Those who remained suffered from increasing rates of inter-personal violence and infection, particularly in marginalised communities who received little protection from a weak, decentralised authority.

It was during these two phases that Cemetery H was utilised, and an ossuary was dug (Area G) outside the city walls just beyond a sewage drain under the southeastern gateway. Both these burial sites indicate post-urban populations were subjected to increasing levels of violence in the stressful time of disintegrating social structure. Those affected were already vulnerable due to their sex, age and social status.

In Cemetery H's older graves, the dead were buried with ceramics but with no other associated grave goods. Funerary jars were used for later interments. The ossuary (18 m x 18 m x 18 m) was located in a low-lying field. Human remains show skeletal injuries received from inter-personal violence with women and children being at greatest risk. The communal nature of this burial of human and animal body parts, with no special distinction for children, suggests the dead may have been victims of an epidemic or a massacre.

The evidence from Cemetery H and especially Area G strongly indicates there were clear differences among groups in access to resources, risk of violence and infection. Traumatic injuries, infection and disease which were present at a low frequency in the urban-period Cemetery R-37, increased dramatically in the post-urban Cemetery H and Area G.

A lead and strontium isotopic analysis of human tooth enamel from Cemetery R and Farmana (Haryana) reveals they came from first-generation immigrants who had arrived at a young age from resource regions to the northwest. This leads to the hypothesis that they were relatives of raw material suppliers who were fostered by elite Harappans to cement economic relationships. This relationship need not have been one of equality, but one that existed without marriage.

Human tooth enamel from individuals buried at Harappa and at the Royal Cemetery of Ur has been analysed for strontium, oxygen, and carbon isotopes.[1] Teeth from animals, such as pig and sheep from both regions dating to the same general time period, were also sampled in order to obtain a local strontium isotope signature for comparison. The isotope ratios between the two regions show significant variation that can be used to identify locals and non-locals. While this process is still ongoing, the study shows substantial variation among Harappans themselves, suggesting significant immigration to the site (Kenoyer 2013).

Continuity (Abro 2016)

The decline and abandonment of Harappan cities did not mark the end of the Harappan cultural tradition but only that of its urban phase. One part of its material culture which shows continuity is pottery. Although there was deterioration in the quality and finish of the end product, there was continuity in methods of manufacture, styles and designs. Late Harappan pottery from Jukhar near Mohenjo-daro continued to use motifs from the Mature Harappan: chequered, ladder and perforated designs, intersecting circles, the pipal leaf and the fish scale. Shapes and colours remained the same, as did firing processes.

Like Harappan pottery, many aspects of the Harappan Tradition passed on into South Asia's later traditions. While its elite, institutions and supporting infrastructure disappeared, other traits that defined the Harappan Tradition – genetic material, artisan skills, agro-pastoral practices, domesticated crops and animals, traditions, beliefs and other cultural aspects – survive to this day.

16

Bronze Age Eurasia

During the centuries when the Harappan region underwent the transformation from the Early Harappan through the Mature Harappan and its decline, there was a churning of new developments in the Eurasian steppes that would eventually reach northwest South Asia and have a profound effect on its linguistic, cultural, religious and genetic history.

The Eurasian steppes comprise a belt of grassland stretching 9,000 kms from the Middle Danube plains in east Europe to northeast Asia (Bokovenko 2005). To its north lies the taiga, deciduous forests adapted to extreme cold winters and the frozen Siberian tundra. There are mountains to its south and deserts. Before the Bronze Age, these treeless grasslands offered a formidable barrier to economic development. It was only with the domestication of the horse and the invention of wagon transport that a complex form of pastoralism evolved and made the steppes productive. This process involved the development of trading networks connecting copper and tin mining areas to processing centres and markets. It converted grasslands from Ukraine through Kazakhstan to Mongolia into crossroads for human population movements, and gave rise to different Eurasian steppe nomadic cultures centred on domesticated horses and cattle. The Early Bronze Age (EBA) saw the emergence of the Yamnaya (Pit Grave) culture in the Pontic-Caspian steppe between 3000–2700 BCE. It gradually spread from the Southern Urals to the BMAC, the Tobol River and the Altai Mountains. The Middle Bronze Age (MBA) saw its progressive transformation to the Poltavka (Catacomb Grave) (2700–2100 BCE), Sintashta (Timber Grave) (2050–

1750 BCE) and Petrovka (1950–1700 BCE) cultures. Between 1900–1200 BCE, the Andronovo culture appeared over a wide area with many regional traits, the prominent ones being Federovo (1800–1200 BCE) and Alakul (1900–1200 BCE). These cultures were formed by a complex interaction between many different ethnic groups (Anthony 2016).

The Yamnaya (Kristiansen 2017; Kuznetsov 2005)

The first inhabitants of the Pontic-Caspian steppes were foragers who lived almost entirely in river valleys. Forests provided shelter, firewood, building materials and wild animals and fish for food. The steppes were dominated by wild horses which became targets for foraging hunters as an attractive source of meat. Beyond the river valleys where the climate ranged from summer temperatures above 40°C to winter temperatures below (-)37°C, there was little else to forage or hunt. It was an inhospitable environment for hunter-gatherers.

The first cattle herders arrived in the Pontic-Caspian region about 5700 BCE from the Danube valley. By c5200 BCE, cattle keeping had transformed the steppe economy and its society. Sheep and cattle converted steppe grass into wool, felt, clothing, tents, milk, yogurt, cheese, meat, marrow and bone and became a source of wealth and status. The regular need for fresh pasture encouraged mobility. Cattle herders were drawn into long-distance trade and a new kind of social and political power equation that involved elaborate sacrifices, gift exchanges and public feasting. Cattle became a kind of currency and came to occupy a principal place in a new set of rituals and religious beliefs.

Cattle and sheep, however, being mobile, were easily stolen and became objects of conflict and contest. Their need for shelter and protection drew related males into close defensive alliances. This connection between animals, brothers and power was the foundation on which new forms of male-centred ritual and politics developed among Indo-European-speaking societies. The cow (and brothers) came to occupy a central place in mythology.

Domesticated animals appeared in the east Eurasian steppes after 3000 BCE; agriculture came much later. Under the influence of southeast European and Caucasian farmers, the Yamnaya, who occupied the Pontic-Caspian steppe (region between the Black and Caspian Seas), adopted domesticated cattle, sheep and goats to become the first fully pastoral economy in Eurasia. In this environment dominated by dry-steppe landscapes and forest patches, they used river valleys and nearby watershed areas and undertook small-scale seasonal migrations between summer and winter grazing lands.

The domestication of the horse increased the range of cattle herders and fuelled the sheep- and cattle-breeding economy. This growth had an adverse effect on the fragile steppe environment and caused an intensified search for new pastures. The use of carts and wagons accelerated movement across the steppe. Yamnaya culture was characterised by intensive cattle breeding, long-distance migrations using wagons, fortified settlements, extensive use of metal tools and burials under mounds (*kurgans*) containing carts, wagons, sacrificed horses and a variety of weapons. These burials attest to sharp distinctions of rank and clans being led by powerful chiefs.

Between 3500–3000 BCE, a significantly drier and colder steppe climate forced the Yamnaya to move further to the north and east in search of pasture land. As reduced water resources began to alter landscapes to semi-desert conditions, seasonal migrations began to extend across hundreds of kilometres (Shishlina n.d.).

The Yamnaya lived on wheels, using wagons for slow bulk transport (water, shelter, food) and horses for rapid light transport (scouting for pastures, herding, trading and raiding expeditions). With a wagon full of tents and supplies, herders could live indefinitely on the open steppes moving between rivers and making territorial claims on wild pastures. A gene mutation that gave the Yamnaya lactose tolerance, which probably emerged first in the steppes west of the Ural Mountains between 4600–2800 BCE, ensured a reliable food resource in milk and its products. This dependence on dairy foods might explain the importance of the cow (PIE-*gwou*) in Proto-Indo-European myth and ritual. The creation of a powerful new set of social, religious and political institutions (guest-host agreements, patron-client contracts, ancestor cults) aided Yamnaya expansion.

The Eurasian steppes preserve evidence of long-distance nomadic migrations coinciding with adverse climatic changes (Bokovenko 2005). These changes appear to have occured in an approximate cycle of 2,400 years. Two such events took place between 4700–3700 and 2500–1200 BCE. Pollen cores across the Eurasian steppes reveal that a markedly cooler, more arid climate began around 2500 BCE and reached its coldest and driest peak between 2250–2000 BCE (Dergachev 2005). Forests, lakes and marshes decreased and grasslands expanded as aridity caused the rich black-soil steppe to change to desert landscapes. This Little Ice Age is documented in botanical studies in Anatolia, the Caucasus and Mesopotamia, as well as in East Africa and India (Weiss 2000).

MBA steppe pastoralists began to establish permanent settlements near marshes in river valleys. Here reeds growing up to 7.6 m remained standing above the ice all winter. They provided good fodder for cattle and sheep and shelter by way of roofing and mat-making materials for log houses from snow and cold winter winds. Their roots were sweet and edible and fish, waterfowl and deer thrived in and around the oxbow lakes where they grew. These were ideal winter habitats and were strongly defended against rivals. These settlements have left no evidence of agriculture but of an economy based on herding and gathering and a population living on a diet based largely on cattle, sheep and goats for meat and dairy products, with an occasional pig, a very few hunted wild animals and plenty of fish.

The Horse – The Agent of Mobility (Anthony 2007: 160; de Barros Damgaard 2018; Gaunitz 2018; Levine 1999; Warmuth 2012)

Wagons and horseback riding brought a multifold enhancement in mobility to steppe populations. It coincides with the Yamnaya expansions from the Pontic-Caspian steppe. The domestication of the horse made possible the exploitation of larger and more diverse landscapes and maintenance of larger families. It increased trading horizons and enhanced military capabilities tremendously. Between 5000–3000 BCE when important cultural, social and economic changes were taking place among steppe populations, horse remains became much more common in archaeological deposits.

The domestication of *Equus ferus*, the wild progenitor, now extinct, of domestic horses, began around 5,500 years ago.[1] Genetic and archaeological evidence points to west central Eurasia (Ukraine and northwest Kazakhstan) as the primary area of horse domestication. From here it spread with a high degree of repeated cross-breeding with local wild populations. Domesticated horses show a high level of matrilineal diversity which suggests that wild females were regularly captured for breeding purposes. The earliest unambiguous evidence for horse domestication comes from the Botai hunter-herder culture in north Kazakhstan c3500–3000 BCE. There is evidence of corralling, harnessing and milking. Botai-related ancestry, however, is present at just about 2.7% in modern domestic horses which suggests that Botai hunter-gatherers were not the first to domesticate horses but learned horse husbandry from an early eastward spread of western pastoralists closely related to the Yamnaya and Afanasievo cultures.

The Afanasievo culture was formed in the Altai region c3000 BCE by Yamnaya-related people who migrated 3,000 kms from the west. This expansion is believed to have been related to the migration of Indo-European-speaking Tocharians to northwest

China. In the Pontic-Caspian steppes, horses were a major part of the meat diet and began to appear in human funeral rituals along with cattle and sheep. Horses were well adapted to the grasslands where they had evolved and easier to feed through the winter than cattle or sheep.[2] This was strong motivation for cattle herders to domesticate horses as a food source during cold winters.

The Wagon (Anthony 2007: 282, 295; Kortlandt 2010; Ringe 2015)

Contact with Mesopotamia may have been instrumental in bringing a revolutionary new technology for land transport to the steppes: wagons. Mesopotamia's enormous appetite for copper, gold and silver resulted in overland routes radiating outward from its cities to sources of supply. Some crossed the Iranian plateau to mines in Zeravshan (Tajikistan), others to the Caucasus Mountains. The first contacts between Mesopotamia and the steppe peoples may have been facilitated by Anatolian middlemen who transported metals from the mineral-rich Kuban basin via the Black Sea. This is where the Maikop culture suddenly appeared. Graves have yielded extraordinary displays of wealth including exotic ornaments made of turquoise and carnelian imported by Mesopotamians from Zeravshan and Harappa. This long-distance trade collapsed c3100 BCE and with it the Maikop culture came to an end.

A Maikop kurgan on the Kuban River has preserved traces of at least two solid wooden disc wheels, perhaps the oldest in Europe.

Expansion into Europe

The Yamnaya expansion into northern Europe brought about the formation of a new social and economic order known as the

Corded Ware Culture (from the cord impressions they made on pottery). It co-existed with late Neolithic cultures and through a gradual process of acculturation and integration that was also marked by episodes of violence brought about the cultural homogenisation of the MBA to northern Europe.

Among other developments, there was the burning of forests on a massive scale to create steppe-like grazing lands for cattle, sheep and horses. A humid climate favoured grasslands and wagon-homes enabled a mobile lifestyle. The economy was based on meat, dairy products, fish and seeds from wild plants with little or no agriculture. Different groups maintained links through extensive exchange systems that secured them access to products outside the pastoral economy, such as metal.

Burial sites reveal that the Corded Ware Culture had spread across much of northern Europe by 2800–2200 BCE. Women were more mobile than men. Between 28–42 % of women were of non-local origin and had a different diet during childhood. Their bones reveal a change in diet to a greater proportion of meat and dairy products. It suggests a pattern of female exogamy by Neolithic women who moved to their husband's settlements and were completely integrated into Corded Ware society. As migrating groups were largely male-dominated, it is likely that many of these women were abducted (Sjogren 2016).

The Mechanism of Spread (Anthony 2007: 191–92; Kortlandt 2010; Kristiansen 2017)

Eurasian steppe pastoral societies have shown remarkable abilities to absorb disparate ethnic and linguistic groups. This is the case with the expansion of Indo-European speaking populations. As a consequence, their languages were adopted by local populations occupying the lands they moved into. Usually, language shift flows in the direction of paramount prestige and power. Horses gave both to the Yamnaya. Horse riding made them more productive in managing bigger herds and exploiting larger pastures. It also gave them a military edge during a period of increased levels of warfare. Breeding of the largest, strongest and most manageable horses may have also made them rich through horse trading.

Yamnaya society had developed a political infrastructure to manage migratory behaviour with institutions like patron-client and host-guest relationships. Proto-Indo-European religion was based on solemn promises bound by oath that obligated gods to provide protection and gifts of cattle and horses to their followers. This extended to the social structure in which chiefs became patrons to their human clients. The strength and sanctity of these institutions allowed them to build ties to new communities without the stress of conflicts. They offered local populations social mobility with advantage and status in the overall structure. The patron-client relationship obligated patrons to protect clients in return for loyalty and service. The host-guest relationship created mutual obligations of hospitality between guests and hosts and extended protection with clearly-defined rights to new groups.

The Yamnaya initially established themselves in pockets from which they exercised authority over the surrounding area. From here, Yamnaya chiefs entered into a patron-client relationship with locals by offering them protection, hospitality and rights to agricultural production in exchange for their loyalty, service and pasture land. In this manner, they extended their claims over large tracts of pastures for their ever-increasing herds and the migration routes that linked them. Their role as patrons encouraged the use of Indo-European languages. Between 3300–2500 BCE, the Yamnaya, their institutions, culture and language, late Proto-Indo-European, spread well beyond the Pontic-Caspian steppes.

There is a darker side to the emergence of Yamnaya Culture to pre-eminence in Europe. It involved violence. There is good evidence that it routinely engaged in warfare and developed social institutions specifically associated with armed aggression and defence. Proto-Indo-European vocabulary contains numerous words associated with such behaviour. It contains words for spear, javelin, dagger and sword and many words relating to aggression, assault, physical violence and trauma. The term *wagros* (Indic *vajra*, Avestan *vazra*) translates to mace or cudgel, an artefact of power and authority in Indo-European societies and the weapon of choice of the Indo-Aryan god Indra. The word for axe, *pelekus*, has cognates in Greek (*pelekus*) and Sanskrit (*parasu*). It was the favourite weapon of Parasurama, the fifth avatar of Vishnu. A possible word for 'warrior' (*yeudhmos*) is found in Sanskrit as *yudhma*, from the verbal root *yeudh*, 'fight' (Mallory 2007: 97).

As with its vocabulary, Indo-European mythology is replete with themes of warfare and the warrior. Indo-European poetry extolls the deeds of warrior knights, their fight against hostile forces, their victories and heroic deaths. Recited at feasts and gatherings, these oral narratives were means of igniting emotions and stirring passions. More tellingly, they open a window on a particulary war-like cult that existed in all Indo-European societies, that of boys initiated at a young age into roaming war-bands known as *mannerbunde* (Germanic), *sodales* or *luperci* (Italic), *fiana* (Celtic), *ephebes* or *kourios* (Greek) and *Vratyas* or *Maruts* (Vedic).

The Cult of the Mannerbunde (Anthony 2016)

The term 'mannerbunde' means 'binding together of a group of men' (IE root *bhendh*, or *bhandh* meaning 'to bind'). This (Proto-) Indo-European war-band was composed of young unmarried elite males aged between 14–20 years tasked primarily with military duties. They lived beyond the usual boundaries of society and were permitted anti-social behaviour as long as it was not directed at the host society. They lived without possessions until they were later fully re-incorporated into society, married and settled down. Their lifestyle was associated with sexual promiscuity, fighting and raiding and also learning poetry. They wore animal pelts, particularly those associated with wolves, and adopted wolf-like behaviour and names associated with wolves and dogs. These animals, the prime predators of the Eurasian steppe, were strongly associated in Indo-European mythology with death and war. The multi-headed dog, Cerberus, guarded the entrance to the Underworld. Rituals associated with death and the colour black had particular significance in the lifestyle of the mannerbunde.

Numerous references to these youthful war-bands appear in daughter Indo-European languages from Ireland to India making it highly probable that such bands existed in large numbers and in cases played a crucial role in history. Romulus, the legendary founder of Rome, along with his twin brother Remus, was said to have been suckled by a she-wolf, and Rome populated by a number of landless young men who raided the Sabines and took their women for wives. The Roman winter festival of Lupercalia preserves an archaic tradition associated with male adolescents, community protection and sexual fertility in which adolescent sons of the nobility wearing or carrying wolf or dog skins ran around Rome's walls and struck women with goat skins.

The Srubnaya settlement of Krasnosamarskoe (1900–1700 BCE) has left evidence of a unique mid-winter initiation ritual of young boys into the war-band. Here, bones have been found of fifty-one dogs and seven wolves which were sacrificed, roasted and apparently consumed in a rite of passage that symbolised a transition to a status associated with the dog/wolf through the consumption of its flesh. Dogs were not normally eaten in the Srubnaya culture. At this site, however, dog and wolf bones together accounted for 30–40% of excavated faunal remains. Such a high percentage has not been found in any other settlement which suggests Krasnosamarskoe was a regional centre were the initiation of youths into war-bands took place.

The Sintashta Culture (Anthony 2009; Johnson n.d.; Pinheiro 2010, 2011)

The Srubnaya culture emerged in the Don-Caucasus region and was contemporary to the Andronovo culture of central Asia. The Andronovo-Srubnaya horizon is characterised by a string of related cultures across the Eurasian steppes from the Danube basin to the Tien Shan and Altai Mountains of China. Formerly isolated regions were drawn into a network that began to experience the spread of technical innovations including bronze casting, chariotry, aspects of pastoral subsistence and settlement types, mining of copper and processing it in the household economy and trade in copper, tin and horses. Language, rituals patterns of distinctive elite behavior and other cultural traits spread throughout.

The Andronovo culture, closely identified with the ancestral Indo-Iranian community, grew out of the Sintashta culture.

The Sintashta period saw the concentration of dispersed MBA mobile herder populations into fortified settlements through an unprecedented level of population mixing and inter-regional north–south steppe movements. The Sintashta culture, characterised by chariot builders, breeders and trainers of horses and producers of sophisticated new weapons, emerged in the southern Urals. Its genetically close relation with Corded Ware populations indicates an eastward migration c2200 BCE.

Intensified warfare and long-distance trade played powerful roles in the origins of the Sintashta culture. Twenty-two heavily fortified settlements excavated in the southern Ural Mountains give insights into its defining character. These well-planned settlements were built on low terraces beside the marshy floodplain of a meandering stream close to winter grazing composed of tall, dense patches of reeds. Their layout reveals coordination of buildings and spaces and standardisation of architectural forms. The best-known settlement, Arkaim, was inhabited by an estimated 1,000–2,000 people. Approximately

150m in diameter, its sixty semi-subterranean dwellings were built in two circles with the outer abutting a defence wall. Units within the first circle were located close to each other and radially oriented with their entrances/exits facing inwards towards an empty space. Houses in the outer circle were also radially oriented towards the centre with their exits facing a circular street. Entrance into the settlement was through four angular passages constructed over moats and protected by gates. Houses contained hearths, cellars, wells and, in some cases, metallurgical furnaces. The swastika was one of the motifs used to decorate Arkaim pottery.

Sintashta's dead were buried in pits with wooden structures and roofs. They have preserved a wealth of materials including vessels, daggers, pins, awls, needles, axes, mortars, pestles, stone tools, bone artefacts, a range of bronze weaponry, spoke-wheeled chariots and the remains of sacrificed horses, cattle, sheep, goats and dogs. Burial of local elites was accompanied by elaborate feasting, ceremonies and rituals that cemented social bonds. The large number of sheep, goats, cattle and horses slaughtered at these feasts provided meat for over 3,000 people.

Such discoveries have raised the question as to how and why the Sintashta culture acquired such a militaristic character. The probable answer lies in the onset of an extremely cold climate and the need to control key locations with access to critical resources in a time of scarcity. The heavily fortified settlements are an indication of fierce competition for available resources. There is evidence that this encouraged active warfare with the development and increased production of new tin-bronze alloy weapons and, perhaps most importantly, the light war chariot.

This escalating cycle of tribal competition was transformed when the Sintashta chiefs made contact with the old and well-oiled trade network that connected west, central and South Asia. These contacts connected the insatiable demand for metals and horses from Mesopotamia to the inexhaustible supply from the steppes. Wealth and prestige goods flowed northwards in exchange for horses and metals, especially copper.

Exports contributed to elite wealth which was used to secure and cement socio-political power. Competition between rival tribal groups encouraged trade for novel insignia and valuables that could be used as gifts in public ceremonial and feasting events where alliances were made. As competition intensified, feasting and ceremonies became more elaborate and led to increased warfare. This development led to the evolution of the Sintashta culture, unique in the steppes: heavily fortified settlements, intensified metal production, a great increase in quantity and variety of new weapons, chariot warfare, elaborate public funeral ceremonies accompanied by massive animal sacrifices, great feasting and eulogistic poetry. For the first time in the steppes, large deposits of weapons were interred with humans. So too horses and war chariots and a new type of spearhead which suggests it was used in close combat as a throwing weapon. All this coincided with the first contacts with the trading network of Central Asia.

The first phase of contact with Central Asia occurred between 2100–2000 BCE. The evidence lies in steppe pottery recovered in Margiana along with horse bones and riding gear. The horse had been decapitated and buried along with a dog and a camel in a grave containing ten humans. Horses were not native to central Asia.

The second phase of contact, 2000–1700 BCE, witnessed a dramatic intrusion of steppe materials and even settlements into central Asia, south of the Zeravshan River which flows a little to the north of Samarkhand. Steppe pottery appeared in many sites of the BMAC and northeast Iran along with horse remains and specific Sintashta type harness parts. About 1800–1700 BCE, at the end of this second phase, Andronovo miners settled the Zeravshan Valley and began to exploit its mineral resources. In central Asia and Iran, there is evidence for increasing horse imports and chariot warfare. By about 1600 BCE, the cities of the BMAC were abandoned as pastoral populations moved in from the north.

Sintashta militaristic innovations, primarily the war chariot, quickly spread to Europe and central Asia. Andronovo populations were genetically closely related to the Sintashta people so that Yamnaya ancestry (Steppe EMBA) now genetically connected Altai in Siberia with Scandinavia in Europe. It is also present in South Asian populations, especially among UP northern Brahmans and Bhumihars, the traditional custodians of early Sanskrit texts. This implies groups with relatively more steppe ancestry had a central role in spreading early Vedic culture. The organised military aristocracy of the Sintashta culture did not die; it travelled with steppe dwellers migrating south to central Asia and the BMAC region. There Sintashta-Arkaim type settlements and new types of graves began to appear together with Indo-Iranian-speaking groups of the Andronovo culture.

17

Expansion of Indo-European Speakers

A sheep that had no wool saw horses, one pulling a heavy cart, one carrying a big load, and one quickly carrying a man. The sheep said to the horses: My heart pains me seeing a man driving horses. The horses said: Listen sheep, our hearts pain us when we see that a man, the master, makes the wool of sheep into a warm garment for himself, and the sheep have no wool. Having heard this, the sheep fled into the plain

(Schleicher 1868).

Schleicher's Fable, *Avis akvāsas ka* (The Sheep and the Horses), was the first attempt to produce an audio text in Proto-Indo-European (PIE) using reconstructed vocabulary. In doing so, Schleicher, a German linguist, relied heavily on Sanskrit. It may have been the first time in 6,500 years that the sounds of the dead language were heard. Another text soon followed. In *The King and the God*, a childless king prays to the god Werunos for a son. His wish is granted when the queen bears a son. Werunos is the god Varuna of Sanskrit texts.

The term Indo-European refers to a language family and not to race. Therefore, it is only logical that any attempt to trace its place of origin and the manner of dispersals from the region must rely primarily on linguistics and then seek corroboration from archaeological and genetic evidence. Over two centuries of extensive research by scholars globally in linguistics, archaeology and genetics point unambiguously to the Pontic-Caspian steppes as the place of origin of Indo-European languages. Lying between the Black and Caspian Seas, this region is part of an expansive steppe landscape from which populations speaking daughter languages of PIE spread westwards to Europe and eastwards to central Asia, Iran and South Asia over a period spanning some centuries. Today, speakers of these languages form a large part of the world's population. While it does not mean these populations are all genetically linked, this language family expansion closely followed that of populations bearing Y-chromosome Hg R1a of which R1a-Z282 in Europe and R1a-Z93 in South Asia form major percentages. The oldest R1a is found in Ukraine.

The Genetic Story (Allentoft et al. 2015; Haak 2015; Hollard 2018; Kristiansen 2017; Lucotte 2015; Narasimhan et al. 2018; Underhill 2014)

Genetic studies of ancient DNA (aDNA) and of modern Eurasian populations corroborate the archaeological and linguistic record that Bronze Age Eurasia (3000–1000 BCE) was a dynamic period characterised by large-scale migrations and population replacements. It transformed the region from Europe to the trans-Ural steppe into a relatively genetically homogeneous population (Steppe MLBA) which harboured a mixture of Yamnaya ancestry (Steppe EMBA) with European farmer populations. Connected to the Corded Ware, Srubnaya, Petrovka, Sintashta and Andronovo cultures, these migrations coincided with the spread of Indo-European languages through these areas. The timing of this expansion also coincided with a period when striking traits of the Yamnaya expansion appeared in the archaeological record.

The pre-eminent Y-chromosome haplogroup connected with this expansion, Hg R1, has two main branches, R1b and R1a. R1b has a greater presence in west Europe, the highest being among the French Basques. R1a is most frequent in eastern Europe. There is a declining gradient of R1b towards the east which suggests migratory waves of later R1a populations from the east replaced earlier populations. Hg R1a shows a declining gradient towards the west and south. It has relatively low frequencies in the Seine and the Rhine basins (3.6% and 3.4% respectively),

Figure 17.1: Expansion of Yamnaya Steppe pastoralists into Europe and Asia

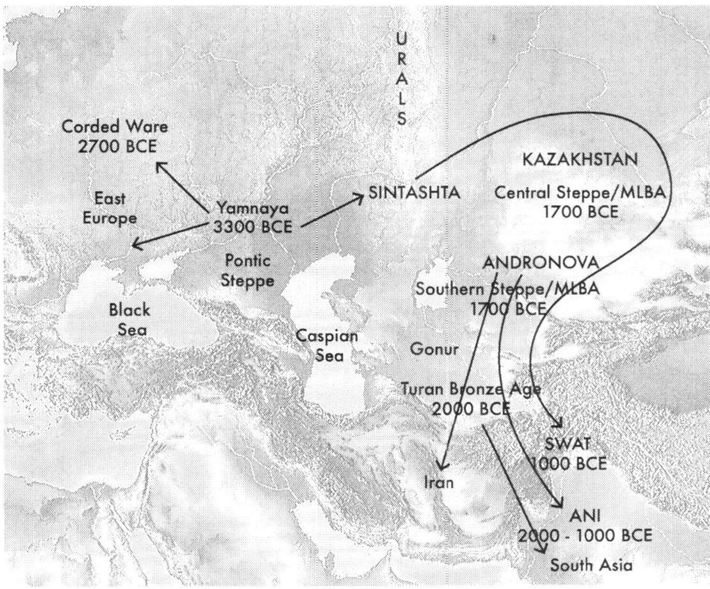

Source: Adapted from Narasimhan et al. (2018).

climbs to 39.3% and 38.9% in the Oder and the Vistula basins and culminates at 44% in the Dnieper basin in the Ukrainian. These values suggest a wide and relatively rapid spread which coincided with that of EBA societies.

More than 10% of men from South Asia to Scandinavia share a common ancestor in Hg R1a-M420. Its highest frequency is found in eastern Europe but it also has a high peak in Punjab. The vast majority fall within the R1a1-M17 subclade which originated c5,800 years ago. It has two major groups, a European branch defined by Z282 and a central and South Asia branch defined by Z93. The earliest European R1a lineages appear in Corded Ware populations and the highest frequencies of R1a-Z282 occur in northern Ukraine, Belarus and Russia. R1a-Z93 is most common in the Altai region of

Russia, Kyrgyzstan and Iran. Its sub-group, R1a-M780, occurs at high frequency in South Asia and Iran.

These genetic findings are consistent with archaeological evidence of connections between material culture in the Kazakh MBA-LBA steppe and early Vedic culture in India. They make a compelling case for the expansion of Yamnaya pastoralist populations from the Pontic-Caspian steppes as having a defining role in the spread of R1a lineages into Europe and Asia. By 3000 BCE, Neolithic farming cultures from Hungary to the Urals appear to have been largely replaced by the Yamnaya culture. This genetic expansion coincided with that of Indo-European speakers and the appearance of kurgans across Eurasia.

The Linguistic Trail (Anthony 2007; Koch 2018)

The Proto-Indo-European language is believed to have existed c4500 BCE and to be the language from which all Indo-European languages, spoken by about three billion people worldwide today, derive. Linguists divide the Indo-European language family into the centum and satem groups which together with Anotalian form twelve major branches. The centum group consists of the western branches – Hellenic, Celtic, Italic, Germanic and Tocharian, while Balto-Slavic, Indo-Iranian, Albanian, Phrygian and Armenian are placed in the satem group. Anatolian does not come under either.

The centum-satem and later satem-ruki classifications are based on the development of certain features of Indo-European languages illustrated by the evolution of the reconstructed PIE word for 'hundred' (Latin-centum, Avestan-satem). 'Hundred' has been reconstructed in PIE as *kmtom*. The centum group retains the hard consonant 'k' in the Celtic and Italic groups while evolving into 'h' in Hellenic and Germanic. In the satem group, 'k' evolved into the soft consonant 's' (Proto-Indo-Aryan – *satam*, Proto-Baltic-Slavic – *simta*, Proto-Slavic – *cto*).

Figure 17.2: Expansion of Indo-European languages

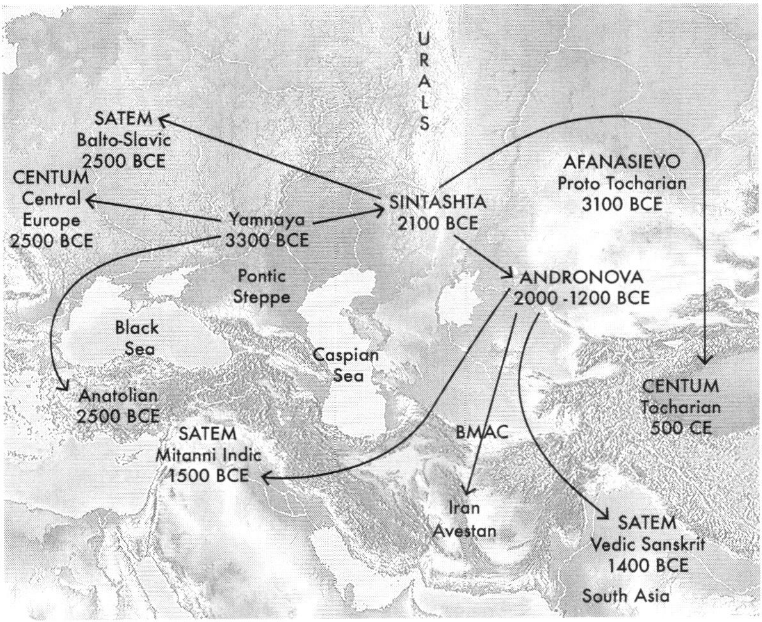

Source: Created by author; various sources mentioned in-text.

The manner in which these innovations developed leave a record of how, when and from where PIE speaker migrations took place.

Linguists have been working on reconstructing the Proto-Indo-European lexicon for about 200 years. Today, the reconstructed PIE vocabulary consists of more than 1,500 words. They open a window into the world of PIE speakers, their environment, social life and beliefs. There are words for wild animals (otter, beaver, wolf, lynx, elk, red deer, horse, mouse, hare, hedgehog), birds (goose, crane, duck, eagle), domestic animals (cattle, cow, ox, steer, sheep, pig, boar, sow, piglet, dog), bee and honey, wool and weaving.

PIE contains at least five words for parts of wheeled vehicles which provide strong and clear evidence for where and when PIE was spoken. There are two words for 'wheel,' one for 'axle,' one for 'thill' (harness-pole), and a verb 'to transport in a vehicle'. The PIE word for wheel was created from a verb that meant 'to turn'. It meant 'the thing that turns'. These root words appear as cognates in most IE languages. In Sanskrit they become *chakra* (wheel; Avestan *caxtra*), *ratha* (chariot; Avestan – *ratha*), *isa* (thill), *aksas* (axle), *vahati* (vehicle). The invention of the wheel-and-axle principle which made the use of wagons and carts possible is dated to c4000 BCE. It means that PIE was then a spoken language. The absence of wheeled chariot vocabulary in Anatolian means it split from PIE before the invention of the wheel.

Anatolian Goes Its Way (Anthony 2007: 138, 227, 258)

Southeast European winters turned colder from c4200 BCE. A bitterly cold spell that began in 3960 BCE and lasted 140 years caused enormous stress on farming settlements. By the time the climate warmed up again, there was a drastic cultural change in the agricultural economy of the lower Danube basin. Farmers abandoned farmsteads and turned to pastoralism. At the same time steppe herders began to move in from the Pontic-Caspian steppes with a powerful new ally in managing larger herds of cattle: horses. It transformed their status from that of raiders to chiefs and patrons who were rich in animal resources, something that a devastated economy badly required. They brought their ideology and lifestyle with them, built new alliances through gifts and feasts, demonstrated muscle power when required and a new language. It spread through southeastern Europe as its population, emerging from an era of warfare, dislocation, migration and economic change, adopted steppe herders as patrons who offered protection and rewards in exchange for service. Together with a pastoral economy, they adopted the new language, Anotalian, named after the land the steppe herders reached via the western Black Sea shore.

Tocharian (Anthony 2007: 264)

Wheels now enter the story. About 3700–3500 BCE, a section of the Volga-Ural steppe population migrated east across Kazakhstan more than 2,000 kms to the Altai Mountains in China to form the Afanasievo culture. It introduced domesticated animals, metal types, pottery types and funeral customs to the region. Their language developed into the Tocharian branch of the IE family. It was spoken in Xinjiang along the Silk Road till about 500 CE. Tocharian included words connected with wheeled wagons suggesting this migration had a role in spreading developments connected to the domestication of horses to these areas. Modern genetic studies of aDNA support this eastward migration. Afanasievo men show close genetic affinity with the Yamnaya.

West into Europe's Heartland

Between 3100–2800 BCE, steppe herders began to move into the lower Danube valley once again. Archaeological evidence suggests it was a large-scale migration, one that could have acquired power and prestige partly just through its numerical weight. It coincides with the expansion of Indo-European branches that evolved into Celtic, Italic and Greek.

The trail is marked by thousands of kurgans which dominated the landscape. Kurgans were highly visible mounds erected over grave pits. The body was laid on its back on a thin bed of reed mats or hide and powdered with red ochre. The knees were bent and raised, hands laid beside the body and head turned to the east or northeast. Grave goods were sometimes interred with the body. They included ceramic pots, bone objects, copper or bronze daggers and awls, flint flake tools and occasionally small ornaments of shell, silver or copper. In rare cases, whole or disassembled wagons were also buried.

The earliest kurgans appeared on low floodplain terraces of rivers. Later, they were constructed on the open steppe on high watersheds between rivers. The kurgan cemeteries of the Yamnaya culture eventually spread from the Danube to the Urals, and Pontic-Caspian steppe to the borders of the northern forests. Their protrusion above the plains converted them into landmarks and their size and the interred grave goods demonstrated social rank and elite status.

Kurgans have yielded two-wheeled spoked chariots, remains of whole horses and an abundance of weapons suggestive of a highly warlike society. Over two dozen warriors who had apparently been killed in battle were found interred in one kurgan, some beheaded, others with skulls crushed and limbs missing.

Yamnaya and Corded Ware cultures bordered each other in the region where Poland meets Ukraine. The resultant interaction spread Germanic, Slavic, Baltic and Yamnaya gene pools into northern Europe together with the defining traits of Yamnaya culture. An estimated three-fourths of Corded Ware ancestry has been traced to the Yamnaya which implies a massive westward migration from the Pontic steppes into the heartland of Europe. Genetic data indicates this migration across a distance of over 2,500 kms was relatively sudden.

The large herds of cattle, sheep and horses possessed by the Yamnaya, their politico-religious culture adapted to territorial expansion and the possible employment of aggressive youthful war-bands in the vanguard of their demographic movement gave them an advantage over Neolithic inhabitants. The successive westward migrations from the Pontic steppes cannot perhaps be described as a military invasion but it resulted in the appropriation of prime pasture lands and the transformation of the newcomers eventually into patrons who offered locals a place in their rituals and political institutions. Inevitably, it resulted in locals adopting Indo-European languages which evolved into the Germanic group.

The Satem Group

The westward push of Germanic groups resulted in a linguistic split with the Balto-Slavic groups who remained in East Europe. These languages gradually adopted the characteristics of the satem group which spread all over the steppes. Around 2200 BCE, groups of Corded Ware populations moved eastward to the Urals to form the Sintashta culture. From there some groups spread south into central Asia and the BMAC. The satem-ruki split developed between Proto-Balto-Slavic and Proto-Indo-Iranian speakers. Very simply, this change involves a change of 's' to 'sh' when it follows the sounds r, u, k, i.

Pre-Indo-Iranian developed from a northeastern set of dialects between 2500–2200 BCE. Indo-Iranian is dated at the latest to about 1700 BCE. Indo-Iranian is the parent of Old Indic (oldest form of Sanskrit) and Avestan (oldest Iranian language) of which the Gathas forms the oldest part. The Gathas and the Rgveda are closely related in both language and thought. They use the same deity names (although Old Indic gods were demonised in the Avesta), employ the same poetic conventions and share specific rituals.

By c2500 BCE, Proto-Indo-European had fragmented into a variety of late dialects and daughter languages and was no longer a spoken language.

18

The Indo-Iranian Speakers

A clause from the treaty signed between the Hittite (Anatolia) and Mitanni (Syria) kings in 1380 BCE states,

> May they ... stand by these words of the treaty, may they hear and may they witness. If thou ... do not keep the words of the treaty, may the gods who are the lords of the oath destroy you ... together with your country, together with your women, and together with your possessions ... (Thieme 1960).

Contracted terms were sacred and binding. Verse 1.2 of the 'Mihr Yasht' (Hymn to Mithra) composed about a millennium later, advises Zarathushtra: 'Break not the contract ... neither the one that thou hadst entered into with one of the unfaithful, nor the one that thou hadst entered into with one of the faithful who is one of thy own faith. For Mithra stands for both the faithful and the unfaithful' (Avesta: Khorda Avesta).

The sanctity of the oath calling upon the gods as witnesses and guarantors had high prominence in Indo-European society. The gods called upon in this case were many. Hittite gods were listed first, then Mitanni and finally five Aryan gods, Mithra, Varuna, Indra and the Nasatya twins. These gods are named together in RV 10.125 in which the goddess Speech claims: 'I roam with the Rudras and the Vasus, I with the Adityas and the All Gods. I bear both Mitra and Varuṇa, I Indra and Agni, I both the Asvins.' The Rgveda was compiled in the Punjab from c1500 BCE. The Mitanni ruled 4,000 kms away, and their reference to the Vedic gods comes over a century earlier.

A non-Indo-European language, Hurrian, was spoken in the territory ruled by the Mitanni. The Mitanni kings, however, all bore Old Indic throne names like Tus'ratta I (Old Indic *Tvesa-ratha* – having an attacking chariot), Artatama I (Rta-dhaaman – having the abode of *r'ta* – cosmic order and truth), Artas's'umara (*Rta-smara* – remembering *r'ta*), and S'attuara I (*Satvar* – warrior). Their capital city was Wassukanni (*vasu-khani* – wealth-mine). The Mitanni kingdom was probably founded by Old Indic-speaking mercenaries in the service of the Hurrian kings, perhaps charioteers, who usurped the throne. The Mitanni word *marya* has the same meaning, warrior, as in the Rgveda (Lamberg-Karlovsky 2002). Mitanni royal names, deities and their terms for horses and chariots give a clue to the location of their original homeland.

The Mitanni Aryan gods

The inclusion of Indo-Aryan gods, not worshipped by the Hittites and Hurrians, in the treaty implies they were family or clan gods of the Mitanni. In Indo-Iranian and Indo-Aryan societies, the five gods were the 'lords of the oath' who protected treaties, promises and oaths.

RV 3.59.1 addresses Mithra as the god who oversees agreements, treaties, marriages and other forms of alliances and who watches over the nations with unblinking eyes. Mithra was the god of heavenly light who saw everything and knew the truth, the ideal witness and enforcer of solemn agreements and oaths and the chastiser of those who broke them. Mithra was made by Ahura Mazda in his own image and likeness. His title 'grass-land magnate' describes his realm, the wide-open steppe. He was the protector of cows, the guarantor of treaties, the lord of wide pastures who, with a thousand ears and ten thousand eyes, was sleepless and ever watchful.

The noun *mitra* means ally. The Rgveda mentions Mithra more than 200 times, ninety of them together with Varuna as Mithra-Varuna. Together, they are invoked to guarantee oaths and solemn verbal undertakings (RV 5.65.6, 7.49.3). The Rgveda calls upon Indra to work together with Mithra and Varuna in enforcing the preservation of the contracted word (RV 7.85.2, 10.89.9). The Nasatyas, known as Asvins in the Rgveda, are called upon to work together with other gods including Mithra and Varuna in smiting rivals, arranging allies and providing progeny and property (RV 8.35.12/13). It made eminent sense for the Mitanni to invoke them as witnesses. The order in which the gods were listed in the treaties, Akkadian, Sumerian, Mitanni and Hurrian, suggests the Mitanni had a higher status than native Hurrians who, however, made up the majority of the inhabitants of the Mitanni kingdom.

The Kikkuli Text (Fournet 2010; Novak 2007; Raulwing n.d., 2009)

The Kikkuli Text reveals that the Mitanni were experts in horse training and used related Indo-Aryan terms. Discovered in the royal archive of the Hittite capital Bogazkoi in Anatolia, it was written c1345 BCE by Kikkuli, a horse trainer, in Hurrian, the language of the Mittani state. The Kikkuli Text contains Indo-Aryan technical terms associated with horse training and the numerals *aika*, *tiera*, *panza*, *sata*, *nava* (one, three, five, seven, nine). Kikkuli's professional title contains the Indo-Aryan word for horse, *asva*. Indo-Aryan was no more spoken at the time of Kikkuli. The continued use of Indo-Aryan terms, therefore, confirms that its speakers were once regarded as experts in the use of horses and chariots in the Syrian-Anatolian region, and possibly Iraq where Indo-Aryan words for horse colours (*p/babru-nnu* – reddish brown, brown, *p/barita-nnu* – grey, *p/binkara-nnu* – reddish brown, reddish yellow, greenish yellow) were found in an archive in Nuzi, Mesopotamia.

The Mitanni dialect linguistically represents one older than Vedic from which it must have separated in the sixteenth century

BCE. Both languages preserve 's', while in Iranian 's' becomes 'h' (Mitanni-Nasaattiia, Sanskrit-Nasatya, Iranian/Avesta-Nahtya; Kikkuli – *satta*, Sanskrit – *sapta*, Iranian – *hafta*, *hapta*; Kikkuli – *aika*, Sanskrit – *eka*, Iranian – *aiva*). Aika and aiva are both used in Proto-Indo-Aryan. While Indo-Aryan preserved the earlier forms, early Iranian innovated (Thieme n.d.).

The Bactrian-Margiana Archaeological Complex (BMAC)

(Lamberg-Karlovsky 2002; Luneau 2019; Narasimhan et al. 2018; Parpola 1988; Salvatori n.d; Sarianidi n.d.)

To the south, the Andronovo region borders the BMAC, a region between the Caspian Sea and the Amu Darya River which had long contacts with both Harappa and Mesopotamia. The material culture of the mature phase of the BMAC (c2250–1750 BCE) was largely homogeneous over northern Iran, Turkmenistan, northern Afghanistan, southern Uzbekistan and southern Tajikistan. The BMAC played a significant role in the long-distance Asian trade network for raw material (gold, lapis lazuli, turquoise, alabaster, tin) and finished items. It was characterised by urban development, social stratification, task specialisation and territorial expansion. Its economy was based on irrigation and agro-pastoralism. The question as to which language these people spoke remains unanswered.

BMAC cities contained monumental structures protected by heavy defensive walls. Their graves have yielded prestige and luxury goods, many imported. Gonur in Margiana is noted for its political, administrative and religious buildings. The last contained fire altars and sacrificial areas for the veneration of fire with architectural features similar to those described in the Rgveda and Avesta.

While the steppes provide ample evidence for the use of horses, wagons and chariots, BMAC settlements do not. This suggests very little contact between the two neighbouring cultures though numerous steppe sites have been found near BMAC settlements. The fortified nature of BMAC cities suggests the existence of a strong warrior class who intentionally avoided steppe populations.

Genetic evidence appears to confirm this. Ancient DNA reveals a southward migration of steppe populations between 2300–1500 BCE but fails to find admixture between steppe and BMAC populations although such admixture exists to the north and south of the BMAC. This indicates a southward infiltration of Andronovo steppe pastoralists who largely bypassed BMAC urban centres. The traditions of the Indo-Iranians, however, reveal that this genetic separation did not prevent a degree of cultural interaction between the two.

The Indo-Iranian Homeland (Eduljee n.d.; Falk 2003)

The earliest textual reference to an Indo-Iranian homeland is found in the first chapter of the Vendidad, the first chapter of the Gathas, the sacred Avestan hymns said to have been composed by Zarathushtra. It lists sixteen districts created by Ahura Mazda. The text, probably composed before 1000 BCE, details a southward migration followed by a branching to the east and west. The first of the sixteen districts is Airyanem Vaejah, an inhospitable place with two months of summer followed by ten of winter. The other fifteen districts as listed in the Vendidad are Gava (Sogdiana), Mouru (Margiana), Baxdi (Bactria), Nisaya (between Margiana and Bactria), Haroiva (Herat), Vaekereta (Gandhara), Urva (probably Gazni), Xnenta (Gorgan), Haraxvaiti (Arachosia), Haetumant (Helmand), Raya (north of Haraxvaiti and Haetumant), Caxra (between Gazni and Kabul), Varena (Buner), Hapta Hendu (Sapta Sindhavaḥ, northeastern Punjab) and Ranha (Rasa, mentioned together with Kubha or Kabul and Krumu or Kurram rivers in RV 5.53.9). The Airyanem Vaejah, the homeland of Zarathustra, was placed at the centre of the world. The first man, Yima, and the 'uniquely created bull' were created on the shores of its river, the Vanuhi Daitya. It was dominated by Mount Hara (Mount Meru in Indic, the Indian branch of Indo-European languages). Mount Hara/Meru was just one of the many shared elements in Indo-Iranian cosmography. It was believed to rise in the middle of the central region (Iranian Xvanirata, Indian Jambudvipa), one of seven regions of the earth (Iranian *karsvar*, Indian *dvipa*). Hara gave light and water to the world. From its peak, the mythical river, the Haraxvaiti, as large as all other earthly rivers combined, flowed to the sea, Vourukasa. This mix of myth, history and geography is a common feature of Indo-Iranian concepts of cosmography concerning mountains, lakes and rivers.

Indo-Iranian-speaking peoples once inhabitated a larger territory. Indo-Iranian loanwords in Finno-Ugric, the prehistoric ancestor of the Uralic languages spoken today in the forest zone north of the Eurasian steppe, prove that the speakers of these languages once lived in territories bordering each other. Uralic has borrowed heavily from Indo-Iranian. Remarkably, the oldest layer of loanwords is only attested in Sanskrit and not in Iranian which suggests the Indo-Aryans came into contact with Uralic speakers before the Iranians. The Indo-Iranian term describing their ethnicity, arya, appeared as a loanword in ancestral Finno-Ugric as *orya* (slave). Evidently there were hostilities between forest-zone Uralic and steppe-zone Indo-Iranian speakers some of whom were captured and enslaved by Uralic speakers. Another loanword *asura* (lord), (*asera* in Finno-Ugric), suggests there were also alliances between the two neighbours. Other borrowings include terms for hundred, bee, honey, tribe/troop, wheel, spindle, bridge and boat (Anthony 2016).

While Finno-Ugric borrowings establish a northern boundary for Indo-Iranian speakers, the Mitanni texts reveal that by 1600 BCE a militarised Indo-Iranian speaking aristocracy with war chariots had established themselves at the southern boundaries of the Andronovo cultural area. Spread over three million sq. kms and lasting for over a millennium, it is believed that this culture was essentially Indo-Iranian and formed a single cultural entity with regional sub-cultures, the main ones being Petrov, Alakul and Fedorovo. Its formation and survival were aided by the large-scale mining and trade in copper and tin throughout Eurasia with pastoral nomads being the agents of dissemination. Specific Indo-Iranian cultural traits of the Andronovo culture, including an agro-pastoral economy, handmade ceramics, horse-drawn chariots, horses, fire and ancestor cults and a high status for charioteers, are reflected in the Rgveda and Avesta (Kuzmina 2007). These considerations would place the Indo-Iranian homeland in the Eurasian steppe lands south of the Urals.

The Indo-Iranian Economy (Kuzmina 2007: 146–61)

A reconstruction of the Indo-Iranian economy based on common Indo-European words preserved in Sanskrit, Avestan and the earliest Vedic literature points to it being predominantly pastoral with an element of farming. This last is revealed by the presence of words for grain (barley but not wheat or rice), crop, plough, grind, pestle, flour, etc. Compared to terms for beef, udder, milk, butter, curds and other dairy products though, they are few and far between.

Cattle-raising occupied the primary place in the Indo-Iranian economy. Sheep and horse-breeding followed. The conditions for such an economy in the Bronze Age existed only in the Eurasian steppes where, Kuzmina writes, one must look for the Indo-Iranian homeland.

The Eurasian steppe environment created unstable conditions for farming, but offered optimum pastures for stock-breeding. Here in the Bronze Age, the climate became milder and forests of birch, lime, aspen and pine appeared together with various grasses and cereals. They provided timber for houses, graves and other uses. By the third millennium BCE, a complex sedentary economy had emerged in the Andronovo steppes centred on the raising of cattle, sheep and horses as bones found in these settlements show. Those of cattle (60%), sheep (24%) and horses (15%) constituted 96% of faunal remains. Over 50% came from animals less than two years old which shows they were kept mainly for their meat and hunting played a minor role. Domestic animals provided meat, milk, wool, skins, fuel and bone for implements. Bactrian camels and dogs were also bred, but not pigs.

There was a constant need for new pastures to sustain this meat-dairy economy as the population grew and existing pastures were over-exploited. Evidence from burial sites shows that settlements were occupied for between twenty-five and fifty years. Andronovo society had developed into nomadic groups breeding cattle, sheep and horses.

Nomadism brought the horse into greater prominence. Their ability to paw away snow to reach grasses beneath made them indispensible to mounted herdsmen seeking ever more remote pastures. Andronovo society developed other innovations that aided steppe nomadism like digging deep wells in the desert, light transportable shelters, wheeled transport using bullocks and draught-horses, using the Bactrian camel for transportation and cheese production.

The common Indo-European term for cattle denoted 'movable property', and Indo-Iranian terms for 'war'and 'booty' literally meant 'cattle stealing'. The Rgveda and Avesta both contain numerous hymns in which the gods are praised as lords of cows, swollen with milk sweet as honey. They are urged to bestow such cattle, equated to wealth, on the worshipper, even seizing them from the enemy. The importance of cattle to the early Iranian economy is shown by the Avestan word for house which also meant 'room for cattle, cattle-shed'. Hymns were composed to pray for rewards in the form of herds of cattle. The wealth of a person was assessed by the cattle he owned.

The Rgveda hints at a nomadic way of life. RV 1.42 prays to Pusan to accompany them on their journey, drive away the evil and malevolent wolf and the highwayman, the robber who knows the crooked ways. The hymn addresses Pusan, the foremost wielder of the golden axe, as the one who spurred their forefathers. It ends with a plea: 'Lead us across the parched places. Make easy passages, easy pathways for us ... Lead us to good pasture, with no new suffering on the road ...' The reference to the wolf brings memories of the Eurasian steppe where it is the dominant predator.

The northern steppe territory being unsuitable for stock-breeding due to the taiga forest zone, the direction of further migration lay south towards the farming cultures of south Central Asia and Iran. By the end of the second millennium BCE, groups of steppe populations had migrated to and assimilated with the genetically alien farming cultures of south Turkmenistan and Bactria. It is here that an element of mixed farming entered the economy.

Possible Reasons for Southward Migrations (Anthony 2016; Cerasetti n.d.; Frachetti 2002; Kuznetsov 2005; Luneau 2019; Rouse 2017; Salvatori n.d.; Wen 2018)

With no market for surplus animals, steppe pastoralists had no incentive to increase herd size, and with cattle being unsuited to long-distance migrations, they had to adopt a more settled lifestyle so that their economies were never self-sufficient. They faced severe problems from winter blizzards which sometimes decimated entire herds and caused famine. This changed with the use of the domesticated horse for herding and utilisation of the wagon for bulk transportation. It made the exploitation of larger pastures possible. Herd sizes increased and pastoralists undertook long-distance migrations in search of more pastures.

From the third millennium BCE, the developing trade in metals drew pastoral herders into the trading network as transporters and guides. It expanded the steppe pastoral economy and as populations expanded into new areas, leaders sought to maximise their political and social power. The demand for imported luxury goods as a means to display elite status grew and spurred steppe pastoralists southwards and brought them into direct contact with the trading networks of the BMAC. It happened at a time of worsening climatic conditions that brought increasing aridity to the steppe.

The delta of the Murghab River, the second largest in Turkmenistan, preserves evidence of drying rivers as flows decreased. Sand encroachment from the north drastically reduced agricultural potential. Agricultural land progressively turned to pasture. Semi-nomadic groups began to move in from the north and occupy marginal zones. Their campsites featuring a typical Andronovo cultural identity have been found alongside agricultural fields. They testify to a degree of interaction with sedentary communities and an exchange of technology in agricultural, metalworking and architectural traditions.

By c1900 BCE, major population centres like Gonur were abandoned and replaced by new settlements all characterised by defensive walls with circular and semicircular towers. Clearly it was also a time of conflict and competition for dwindling resources. Long-distance trade dropped off, burial practices changed, site sizes decreased and new architecture and settlement patterns emerged. Steppe pottery styles became more frequent. By 1750–1500 BCE, populations had adopted a complex agro-pastoral lifestyle.

Sand dunes continued to push southwards. Decreasing site numbers point to forced southward migrations even as steppe pastoral groups continued to move in from the north. The international trading network shrank; only the Indus Valley corridor continued to be operational.

Haraxvaiti, Haetumant, and Hapta Hendu (*Encyclopædia Iranica*; Falk 2003; MehrAfarin 2010)

The lands south of Turkmenistan are dominated by tall east–west running mountain ranges. Their slopes are steep, arid and strewn with boulders that have rolled down unstable mountainsides. They offer little to humans except a breathtaking panorama capped by azure skies and isolation in an enormous, silent world. In winter, snow-capped mountain tops add visual emphasis to the bitter cold brought by harsh winds. This is the land described in the Vendidad as the Airyanem Vaejah: 'There are ten winter months there, two summer months; and those are cold for the waters, cold for the earth, cold for the trees. Winter falls there, with the worst of its plagues' (*The Zend-Avesta*, Fargard I.4). The fertile lands to the south, Haraxvaiti, Haetumant and Hapta Hendu, beckoned.

Haraxvaiti, modern Khandahar, is the etymological equivalent of Vedic Sarasvati (provided with many ponds/lakes; *saras* – lake, pond, *vat* –possessing, abounding) (*The Free Dictionary*). The province was named after its main river, the Haraxvaiti (Arghandab). In later Achaemenid royal inscriptions, the province was identified as a neighbour of the Indus province and a source of ivory. It was a fertile land with valleys cultivated and mountain slope pastures used for cattle-breeding. It was, however, inhabited by too many foreign people who buried their dead, a practice abhorred by the Avestans as it was considered to defile the earth. The Haraxvaiti River joins the Haetumant (Helmand) which flows through the province named after it.

Haetumant (Sistan), the eleventh land created by Ahura Mazda, receives exceptional praise in the Vendidad. The Haetumant River transformed it into a granary endowed with flocks of goats, sheep and cows. The river and the region therefore earned pre-eminent status bordering on sanctity in Zoroastrian tradition, one not received by any other in Avestan geography. The Haetumant is considered one of the holiest rivers, blessed by the presence of 'Divine Grace' within it. It is believed that Zarathustra emigrated from the Airyanem Vaejah to Sistan due to the enmity of the people there, and the Zoroastrian religion took shape in Haetumant with the blessing of this divine light.

The name Haetumant is derived from *haetu* (bridge, dam; Vedic *setu*) and *mant* (possessor). 'Zamyad Yasht' (Hymn to the Earth) 9-65-8 describes the Haetumant as a magnificent river with white, rebellious waves flowing with a force powerful enough to submerge non-Iranian nations. The text mentions eight other rivers that flow through the Sistan, seasonally overflowing their banks and flooding the flat land. They end their journey in an inland delta, the Hamun-e-Helmand, formed by three lakes which during the high season transform into one great lake known as Kansaoya (Hamun).

Considered holy, this lake attracted kings and sages seeking its divine light. It was believed that, at its bottom, Lake Kansaoya protected the seed of the prophet and cared for it with the assistance of a host of powerful supernatural beings. From this seed would be born a saviour who would continue the fight against evil after the death of Zarathustra.

There are remarkable similiarities in the traditions of these two regions with the Hapta Hendu, described in the Vendidad as a land of wide expanses, violence, rage and hot weather. Hapta Hendu was the Avestan name for the Sapta Sindhu (Seven Rivers – Indus, Kabul, Kurram, Jhelum, Chenab, Ravi, Beas/Sutlej), the Punjab. It is here that the Vedic arya first settled down. The country was just recovering from the 4.2 ka megadrought which was one of the prime reasons for the Harappans abandoning a highly urbanised region and migrating from the stricken centre. As the arya moved further into South Asia, they encountered a land very different from the one they had left, heavily populated by diverse ethnic groups. While their language and other cultural traits underwent changes in the encounter that ensued, the links to the Indo-Iranian past remained. As the Vedic names they gave to Indian rivers reveal, there was a process of post Indo-Iranian mythic relocation (Skjaervo 2015).

Language (Erdosy 1995; Lubotsky 2001: 301–17)

The Indo-Iranian and Indo-Aryan substratum represent the same or two dialects of the same language, evidence that the Indo-Iranians formed a unified language group before they split. The later spread of the Mitanni to the south-west and the Vedic group to the south-east to Punjab further suggests the Indo-Aryans formed the vanguard of the Indo-Iranian southward movement, with the Iranians following. The former groups pressed on while the Iranians remained in Central Asia and later spread over the Iranian plateau. The change from 's' to 'h' in the names of Indo-Iranian borderland rivers and regions (Vedic Rasa – Avestan Ranha; Sarayu – Haroiuua; Sarasvati – Haraxvaiti; Sindhu – Hindu) point to their initial occupation by Indo-Aryans followed by Iranians.

The Indo-Aryans would therefore have been the first to come into contact with the original inhabitants of the Central Asian towns and borrow words from their languages before passing them on to the Iranians. Indo-Iranian has a small body of loanwords that reflect changes in environment and way of life as they arrived in this new land. There are no new terms for plants or landscape which means the new environment was quite similar to that of their original homeland. Loanwords for new animals like camel, donkey and tortoise, however, show that the new land was situated more to the south. The urban civilisation of Central Asia has enriched the Indo-Iranian lexicon with building and irrigation terminology, with terms for clothing and hairdo, and for some artefacts. The lack of words related to agriculture means the Indo-Iranians continued to be pastoralists and the scarcity of new terms for military technology can be interpreted as an indication of their military supremacy.

Rituals (Falk 2003; Heidarpoor 2016; Sadovski 2018)

The formulae and sequences of Vedic and Avestan ritual practices show many parallels with both often invoking the same groups of divine entities in the same order. The sacrifice ritual (Vedic *yajna*, Avestan *yasna*) is one of the most important religious ceremonies of both traditions. They share common features, the most important being the element of fire, the Iranian *haoma* (a mildly intoxicating drink used in Avestan rituals) or Indian soma drink, sanguinary or non-sanguinary sacrifices and the recitation of eulogistic poetry. Water, so vital to life in the steppes, was deified in the river goddesses Ardvi, Sura, Anahita and Sarasvati. Fire, critical in the bitter cold winters, was worshipped as the Vedic god Agni and Avestan Atur. Their common root goes back to the period before the separation of the two peoples.

Indo-Iranians believed a natural law governed the regular operation of the universe and everything within it. Vedic people knew this law as *rta* or *arta*, Avestans as *asha*. Many divinities were responsible for the proper functioning of the world. They had to be pleased by praise and prayer, sacrifices and offerings. Yajnas/yasnas additionally made the gods more powerful and helped them in maintaining the world order. In return, the gods favoured the sacrificer with material possessions. Sacrifice was therefore seen as a contract between sacrificer and the god for whom the sacrifice was offered. Conducted by priests, yajnas/yasnas included the sacrificial fire which became the intermediary between man and god. Offerings of milk, water, haoma/soma sap, fruits, vegetables, butter and animals, the most prized being the horse, were made and hymns recited. Seven priests were usually involved, the most important being the Vedic *hotri* or Avestan *zaotar*.

The Soma/Haoma Ritual (Falk 2003; Lubotsky 2001: 301–17; Nyberg 1995; Sarianidi 2003; Skjaervo 2015)

The soma/haoma ritual was a principal part of the yajna/yasna ceremonies. It was devoted to the deity Soma/Haoma, the personification of an intoxicating drink. The name soma/haoma referred to both the plant and its divinity. The ritual involves the preparation of a mildly intoxicating drink by pressing and filtering an as yet unidentified plant and offering it to the gods. It was believed the refreshing drink would have a pleasing effect on them and induce them to grant favours. Terming haoma 'master of knowledge', Avestan texts declare it induces excitement and feelings of victory, health, prosperity, growth, strength and knowledge (Yasna 9.26, Yasna 9.17). It kept one awake and alert and stimulated intellectual creativity and religious insight apart from giving humans strength in battle. In the Iranian tradition, haoma was apparently taken as a stimulant before going into battle. In the Rgveda, soma was mainly reserved for the gods, especially Indra, the warrior god.

While there were several varieties of haoma (Yasna 10.12+ 17), there is strong evidence for identifing the plant chiefly with the genus ephedra. Ephedra is known in many regions by names derived from haoma/soma: Nepali – *somalata*, Pashto – *oman*, Baluchi – *hum/huma*, Persian – *hom/umah*, Punjabi – *amsania*). The plants are bushes of variable height (0.2–4.0m) with a tree-like twisted trunk and numerous leafless, green or yellowish stems. There are about forty, mainly Eurasian, species. They do not thrive in lowland, semi-humid or humid climates.

Originally, soma/haoma was not the name of the plant but the extract produced by the ritual pressing. Vedic soma and Avestan haoma are nouns derived from the roots *su-/sau-* (*hu-/hau-*) 'to press or extract (juice from something)'. The bitterness of the ephedra extract was probably neutralised by adding honey and/or milk. Eephedra stems are often brown in colour.

In Vedic texts, *babhru* (greyish brown) is used exclusively to describe the soma extract.

The archaeological evidence for the cult comes not from India or Iran but from Gonur in Margiana where urbanised populations built monumental temples dedicated to the soma/haoma god. Ephedra, cannabis and poppy, plants used for making narcotics, grew in large clumps near the temples. Their remains have been found in huge vats, stone grinders and vessels recovered from the temples. These show the plants were processed in a manner similar to that described in the Avesta and Rgveda. After soaking, the plants were pressed with stone pestles. In Avestan, haoma is translated as 'the thing that is squeezed'. The pressed plants were mixed with barley, milk and water and allowed to ferment for several days. After the fermentation, the intoxicating drink was strained to separate stems and seeds and poured into cult vessels during ritual ceremonies to the accompaniment of hymns.

A hand-made vessel typical of the nomadic Andronovo culture recovered from one temple testifies to contacts between the agricultural and nomadic people in Margiana. Two of these temples had fire altars. The archaeology of Gonur suggests the interaction of Indo-Iranians with BMAC populations appears to have included the borrowing of the soma/haoma cult, and possibly the fire cult as well.

The Split

South of the BMAC, Indo-Iranian groups expanded into new territories with Indo-Aryan speakers forming the vanguard. While a small elite group of charioteers, the Mitanni, moved westwards, the major section moved south into Iran and southeast towards South Asia. Archaeological evidence suggests that the earliest groups may have crossed into South Asia via the Bolan Pass c2000 BCE. They followed in the footsteps of the Harappans who had abandoned large swathes of Sindh to cross into Gujarat and onwards to the east and northwestern Deccan. The languages of these early Indo-Aryan speakers evolved into the Outer Indo-Aryan family. Major migrations took place some 500 years later via the Khyber Pass. A small part of this group settled in northeast Afghanistan, the ancestors of the Nuristani-speaking population still living there. The main thrust consolidated in the Punjab. These were the speakers of Vedic Indo-Aryan, the composers of the Rgveda.

The BMAC, once occupied by Indo-Aryan speakers, was colonised by Iranian speakers following from the north. They created the world's first great empire, that of the Achaemenids (550 –330 BCE).

19

The Early *Arya* in South Asia

I am Darius the Great King, King of Kings, King of countries containing all kinds of men, King in this great earth far and wide, son of Hystaspes, an Achaemenian, a Persian, son of a Persian, an Aryan, having Aryan lineage.

(Rock inscription at Naqsh-e-Rostam of Darius I, third Achaemenid king, reigned 522–486 BCE)

Darius's empire stretched from the Mediterranean to Sindh, an empire of about fifty million people, the largest the world had then seen. Founded by Cyrus the Great in the sixth century BCE, Darius, the greatest of the Achaemenid kings, secured his throne by ruthlessly slaughtering his rivals and suppressing rebellions. He divided his empire for administrative purposes into seven regions. One of them comprised the eastern borderlands which included Arachosia (Haraxvaiti) and Sindh (Hindu). Though firmly believing his powers derived from Ahura Mazda, Darius patronised the multitude of religious faiths his subjects followed as long as they were submissive and acknowledged his authority.

Darius's proud assertion of his Aryan lineage highlights the fact that the descendants of the Proto-Iranians, within a few centuries of their moving south and west from the BMAC, had employed a powerful militaristic tradition to create a vast empire radiating outwards from the Iranian plateau. By this time, the descendants of the Proto-Indo-Aryans had moved beyond northwest South Asia into the Ganges basin and the Deccan. Like Darius, though having undergone close to a thousand years of admixture, they identified themselves as arya, a term that came to denote a multitude of ethnic groups subscribing to a newly emerging ideology in a geographic region bounded by the Indus and Sarasvati rivers.

The Indo-Iranian Diaspora (Masica 1991)

Linguistic and archaeological evidence appear to converge in determining the chronology of the Indo-Iranian diaspora. Sometime around 2000 BCE, as indicated by the distribution of daughter languages of Vedic, Avestan and Nuristani languages today, a north/south split occurred between Indo-Aryan and Iranian speakers. The southern branch, the Proto-Indo-Aryans, moved south via Central Asia into the BMAC and Iran. The last group became the ancestors of the Mitanni kings whose language indicates a pre-Vedic phase of Indo-Aryan. Around the same time or shortly after c1500 BCE, Proto-Indo-Aryans from Afghanistan and Bactria began moving into northwest South Asia to eventually form the Vedic branch. The northern branch, the Proto-Iranian, moved from Central Asia around the fourteenth century BCE into northeastern Iran and Bactria. Here Zarathustra was born. His religious reforms created a fiery religious movement that converted or extirpated the remaining pockets of Proto-Indo-Aryans who followed the old beliefs. Some of them found refuge in inaccessible valleys of the Hindu Kush and became the ancestors of the Nuristani (Kafiri) tribes, isolated from the Vedic Aryans.

Vedic texts contain little direct reference to these migrations into South Asia. One explanation is that the movements were gradual, undertaken by different clans, and spread over many generations mainly between 1700–1200 BCE with some early incursions dating from c2000 BCE.

Archaeological Evidence for the Earliest Indo-Aryans in South Asia (Allchin 1996; Parpola 1988)

Excavated graves at Mehrgarh show that Indo-Aryan-speaking clans began moving into South Asia via Baluchistan from c2000 BCE. Interred goods and burial modes totally different from earlier local traditions attest to this. Dated to c2000–1900 BCE, they are practically identical to those in northeastern Iran, southern Turkmenistan and Afghanistan, a region which shared a fairly uniform culture at the end of the third millennium BCE. This culture had evolved locally with a strong Proto-Elamite influence and with some contact with the Harappan region. It was characterised by monumental architecture, distinctive small ritualistic stone columns, long stone sceptres, seal-amulets with distinctive shapes and iconographic motifs, luxury artefacts, pear-shaped terracotta goddess figurines and cenotaph-marked flexed (legs flexed at angles as opposed to supine) burials containing weapons. Horse and chariot remains indicate it was controlled by semi-nomadic military elite groups.

At Pirak, near Mehrgarh, distinctive terracotta figurines of two-humped camels and horse-riders testify to the arrival of the horse and the Bactrian camel in northwest South Asia c1800 BCE. This is the earliest evidence for the use of the horse in South Asia. The horsemen have curiously beaked heads, similar to representations of an Iranian eagle-headed deity who fights snakes. The camel figurines are also new, but have close parallels in Margiana.

With the central Indus and Gaggar-Hakra basins being largely deserted, Sindh would have been the most feasible route of dispersal of these immigrants into India. It is possible they had a disruptive, if minor, role in the ongoing disintegration of Harappan political and cultural unity. There is evidence of their presence and assimilation into the local cultures of southern Rajasthan and the Deccan. The Banas-Ahar culture (c1800 BCE) in Rajasthan and the Malwa Culture (c1700–1400 BCE) to its immediate southeast have produced ceramics and copper objects resembling those of the Bronze Age culture of Greater Iran. The Malwa culture evolved into the Jorwe culture (c1400–1100 BCE) which spread into what is now Maharashtra where, at Daimabad, a cylinder seal with a horse motif was found. At the same time in the upper Ganges valley, along with objects clearly of Harappan ancestry, the appearance of swords and dirks identical to those found in north Afghanistan point to the presence of new arrivals, a warring people.

Nuristani (Deneger 2002; Hock 2016: 14)

A small population inhabiting the relatively isolated mountainous region northeast of Kabul in Afghanistan today speaks what may be a third branch of Indo-Iranian, Nuristani.

A few mountain ranges separate the Nuristani homeland from the Swat Valley in Pakistan. The snows that whiten their peaks feed rivers that flow through the deep valleys and form highways for pastoral nomads moving eastwards from the BMAC. One such is the Kabul River mentioned in the Rgveda. Its source lies not far from that of the Helmand.

Nuristani (Kafiri) languages consist of several dialects. Located at the border of Iranian and Indo-Aryan speakers, it shares more features with Indo-Aryan than Iranian, which suggests it descended from Proto-Indo-Aryan but came under the later influence of the Iranian family.

Proto-Indo-Aryan and pre-conversion Nuristani society had many common features. Status, for instance, depended on the ownership of property and the number of warriors clans could muster. Ranks and privileges came from success in warfare and giving feasts. Nuristani society was composed of three classes: priests, a ruling class of cattle-owning warriors and socially segregated artisan-slaves who could not own land.

The term for god, *de*, derives from Vedic *deva*, and for sky from *devaloka*. Gods included Yamra (yamaraja), Indr (Indra) and Mon (Mahadeva), and demons, *yos* (*yaksa*) and *dani* (*dakni*). These concepts suggest that Proto-Nuristani and Proto-Indo-Aryan peoples migrated together from BMAC but the former remained behind long enough to come in contact with the later Proto-Iranian Yaz culture.

Vedic Aryans (Pusalkar 1951: 254–66)

South Asia's earliest literature, a legacy of the Vedic arya, contains tantalising bits of information from which some of the history of those times can be reconstructed. A striking revelation is the total lack of any mention of Harappan cities. Rather, they speak only of their long-neglected ruins. The decline of Harappan cities intensified from 1900 BCE and took a few centuries for total abandonment and desertification. This adds credibility to the view that the Rgveda was composed some centuries after the decline, perhaps c1500 BCE, a view which finds support from the Mitanni treaties suggesting the presence of Indo-Aryans in the area south of the BMAC a little before that time. Considered together, they provide a plausible date for the movement of Vedic tribes into northwest South Asia.

The most well-known of Rgvedic tribes were the Bharatas, led by their legendary king, Sudas, the son of Divodasa, leader of the Trtsu clan. Divodasa had a reputation for being a warrior king who fought other tribes, the Purus, Yadus and Turvasas, as well as the dasa king Sambara and the Panis. The Bharatas were settled between the Sarasvati and the Yamuna and were closely allied with the Trtsus. Together they performed sacrifices on the land watered by the Sarasvati, Drishadvati and Apaya, later to be known as Kurukshetra. By this time, the Bharatas and Trtsus had coalesced with their neighbours and one-time rival the Purus to form the mega-tribe, the Kurus. The Kurus were often mentioned together with their neighbours the Panchalas as the Kuru-Panchalas.

We meet other Rgvedic tribes as participants in the Dasarajna (Battle of the Ten Kings) in which the Bharatas and the Trtsus, supported by the Purus and probably the Srinjayas, defeated a tribal confederacy that included the Yadus, Turvasas, Anus, Druhyus, Simyus, Bhrgus, Matsyas, Alinas, Paktas, Bhalanases, Sivas and Vishanins. The battle was fought on the west bank of the Ravi which implies that the tribal confederacy occupied different regions of western Punjab, Sindh and the frontier regions of the northwest.

In another battle on the Yamuna, Sudas defeated three non-arya tribes, the Ajas, Sighras and Yaksus. The arya were in perpetual conflict with the non-arya. Among them were the Panis, cattle-owning merchants, described as selfish, greedy and of cruel speech. They did not sacrifice to or worship arya gods or reward priests. Rgvedic poets did not have much regard for them. The dasas were enemies, wealthy, who lived in fortified settlements. They consisted of many tribes (Kirata, Kikata, Chandala, Parnaka, Simyu) and many kings (Chumuri, Sambara, Pipru, Varchin, Ilibisa, Dhuni, Pramaganda). The dasyus were mostly mentioned with the prefix '*a*' (non). They were rite-less (*a-karman*), indifferent to the gods (*a-devauu*), without devotion (*a-brahman*), non-sacrificers (*a-yajvan*) and lawless (*a-vrata*).

The Dasarajna (Battle of the Ten Kings)

The Dasarajna took place when Sudas crossed the Ravi and was confronted by a hostile alliance of arya tribes that outnumbered his forces. The poet Vasistha appears to have witnessed the battle and describes it in RV 7.18. The actual denouement is confusing, clouded by the proximity and panic of a closely-fought contest between former comrades.

As Sudas's priest, Vasishta mediates with Indra, praises him and makes him an ally; he sends his 'sacred formulations' to steel him for the coming battle. The hostile alliance's strategy of diverting the river backfires and results in the drowning of many of their warriors including the priest of the Turvasas. Vasishta induces Indra to make fords in the floods to give Sudas an easy crossing. Indra descends on the confused ranks of the alliance, 'cows without a cowherd', with all the energy of a newly-created flood. The cow-seeking Anu and Druhyu are slaughtered. Indra uses his vajra to smash seven fortified enemy strongholds. Another hymn, RV 1.63.7, credits the Purus with being instrumental in the destruction and capture of the seven fortifications during this battle in which Indra 'twisted them (the enemy) like ritual grass for Sudas'. The spoils of war were plentiful. Sudas lavished rewards on Vasishta who joyously claims to have outwitted the Purus 'of scornful speech' when the spoils were being distributed.

It has been suggested that the seven fortifications were located in the city of Harappa, east of the Ravi (Stuhrmann 2016). Harappa's ruins survive on a series of mounds numbered from A to F. Between 1800–1500 BCE, Harappa's extent had been reduced to eight ha from a peak of 150 ha. Cemetery H and the ossuary (Area G) dating to the post-urban period (1900–1300 BCE) have preserved bones of men, women, children and animals buried unceremoniously. Many of the dead had suffered fractures. Some of these fractures had healed. These individuals were victims of violence, some of blunt force trauma inflicted by club-like instruments. The opinion of researchers is that these injuries were a reflection of the increasing lawlessness of the post-urban period when the city experienced migrations and economic collapse together with an absence of administrative control (Schug 2012). Could they also have something to do with the Dasarajna?

Vasishta concludes the hymn with unrestrained adulation of Indra and commends Sudas to the protection of the Maruts, '... you superior men, you Maruts'. Sudas's victory brought the

Bharatas to pre-eminence among the arya tribes of the Punjab as the push to the east intensified, a move that now required the crossing of eastern tributaries of the Indus.

The rivers of the Punjab constituted a formidable natural obstacle in the eastward migration of the arya. RV 3.53.9 credits the sage Visvamitra with facilitating Sudas's crossing of the flooded river before their parting of ways. Another haunting hymn, RV 3.33, presents us with a picture of the daunting nature of such crossings. The scene takes us to the confluence of the Vipas (Beas) and Sutudri (Sutlej) Rivers on the western banks of which the Bharata clans had been stopped by the rivers in flood. Visvamitra steps forward, a puny figure before the raging waters, to cajole and plead with them to calm their turbulent flow and allow them a smooth crossing. He begins by showering them with accolades, comparing them to 'two mares unloosed, resplendent, licking each other' eagerly racing 'clashing together, swelling with your waves' in a mad, exuberant rush from the mountains to the sea. A dialogue between him and the rivers ensues in which he pleads with them to stop awhile and allow the cattle-seeking Bharatas cross over. The rivers reply that Indra had created their channels with his mace, smashing away all obstacles, and ask the bard to sing well of them in his hymns. Visvamitra responds: 'Listen well to the bard, sisters. He has driven to you from afar with his wagon and chariot. Bow down; become easy to cross, staying below his axle(s) with your currents...' The rivers oblige, one bowing down like a young woman swollen with milk to her infant, the other bending like a maiden to her knight. The Bharatas cross over and the rivers swell once more and resume their wild journey.

Indra and the Vajra

The Rgveda eulogises the vajra, Indra's weapon. In verse RV 8, he, 'the best soma-drinker', is offered soma and praise and urged to use his vajra to destroy the enemy completely and seize their wealth. The Rgveda describes the vajra as a four-edged object with a cow-hide strap, honed to a glistening, piercing sharpness (RV 4.22.2, 1.121.9, 1.55.1). It must, therefore, have been made of metal, probably copper or bronze. Indra rides into battle on a golden horse with his weapon, the golden mace, in his arms (RV 3.44.4). In battle, the weapon was believed to be rotated and hurled at the enemy so that it smashed his body and fractured and splintered his bones.

Just such a weapon has been recovered from an EBA kurgan in the middle Volga steppes (Kuznetsov 2005). Dated between 3000–2900 BCE, it contained the skeleton of a 176 cm tall sturdily-built male, thirty-five to forty years old with long forearms, wide shoulders, and well-developed muscles. Resting on the crook of the left arm was a large copper object 48.7 cm long weighing 750 gms. The rectangular handle, 12.6 cm long, had polished edges and was once covered by an organic material, probably a leather strap. The diamond-shaped blade broadened towards the end, and had blunt edges at sharp angles. It appears the object was cast in one piece and the handle forged. This object may have been a ritual symbol of sacred power or a weapon that was used to shatter a target. Its discovery has been interpreted as evidence that the roots of the Indo-Iranian people go back to the north Eurasian steppe.

When Indra wielded his vajra, his faithful followers, the warrior Maruts, were close behind.

The Maruts and the Vratyas (Heesterman 1962: RV 1.64, 1.85–88, 3.47; White 1991; Witzel 1995)

The Proto-Indo-European term for 'war-god' *mawort* has been argued to be the source word for the names of both the Roman war-god Mars and Rgvedic storm-gods, the Maruts (Mallory 2007).

The Maruts receive fullsome praise and adulation in the Rgveda. It depicts them as a youthful, playful, irrepressible and boisterous band of youngsters riding dappled horses with mastery. The poets strive to do justice to the prowess of these powerful, lordly, unblemished and consummate warriors of frightful form. They are like buffalos, masters of artifice, and wild elephants chewing up the forest, like roaring lions, and beautiful spotted deer. These unruly battlers are armed with arrows and glinting spears. They pound the earth and its mountains with foot and chariots fitted with lightning bolts as they accompany Indra to the soma-pressing rite. Fired by soma, the Maruts reach a peak of exhilaration and join forces with Indra, falling like a thunderstorm on the enemy like flash floods created by storm clouds, blazing fires and whirlwinds.

Sons of Rudra, they project power and strength and are the best protectors of their patrons on whom they confer wealth, fame and a thriving peaceful life. Rudra, their father, has a dual nature. He is quick to anger; he shoots his arrows at those who enrage him. He also provides healing remedies and bestows good luck. The poets are wary of turbulent Rudra:

> Let us not anger you, Rudra, through our acts of reverence, nor through poor praise, nor through an invocation shared (with other gods), o bull ... Surely there exists nothing more powerful than you, Rudra, sitting upon the high seat, the mighty one, pouncing like a terrifying wild beast. Being praised, have mercy on the singer, Rudra (RV 2.33).

Indra and Rudra are associated with canine imagery and groups of wandering ascetics. During a famine that lasted twelve years, Indra in his alias as the beggar Sunahsakha (friend of dogs) encounters the Seven Rishis. Regarded as the patriarchs of the Vedic religion, they have been variously named as Kashyapa, Atri, Vasishta, Visvamitra, Gautama, Jamadagni, Bharadvaja, Agastya, Shandilya, Bhrigu and Gungu. Sunahsakha, fat, well-fed, and accompanied by a dog, joins them. They reach a lake haunted by an ogress, Yatudhani, who does not allow them to harvest lotus for food until they explain the meaning of their names. Sunahsakha refuses and kills the ogress with his 'triple stick'. He then reveals that he is Indra come to earth to destroy Yatudhani and sends the Seven Rishis to the skies where they become the seven stars of the Great Bear (Ursa Major).

This tale illustrates Indra's role in performing a function attributed to the Maruts, that of a forest-based non-brahman sacrificer. When all else have been weakened by famine, he remains the only well-fed creature, a result of his sacrifices. By sending the Seven Rishis to heaven, he does what the Vratyas do for nature with their mid-winter *sattras* (sacrificial forest rituals). They set nature, wilting in the grip of cold and darkness, into a journey of revival that ends in the bright firmament.

Rudra leads the Vratyas. His name is derived from the root *rud* meaning to cry, howl (Sanskrit: *rudrah* – the howler, roarer; Latin: *rudere* – to roar, bellow; Lithuanian: *rauda* – wail, lamentation; Old English: *reotan* – to wail, lament). One can imagine the inspiration for such a name in the context of canine imagery associated with Rudra: the long howl of a lone wolf in the remote fastness of a darkened forest bordering the steppe answered by his faithful pack. Their wailing howls echo across the barren wastes, the shadows gather and the fears199 c and anxiety of those who hear grow. So it is with Rudra, a god feared even by other gods, a god who haunts graveyards and wears skulls, a god kept at a distance. It was Rudra who shot his arrow at the Father mating with his virgin daughter in the act of primordial creation. Immersed in his lust, the Father did not notice the approaching hunter until the arrow had left the bow and found its mark. Reacting in alarm and surprise, he spilt his seed, the seed of Creation, upon the earth (RV 10.61).

This Rudra is father to the Maruts who appear in human form as the Vratyas, archaic Vedic sacrificers who lived as a troop like the Maruts. Sons of Kuru-brahmans in the Vedic homeland, Kurukshetra, Vratyas set out on an expedition of conquest (*digvijaya*) in the easterly direction during the cold season. They returned at the end of the hot season before the rains with seized barley, having meanwhile fed themselves and their animals during their long journey on crops raised in the lands they had raided. Referred to as dogs, their organisation had close parallels to that of the mannerbunde associations of Eurasia. They wore their hair long and grew long nails. During the darkest and leanest part of the year in winter they performed their rites secretly in the forest. Called sattras as opposed to brahmanic yajnas, these sacrifices involved bovine, or even human, victims, and were thereby considered violent. Sattras were held over twelve days just like other Indo-European rituals (the Roman Lupercalia and the twelve nights of Christmas) during which the wild hunter Wode-Wodin roared through the forests of northern Europe. The wild hunter of the Vedic forest was Rudra, the 'howler'.

Vratyas kept the sacrificial present (*dakshina*) for themselves and were therefore competitors to brahmans. As society gradually turned away from blood sacrifices, Vratyas and their secret forest sacrifices were degraded, with sattras being portrayed as violent sacrifices and tantamount to eating human flesh (Baudhayana SS. 18.26, vol. 3). Brahmans gradually replaced them as sacrificial specialists.

The *Chandogya Upanishad* contains a passage which may be interpreted as a Vratya counter attack against brahmans who mindlessly mouth mantras in return for rewards. A group of hungry dogs confronts a priest Baka Dalbhya (a sage who murmurs and hums) with a plea: 'Sir, sing and get us food, we are hungry.' The priest does not respond. The dogs return the following day, walking in single file, each dog holding in its mouth the tail of the one in front in imitation of a group of priests. They sit before Baka Dalbhya and chant 'Om, let us eat! Om, let us drink! Om, may the divine Varuna, Prajapati, and Savitri bring us food! O Lord of food, bring hither food, bring it! Om' (*Chandogya Upanishad* 1.12.1–5).

Visvamitra is also linked to the mythology of the dog. The *Mahabharata* relates how during a twelve-year drought, sages and seers forsook their studies and hermitages in search of food. Wandering homeless and hungry, Visvamitra came to a village of dog-eating Candalas (outcasts). Overcome by hunger, he cooked and ate meat from the hindquarters of a dog that had been killed for food by a Candala despite the latter's urging that such food was taboo for a brahman. Visvamitra justified his decision by saying one must use one's intellect to seek solutions in extreme cases even if they go against the cosmic order. In this case, the dog's flesh, food of the reviled Candala, was necessary to keep him, a brahman, alive so as to preserve the sacred texts and prevent the earth from being dasyu-fied. Indra applauded Visvamitra, and as a reward drenched the parched earth with rain. So ended the crisis the drought had created.

Visvamitra was not born into the status of rishi but attained it. He quarrelled constantly with his rival, Vasistha, a highly orthodox rishi. Visvamitra was a kshatriya who, being worsted by Vasistha in a forest encounter, realised that his warrior powers were unequal to the spiritual powers employed by a brahman. Through intense penance and sacrifice he attained brahmanical powers but his status always remained somewhere in between. It was the same with the Vratyas who fought like kshatriyas and sacrificed like brahmans. Eventually, the Vratyas became marginalised; their sattras and canine symbolisms gave way to brahmanical yajnas and the sacred cow.

The First *Aryavarta*

As Sudas's purohit, Visvamitra confidently predicted Sudas would smash all obstacles to 'sacrifice on the best part of the earth' (RV 3.53.11), a process that would naturally deprive the earlier inhabitants like the Kikatas of these places (RV 3.53.14). With his mantras, Visvamitra drew Indra and other gods into an alliance to ensure Sudas's resolve and the journey would not be hampered:

> Let the two oxen be steadfast, the axle firm; let the chariot-pole not be torn off, nor the yoke be broken off ... You with indestructible wheel-rims, escort us. Put power in our bodies, power in our draft-oxen, Indra ... for you are the giver of power. ... Don't make us leave off from this journey (RV 3.53.19).

Sudas's journey brought the Bharatas to the sacred land between the Sarsuti and Chautang rivers where even the gods performed sacrifices. Here, they paused and consolidated. This, the first *aryavarta* (land of aryas) was named Kurukshetra (the land of the Kuru) after the Kuru mega clan. It is here that the Mahabharata battle took place.

The Kuru emerged in the post-Rgvedic period through a process of unification of various smaller clans. They used a number of strategies to maintain their new status (Witzel 1995). Power was centralised and emphasised by elaborate rituals which underlined the enhanced status of kings and strengthened their position. The traditional collection and distribution of booty from external lands was supplemented by the collection of taxes (one-sixteenth as per Atharvaveda 3.29.1), and used by the king to provide infrastructure and protection for his people and thereby project his benevolence. Tax revenue was also used to bolster the centralised power structure and pay officials employed to do this.

As the land between the rivers was settled, production increased by the benevolence of Agni Vaisvanara who 'sweetened the country as to make it suitable for agriculture'. Increasing production of goods led to craft specialisation and stratification of society into four main divisions dominated and exploited by the brahman-kshatriya alliance. Kings used a variety of strategies to dominate this alliance.

Rituals became more diversified, elaborate and complex effectively sub-dividing brahmans according to their area of sub-specialisation. Major poetic and ritual texts were collected to showcase the king's care for traditional lore and knowledge, and while seemingly preserving the old, minute changes were often made so as to serve the new ruler's goals. Kurukshetra was projected as the sacred land where the gods sacrificed in order to overcome their perpetual foes, the asuras. Through it flowed the sacred Sarasvati, the heavenly river, the personification on earth of the goddess Sarasvati, from the centre of heaven and earth to the sea.

The formation of the Kuru state brought about important changes in ideology, religion and mythology that formed the foundation for further expansion.

Beyond Kurukshetra

The stratification of Kuru society into distinct castes not only provided each member of society with a clear and fixed identity but also allowed society to eliminate much of intra-tribal and inter-tribal strife, such as constant cattle rustling, and to turn its activities outwards. Military expansion quickly established the Kuru as the only major force in eastern Punjab, Haryana and west Uttar Pradesh. Vedic texts describe this expansion in two directions: the territories of the lesser advanced chalcolithic cultures of the Ganges basin to the east and the Banas/Malwa cultures to the south.

To the east, the Kurus cemented ties with the Panchala by intermarriages between royal families. Polygamy multiplied and extended such ties to powerful subgroups. The *Satapatha Brahmana* (1.4.1.10) relates the migration of Videgha Mathava and his *purohit* (priest) Gotama Rahugana from the banks of the Sarasvati deep into eastern territories with Agni Vaisvanara, the ritual fire, in the vanguard. The marshy eastern country was converted to arable land suitable for brahman settlement. It was not just physical colonisation, but cultural and ritual as well, a process of 'Sanskritisation' which quickly expanded all over northern India, and subsequently across the Vindhyas to south India and later overseas to Southeast Asia.

In time, the Kurus disappeared from the stage. A passage in the *Sathapata Brahmana* (14.6.3) asks what has become of the Pariksitas, the Kuru royal family, and receives the reply, 'they have, in truth, gone whither the offerers of horse sacrifice go.'

The Eastward Progression as Portrayed by Vedic Sacrificial Rituals (Woodard 2006: 67–70, 243, 4.3.1, 48)

The eastward migration is symbolically re-enacted in the Vedic sacrificial rite (Woodard 2006: 82, 143, 66–70, 146–47). Vedic ritual revolves around sacrifice to the gods in return for favours. One of the most impressive is the soma pressing ritual. A central feature of this rite is the crafting of the yupa post, the antecedent of the *shivalinga*, and its installation. The sacrificial victim is tied to this post which marks the eastern boundary of the great sacrificial space called the *mahavedi* (great altar), the border between the ordered realm of the sacrificial cult and the disordered and menacing domain of the wilderness inhabited by rakshasas beyond. Connecting the divine and earthly worlds, the yupa, associated with Indra, is identified as an eight-edged weapon.

The rite invokes Agni's assistance to protect the sacrificial space and destroy the demonic rakshasas. Situated at the highest spot on earth, it links the world of humans with that of the gods. While the yupa is associated with Indra whose weapon is the vajra, the thunderbolt, it also belongs to Vishnu. The yupa is fashioned from the trunk of a tree felled in a forest after its anointing with ghee to the recitation of prayers. A smaller sacred space, the *devayajana*, is laid out to the west of the mahavedi. The soma sacrifice begins here. Its basic form is called the *agnistoma*. Three canonical fires play a vital role in this *srauta* (public) Vedic ritual. The *garhapatya* (the round fire of the master of the house) and the *ahavaniya* (the quadrangular fire of offering) lie along an east-west axis, and to the south of this axis is the guardian fire, the *daksinagni*. These three fires lie within the devayajana. A fourth fire is positioned on that same east-west axis in the mahavedi at its eastern boundary adjacent to the yupa.

As the ceremony progresses, fire from the ahavaniya is moved eastwards to the mahavedi in the rite called the *agnipranayana* (the carrying forth of fire). It is accompanied by the movement of two soma carts from the devayajana to the mahavedi after the sacrificer's wife anoints the lynchpins of two carts, only on their eastern side. Here the final rites are performed with fire and soma. As the carts are drawn ceremoniously to the mahavedi, the *Taittiriya Samhita 1.3.4.c* is recited:

> May Agni here make room for us;
> May he go before us cleaving the foe;
> Joyously may he conquer our foes;
> May he win spoils in the contest for spoils.

The war chariot has a special place in the migratory history of Indo-Iranian speakers. Along with the horse, it spearheaded their southward expansion from the southern Urals where the earliest evidence of chariots has been found (in Sintashta burials). The movement of the soma carts, fire, soma, cultic implements, priests and the sacrificer from the smaller devayajana to the much-enlarged mahavedi 'was clearly presented as a journey, or more precisely, a migratory conquest ... The priestly procession into the great sacred space is an invasion, divinely led and bent on acquisition of space and spoils' (Woodard 2006: 147). The direction of progress was the east, the region that belonged to the gods according to the *Sathapata Brahmana*. Offerings to the gods, therefore, were made while facing east. The east was Agni's region and under his protection. The east was also the direction of the arya advance into Gangetic basin, the north Indian heartland.

The soma pressings, held in the mahavedi, were conducted in the morning, at midday and in the evening. Agni was invoked in the morning when two goats were sacrificed. A ram was sacrificed during the midday pressing which was dedicated to Indra and the Maruts. A chariot race was then held. The evening pressing was accompanied by the sacrifice and offering of a sterile cow to Mithra and Varuna and the offering of the cow's embryo to the Maruts.

Eleven posts were erected beyond the eastern boundary of the sacrificial space for these animal sacrifices. A twelfth, rough-cut, was left lying on the ground. These posts represented Indra's weapon, the thunderbolt, by means of which the sacrifice took possession of the earth. The brahmans, afraid of being disturbed by asuras and rakshasas while performing the sacrifice, placated and threatened them. The blood, stomach and excrement of the victim were thrown into a pit beyond the great sacrificial space, as an inducement for the rakshasas to stay away. A blade of grass dipped in the animal's blood on both ends was thrown down with the mantra, 'Repelled is the rakshas!', 'Scorched is the rakshas!', 'Scorched are the enemies!' (*Satapatha Brahmana* 1, 1, 2, 15; 1, 4, 4, 8; 1, 1, 2, 8). This was believed to drive them away and confine them in the darkness of the underworld.

The priests received gifts (*dakshinas*) for the sacrifice. Some texts specify a fee of 100 cattle for the soma sacrifice. RV 8.46.32 tells us that a local chief of dasa origin who had joined the arya fold, gifted 100 camels as dakshina. The gifts given to the priests were truly impressive and the sacrificial meat fed many people. These public displays of wealth and command of divine fire by clan leaders and other individuals established them as patrons worthy of serving and allying with.

Like the soma agnistoma, the Vedic *yattsatra* dedicated to the goddess Sarasvati was another ritual demonstrative of progressive eastward expansion of the mahavedi along the course of the Sarasvati River. It began in the desert where the river disappeared and continued to its source, a journey of forty days on horseback. Sattras had various objectives like obtaining wealth, cattle offspring or a prosperous marriage. A herd of 100 cattle and one bull was taken on the journey, a reflection of transhumant nomadic activities. It may also be thought of the sacrificer's journey to the heavenly world with the river being the pathway to the gods (*Panchavimsha Brahmana* 25.10.16–17).

The Shifting Aryavarta

The Vendidad (1200 BCE) cites the Hepta Hindu, the northern Indus basin, as the only land occupied by the arya in South Asia. Vedic literature projects Kurukshetra, at its eastern frontier, as a sacred land where arya society re-grouped and created a powerful identity before expanding further east and south. By the time Baudhayana compiled his *Dharmasutra* (600–300 BCE), the aryavarta had shifted well to the east of the Sarsuti, to the Yamuna-Ganga doab (Kane Vol. 2-1). The neighbouring lands were considered impure and persons who travelled there were required to perform purification rites. Some of these lands can be identified: Avanti (Malwa), Anga (Bengal), Magadha (Bihar), Saurashtra, Deccan, Sindh and the Sauviras (southwest Punjab?), Aratta (Punjab), Vanga (Bengal) and Kalinga (Odisha).

Composed some centuries later, the *Manusmriti* (c200 BCE–200 CE) gives the name Brahmavarta to the land between the Sarsuti and Chautang, adding its customs were those of virtuous men. Manu's aryavarta had expanded greatly. It lay between the Himalayas and the Vindhyas, and extended 'as far as the eastern and the western oceans'. It was here that the 'twice-born' (brahman, kshatriya, vaishya), Manu advised, should strive to live.

By 600 BCE, sixteen greater political divisions or *mahajanapadas* had emerged in this territory: Kamboja, Gandhara, Kuru, Panchala, Surasena, Matsya, Avanti, Chedi, Kosala, Malla, Kashi, Videha, Anga, Magadha, Vatsa, Assaka. These political entities spread from Afghanistan in the west to Bihar and Bengal in the east, and from Nepal in the north to Central India in the south. By this time, the great admixture of populations, mixing and churning of political, religious and other cultural concepts, and of languages of hunter-gatherer, Harappan and steppe nomadic peoples that had been going on for the past 1,000 years had begun to express themselves in distinctive traits. While the core regions of the aryavarta coalesced into a rigidly stratified society, from the eastern edge of this political formation new and powerful religious forces, Buddhist, Jaina and Ajivika, began to question and challenge the brahman-kshatryia dominance.

It was in this new aryavarta that South Asia's second urban culture took root and flourished, then spread to other areas.

20

Fashioning a New Order

About 4,000–3,500 years after the expansion of populations from the Pontic-Caspian steppes had carried elements of the Yamnaya pastoralist gene pool, language and culture in opposite directions to the Atlantic shoreline and South Asia, the descendants of these two branches were to confront each other in South Asia. Both branches have played prominent roles in South Asian affairs, influencing its languages, cultures, religious practices, institutions and, in the case of the Indo-Aryans, its gene pool. There are parallels in the processes by which it happened, and reasons why one became an integral part of the land and the other did not. The latter being more recent and better documented and understood provides insights on the former which occurred sufficiently long ago to obscure the process within the mists of time. Until now a literary resource and mythology largely created by dominant elements associated with this group has been our main window, albeit a narrow one, into how its cultural traits came to such pre-eminent status in South Asian society. A comparison of the processes by which the latter encounter was able to make such a deep impression on Indian society in such a short time may provide insights on how the earlier one happened.

The Arrival of the British (National Archives, UK Government)

The attraction of a richly fabulous land in the east survived in Europe from the time of Alexander and the Romans. At the beginning of European colonial expansion, India became the guiding star of merchant ships that left European ports with the objective of returning laden with enormous wealth. The first to arrive were the Portuguese. While they had little territorial impact, being confined to tiny coastal pockets, primarily Goa, they influenced India in many other ways. Through the sixteenth century Portuguese warships ruled the Indian Ocean; ships of other nations were forced to pay a fee (*cartaze*) or face seizure. A pidgin Portuguese became a sort of lingua franca in India's port cities among the trading class. Local rulers hired Portuguese mercenaries, specialists in new martial technologies like the use of artillery. A little-acknowledged result of this encounter was the adoption and cultivation of a number of new crops brought by Portuguese sailors from South America, Africa and the Pacific Ocean periphery. Without these crops (potato, tomato, chilli, cashew, okra, breadfruit) India's agricultural economy, and population statistics, would look very different today. A far lesser impact was made by the Portuguese religion, Catholicism, which remained largely restricted to small coastal populations.

The most significant encounter came with a later arrival from a small island nation separated from India by thousands of kilometres of ocean and many sailing months. For roughly 200 years from the time (1765) when the Mughal Emperor conferred the *diwani* (office of the revenue collector) for Bengal, Bihar and Odisha on the East India Company, South Asia was progressively brought under direct or indirect British control.

Thomas Roe landed at Surat in 1601 seeking an appointment with the greatest sovereign of those times, the Mughal Emperor Jehangir. He had brought a letter from Queen Elizabeth I seeking trade concessions on behalf of the East India Company. He had to wait over two months travelling from Surat to the court at Agra before he was given an audience. It led to little benefit in the early decades. Within 200 years, however, the East India Company defeated one of the most powerful states in India at that time, Tipu Sultan's *sultanat-i-khudadad*, and captured its capital Srirangapatna in south India's heartland. By then it had wrenched administrative control of a large territory in eastern India, Bengal, Bihar and Odisha, had established firm footholds in Bombay and Madras and made alliances, mainly in its favour, with a number of Indian states. Tipu's defeat led to a rapid expansion of this territory. By 1857, the Company was in effective control of a large part of India through direct governance or alliances with local rulers at whose court the English Resident kept close watch and furthered the Company's interests. That year a major section of the army and a number of local rulers revolted. Not long after it was put down the following year, India came under the direct rule of the British sovereign, and became the 'brightest jewel in the British Crown'. The fabulous Kohinoor diamond adorned that crown.

The British sovereign's rule lasted for ninety years, till 1947. When the British finally departed, the land divided between India and Pakistan had a population of close to 400 million. The last census compiled by the British administration, in 1941, came up with a figure of 389 million spread over 2.5 million sq. kms (Census of India 1941, Vol 1. 1943). The 1861 census counted 125,945 Britons in India, of whom 41,862 were civilians. In 1880, the standing Indian Army consisted of 66,000 British soldiers, 130,000 Indians, and 350,000 soldiers in princely armies. The total number of Britons in India never increased substantially. In 1921, they numbered 165,485 in a total population of 307 million.

How did such a minuscule number govern such a large population inhabiting such a vast, diverse land? The answer, as was demonstrated in districts where one British magistrate effectively dispensed justice over a million people, may aptly be stated as 'more by bluff than by force' (Mason 1985). Britain controlled India with the co-operation of Indian princes and local leaders, as well as huge numbers of Indian troops, police officers, civil servants, the merchant class, the servant class and others. While 584 local princes still ruled in India in 1947, treaties and military and trading alliances tied them to British interests; loyal princes gained much. Added to this, Indian society was so divided that it could not unite against the British. Britain encouraged these divisions. The wealthier classes, educated in English-speaking schools, formed the backbone of administrative institutions effectively joining the British in ruling their poorer fellow Indians. Big landowners, money lenders and the middle classes all gained in terms of jobs, business opportunities and careers. Others earned a living by serving the British and upper classes in various manual capacities for a subsistence.

Britain took pains to portray its rule in a benign light, as one of a civilising exercise that brought good government and economic development in the form of education, railways, irrigation, medicine, etc. to millions of Indians mired in dirt and poverty. In reality, Britian gained enormously from ruling India. India's huge population became a captive market for British industry. In the 1880s, for example, about 20% of Britain's total exports went to India. In return, they imported huge quantities of goods at low prices including a range of cash crops like tea, jute, coffee and cotton, much of which was processed and repackaged for export at great profit. India's grain fed Britain's wartime armies even at the expense of the very farmers who grew it; famines followed. Indian labourers were indentured for the construction of critical infrastructure in other colonies enabling Britain to control and exploit them more efficiently. An estimated 40% of India's wealth was spent on the Indian army, probably Britain's single greatest resource. Used all over the world, it became the backbone of British imperial power.

India became Britain's *kamadhenu*, the mythical sacred cow which grants all wishes and desires.

The Timing

India's political identity was created in 1947 when its diverse regions and peoples were drawn into a unified nation governed by a constitution. Before that it was a conglomeration of political entities confined to a geographical space. It has been so for much of its history. Only brief periods when large extents were drawn into dynastic empires mark that history. The Mughal Empire was one such.

The Indian political order fragmented following the Mughal Emperor Aurangzeb's death in 1707. In the vacuum, regional rulers manoeuvred for territory. The East India Company had three tiny trading enclaves in Madras, Calcutta and Bombay separated from each other by large expanses of territory. They had, however, effective communication between each other and with Britain by sea. While Indian states remained static, land-based, politically isolated entities, Britian's unrestricted mobility across vast ocean tracts enabled it to mobilise and effectively utilise concentrated military force against its opponents with devastating effect. Haider Ali realised this when he confided to his advisers, 'I can ruin their resources by land, but I cannot dry up the sea ...' (Wilks 1817: 373).

The Company employed a small armed force to protect its trading establishments. Largely drawn from local *topasses* (mixed Indian-Portuguese parentage) and martial classes, they were commanded by British officers and disciplined along European military norms with uniforms, drills and muskets to operate in closely-knit formations and unquestioningly follow orders from their immediate commanding officers. The essence was loyalty to the group, not to individual leaders as was the norm in Indian armies. A wounded soldier could be quickly replaced by another without breaking the formation. The uniform ensured their group identity. They proved an effective force superior to that employed by local rulers.

As the East India Company's profits soared, its operations expanded. So did its forces and the costs of maintaining them. It led to an ever-growing, ever-widening cycle in which the Company lent the services of its troops under the guise of 'protection' to local rulers in return for money and further trading concessions. In time, these rulers became lackeys of the Company and the very forces they had hired to guard them were used by the Company to wrest control of their territories. These forces grew into the formidable British Indian army which was employed throughout Britain's colonial empire so effectively.

Something similar can be visualised with Indo-Aryan speakers 3,500–4,000 years ago. Their first encounters were with a region fragmented by de-urbanisation, and with a largely subsistence agricultural economy. These first contacts were made by individual transhumant nomadic clans who almost certainly acted as carriers of goods between the Harappans and the Iranian plateau. The earliest archaeological evidence, apart from a trail of distinctive pottery, of their presence comes from the remains of horses and camels in Pirak, near the Bolan Pass. These animals carried goods in caravans. As Cholistan reverted to desert and the Harappans abandoned their settlements and moved away from the centre, these nomads were drawn further into South Asia, primarily through Sindh towards Gujarat where the lower Indus Harappans had moved. The tempo of migration increased with deteriorating climate pushing Central Asia into severe aridity. The shorter northern routes via the Khyber Pass now took precedence and brought the forebears of Vedic culture. This main thrust encountered a previously highly urbanised population dispersed into smaller, relatively isolated agricultural settlements of the hinterland. Like in the BMAC, there were many interstices in between providing space for nomadic pastoralists. That contacts were still being maintained with Iran is clear from the inclusion of the Punjab, the Hepta Hindu, in the sixteen sacred arya lands of the Vendidad. The horse, the camel and a trading and nomadic pastoral economy brought mobility to the newcomers among static sedentary populations.

The Rgveda suggests this interaction was not without conflict. Many passages eulogise and appease Indra with soma sacrifices and appeal for his help in defeating resident populations and acquiring territory. Indra's storm troopers, the Maruts, were boisterous and eager to race into battle on their chariots under the inspiration of Rudra. The human manifestation of the divine Maruts, the Vratyas, lived on the borders of Indo-Aryan society, though yet an integral part of it. They formed the vanguard of the Indo-Aryan advance, employing tactics suitable to their tempestuous nature. They played the role enacted by the East India Company's troops during the initial inroads into India.

The Changing Nature of the Two Expansions

The initial expansions into new territories were limited, fortified trading establishments in the case of the East India Company and nomadic camps in the case of the Indo-Aryan tribes. Though small, they were characterised by features that differed from those in the local environment and sufficiently impressive to gain clients. A pervading element of bluff and the availability of larger unseen retributive forces that could be called upon by isolated garrisons must have always made disaffected elements wary.

Identified from afar by fluttering flags, British camps stood out from the local scene. Closer, they were conspicuous, aloof and impressive. They exuded the air of a superior power with the strict discipline of a British camp, armed soldiers parading to drums and fifes in distinctive uniforms and close-knit formations, weaponry, individual Englishmen in alien attire moving around on horseback without fear, purchasing power to stock warehouses and ships, and a continual arrival of new soldiers and men. They were patrons who could be served.

As Company interests grew and the territories they controlled expanded, the need arose for expertise required to administer them. Revenue collection, commercial transactions and the administration of justice required a rapidly growing number of clerks, professionals and servants. In return for such service, the British offered, apart from a regular income, the means for locals to aspire and attain these positions which opened pathways to superior status within their own society. In effect, they became part of the British world in various capacities in the running of empire and governing other Indians. It involved the adoption of many things British primarily language and, for the upper echelon, an English education. To varying degrees, it meant the adoption of English values and institutions, though not necessarily Christianity. Without this vast number of Indians in British service, a few thousand Britons could never have governed India. This patron-client relationship eventually expanded right across South Asia.

Something similar occurred with Indo-Aryans. As the numerous Rgvedic invocations to Indra and the Maruts show, armed confrontation played a role in the initial stages of expansion. These were accompanied by elaborate soma sacrifices, very impressive with chariot displays and animal sacrifices. There was plentiful soma to get intoxicated on and plenty of meat to go around. The yatsattras would have been equally eye-catching with herds of lowing cattle being driven across the plains for forty days. They demonstrated wealth and hidden powers to which only the sacrificers had access to.

It must truly have been spectacular. The Rgveda cites one example, that of the dasa Balbutha who rewarded the priest with 100 camels. How many more Balbuthas were there who eventually joined the arya fold? Clearly there were many, for Indo-Aryan society was nomadic in nature which offered permeability and upward status movement. This is clearly brought out in the free population admixture that occurred in this period. Such admixture was aided by intermarriage with local women. A stratified caste system took many centuries to fall in place.

In the case of the arya, eastward expansion meant the adoption of agriculture and a sedentary lifestyle as contacts with Iran diminished and admixture increased. The presence of loanwords from Harappan languages in the Rgveda reveals interaction with local farmers which required accommodation and the toning down of the initial militant encounter. Nomadism gave way to sedentism and the resolution of conflicts by less violent means. Indra and the Maruts, the warrior gods of the Vedic pantheon, gradually gave way to other gods more suitable to new patron-client relationships. As the spread of

Indo-Aryan languages and the genetic paternal Hg R1a reveals, the arya maintained a dominant role.

Admixture

Although the initial British presence in India was overwhelmingly male-dominated with the resultant promiscuity with local women, the numbers were too little and the time too short to create a significant impact in the South Asian paternal genome. In the early years, some Englishmen adopted an unabashedly extravagant and lavish lifestyle imitating an oriental court. David Ochterlony, the British Resident at the court of the Mughal Emperor in Delhi, paraded his thirteen Indian wives daily seated on the back of elephants sauntering around the Red Fort. He had joined the British army in 1777 and arrived in India as a cadet, was appointed the British Resident at Delhi in 1803 for three years and again after a successful military career in 1818.

Soon, however, British society in India came under the increasing influence of Christian missionaries. Strict monogamy was enforced. Later, when British administration spread across India, the maintenance of social distance between ruler and ruled became the norm and mixed marriages became largely something of the past. Instead, annual 'fishing' boats arrived from England with young maidens eager to marry India's new nabobs. Segregation in British institutions like clubs and cantonments and promotions in military and government circles emphasised this separateness. Churches were visible statements of a different god, white, cold, and aloof amidst a colourful, warm, sometimes quarrelsome and diverse Indian pantheon.

The migration of Indo-Aryan speakers into South Asia was similarly male-dominated. It is characterised by the paternal Y-chromosome Hg R1a-Z93. For over a millennium, there was free admixture with local populations which changed to strict endogamy after the establishment of caste stratification. Such admixture is visible in tribal populations. The Chenchu and other tribes living today in isolated jungle pockets of southern and central India carry a high percentage of Hg R1a. It is closely linked with that of Tiwari Brahmans of Uttar Pradesh. The earliest Chenchu Hg R1a dates to 3,000 years ago. Chenchu paternal genes are not found among Brahmans, indicating a one-way transfer. These two populations must once have lived in the same territory and had a patron-client interaction before a parting of ways.

The Maternal Influence in the Spread of Indo-Aryan Languages, Religion and Institutions

Arya society was patriarchal. Males inherited property and remained in the same place to look after it. Their Y-chromosome became localised. Daughters went to their husbands' homes; their mtDNA spread. Here, a woman learned the husband's Indo-Aryan dialect and modified her religious beliefs to accommodate those of the new household. Until strict endogamy set in, some of her old beliefs and mother tongue found a place in her husband's home.

Certain kinship structures arising from Dravidian principles adopted by Indo-Aryan languages reveal that a close relationship once existed between speakers of the two language families. Dravidian structural features, particularly the emergence of retroflex sounds [pronounced with the tip of the tongue curled up towards the hard palate] in OIA, further indicates extensive interaction between the respective speakers, an interaction in which the majority of OIA speakers had Dravidian as their first language, and which they shed after a period of bilingualism. The marriage of Dravidian-speaking women into patriachal arya society fits in perfectly with such evidence.

The South Asian genetic profile reveals that while over 80% of maternal genetic heritage derives from the earliest settlers, roughly 66% of its paternal heritage arrived with the Neolithic, of which Hg R1a constitutes about half. It implies Indo-Aryan-speaking males married local women to a large extent. Possibly most of them were Dravidian speakers. The initial bi-linguism gradually died out with succeeding generations. Another inference is that though there was admixture with hunter-gatherer populations, their women were not absorbed into arya society. They were most likely kept as slaves and bonded labourers for limited time periods during which advantage was taken of them. Eventually they moved away into isolated jungles.

Religion (Carson 2012)

There was a marked difference in the approach to religion by two distant branches, the British and the arya, of the Indo-European family. To both, the religions of South Asia were alien. Britain was a Protestant Christian nation; the arya followed a cult that had evolved in the alien geography and climate of the Eurasian steppe where cattle dominated the economy, not agriculture.

Britain's approach was complicated by a number of factors. The initial contact was made by a merchant company whose primary interest was trade and profit. As the East India Company made ever deeper inroads, it was confronted by the problem of how to deal with societies following diverse faiths in ways different from their own without upsetting the primary commercial object. It required the delicate art of peaceful administration and accommodation.

Initially the British used the word *gentoo* (Portuguese *gentio* – gentile) to describe the bulk of the people who seemed to follow such a profusion of sects and cults. In time they clubbed all these together and began to refer to the 'Hindoo' religion, a term first used by Arab geographers to identify a people who lived to the east of the Indus (Sindhu or Hindu in Persian).

It was a convenient categorisation for the followers of an all-embracing religious system.

Depending on the loyalty of its sepoy army to defend its interests, the Company believed that it would be counter-productive to interfere with Indian religious beliefs and practices and assured Indians they would be allowed freedom of worship. The army also included Roman Catholics, Indian and European, who did not subscribe to the growing view of evangelical forces in Britain who believed that the acquisition of empire carried with it a duty to promote a Protestant version of Christianity.

The issue of how far the Company could go in enforcing military discipline when it came in conflict with sepoy religious beliefs came sharply into focus in 1806 in Vellore where Tipu's family was being held in the fort. In an uprising by the sepoys who guarded the fort, 200 Englishmen were killed. Further disturbances occurred in other southern garrisons. All were put down. It was believed that the sepoys were incited by rumours that they were to be converted to Christianity when new dress regulations for uniforms forbade the use of caste marks and earrings, ordered the trimming of beards and the wearing of a new headdress made with leather. Visibly increasing signs of missionary activity added to these rumours.

The mutiny demonstrated the fragility of British rule and its dependence on the loyalty of the sepoys. The anti-missionary lobby forcefully argued that Indian religious prejudices were easily excited and that the greatest caution was to be exercised when handling them. Under the lobbying of evangelical forces, however, in 1813, Parliament directed the Company to provide for the 'religious and moral improvement' of its Indian subjects. Many Indians now came to believe that the British intended to convert them forcibly. Growing unease eventually led to a violent uprising by sepoys and Indian rulers in 1857/58 which was ruthlessly countered by the Company's troops. Men, women and children were slaughtered on both sides in what was, at least in part, a war in which religious rhetoric found expression in both camps. The uprising brought the East India Company's rule to an end.

Under sovereign rule, Britain's approach towards South Asia's many religions became one of tolerance, not accommodation. Christianity remained superior and aloof, its church spires rising impressively unguarded over open ground, projecting the hidden power of a ruling elite who gathered weekly and on other solemn occasions, arriving on horseback, chariot and motor car, in formal dress to honour and worship their god.

In South Asia, the arya gods of the Eurasian steppe met those who had evolved in totally different cultures. The initial arya approach recognised the differences in the religious practices of the people they encountered. Vedic texts mention phallus worshippers, non-sacrificers, disrupters of Vedic sacrificers who had to be appeased or threatened with reprisals, female sakti deities, spirits and deities of the forest who had to be placated and kept in good humour and many others.

The *Nasadiya Sukta* (Creation Hymn) makes the startling revelation: 'The gods themselves are later than creation' (RV 10.129.6, Basham, A. L. tr.). This concept of a number of gods appearing after the creation of the universe is fundamentally different from that of a Christian God who created the universe and all within it, with Man being created to love, honour and serve the Creator whose existence pervaded everything but was yet an aloof entity. Arya gods were more human, with limited powers and approachable; they could be cajoled with soma and sacrifice; in fact, they depended on the correctly executed sacrificial ritual to perform their functions.

As arya society pushed further into South Asia, they encountered other gods more attuned to meet the requirements of a people subsisting on an agricultural or forest economy. When arya males married local women, these gods accompanied them into arya homes, though perhaps not receiving the same primacy. Reflecting the admixture of populations in South Asia, the gods of the wide-open Eurasian steppes began to be integrated into an array of deities, *kuladeva*s (clan gods), village and forest gods in charge of particular functions, sakti goddesses with particular powers. As nomadic society changed to a sedentary lifestyle, as the initial confrontation changed to accommodation in the home and outside, some of this bewildering array of gods became redundant and receded into the background or metamorphosed while others became more prominent.

Indra was one of those who faded away and with him the Maruts and soma. There are few or no temples dedicated to Indra; temples were rare in nomadic societies. The images we have of Indra were sculpted centuries after his decline from the heights of Rgvedic honour, placed in temples dedicated to other gods. One is found in the temple cave complex of Ellora. Others are preserved in a Danang museum in distant Vietnam (Huynh Thi Duoc 2009). They date from the tenth century CE. They depict a muscular male with a belly leaning to portliness seated on his elephant Airavata.

Was Indra, the smasher of obstacles, replaced by the pot-bellied god Ganesha, the remover of obstacles? Ganesha's *vahana* is the rat, an animal that can penetrate holes and corners. The head of this much-loved god is not human but that of an elephant. He is the son of Shiva, the peaceful manifestation of war-like Rudra, the father of the Maruts. If Indra lived on as Ganesha, the transformation of a war-like soma-drinking god to a docile, obese, *kadabu* [a fried sweet]-loving god, from a smasher to a remover of obstacles, is a stark reflection on the dramatic change in society as the arya integrated himself into the new situation. The head and attire are Indian, the father is Shiva not Rudra, the purpose of the god (the removal of obstacles) remained the same, but the manner of doing so had changed from the use of force to, as Ganesha's giant head suggests, the use of the brain in an environment where brute force had given way to ideology and diplomacy to achieve the same ends.

Rudra, his father, the wild god howling like a wolf, wandering in cemeteries, the only god unafraid to shoot an arrow and disrupt the mating of Prajapathi with his virgin daughter, assumed the peaceful form of the great god Shiva. Unlike the fair-skinned gods of the cold Eurasian steppe, Shiva is dark blue, tanned in the tropics. Together with Brahma and Vishnu, Shiva is one of the three most important gods of the epics and puranas, the texts that follow the Rgveda.

These three gods, the *trimurti*, are said to represent the trifunctional ideology of arya society, which is also characteristic of many branches of Indo-European mythology (Mejia 2009; Bailey 1983: 40). Brahma represents the first function, sovereignty, the sacred and wisdom. Vishnu represents the second function, the dynamic aspect of kingship and martial force. Shiva represents the third function, fecundity and wealth. They came to prominence as Prajapathi, Mitra and Varuna lost theirs. These changing statuses are a reflection of the formation of new groups and identities with loyalties to gods more suitable to their new condition in a time of flux.

In arya society, these three functions defined the duties of the 'twice-born'. The brahman was its channel to the gods, the sacrificer, the advisor to kings and the keeper of the sacred texts. The kshatriyas represented the role of kingship and were the defenders of the realm. The vaishyas were the creators of wealth through agriculture and commerce. In South Asia, a fourth class was added, the shudra, whose function, it was decreed, was to serve the other three. A fifth, the hunter-gatherer nisada, stayed beyond.

Vedic texts make little references to Brahma. Instead, it is Prajapathi who is the creator, the repository of the sacrificial ritual and the keeper of *rta*, the cosmic order. As the first post-Vedic political entities began to emerge, the brahman-kshatriya alliance was cemented, united in their resolve to dominate other castes, but at times caught up in jockeying for the upper hand. Rituals and symbolisms assumed more importance in establishing legitimacy. Vishnu, the warrior god, grew in importance, and so did Brahma.

While the brahman and kshatriya achieved dominant status, they still depended on the wealth-generators – the vaishya. This is where the peaceful side of Shiva-Rudra assumed primacy. While

Rudra's ferocious aspect was passed on to a retinue of *ganas* and *bhutas*, classes of localised divine beings who had to be placated by sacrifice, the need for the generation of wealth brought the role of fertility to the fore. Shiva's association with the *shivalinga*, a symbol of procreation and fertility, became more important. The shivalinga was not new. Harappan society has left evidence of what may possibly be considered as *linga* (phallus) worship. The Rgveda ridicules the worshippers of the linga, but through its association with fertility and agriculture, its worship gained importance. So did Shiva.

Even as these deities were drawn into the pantheon of Indian divine entities, they were assigned positions reflective of the social status of their followers. In Tulunad, Karnataka, for instance, bhutas are honoured and consulted during the *bhutaaradna* which is conducted by a person belonging to their original caste of worshippers, but they remain temple guardians, not permitted entry inside. Vedic texts have few female deities, but the country to which the arya came had very many. These sakti goddesses were powerful and often depicted as fiercely aggressive in the fight against diseases and evil entities. They were progressively drawn into the new pantheon, many as wives of Shiva or Vishnu (Durga, Chamundi, Meenakshi), but like the women of South Asia who were drawn into arya households as wives, assigned subordinate roles.

Time tamed some. Shantadurga, a revered goddess in Goa, is another form of Durga, the warrior goddess who threatens and combats demons endangering the stability of the established order. Durga is associated with blood sacrifice, meat-eating and fertility, and is a violent and powerful defender of her devotees. She is not found in the Vedic tradition. In Goa, she became Shantadurga, peaceful and gentle. Here, she gradually assumed some of the qualities of another goddess from neighbouring Karnataka, Shantala Devi, known in Goa as Santeri. She is associated with the earth and the anthill (*rohn*), a link between the earth and sky. Santeri has close links to four other goddesses, with other powers, who together protect villages. Such groups of five or seven sister sakti goddesses continue to protect villages throughout south India (Newman, 2019: 107).

End Comment

Within a period of about 2,000 years, Indo-European-speaking populations had expanded from the Pontic-Caspian steppe to settle a region that stretched from Ireland to the Central Asian steppe and from Scandinavia to the Indian Ocean shores and the South Asian heartland. In addition to their nomadic heritage and command of horse, wagon and chariot, this society possessed common institutions and a martial character that facilitated a rapid global spread in lands that till then were dominated by isolated farmsteads.

Britain's significant physical presence in South Asia lasted just about 200 years, but its legacy still remains strong in areas such as language and attire, government institutions like parliament and judiciary, education and scientic temper, industry and many other spheres. The arya influence, with a presence of 3,500 years, runs much deeper in genetics, religion, culture and languages.

Mythology has been a critical component of this process. Britain, while making genuine efforts to unravel South Asian history with rigorous scientific temper, also emphasised aspects that suited its rule. Colonial historians created myths about Britain's benign and enlightened rule while ignoring many of its adverse aspects. Bengal's people died in millions due to famine in the early years, as well as during World War II; no history highlighted that. Bengal's wealth flowed down the Hoogly and up the Thames to fuel Britain's Industrial Revolution; no history highlighted that. Wellesley ruthlessly violated principles of statesmanship in instigating the final war on Tipu; no history highlighted that. Britain's colonial historians wrote, like Rawlinson, a flawed one-sided version.

The arya too created such myths. Vedic texts glorify the marauding exploits of the Maruts, not the miseries of the people affected by their actions. The burning of the Khandava forest is portrayed as a monumental achievement, the agony of death and destruction of its denizens is overlooked. The expropriation of the nisada chieftain Pramaganda's wealth is justified and prayed for, the resulting destitution of his people ignored. All this was justified by creating myths of martial, ritual and pre-ordained superiority. We shall investigate an enduring one in the next chapter.

21

A Forgotten History and a Lost River

The Harappan legacy lived on though its history had been lost for close to 4,000 years. Like its history, its cities lay buried and forgotten, cocooned in a vacuum, unseen and unsuspected.

Its history had been lost because it left no texts and its abandoned cities and its artefacts were buried under sand; the vacuum was filled by other narratives. In the early years of British colonial rule, one of these gained in importance and has come to dominate the narrative of South Asia's early history.

When British interests expanded beyond trade, loot and conquest into administering extensive lands inhabited by people with very different cultures, the problem arose of how this was to be done, particularly, what laws were to be framed for the application of justice. They found no standard histories to fall back upon except for those compiled by Indo-Muslim dynasties, many of which were written as court histories in the Islamic traditions as a means of legitimising their rule. The British did not want themselves to be seen as successors to this tradition; they needed to reach beyond, to periods before the earliest Indo-Muslim rulers. There were serious difficulties in this; the pre-Indo-Muslim history of South Asia was shrouded in a darkness whose existence was suggested only by faint, flickering and elusive light.

This dilemma was succinctly expressed in 1803 in the preface to *The History of Hindostan*: 'The Mahommedans know nothing of Hindoo learning ... But whether the Hindoos possess any true history of greater antiquity than other nations, must altogether rest upon the authority of the Brahmans, till we shall become better acquainted with their records' (Dow 1803: iv). The writer continues:

> The aversion of the Indians themselves to disclose the annals of their history, which are interspersed with their religious tenets, to strangers, has ... involved their transactions, in ancient times, in impenetrable darkness. The only light to conduct us, through the obscure oaths of their antiquities, we derive from an historical poem ...

This 'historical' poem, the *Mahabharata*, was also cited as a source by a sixteenth century Muslim chronicler (Dow 1803: 1).

The Aryan Identity

In 1783, William Jones assumed his responsibilities as judge in the Bengal Supreme Court in Calcutta and began the task of formulating an English version of Indian laws. He turned to Sanskrit sources preserved for centuries by brahmans and soon discovered an ancient link between Sanskrit, Greek and Latin. His many translations of ancient Sanskrit texts including the *Manava-Dharmasastra* (*Laws of Manu*) exposed Englishmen to India's vast literary heritage though only through the limited medium of just one language, Sanskrit, the ritual brahamanical language. It was like using Greek and Latin classical literature exclusively to write European history. Yet, until the first ruins of Harappa were discovered a little over a century later, they formed the primary building blocks on which early Indian history was written.

One of the most far-reaching results of this effort was the creation of the 'Aryan' identity that came to define a racial group. This is contrary to early Sanskrit texts which used the term arya to define upper-caste status, not race. It referred to people considered respectable, honourable and faithful who used certain social and linguistic norms defined by the use of Sanskrit, performance of sacrifice-based rituals and occupation. Non-arya spoke a variety of other languages, practised *linga* (phallus) worship and worked in occupations deemed as lowly. RV 1.51.8 calls on Indra to 'Distinguish between the Aryas and those who are Dasyus. Chastising those who follow no commandment, make them subject to the man who provides ritual grass.'

Max Muller first applied the term 'Aryan' to the family of languages (now called Indo-European) and the peoples speaking them. The members of this family were first identified by Jones in 1786 as consisting of Sanskrit, Latin, Greek, Gothic, Celtic and Old Persian. The name 'Aryan', though not given by Jones, seemed most suitable as it was spoken by the arya and also in Iran (land of the Aryas) (Trautmann 1997: 13). *The Zend-Avesta* uses the term *airya* both to mean venerable and as the name of a people who occupied an extensive territory radiating out from the Airyanem vaejah (Aryan seed) (Muller 1885: 277–80).

In 1847, Max Muller proclaimed that the British, 'descendants of the same [Aryan] race, to which the first conquerors and masters of India belonged, (had) return(ed) ... to accomplish the glorious work of civilization, which had been left unfinished by their Arian brethren' (Muller 1847: 349). This task, he suggested, was to be accomplished in collaboration with Indians who were considered inheritors of the Aryan legacy. Caste was to be the main criterion for selecting these Indians with the foremost being Brahmans, 'the spiritual aristocracy'. Muller wrongly believed that the Vedic caste system comprising the 'twice-born' (aryas) and shudras (slaves) formed the true essence of Indian society.

Such pronouncements inspired sections of the upper caste in the last quarter of the nineteenth century to begin to project India as a homogeneous state that traced its legitimacy primarily to a glorious civilisation of Vedic Aryans. In a multilingual land in which Sanskrit had never been popular among the common people, this could not be done on the basis of language. Instead, Hinduism, the term used by the British to denote the religion of those who were not Muslim, Jain, Buddhist, Jew or Christian, was promoted as a common basis for nationhood. This approach fell neatly into a political strategy that attempted to win the support of a perceived Hindu majority which the upper castes could dominate and thereby have greater access to resources of the state and control the socio-economically disadvantaged groups and lower castes (Roy 2016).

Max Muller's writings were used by Indian leaders in various ways for political gain. In South Africa, Gandhi quoted his theory of Aryan brotherhood with the British in his campaign for the rights of Indians. Max Muller's glorification of Aryan/ Hindu spirituality influenced Nehru's *Discovery of India* in which he cites India's history as an ancient and predominantly Hindu civilisation whose spirituality remained unconquered despite multiple invasions and foreign rule. Perhaps Max Muller's greatest influence was on Savarkar, the foremost ideologue of *Hindutva* (politicised Hinduism). Savarkar maintained that Hindus descended from the Aryans, defended the caste system and adopted a harsh approach to the lowest castes and indigenous tribes as people who had not contributed anything to the glories of Hindu civilisation. He depicted Muslims as invaders who oppressed Hindus but portrayed the British colonisers as comparatively benign. Following Muller, Savarkar included in the Hindu civilisation Buddhism, Jainism and Sikhism since they had originated in India and were therefore 'culturally and racially Hindu'. Christianity and Islam were not part of the Hindu/Indian civilisation since they had originated outside India (Roy 2016).

Max Muller's view that the Teutonic Aryan was 'the most vigorous and enterprising of all the members of the Aryan family' had devastating consequences in twentieth-century Germany when Hitler's Nazis adopted it as state policy (Muller 1885: 348). It resulted in the deaths of over twenty million people including six million Jews. Before that, however, his assertion that Indians and Europeans were long-lost cousins, and that Britain was in India on a civilising mission, met with increasingly adverse reaction. Academic circles refuted the view that language could be correlated with race. Politcial groups viewed it as undermining the policy of a governing class keen to emphasise Britain's separateness and superiority (Trautmann 1997: 12, 178–81, 190). In later life, Max Muller distanced himself from the concept that linguistic categories could be equated with ethnological or racial classifications. But his many statements concerning the so-called superiority of 'Aryan' nations provided ample fuel for those who had a purpose in distorting history for furthering their political interests.

Such a scenario had been foreseen as far back as 1875 by Sir Henry Maine who wrote:

> Sanscritic study has been the source of certain indirect effects, not indeed having much pretension to scientific character, but of prodigious practical importance. There is no question of its having produced very serious political consequences ... the new theory of Language has unquestionably produced a new theory of Race ... That peoples not necessarily understanding one another's tongue should be grouped together politically, on the ground of linguistic affinities assumed to prove community of descent, is quite a new idea. Nevertheless, we owe to it, at all events in part, the vast development of German nationality ... (Maine 1875: 10).

The invention of the Aryan race became fundamental to the reconstruction of Indian history for upper-caste nationalists who sought legitimacy and identity from a past perceived as conferring self-esteem and exclusive status. It argued that the colonised were linguistically and racially of the same stock as the colonisers. Brahmans, who played a central role in this reconstruction, used it to re-assert the superiority of the upper castes. Origins and the strident insistence that the Aryan should be indigenous to India therefore became crucial (Thapar 1996: 7–9; n.d.: 39).

These attempts, depending almost solely on literary evidence, floundered when archaeologists uncovered the buried cities of Harappa in the 1920s.

The Case for a Multi-Disciplianry Approach to Writing History

Until recently, historians depended primarily on two types of evidence, archaeological and literary. The attempt to rewrite Indian history giving primacy to an Indian origin for the Aryan depends on the latter type of evidence which, not surprisingly, derives almost exclusively from Vedic sources. Archaeological excavations, however, make it evident that Harappa preceded the Aryan presence in India by millennia. Today we have evidence from many more disciplines that needs to be considered to arrive at a more accurate interpretation of Indian history.

We have sparse knowledge about the history of the hunter-gatherers who inhabited India exclusively until the Neolithic, that is, for the greater part of its early colonisation by humans. They find little place in South Asia's history; their story is largely unknown, unwritten and uncared for. Yet, much of their culture and beliefs survive in modern societies. The origins of religion and dietary preferences, for instance, as archeobotany, stone tool evolution and rock art show, have their roots in the pre-Neolithic era of human existence.

The same was the case with Harappa. Nothing was known about it until about a century ago. Yet, it was never really lost. Yes, the archaeological and material evidence was not visible, but the cultures and traditions, beliefs, agro-pastoral practices, artisan skills, the domesticated crops and animals still nurture Indian civilisation. Like the ancient bricks that were once used to build the finest cities of the ancient world and now form the foundation on which Sindh's railway lines have been laid, these constitute the base on which much of modern Indian culture, even its genetic composition, has been built. There is continuity, but there is also much more to know, a vacuum that needs to be filled.

Nature abhors a vacuum; vacuums are soon filled by surrounding air and whatever it carries. So too history; myth, hypotheses and narratives, some compiled through ignorance, others through motivated agendas, fill blank spaces.

The Lost River

Such is the case with the Lost River. Ancient texts refer to a sacred and mighty river whose life-giving waters were also the waters of wisdom. Its name was associated with a goddess. Sacred texts said to have been composed on its banks have inspired generations and have been woven into the early history of an 'Aryan' South Asia.

That river does not flow today, and the bed that provided a channel for its sacred waters cannot be located. Most of the other rivers referred to by these earliest texts have been identified: Sindhu (Indus), Ganga (Ganga), Yamuna (Yamuna), Sutudri (Sutlej), Parusni (Ravi), Asikni (Chenab), Marudvrdha (Maruwardwan), Vipas (Beas), Vitasta (Jhelum), Suvastu (Swat), Susoma (Sohan/Suwan), Kubha (Kabul), Gomati (Gomal), Krumu (Kurram). Others like Arjikiya, Tristama, Susartu and Mehatnu are believed to be minor tributaries of the Indus (Witzel n.d.). Strangely, it is the river most praised and cited, the Sarasvati, that does not correspond to any current watercourse. It is mentioned as being located between the Yamuna and Sutlej, but it is also described as a tempestuous, snow-fed, mountain-shattering river flowing all the way to the sea. Only the Sarsuti-Ghaggar-Hakra flows in this geographical location, but its puny status in no way fits the glowing description of the ancient texts. There was a vacuum that needed to be filled.

The Periplus of the Erythraean Sea, written c60 CE as a guide for traders sailing to India from Egypt along the coast, writes of the Sinthus (Indus) as marking India's boundary. The river, it wrote, brought down an enormous volume of water, 'so that a long way out at sea, before reaching this country, the water of the ocean is fresh from it. Now as a sign of approach to this country...there are serpents coming forth from the depths to meet you ...' (*The Periplus of the Erythrean Sea*: 37).

The name Indus is derived from the Sanskrit word Sindhu which means 'a large body of water, a sea or an ocean' (Mountjoy 2005). The river carries great volumes of silt which colours the sea for a long distance from the shore. Deposited silt creates shifting sand banks along the coast that make sailing hazardous. During one monsoon season alone, the Indus carries an estimated ninety-one million cubic cm of silt to the sea, sufficient to cover about 100 sq. kms of land to a depth of about one metre. Between 1873 and 1904, about 250 sq. kms of new land has been formed at the mouth of the Indus (Lambrick 1986: 22–23).

Most of the Indus's silt, however, is deposited on its bed causing it to rise year on year. It obstructs smooth flows. During the monsoon, the river and its tributaries overflow their banks to create a turbulent flood-prone ecosystem. At Mohenjo-daro, the land has risen by about ten metres. Mohenjo-daro's lowest levels have never been reached due to a low water table and consequent inundation. Such unpredictable and devastating floods, extensive and voluminous beyond the imaginings of humans a few millennia ago, made settled life along the river banks hazardous. The effort of a generation could be wiped out by flooding during one monsoon season.

The Indus Valley Civilisation was so named because the first major discovered sites were located along the banks and tributaries of the river Indus. Subsequent explorations, however, unearthed a large number of Early and Mature Harappan sites along the Sarsuti-Ghaggar-Hakra palaeochannel,[1] often identified as the mythical Rgvedic Sarasvati, that runs to the east of the Indus, and, in places, roughly parallel to it. This dense concentration led to the assumption that it had once been a large glacier-fed river with perennial water flow, and that its diversion or drying up triggered the decline and abandonment of these urban settlements. It led to a move to rename the Indus Valley

Civilisation as the Indus-Sarasvati or Sarasvati Civilisation thereby relocating its focus from the Indus, now flowing through Pakistan, to the Indian states of Haryana and Punjab.

This, however, writes Kenoyer,

> is based primarily on the misconception that a significant or even greater proportion of the ancient 'Indus' sites were situated along the bed of the now dry Saraswati-Ghaggar-Hakra-Nara River. In fact, most sites along the dry river channel are relatively small and even the few large ones are not as large as the major cities on the Indus or its tributaries. The discovery of these sites is mainly due to the rapid abandonment of the region after the river began drying up during the Late Harappan period. The lack of later occupation and the fact that no more silt was brought down with annual floodwaters has left these sites exposed and therefore easily identified by archaeologists. In contrast, the Indus settlements in other parts of the Punjab, Sindh and Gujarat have been buried by annual flood sediments or by later historical villages and cities (Kenoyer n.d.a).

The densest site concentration lies roughly equidistant between Harappa and Mohenjo-daro, in the deserts of Cholistan, around Ganweriwala. These sites represent some of the earliest settlements on the Indus plains. However, it is yet to be determined how many were occupied simultaneously. Stream flows, especially in the Derawar inland delta, have constantly shifted as silt deposits and wind-blown sand have raised sand banks and clogged and diverted water channels. There is good reason to believe that, deprived of water, populations have abandoned sites and moved to wetter locations. Population density along the Ghaggar-Hakra could therefore have been considerably less than the exposed site distribution would imply.

Northeast of Ganweriwala along the channel, another concentration is centred around Kalibangan, and still beyond, on the banks of the tributary to this palaeochannel, the Chautang, lies Rakhigarhi.

The stimulus for these settlements along the Ghaggar-Hakra came from a long-term declining trend in the summer monsoon which reduced water flows, flooding and course changes. It created a stable environment for settlement. Ironically, 'it was the departure of the river, rather than its arrival, that triggered the growth of Indus urban settlements here ... a stable abandoned valley, still able to serve as a water source but without the risk of devastating floods ...' (Singh 2017).

The Ghaggar is very much smaller than the Sutlej and Yamuna as the following comparison shows:

Table 21.1: Comparison of Sutlej, Yamuna, and Ghaggar rivers

	Sutlej	Yamuna	Ghaggar
Upstream drainage area	10,616 sq. kms	10,542 sq. kms	485 sq. kms
Bed depth	Up to 20 m	Up to 20 m	2–5 m
Active channel width	300–900 m	900–1,500 m	60–100 m
Valley width	7–50 kms	7–50 kms	5–8 kms
Floodplain	10–20 kms	10–20 kms	5 kms

Source: Maemoku (2012); van Dijk (2016).

The Ghaggar-Hakra palaeochannel lies between the Sutlej and Yamuna. Its floodplain is too small to explain large discharges in the past or present, the size of a floodplain being directly proportional to the volume of annual river discharge. Further, this width has been enhanced by the channel's shallow bed. Still further, OSL[2] dating reveals this width has been restricted by sand dunes that formed on either side from c10–15 ka. Harappan sites located on these dunes and on the bed and floodplain confirm that the region never suffered from devastating floods during their settlement.

The upper course of the Ghaggar is known as the Sarsuti, a stream that has its source in the Siwaliks. The Chautang, identified as the ancient Drishadvati, flows parallel to it and joins the Ghaggar at Kalibangan. The Ghaggar bed is dry for much of the year and, in the rainy season, flows for a distance of about 465 kms from its source. It continues across the Pakistani border as the Hakra where, approaching Derawar in Cholistan, it loses itself in a delta of smaller channels and a confusion of dry palaeochannels. About 350 kms downstream, near Sukkur in Sindh, the Nara channel emerges and following the general direction of the Indus at a distance varying between forty and 100 kms to its east, flows along the edge of the Thar and finally empties itself into the Rann of Kutch. This channel occupies the lowest valley-line east of the Indus, and in times of flood, has sometimes received immense volumes of Indus water (Lambrick 1986: 28). In some circles, the Nara is believed to be a continuation of the Hakra.

The special interest in the Ghaggar-Hakra-Nara palaeochannel arises from the belief that the dry bed may be that of the Sarasvati mentioned in Vedic texts. One of the earliest published references to the 'Lost River' comes from an article in *The Calcutta Review* of 1874 (Oldham 1874). It cites local traditions attributing the desolation of a once flourishing country to the drying of a large river close to 1000 kms in length. The channel was known by different names along its course, the main sections being the Ghaggar, Hakra and Nara. The course of this lost river was marked by scattered mounds, great and small, that were once cities and towns, many of considerable importance. These ruins contained huge quantities of bricks of a type that had not been manufactured for centuries, and the old river bed was littered with fresh-water shells similar to those found in the Sutlej and Indus. The small number of people who lived in this inhospitable region knew little of its past; not much more than a few legends remained.

A survey in 1940 referred to the modest nature of the Ghaggar-Hakra palaeochannel (Stein 1942). It observed that the Ghaggar flowed for only some months in the year in a wide sandy bed that contrasted greatly with the paltry volume of water it brought down from the Siwaliks. Both sides of the bed were lined by dunes formed by wind-borne sand. They showed no marks of erosion, and there was a clear difference between the firm loamy soil on the bed and the light dune sand on either side. Clearly, the river had rarely overflown its banks in this region of scanty rainfall. Of particular interest was the large number of ancient mounds located along the palaeochannel, bare of vegetation and littered with numerous pieces of broken pottery. Wind erosion had brought shards from different layers to the surface. They formed so thick a cover that the mounds could be recognised from a distance. Their large number contrasted strikingly with the few hamlets that were presently there.

The Ghaggar-Hakra palaeochannel ended in a profusion of ancient mounds, some of great proportions and littered with pottery shards, in Derawar. This area of about 250 sq. kms was overrun by dunes separating long stretches of dry river beds, giving it the appearance of a delta. The archaeology of the mounds along the palaeochannel showed they had been abandoned much earlier on the Hakra than on the Ghaggar.

Recent Scientific Investigations

In recent years, scientific investigations have used a number of different technologies to study the Ghaggar-Hakra and its history. Remote sensing satellite imagery has uncovered an 8,000 kms network of palaeochannels in the Sutlej-Yamuna interfluve (Punjab, Haryana, north Rajasthan) of which the Ghaggar-Hakra network comprises about 2,200 kms (Orengo 2017; Review – Palaeochannels 2016). These palaeochannels have been formed by snow-fed Himalayan rivers frequently changing their courses. A high-resolution map of the western region of the Indo-Gangetic Plain using the SRTM[3] database shows wide, shallowly incised valleys separated by interfluves in the Indus basin, but none in the Ghaggar-Hakra interfluve. This means similarly large glacier-fed rivers did not flow there in the past (Giosan 2012).

OSL dating of a section of the Ghaggar-Hakra reveals a flowing water channel with several lakes and ponds in the surrounding areas c4000–2000 BCE (Saini 2010; Chatterjee 2017). Electrical resistivity soundings beneath the surface of the Ghaggar-Hakra palaeochannel also confirm a once flowing river but not its size or age (Sinha 2012). Reduced discharge led to its degeneration between 2000–1400 BCE. It has been dry since then. Geochemical analysis of bed sediments has revealed two distinct origins: older grey micaceous sand (c70–4.3 ka) from melting Himalayan glaciers and younger yellowish-brown sand and brown silty clay (c16–0 ka) from the Siwaliks. There was a gradual disappearance of the river's perennial water sources and increasing dependence on monsoon rainfall. Pottery samples from the Mature Harappan period (2600–1900 BCE) at Kalibangan contain only the newer sediments confirming the Ghaggar had transitioned from being a glacier-fed to a rain-fed river by then.

Strontium and neodymium isotope sediments in the Ghaggar-Hakra palaeaochannel confirm a sub-Himalayan catchment area (Tripathi 2004). From c3500 BCE, a progressively weakening monsoon reduced its flows and the river gradually shrank northwards. Scientists now believe that a weakening monsoon created a more stable environment in the northwest and the stimulus for intensive agriculture and resultant urbanisation in the Harappan region. The explanation is straightforward. About 45% of Indus waters comes from melting snows, but most sediment is delivered by monsoon floods. When the monsoon weakens, sedimentation decreases in comparison to water discharge. This creates faster water flows that cause channel incision. River beds deepen. This restrains rivers from overflowing their banks. The Sutlej incised primarily between c8000–6700 BCE.

U-Pb dating of zircon sand grains of the Ghaggar-Hakra bed in the Cholistan section contains at least two groups of sediments with similarities to the Beas, Sutlej and Yamuna Rivers confirming it once received water from these rivers (Clift 2012; Lambrick 1986: 30; Singh 2017).[4] The Chautang palaeochannel, two kms in width in places, was once the bed of the Yamuna.

The Sutlej, as its name suggests, has had a turbulent history. In Sanskrit literature, the Sutlej is known as Sutudri or Satadru (flowing in 100 channels). The Sutlej appears to have joined the Ghaggar-Hakra palaeochannel from c23 ka in three widely separated places, the furthest upstream junction being above that with the Chautang. The subsequent diversion of these rivers to their present courses re-routed water away from the Ghaggar-Hakra palaeochannel. The Yamuna changed its course c49 ka, and the Beas-Sutlej between 15–8 ka. The Ghaggar-Hakra ceased to be an active Himalayan glacier-fed river well before Harappan times. As one investigator states:

> ... contrary to earlier assumptions that a large glacier-fed Himalayan river, identified by some with the mythical Sarasvati, watered the Harappan heartland on the interfluve between the Indus and Ganges basins ... only monsoonal-fed rivers were active there during the Holocene. As the monsoon weakened, monsoonal rivers gradually dried or became seasonal, affecting habitability along their courses. Hydroclimatic stress increased the vulnerability of agricultural production supporting Harappan urbanism, leading to settlement downsizing, diversification of crops, and a drastic increase in settlements in the moister monsoon regions of the upper Punjab, Haryana, and Uttar Pradesh (Giosan 2012).

Using floodplains for agriculture requires expert knowledge of their behaviour and adaptation to floods and changing water courses. Harappans adapted by building only a few large urban centres among many smaller towns and villages. Significantly, many were located on elevated sites above the floodplains, or without direct access to perennial water. Apart from reducing the risk of flooding or river avulsion, land areas some distance from the flood-prone plains offered better soils with fine sediment, more organic matter and a higher moisture-retention capacity. This explains, in part, the Harappan preference for the Ghaggar-Hakra palaeochannel over the Indus and its tributaries.

The Harappan region passed through alternating wet and dry phases spreading over centuries. The last, beginning with the 4.2 ka global megadrought, resulted in a drastic reduction in the Indian summer monsoon rainfall for two centuries (Kathayat 2017; Berkelhammer 2012; Dixit 2014; Staubwasser 2003). The evidence lies in the oxygen isotope values of a calcitic stalagmite collected from Mawmluh Cave in Cherrapunji, Meghalaya. They show a precipitous rise between c2071–2049 BCE which confirms a reduction in monsoon rainfall. It lasted for about 180 years before rapidly returning to previous values in 1888 BCE. Oxygen isotope records of gastropod shells from Thar paleolake sediments confirm this weakening of the monsoon with a peak reduction in rainfall occuring c2100 BCE. Planktonic oxygen isotope ratios off the Indus delta record these spells of aridity during the last 6,000 years with the most prominent change occuring 4.2 ka. It resulted in a significant reduction in discharge from the Indus.

By c1900 BCE, river beds had gone dry. Rain-based farming and urbanism declined especially along the Ghaggar-Hakra palaeochannel with a downsizing in settlements until the region became depopulated. People moved to the dense stream network on the upper channel in Punjab and Haryana where the monsoon was more consistent. In lower Punjab and Sindh, the number of sites decreased over the same interval as populations moved to Kutch and the Deccan. The abandoned Cholistan section of the Ghaggar-Hakra turned to desert. It is this seasonally active monsoon-fed river that is believed to be the Rgvedic Sarasvati.

The Rgvedic Sarasvati

The Rgveda knows Sarasvati both as a river and a goddess, a mother, sister, wife, daughter and friend. One of her foremost functions as a goddess is the bestowing of wealth, pleasure and, as the presiding deity of fertility and growth, progeny. In RV 2.41.16, she is called upon after the gods Vayu, Indra-Vayu, Mithra-Varuna, Asvins, Indra and the All Gods to attend the morning soma pressing and grant favours: '*ambitame*, *naditame*, *devitame*, Sarasvati (O best mother, best river, best goddess, Sarasvati) ... make a laud for us, mother ... Allot offspring to us, goddess'. Other hymns urge her to descend from the heavens and high mountains to attend the sacrifice, accept the offered ghee and listen to devotional hymns (RV 5.43.11) and, along with the gods, grant favours (RV 5.46.2).

The Rgveda glorifies the northern rivers, especially the Sindhu and lists them from east to west beginning with the Ganga. Calling her a daughter of the Sindhu, it describes her as flowing from the mountains to the sea (RV 10.75, 7.36.6, 7.95.2). RV 6.61, exclusively devoted to the Sarasvati, glorifies it as the best of seven sisters and ends with a plea that she does not abandon her worshippers.

Later Vedic texts, the *Panchavimsha Brahmana* (25.10.1) and *Jaiminiya Upanishad Brahmana* (4.26.12) among others, however, speak of the disappearance of the river in desert sands at a place, near Patiala, known as Vinasana (disappearance) and reappearance at a place called Plaksa Prasravana at a distance requiring a journey of forty-four days (Macdonell 1912. Vol II:300/55; *Panchavimsha Brahmana* xxv.10,6, xxv.10,16.22; *Jaiminiya Upanishad Brahmana* iv.26, iv.26.12). The *Mahabharata* explains why this happened:

> Here is the beautiful and sacred river, Saraswati, full of water: and here ... is the spot known as Vinasana, or the place where the Saraswati disappeared. Here is the gate of the kingdom of the Nishadas and it is from hatred for them that the Saraswati entered into the earth in order that the Nishadas might not see her ..." (*Mahabharata*, Book 3: *Vana Parva*, Section CXXX).

The Sarasvati, still the guardian of the waters and wisdom, flowed only for the benefit of the select few.

The Haraxvaiti and the Airyanem Vaejah

Like the Sarasvati, another river that cannot be located today is the Rasa. It is mentioned in three passages of the Rgveda and also appears in the Vendidad as the Ranha, a stream in the extreme northwest of Indo-Aryan territory. The Rgveda knows the Rasa as a mythic stream flowing at the ends of the earth. Originally, the name appears to have referred to the 'flavour' of the waters and so could be applied to every river.

There are remarkable parallels between the geography and mythology of the Sarasvati, and the Haraxvaiti/Haetumant River, which flows through Iran and Afghanistan. Both names came to be applied to life-giving rivers, flowing down from the mountains and feeding all other rivers.

In the Avesta, Aradvi Sura Anahita is venerated as the female guardian of waters (Aban), associated with fertility, healing and wisdom (Boyce 1996: 71–73; Lommel 1954; Harrassowitz). The Haraxvaiti/Haetumant River was particularly associated with the goddess Aradvi Sura Anahita. *Sura* means 'strong, mighty', *anahita* 'undefiled, immaculate', and *ardvi* 'moist, humid'. In Indo-Iranian times, the goddess was more properly known as Sarasvati (she who possesses waters), a name by which she is still worshipped in India (Lommel 1954: 405–13). The 'Aban Yasht' (Hymn to the Waters), one of the longest and best-preserved Avestan hymns, celebrates the Haraxvati as the personification of a great mythical river which plunges down from Mt Hara into the Vourukasa Sea. It is the source of all the waters of the world. The river-goddess is a powerful diety, a beautiful, strong maiden clad in beaver-skins who drives a chariot drawn by four horses: wind, rain, clouds, sleet (Zand-i Vohuman Yasht, 2.5.5–6). This water-divinity bestowed fertility, purified the seed of males and the wombs of females and made the milk which nourished their young flow. She nurtured crops and herds and imparted knowledge, bestowed chariots, arms, household goods and victories in battle and destroyed foes.

In the 'Aban Yasht', Ahura Mazda asks Zarathushtra to offer a sacrifice to Aradvi Sura Anahita saying:

> *From this river of mine alone flow all the waters that spread all over the seven Karshvares; this river of mine alone goes on bringing waters, both in summer and in winter. This river of mine purifies the seed in males, the womb in females, the milk in females' breasts ...*
>
> *The large river... that is as large as the whole of the waters that run along the earth; that runs powerfully from the height Hukairya down to the sea Vouru-Kasha ...*
>
> *... she, Ardvi Sura Anahita, who has a thousand cells and a thousand channels: the extent of each of those cells, of each of those channels is as much as a man can ride in forty days, riding on a good horse.*[5]

Like Aradvi Sura Anahita, Sarasvati is the guardian of the waters and wisdom; she protects the study of the Vedas. Sarasvati literally means 'abounding in pools', a name that could be applied to many other rivers of the Indus system where continuous sedimentation, especially during the monsoon, creates many ponds (Macdonell Vol II: 434; Meier-Brugger 2003: 299; Vendidad; Eduljee). The same can be said of the Haraxvaiti region.

The Haraxvaiti (Helmand), 1,300 kms long, rises in the mountains about 80 kms west of Kabul, and about 50 kms from the River Kabul. Leaving the mountains, it flows over a gravelly bed across a flat country until it empties into an inland lake, the Hamun-e-Saban, in Sistan (Kochar n.d.). There are a number of other lakes here, like the Hamun-e-Helmand, which make it a rich and fertile area surrounded by desert and mountains. The Helmand's major tributary is the 560km-long Arghandab. Other rivers with their source in the mountains also flow into the Sistan lake region, the main ones being Arghastan, Khash and Farah. Melting snows in spring bring floods. There are similarities between the Haraxvaiti/Haetumant region and the Hapta Hindu: the snow-fed rivers arising in the mountains to the north; the spring floods; the Sistan and Derawar inland lake deltas.

As a rule, place names originate from general appellatives. The Vedic name for Indus (Sindhu) was originally an appellative that meant 'river', and Vedic Sarasvati and Avestian Haraxvaiti 'river or region where there are many swamps'.

So too, there are similarities between the attributes assigned to the goddesses Aradvi Sura Anahita and Sarasvati. A narrative in the *Mahabharata* (Book Nine, the *Shalya Parva*) strikingly illustrates this similarity.[6] Dadhicha rishi, a wise sage and brahmachari who had complete control over his senses, lived the life of an ascetic performing extreme penance on the banks of the Sarasvati. Fearing the powers he was accumulating, the god Indra attempted to distract him by offering various rewards. He failed. Dadhicha was steadfast until Indra tempted him with the beautiful and celestial *apsara*, Alambusa. Seeing her, Dadhicha was driven by lust to spill his seed into the waters of the Sarasvati. The river/goddess received it and nurtured it in her womb. In time, the child Sarasvata was born. Dadhicha blessed the river, saying it would always be the foremost of all sacred rivers. He predicted his son would one day teach the Vedas to many brahmans.

Sometime later, a great drought afflicted the land for twelve years. While brahmans all over abandoned their profession in the struggle for survival, the river goddess Sarasvati kept her son by her side, feeding him fish from her waters, so that he could continue studying and mastering the sacred texts. By the time the drought passed, the brahmans had forgotten the Vedas. They, therefore, approached Sarasvata, 'of unrivalled splendour and god-like mien', to teach them. So it was, that despite his tender years, 60,000 brahmans became Sarasvata's disciples and learned the Vedas at his feet.

In this story, Sarasvati performs the same functions attributed to Aradvi Sura Anahita. She is ambitame, the best of mothers, the purifier of the male seed and female womb, who raises her son with abundant and nutritious food in a land devastated by drought and famine. She is naditame, the best of rivers, whose waters continue to flow and is full of fish when drought has dried the others. She is devitame, the best of goddesses, who preserves sacred knowledge and wisdom. Her waters are holy and bless those who seek it. But where does one seek it?

RV 10.75 places the Sarasvati between the Yamuna and Sutlej. There is, however, no opening in the Himalayan foothills between the Yamuna and Sutlej through which a large river can enter the plains (Oldham 1874: 7). Of the rivulets that have their source there, the Sarsuti, a corruption of Sarasvati, is one. In no way does it do justice to the majestic description, of river and goddess, given in RV 6.61. The turbulent, obstacle-smashing river, dearest of seven sisters, flowed ever roaring in a golden course, her powerful waves broke the back of mountains and smashed foreigners. The poet panders to her yearning for praise and urges goddess Sarasvati to tear down the scorners of the gods and lead her worshippers to a better state, ending his paen with a plea, 'Take delight in our partnerships and communities. Let us not go from you to alien dwelling places.'

So why does the Sarsuti-Ghaggar-Hakra channel, drying and diminishing even in Rgvedic times, get praised and glorified so much more than the bigger rivers flowing to its west and east? Did that glory once apply to another river and get transferred to the Sarsuti-Ghaggar-Hakra?

River names and locations can reveal details of the linguistic and ethnic history of places (Witzel n.d.: 2001). They can be derived from local languages or reflect the migration of peoples. In the northwest, Indo-Aryan names have largely replaced earlier local names. Many of these names relate to rivers flowing through the lands identified as Aryan in the Vendidad: Sarasvati-Haraxvaiti; Rasa-Ranha; Sarayu-Haroiiu; Gomati-Gomal. The latter two have been located further east to the Gangetic basin by Indo-Aryan speakers. The earlier non-Indo-Aryan local name for the Sarasvati has been tentatively reconstructed as *visambal/pal* (*Vaisambhalya/phalya*). It was the river that flowed through Kurukshetra, the heartland of Rgvedic and post-Rgvedic culture, its mythical, religious and political centre. This was a region of several lakes and ponds, a possible inspiration for the Sankritised renaming of the river to *saras-vati*, or equally for the Haraxvaiti.

A Matter of Perception

To the Harappans, it was the size not the location of the river that mattered. While the snow-fed Indus rivers brought floods and devastation across their flood plains, the monsoon-fed Ghaggar river system provided a more stable environment with adequate water for summer and winter crops.

To the Rgvedic people, it was the location not the size of the river that was of prime concern. The Sarasvati flowed through Kurukshetra, the frontier region during the centuries before the onward move into the Gangetic basin. To its south lay nisada territory, once ruled by Pramaganda. Was the insignificant Sarsuti transformed into the mighty and sacred Sarasvati, the raging, tumultuous river and the guardian of water and wisdom, but only for the Vedic people and not for Pramaganda and his nisadas? The river disappeared at Vinasana before it reached his territory.

The 1,028 hymns of the Rgveda were composed over a considerable period of time by a number of poets belonging to the Grtsamada, Visvamitra, Vamadeva, Atri, Bharadvaja and Vasistha family lineages, all part of an elaborate patronage system.

The overwhelming majority of their hymns are intended to praise the god(s) to whom the hymn is dedicated and thereby induce them to favour their worshippers (Jamison 2014: RV 7. 9–10). RV 10.75; the 'nadistuti', for example, lavishes praise on the Sindhu while making just a single, minor reference to the Sarasvati. The Sindhu bestowed abundance on her worshippers. She had lovely horses, chariots and garments, was golden, well-fashioned and rich in prize mares. Her tributaries rushed to her bellowing like mothers to their young, like milk-cows with their milk. RV 6.61 does the same for Sarasvati. Which hymn gives a more accurate geographic description?

The Rgveda was never intended to be a lesson in geography. It can, at best, give limited information on that subject, information that needs to be reconciled with the increasing scientific field and laboratory research that is today unravelling the secrets of the lost river of the desert, a relatively small river that gained a far bigger reputation than all the others put together.

History, like nature, abhors a vacuum.

Notes

Chapter 1: India's First Humans

1. The term 'hominin' refers to humans and their direct ancestors. 'Hominid' includes orangutans, gorillas, chimpanzees and humans.

2. Similar doubts have arisen in regard to the Narmada hominins and the results have been questioned by other researchers.

3. Genetic research reveals that early modern humans admixed with other hominin species, like the Neanderthals and Denisovans, who had already colonised large parts of Earth before their exodus from Africa. See Chapter 3.

Chapter 4: Populating the Earth – the Genetic Evidence

1. Genetic terms: admixture –exchange of genes; clade – a group that includes all the descendants of a common ancestor; coalescence age – merging of genetic lineages backwards in time to the most recent common ancestor; genome – entire genetic material in a chromosome set. The human genome is composed of forty-six chromosomes; haplotype – set of numbers defining Y-chromosome or mtDNA; haplogroup – group of similar haplotypes, assigned letters and numbers, that share a common ancestor; haplotree – chart showing the different lineages within a haplogroup; marker – specific place on a chromosome with two or more forms, called alleles, the inheritance of which can be followed from one generation to the next; mitochondrial DNA (mtDNA) – energy-releasing component of cells which contain their own DNA. Only females pass on their mtDNA; mutation – spontaneous change in DNA; Y-chromosome – male sex chromosome. Only males have a Y-chromosome, inherited from their father.

2. A 'relict' population is one that is geographically isolated today but once inhabited a far wider territory.

Chapter 5: South Asia – the Genetic Story

1. On the physical similarity between Australian Aborigines and South Indians, T. H. Huxley wrote in the nineteenth century:

> An ordinary cooly ... would, if stripped, pass very well for an Australian, although the skull and lower jaw are generally less coarse ... We are ... undoubtedly confronted with a number of characters – skull formation, features, wavy curled hair – in common between the Australians and Dravidians ... a number of points of resemblance between the Australian and Dravidian languages have been discovered, and this despite the fact that the homes of the two races are so far apart, and that a number of races are wedged in between them, whose languages have no relationship whatever to either the Dravidian or Australian. There is much that speaks in favour of the view that the Australians and Dravidians sprang from a common main branch of the human race (Thurston 1909: xxx).

2. Tribes have been described as 'a segmentary system where it has a particular type of clan and lineage structure' (Beteille 1986). This social structure is distinctly different from that of castes. Beteille writes: 'Tribal society is homogeneous, undifferentiated and unstratified; Hindu society is heterogeneous, differentiated and stratified.'

3. The dairy economy had grown to significant importance in Sumer by the 4th millennium BCE. At the temple of Tel al-Ubaid, a stone frieze depicts how milk was churned to produce butter c2500 BCE (Mcintosh 2005:63).

Chapter 6: Tales Languages Tell

1. Most words have about a 50% chance of being replaced by a new non-cognate word roughly every 2,000–4,000 years. However, for some words (numerals, pronouns, special adverbs, e.g. I, you, here, how, not, there, what, two, five) this period extends to every 10,000–20,000 or more. Such ultra-conserved words point to deep language ancestry across Eurasia.

Chapter 8: Foragers – the Retreat

1. *nisadas – jana*; *jati – arya* or freemen (brahmans, kshratriyas, vaishyas) and slaves (shudras).

Chapter 9: Discovering a Buried Past

1. Harappan ships carried crows on board. They were released if a ship drifted off course towards the open sea, and sailors followed their flight towards land. (*Harappa.com*; Parpola 1994: 14).

Chapter 12: The Beginnings

1. Genetically, the world's domestic cattle belong to two lineages. One includes both European and African breeds; the other is the Indian zebu (*Bos indicus*).

Chapter 13: The Maturing

1. Urbanisation has been defined as a process through which the number and/or size of population concentrations increase(s). It involves a shift from agrarian to non-agrarian occupations. Those not directly involved in the agrarian economy would therefore become dependent on others for their food supply.

2. The man-days used to construct Mohenjo-daro's monumental platform, for instance, is calculated at around four million (McIntosh 2008: 389).

3. Kathayat 2012 suggest an alternate possibility: the Mature Phase began around an abrupt intensification of the Indian Summer Monsoon c2550 BCE that continued for nearly 700 years to c1850 BCE. During this period, the monsoon reached its maximum over the past 5,700 years. It is possible that this created conditions for reliable, expanded agricultural surpluses that supported population expansion and the development of urban centres.

4. There is a long gap between the first evidence for the cultivation of wild rice at Lahuradewa c8000–6000 BC and the exploitation of fully domesticated rice by c1800–1600 BCE.

Chapter 14: The Mechanisms of Control

1. The term *pashu* refers more appropriately to domesticated animals. The term *pashupati* (*pati* – master), therefore, does not convey the true potency that the scene attempts to project.

Chapter 15: The Decline and Dispersal

1. Tooth enamel preserves strontium and lead ingested in food, water and dust. Their isotope ratios remain unchanged in the process and analysis of these ratios can be used to deduce the geographic region where the individual was living.

Chapter 16: Bronze Age Eurasia

1. Bit wear is important evidence for early horse domestication. Bits are used to control horse movement; they cause teeth wear which can be analysed from skeletal remains.

2. Cattle and sheep push snow aside with their noses and can starve when grasslands are covered by heavy snow and ice. Horses paw away frozen snow with their hard hooves and feed themselves.

Chapter 21: A Forgotten History and a Lost River

1. Glossary of terms referring to rivers: palaeochannel – bed of once active river or stream; interfluve – region of higher land between two rivers of the same drainage system; incise – narrow erosion of the

river bed; avulsion – change in the course of a river; floodplain – the part of a fluvial plain that can be inundated by floodwater; thin loamy sand or silt is usually deposited on it.

2. The OSL (Optically stimulated luminescence) technique determines the time since sediment grains were deposited and shielded from further light.

3. The Space Shuttle Radar Topography Mission (SRTM) was flown into space aboard the space shuttle Endeavor in February 2000. On an eleven-day mission, it captured Earth's topography at 1 arc-second (30 metres) for over 80% of its surface.

4. Zircon is particularly suitable for age dating as it often contains relatively large amounts of uranium and lead. The U-Pb (uranium-lead) dating method uses the characteristics of uranium's decay to lead over time.

5. Note the similar manner in which the length of the river is specified in the 'Aban Yasht' (the distance a man can ride in forty days) and the *Panchavimsha Brahmana* XXV 10.16 (forty-four *asvina*s, an asvina denoting the distance covered by a horseman in one day).

6. Note the remarkable parallel in the Avesta concerning Lake Kanosoya being the guardian of Zarathustra's semen.

BIBLIOGRAPHY

Abdi, Kamyar. 2003. 'The Early Development of Pastoralism in the Central Zagros Mountains'. *Journal of World Prehistory*.

Abro, Tasleem et al. 2016. 'Pottery Designs as an Evidence of Continuity and Change: Mature to Late Indus'. *Heritage: Journal of Multidisciplinary Studies in Archaeology*.

Abu-Amero, Khaled. 2008. 'Mitochondrial DNA structure in the Arabian Peninsula'. *BMC Evolutionary Biology*.

Aghakhanian, Farhang et al. 2015. 'Unravelling the Genetic History of Negritos and Indigenous Populations of Southeast Asia'. *Genome Biology and Evolution*.

Akhilesh, Kumar et al. 2018. 'Early Middle Palaeolithic culture in India around 385–172 ka reframes Out of Africa models'. *Nature*.

Algaze, Guillermo. n.d. *Ancient Mesopotamia at the Dawn of Civilization*. The University of Chicago Press.

Allchin, Bridget. 1987. 'South Asian Rock Art'. *Journal of the Royal Society of Arts*.

Allchin, Bridget and Frank Raymond Allchin. 1968. *The Birth of Indian Civilization*. Penguin Books.

———. 1996. *The Rise of Civilization in India and Pakistan*. New Delhi: Cambridge University Press.

Allentoft, M. et al. 2015. 'Population genomics of Bronze Age Eurasia'. *Nature*.

Ameri, Marta. 2013. 'Regional Diversity in the Harappan World: The Evidence of the Seals'. In *Connections and Complexity – New Approaches to the Archaeology of South Asia*, ed. Shinu Abraham et al. Left Coast Press.

Anderson, Gregory ed. 2008. *The Munda Languages*. Routledge.

Anthony, David. 2007. *The Horse, the Wheel, and Language: How Bronze-Age Riders from the Eurasian Steppes Shaped the Modern World*. Princeton, NJ, USA: Princeton University Press

———. 2009. 'The Sintashta Genesis: The Roles of Climate Change, Warfare, and Long-Distance Trade'. In *Social Complexity in Prehistoric Eurasia*. Cambridge, Mass., USA: Cambridge University Press.

Anthony, David. 2016. 'The Samara Valley Project and the Evolution of Pastoral Economies in the Western Eurasian Steppes'. In *A Bronze Age Landscape in the Russian Steppes, The Samara Valley Project*. UCLA, Cotsen Institute of Archaeology Press.

Archaeological Survey of India. 2003. 'Rock Shelters of Bhimbetka'. *Excerpt from the Report of the 27th Session of the World Heritage Committee.*

Armitage, Simon et al. 2011. 'The Southern Route "Out of Africa": Evidence for an Early Expansion of Modern Humans into Arabia'. *Science.*

Arun Kumar Ganesh Prasad et al. 2012. 'Population Differentiation of Southern Indian Male Lineages Correlates with Agricultural Expansions Predating the Caste System'. *PLOS ONE* 7(11).

———. 2015a. 'A late Neolithic expansion of Y chromosomal haplogroup O2a1-M95 from east to west'. *Journal of Systematics and Evolution.*

———. 2015b. 'Genome-wide signatures of male-mediated migration shaping the Indian gene pool'. *Journal of Human Genetics.*

Atkinson, Quentin et al. 2008. 'mtDNA Variation Predicts Population Size in Humans and Reveals a Major Southern Asian Chapter in Human Prehistory'. *Molecular Biology and Evolution'* (henceforth, *Mol. Biol. Evol.*).

Avesta: Khorda Avesta (Book of Common Prayer). 1898. Translated by James Darmesteter. *Sacred Books of the East*, American Edition.

Badaeva, Ekaterina. 2015. 'Chromosomal Passports Provide New Insights into Diffusion of Emmer Wheat'. *PLOS ONE* (Public Library of Science).

Bae, Christopher et al. 2017. 'Human Colonization of Asia in the Late Pleistocene – An Introduction to Supplement 17'. *Current Anthropology.*

Bailey, Greg. 1983. *The Mythology of Brahma*. New Delhi: Oxford University Press.

Bar-Yosef, Ofer, et al. 2001. 'From Africa to Eurasia – early dispersals'. *Quaternary International.*

———. 2013. 'Following Pleistocene road signs of human dispersals across Eurasia'. *Quaternary International.*

Barik, S. S. et al. 2008. 'Detailed mtDNA Genotypes Permit a Reassessment of the Settlement and Population Structure of the Andaman Islands'. *American Journal of Physical Anthropology.*

Basu, Analabha, et al. 2003. 'Ethnic India: A Genomic View, With Special Reference to Peopling and Structure'. *Genome Research*.

———. 2016. 'Genomic reconstruction of the history of extant populations of India reveals five distinct ancestral components and a complex structure'. Proceedings of the National Academy of Sciences of the USA (*henceforth* PNAS).

Bates, J., et al. 2016. 'Approaching rice domestication in South Asia: New evidence from Indus settlements in northern India'. *Journal of Archaeological Science*.

Bednarik, Robert. 2001. 'The Oldest Known Rock Art in the World'. *Anthropologie*.

———. 2008. 'Lower Palaeolithic Rock Art of India and its Global Context'. *Man in India* 88(2). https://www.researchgate.net/publication/288628000 (accessed May 2024).

———. 2010. 'Indian Pleistocene rock art in a global context'. *Symposium Asie*.

———. 2013. 'Pleistocene Palaeoart of Asia'. *Arts*.

Bednarik, R. G., G. Kumar, A. Watchman and R. G. Roberts. 2005. 'Preliminary results of the EIP Project'. *Rock Art Research* 22(2): 147–197.

Bellwood, Peter. 2011. 'The Checkered Prehistory of Rice Movement Southwards as a Domesticated Cereal – from the Yangzi to the Equator'. *Rice* 4: 93–103. DOI 10.1007/s12284-011-9068-9. Springer Science+Business Media (accessed April 2024).

Bergstrom, Anders et al. 2016. 'Deep Roots for Aboriginal Australian Y Chromosomes.' *Current Biology* 26(6). http://dx.doi.org/10.1016/j.cub.2016.01.028 (accessed April 2024).

Berkelhammer, M. et al. 2012. 'An Abrupt Shift in the Indian Monsoon 4000 Years Ago. Climates, Landscapes, and Civilizations'. *American Geophysical Union*.

Beteille, Andre. 1986. 'The concept of tribe with special reference to India'. *Archives Européennes de Sociologie* XXVII(2): 297–318.

Beyin, Amanuel. 2006. 'The Bab al Mandab vs the Nile-Levant: An Appraisal of the Two Dispersal Routes for Early Modern Humans Out of Africa'. *African Archaeological Review* (henceforth, *Afr. Archaeol. Rev.*) 23: 5–30 DOI 10.1007/s10437-006-9005-2. Springer Science+Business Media (accessed April 2024).

———. 2011. 'Upper Pleistocene Human Dispersals out of Africa: A Review of the Current State of the Debate'. *International Journal of Evolutionary Biology*.

Beyin, Amanuel. 2015. 'Human Origins, Dispersal and Associated Environments: An African Perspective'. *EOLSS* (Encyclopedia of Life Support Systems) *Publications*.

Black, J., et al. 1998. *The Electronic Text Corpus of Sumerian Literature*, Oxford. https://etcsl.orinst.ox.ac.uk/ (accessed April 2024).

Blench, Roger. 2001. 'You can't go home again: Pastoralism in the new millennium'. London. A paper prepared with financial support from the Food and Agriculture Organisation of the UN.

———. 2007. 'Re-evaluating the linguistic prehistory of South Asia'. Presented at a workshop titled 'Landscape, demography and subsistence in prehistoric India: Exploratory workshop on the middle Ganges and the Vindhyas ', University of Cambridge.

———. 2008. 'Agriculture and phylic dispersals; reevaluating the evidence'. In *Us and Them: Modelling past genetic, linguistic, and cultural boundaries*. Bordeaux. Paper presented at meeting held 15–17 May.

Blinkhorn, James et al. 2013a. 'A new synthesis of evidence for the Upper Pleistocene occupation of 16R Dune and its southern Asian context'. *Quaternary International*.

———. 2013b. 'Middle Palaeolithic occupation in the Thar Desert during the Upper Pleistocene: The signature of a modern human exit out of Africa?'. *Quaternary Science Reviews*.

———. 2015. 'Middle Palaeolithic point technologies in the Thar Desert, India'. *Quaternary International*.

———. 2017. 'Environments and Cultural Change in the Indian Subcontinent –Implications for the Dispersal of Homo sapiens in the Late Pleistocene'. *Current Anthropology*.

Boivin, Nicole et al. 2013. 'Human dispersal across diverse environments of Asia during the Upper Pleistocene'. *Quaternary International*.

Bokovenko, N. 2005. 'Migrations of Early Nomads of the Eurasian Steppe in a Context of Climatic Changes'. In *Impact of the Environment on Human Migration in Eurasia*. NATO Science Series IV, Earth and Environmental Sciences, Kluwer Academic Publishers.

Boyce, M. 1996. *A History of Zoroastrianism*. Volume One, The Early Period. Brill.

Brandt, Guido et al. 2013. 'Ancient DNA reveals key stages in the formation of Central European mitochondrial genetic diversity'. *Science*.

Breeze, Paul et al. 2016. 'Palaeohydrological corridors for hominin dispersals in the Middle East ~250–70,000 years ago'. *Quaternary Science Reviews*.

Buck, Trudi. 2007. 'Dispersal of Homo sapiens around the Indian Ocean rim: a geometric morphometric study of craniofacial diversity'. Durham theses. Available at Durham E-Theses Online: http://etheses.dur.ac.uk/2845/ Durham University (accessed April 2024).

Buhler, G, tr. 1886. *The Laws of Manu*. Oxford: Clarendon Press.

Burrow, Thomas. 1995. *The Sanskrit Language*. Delhi: Motilal Banarsidass Publishers.

Butters, Luis et al. 1996. 'Ideology, Materialization, and Power Strategies'. *Current Anthropology*.

Carson, Penelope. 2012. *The East India Company and Religion, 1698–1858*. Woodbridge, UK: The Boydell Press.

Carter, Elizabeth et al. 'Elam Surveys of Political History and Archaeology'. University of California Press, 1984.

Census of India 1941, Vol 1. Delhi, 1943.

Cerasetti, Barbara. 2012. 'Remote Sensing and Survey of the Murghab Alluvial Fan, Southern Turkmenistan: The Coexistence of Nomadic Herders and Sedentary Farmers in the Late Bronze Age and Early Iron Age'. Proceedings of the 7th International Congress on the Archaeology of the Ancient Near East, 12 April–16 April 2010, the British Museum and UCL, London. Volume 1. *Mega-cities & Mega-sites: The Archaeology of Consumption & Disposal Landscape, Transport & Communication*. Edited by Roger Matthews and John Curtis. Harrassowitz Verlag· Wiesbaden.

Chanda, Ramaprasad. 1976 reprint. *The Indo-Aryan Races*. New Delhi: Indological Book Corporation.

Chandrasekar, A., et al. 2007. 'YAP insertion signature in South Asia'. *Annals of Human Biology*.

Chandrasekar A, S. Kumar, J. Sreenath, B. N. Sarkar, B. P. Urade, et al. 2009. 'Updating Phylogeny of Mitochondrial DNA Macrohaplogroup M in India: Dispersal of Modern Human in South Asian Corridor'. *PLOS ONE*. 4(10): e7447.doi:10.1371/journal.pone.0007447 (accessed April 2024).

Chatterjee, A. et al. 2017. 'Geochemistry of Harappan potteries from Kalibangan and sediments in the Ghaggar River: Clues for a dying river'. China University of Geosciences (Beijing) and Peking University. Production and hosting by Elsevier B.V. Geoscience Frontiers 9 (2018) 1203–121: 2017.

Chaubey, Gyaneshwer. 2010. Dissertationes Biologicae Universitatis Tartuensis 185. 'The demographic history of India: A perspective based on genetic evidence'. Tartu, Estonia. Tartu University Press: 2010.

———. 2011. 'Population Genetic Structure in Indian Austroasiatic Speakers: The Role of Landscape Barriers and Sex-Specific Admixture'. Dissertationes Biologicae Universitatis Tartuensis 185. Tartu, Estonia. Tartu University Press: *Mol. Biol. Evol.*

Chaubey, Gyaneshwer, and Endicott. 2013. 'The Andaman Islanders in a Regional Genetic Context: Re-examining the Evidence for an Early Peopling of the Archipelago from South Asia'. *Human Biology* 85(1): Article 7, http://digitalcommons.wayne.edu/humbiol/vol85/iss1/7 (accessed April 2024).

Chaubey, G., A. Kadian, S. Bala, V. R. Rao. 2015. 'Genetic Affinity of the Bhil, Kol and Gond Mentioned in Epic Ramayana'. *PLOS ONE* 10(6): e0127655. doi:10.1371/journal.pone.0127655 (accessed April 2024).

———. 2016. 'Genetic affinities of the Jewish populations of India'. *Scientific Reports.*

Clarke, Joanne et al. 2016. 'Climatic changes and social transformations in the Near East and North Africa during the "long" 4th millennium BC: A comparative study of environmental and archaeological evidence'. *Quaternary Science Reviews.*

Clarkson, Chris et al. 2009. 'The oldest and longest enduring microlithic sequence in India: 35,000 years of modern human occupation and change at the Jwalapuram Locality 9 rock shelter'. *Antiquity* 83: 326–48.

———. 2011. 'Continuity and change in the lithic industries of the Jurreru Valley, India, before and after the Toba eruption'. *Quaternary International.*

———. 2013. 'East of Eden Founder Effects and the Archaeological Signature of Modern Human Dispersal'. DOI: 10.1017/CBO9781139084741.007 (accessed May 2024).

Clift, P., et al. 2012. 'U-Pb zircon dating evidence for a Pleistocene Sarasvati River and capture of the Yamuna River'. *Geological Society of America*.

Costantini, L. 2006. 'The First Farmers in Western Pakistan: The Evidence of the Neolithic Agro-pastoral Settlement of Mehrgarh'. Paper presented at the international seminar on the 'First Farmers in Global Perspective', Lucknow.

Cordaux, Richard et al. 2004. 'Independent Origins of Indian Caste and Tribal Paternal Lineages'. *Current Biology*.

Cortesi, E. 2008. 'Cultural Relationships Beyond the Iranian Plateau: the Helmand Civilization, Baluchistan and the Indus Valley in the 3rd Millenium BCE'. *Paleorient*.

Dalfes, H. ed. 1997. *Third Millennium BC Climate Change and Old World Collapse*. NATO ASI Series, Springer.

Dambricourt-Malasse, Anne et al. 2013. 'Orsang Man: A robust Homo sapiens in Central India with Asian Homo erectus features'. *Evolving humanity, Emerging Worlds*. 17th World Congress of the International Union of Anthropological and Ethnological Sciences, Manchester.

Darabi, Hojjat. 2012. 'Towards reassessing the Neolithisation process in Western Iran'. *Documenta Praehistorica*.

de Barros Damgaard et al. 2018. 'The first horse herders and the impact of early Bronze Age steppe expansions into Asia'. *Science*.

de la Torre, Ignacio. 2011. 'The origins of stone tool technology in Africa: A historical perspective'. *Phil. Trans. R. Soc. B*.

Deneger, Almuth. 2002. 'The Nuristani Languages'. Proceedings of the British Academy.

Dergachev, V et al. 2005. 'Large-scale Periodicity of Climate Change during the Holocene'. In *Impact of the Environment on Human Migration in Eurasia*. NATO Science Series IV, Earth and Environmental Sciences. Kluwer Academic Publishers.

Diakonoff, I. n.d. 'More on the Possible Linguistic Connections of the Sumerians'.

———. 1997. 'External Connections of the Sumerian Language'. St Petersburg: Mother Tongue III.

Diamond, Jared et al. 2003. 'Farmers and Their Languages: The First Expansions'. *Science*.

Dixit, Y. 2014. 'Abrupt weakening of the summer monsoon in northwest India ~4100 yr ago'. *Geology* 42(4): 339–342; Data Repository item

2014129 | doi:10.1130/G35236.1. Published online 24 February 2014. Geological Society of America.

Dow, A. 1803. *The History of Hindostan*. London

Dubey-Pathak, Meenakshi. 2014. 'The Rock Art of the Bhimbetka Area in India'. *Adoranten*.

Dutt, Romesh. 1900. *The Civilisation of India*. London.

Eaaswarkhanth, Muthukrishnan et al. 2009. 'Diverse genetic origin of Indian Muslims: Evidence from autosomal STR loci'. *Journal of Human Genetics*.

Eduljee, K. 'Zoroastrian Heritage'. http://www.heritageinstitute.com (accessed May 2024).

Encyclopædia Iranica. www.iranicaonline.org (accessed May 2024).

Endicott, Phillip et al. 2003. 'The Genetic Origins of the Andaman Islanders'. *Am. J. Hum. Genet.*

———. 2007. 'Genetic evidence on modern human dispersals in South Asia: Y chromosome and mitochondrial DNA perspectives: The world through the eyes of two haploid genomes'. In *The Evolution and History of Human Populations in South Asia*, M.D. Petraglia and B. Allchin, eds, 229–44. Springer.

Erdosy, George. 1995. 'Language, material culture and ethnicity: Theoretical perspectives'. In *The Indo-Aryans of Ancient South Asia: Language, Material Culture and Ethnicity*. George Erdosy, ed. Berlin. New York. Walter de Gruyter.

Erlandson, Jon et al. 2015. 'Coasting out of Africa: The potential of mangrove forests and marine habitats to facilitate human coastal expansion via the Southern Dispersal Route'. *Quaternary International*.

Falk, Harry. 2003. 'Decent Drugs for Decent People: Further Thoughts on the Nature of Soma'. Berlin. *Orientalia Suecana* LI-LII.

Faris, Justin. 2014. 'Wheat Domestication: Key to Agricultural Revolutions Past and Future'. In *Genomics of Plant Genetic Resources*. R. Tuberosa et al. eds. *Springer*.

Ferishta, M. n.d. *History of the Rise of the Mahomedan Power in India*, Vol 1. John Briggs tr. 1829. London.

Fernandes, Veronica et al. 2012. 'The Arabian Cradle: Mitochondrial Relicts of the First Steps along the Southern Route out of Africa'. *The American Society of Human Genetics*.

Foley, Robert. 2001. 'The Evolutionary Consequences of Increased Carnivory in Hominids'. In *The Early Human Diet: The Role of Meat*. C. Stanford, H. Bunn eds. Oxford University Press.

Foley, Robert. n.d. 'Hominids, humans and hunter-gatherers: an evolutionary perspective'. In *Hunters and Gatherers: History, evolution and social change*. T. Ingold et al. eds. Oxford.

Foote, Robert. 1916. *The Foote Collection of Indian Prehistoric and Protohistoric Antiquities*. Madras: Government Press.

Fortier, Jana. 'The Ethnography of South Asian Foragers'. *Annual Review of Anthropology*. 2009. 38:99–114.

Fournet, A. 2010. 'About the Mitanni-Aryan Gods'. *The Journal of Indo-European Studies*.

Frachetti, Michael. 2002. 'Bronze Age Exploitation and Political Dynamics of the Eastern Eurasian Steppe Zone in Ancient interactions: East and west'. In *Eurasia*. Katie Boyle et al. eds. McDonald Institute for Archaeological Research.

Franke, Sabina. 1995. 'Kings of Akkad: Sargon and Naram-Sin'. In *Civilizations of the Ancient Near East*, Vol II. Jack Sasson ed. New York: Simon & Schuster.

The Free Dictionary www.thefreedictionary.comFreewalt, Jason. 2014. 'Sargon the Great of Akkad: The First Empire Builder of Mesopotamia'. Charles Town, WV. *American Military University*.

Frenez, Dennys. 2016. 'Bronze Age Salut (ST1) and the Indus Civilization: recent discoveries and new insights on regional interaction'. *Proceedings of the Seminar for Arabian Studies*.

Fuller, Dorian Q. 2001. 'Ashmounds and hilltop villages: the search for early agriculture in southern India'. *Archaeology International*.

———. 2003. 'African crops in prehistoric South Asia: a critical review'. In *Food, Fuel and Fields: Progress in African Archaelbotany*. Katharina Neumann, ed. Koln. Heinrich Barth Institute.

———. 2006. 'Dung Mounds and Domesticators: Early Cultivation and Pastoralism in Karnataka'. Catherine Jarrige and Vincent Lefevre, eds. *South Asian Archaeology*.

———. 2011. 'Finding Plant Domestication in the Indian Subcontinent'. *Current Anthropology*.

———. 2012. 'Pathways to Asian Civilizations: Tracing the Origins and Spread of Rice and Rice Cultures'. *Rice* 4: 78–92, Springer.

Gangal, Kavita et al. 2010. 'Spatio-temporal analysis of the Indus urbanisation'. *Current Science*.

———. 2014. 'The Near-Eastern Roots of the Neolithic in South Asia'. *PLOS ONE*.

Garnier, Romain, Laurent Sagart, Benoît Sagot. 2017. 'Milk and the Indo-Europeans'. In *Language Dispersal Beyond Farming*. Martine Robbeets, Alexander Savalyev, eds. Amsterdam. John Benjamins Publishing Company, 291–311, 10.1075/z.215.13gar. hal-01667476 (accessed May 2024).

Gaunitz, Charleen et al. 2018. 'Ancient genomes revisit the ancestry of domestic and Przewalski's horses'. *Science*.

Gauniyal, Mansi et al. 2010. 'A Genetic Study of Four Population Groups of Uttara Kannada District of Karnataka'. *Anthropologist*.

Gayden, Tenzin et al. 2009. 'Genetic insights into the origins of Tibeto-Burman populations in the Himalayas'. *Journal of Human Genetics*.

Giosan, Liviu et al. 2012. 'Fluvial landscapes of the Harappan civilization'. *PNAS*.

———. 'Neoglacial Climate Anomalies and the Harappan Metamorphosis'. *Climate of the Past* Discussion. https://doi.org/10.5194/cp-2018–37.

Gross, Briana et al. 2014. 'Archaeological and genetic insights into the origins of domesticated rice'. *PNAS*.

Groucutt Huw et al. n.d. 'First Arabians'. *Current World Archaeology*, Issue 75;

———. 2012. 'The Prehistory of the Arabian Peninsula: Deserts, Dispersals, and Demography'. *Evolutionary Anthropology*.

———. 2014. 'An Arabian Perspective on the Dispersal of Homo Sapiens Out of Africa'. In *Southern Asia, Australia and the Search for Human Origins*, R. Denell and M. Porr eds. *Cambridge University Press*.

———. 2015. 'Rethinking the Dispersal of Homo sapiens out of Africa'. *Evolutionary Anthropology*.

———. 2015a. 'Stone tool assemblages and models for the dispersal of Homo sapiens out of Africa'. *Quaternary International*.

———. 2015b. 'Human occupation of the Arabian Empty Quarter during MIS 5: evidence from Mundafan Al-Buhayrah, Saudi Arabia'. *Quaternary Science Reviews*.

Grugni, Viola et al. 2012. 'Ancient Migratory Events in the Middle East: New Clues from the Y-Chromosome Variation of Modern Iranians'. *PLOS ONE*.

Gunnell, Yanni et al. 2007. 'Response of the South Indian runoff-harvesting civilization to northeast monsoon rainfall variability during the last 2000 years: instrumental records and indirect evidence'. *The Holocene*. http://hol.sagepub.com/cgi/content/abstract/17/2/207.

Gutala, Ramana et al. 2006. 'A Shared Y-chromosomal Heritage between Muslims and Hindus in India'. *Human Genetics*.

Haak, Wolfgang et al. 2015. 'Massive migration from the steppe is a source for Indo-European languages in Europe'. *Nature*.

Hahn, F. 1911. *Kurukh Grammar*. Calcutta.

Hamblin, W. 2006. *Warfare in the Ancient Near East to 1600 BC*. Routledge.

Harari, Yuval. 2011. *Sapiens A Brief History of Humankind*. London: Vintage. Harcourt, Alexander. 2017. 'Human phylogeography and diversity'. *PNAS*.

Harrassowitz, Otto. n.d. 'Anahita: The Deity of Water, Fertility, Healing and Wisdom. www.caissoas. com.

Harrod, James. 2007. 'The Bhimbetka Glyphs'. In *Exploring the mind of ancient man: Festschrift to Robert G. Bednarik*. Peddarapu Reddy ed. New Delhi.

Haslam, M. et al. 2010. 'The 74 ka Toba super-eruption and southern Indian hominins: archaeology, lithic technology and environments at Jwalapuram Locality 3'. *Journal of Archaeological Science*

———. 2012. 'A southern Indian Middle Palaeolithic occupation surface sealed by the 74 ka Toba eruption: Further evidence from Jwalapuram Locality 22'. *Quaternary International*.

Heesterman, J. 1962. 'Vratya and Sacrifice'. *Indo-Iranian Journal*.

Heidarpoor, Azadeh et al. 2016. 'Commonalities between Yajna Ritual in India and Yasna Ritual in Iran'. *Indian Journal of History of Science*.

Herrenschmidt, Clarisse. 1996. 'Elamite Civilization and Writing'. In *Ancestor of the West: Writing, reasoning, and religion in Mesopotamia, Elam, and Greece*, Teresa Fagan tr. The University of Chicago Press.

Hock, Hans, and Elena Bashir eds. 2016. *The Languages and Linguistics of South Asia: A Comprehensive Guide*. Berlin: Walter de Gruyter GmbH.

Hole, Frank. 1983. 'Symbols of Religion and Social Organization at Susa'.

Hollard, C et al. 2018. 'New genetic evidence of affinities and discontinuities between bronze age Siberian populations'. *American Journal of Physical Anthropology*.

Huang, Xuehui. 2012. 'A map of rice genome variation reveals the origin of cultivated rice'. *Nature*.

Hudjashov, Georgi et al. 2007. 'Revealing the prehistoric settlement of Australia by Y chromosome and mtDNA analysis'. *PNAS*.

Hunter, G. 1932. 'Mohenjo-Daro – Indus Epigraphy'. *Journal of the Royal Asiatic Society*.

Huynh Thi Duoc. 2009. *Cham Sculpture and Indian Mythology*. Danang Publishing House.

Ingman Max et al. 2003. 'Mitochondrial Genome Variation and Evolutionary History of Australian and New Guinean Aborigines'. *Genome Research*.

Jain, S. 2003. 'Pristine Jainism (Beyond rituals and superstitions)'. Varanasi: Parshwanath Vidyapeeth.

Jamison, Stephanie, and Joel Brereton, trs. 2014. *The Rigveda: The Earliest Religious Poetry of India*. Oxford University Press.

Jansen, Michael. 1985. 'Mohenjo-Daro, city of the Indus'. *Endeavour*.

———. 1989. 'Water supply and sewage disposal at Mohenjo-daro'. *World Archaeology*.

———. 1993. 'Mohenjo-daro: Type Site of the Earliest Urbanization Process in South Asia: Ten years of research at Mohenjo-daro, Pakistan and an attempt at a synopsis'.

Jarrige, Catherine et al. 2006. 'The figurines of the first farmers at Mehrgarh and their offshoots'. Paper presented at the international seminar on 'First Farmers in Global Perspective', Lucknow.

Jarrige, Jean-Francois et al. 2006. 'Mehrgarh Neolithic'. Paper presented at the international seminar on *First Farmers in Global Perspective*, Lucknow.

———. 2011, 'Shahr-i Sokhta and the chronology of the Indo-Iranian regions'. *Paleorient*.

Jennings, Richard et al. 2015. 'The greening of Arabia: Multiple opportunities for human occupation of the Arabian Peninsula during the Late Pleistocene inferred from an ensemble of climate model simulations'. *Quaternary International*.

Johnson, J. et al. n.d. 'Society, Demography and Community: Reassessing Bronze Age Sintashta Populations in the Southern Urals, Russia (2100–1700 BC)'. In *Beyond Elites, Alternatives to Hierarchical Systems in Modelling Social Formations*, 355–67. International Conference at the Ruhr-Universitt, Bochum. Germany, 2022. Verlag Dr. Rudolf Habelt GmbH, Bonn.

Jones, Sacha. 2007. 'The Toba supervolcanic eruption: Tephra-fall deposits in India and paleoanthropological implications'. In

The Evolution and History of Human Populations in South Asia. M. Petraglia and B. Allchin, eds. Springer.

Jones, Sacha. 2009. 'The Palaeolithic of the Middle Son valley, north-central India: Changes in hominin lithic technology and behaviour during the Upper Pleistocene'. *Journal of Anthropological Archaeology*.

———. 2012. 'Local- and regional-scale impacts of the 74 ka Toba supervolcanic eruption on hominin populations and habitats in India'. Quaternary International 258 (2012), 100–118

Kane, Pandurang. 1941. *History of Dharmasastra*, Vol. II Part I. Poona: Bhandarkar Oriental Research Institute.

Kathayat Gayatri et al. 2017. 'The Indian monsoon variability and civilization changes in the Indian subcontinent'. *Science Advances*.

Kenoyer, Jonathan et al. n.d.a. 'Cultures and Societies of the Indus Tradition'. https://www.harappa.com/category/article-/author/jonathan-mark-kenoyer?page=8 (accessed April 2024).

———. n.d.b. 'Early City States in South Asia'.

———. 1994. 'The Harappan State: Was it or wasn't it?'. In *From Sumer to Meluhha. Wisconsin Archaeological Reports*, Volume 3.

———. 2004. 'Chronology and Interrelations between Harappa and Central Asia'. https://www.harappa.com/content/chronology-and-interrelations-between-harappa-and-central-asia.

———. 2011. 'Changing Perspectives of the Indus Civilization: New Discoveries and Challenges'. *Journal of the Indian Archaeological Society*.

———. 2013. 'A new approach to tracking connections between the Indus Valley and Mesopotamia: initial results of strontium isotope analyses from Harappa and Ur'. *Journal of Archaeological Science*.

———. 2016. 'The Indus Civilization: Changing Perspectives on Regional Origins, Diverse Character and Complex Legacy'. Lecture, UC Berkeley.

———. 2020. 'Origin and Development of the Indus Script: Insights from Harappa and other sites.' https://www.harappa.com/content/origin-and-development-indus-script-insights-harappa-and-other-sites (accessed April 2024).

Khan, Aurangzeb et al. 2013. 'Bricks and urbanism in the Indus Valley rise and decline'. *American Journal of Archaeology*.

Kingwell-Banham, Eleanor et al. 2015. 'Early agriculture in South Asia'. In *The Cambridge World History*. Cambridge University Press.

Kivisild, Toomas. 1999. 'Deep common ancestry of Indian and western-Eurasian mitochondrial DNA lineages'. *Current Biology*.

———. 2002. 'The Genetics of Language and Farming Spread in India'. In *Examining the Farming/Language Dispersal Hypothesis*. P. Bellwood and C. Renfrew (eds). Cambridge: McDonald Institute for Archaeological Research.

———. 2003. 'The Genetic Heritage of the Earliest Settlers Persists Both in Indian Tribal and Caste Populations'. *The American Journal of Human Genetics*.

———. 2005. 'Maternal ancestry and population history from whole mitochondrial genomes'. *Investigative Genetics*.Klyosov, Anatole. 2011. 'R1a1 history-TurkicWorld'. 'Haplogroup R1a as the Proto Indo-Europeans and the Legendary Aryans as Witnessed by the DNA of Their Current Descendants'. *Advances in Anthropology*. Vol. 2, No.1, 1–13. Published Online February 2012 in SciRes (http://www.SciRP.org/journal/aa) http://dx.doi.org/10.4236/aa.2012.21001.

Kochar, R. n.d. 'On the Identity and Chronology of the Rigvedic River Sarasvati'. Indian Institute of Astrophysics. https://www.webpages.uidaho.edu/ngier/306/contrasarav.htm

Korisettar, Ravi. 2011. 'Paradigm Shifts in the Geo-Archaeology of the Palaeolithic of the Indian Subcontinent: Building a Grand Pleistocene Cultural Sequence'. Dr A. P. Khatri Memorial Lecture delivered at Thiruvananthapuram.

Kortlandt, F. 2010. 'Studies in Germanic, Indo-European and Indo-Uralic'. Amsterdam – New York: Rodopi B.V.

Kramer, Andrew et al. 2001. 'Out of Africa and into the Levant: replacement or admixture in Western Asia?'. *Quaternary International*.

Krishnamurti, Bhadriraju. 2003. *The Dravidian Languages*. Cambridge University Press.

Kristiansen, Kristian, et al. 2017. 'Re-theorising mobility and the formation of culture and language among the Corded Ware Culture in Europe'. *Antiquity* 91(356): 334–47.

Kuiper, F. n.d. 'The Sources of Nahali Vocabulary'. http://sealang.net/sala/archives/pdf8/kuiper1966sources.pdf (accessed April 2024).

———. 1948. *Proto-Munda words in Sanskrit*. Amsterdam: Nederlandsche Uitgevers Maatschappij.

Kumar, Vikrant et al. 2007. 'Y-chromosome evidence suggests a common paternal heritage of Austro-Asiatic populations'. *BMC Evolutionary Biology*.

Kuz'mina, Elena. 2007. *The Origin of the Indo-Iranians*. Leiden, Boston: Brill.

Kuznetsov, P. 2005. 'An Indo-Iranian Symbol of Power in the Earliest Steppe Kurgans'. *Journal of Indo-European Studies*.

Lambeck, Kurt et al. 2011. 'Sea level and shoreline reconstructions for the Red Sea: isostatic and tectonic considerations and implications for hominin migration out of Africa'. *Quaternary Science Reviews*.

Lamberg-Karlovsky, C. 2002. 'Archaeology and Language: The Indo-Iranians'. *Current Anthropology*.

Lambrick, H. 1986. *Sind: A General Introduction*. Hyderabad: Sindhi Adabi Board.

Laursen, Steffen. 2009. 'The decline of Magan and the rise of Dilmun: Umm an-Nar ceramics from the burial mounds of Bahrain, c2250–2000 BC'. *Arabian Archaeology and Epigraphy* 20: 134–155. https://doi.org/10.1111/j.1600-0471.2009.00317.x

Law, Randall. 2006. 'Moving Mountains: The Trade and Transport of Rocks and Minerals Within the Greater Indus Valley Region'. In *Space and Spatial Analysis in Archaeology*. E. Robertson et al., eds. Calgary, Alberta, Canada: *University of Calgary Press*.

Laybourn, S. et al. 2016. 'Genetic analysis of novel Alu insertion polymorphisms in selected Indian populations'. *American Journal of Human Biology*.

Lemmen, Carsten et al.2012. 'A simulation of the Neolithic transition in the Indus valley'. *American Geophysical Union*.

Levine, M. 1999. 'Botai and the Origins of Horse Domestication'. *Journal of Anthropological Archaeology*.

Liu, Wu et al. 2015. 'The earliest unequivocally modern humans in southern China'. *Nature*.

———. 2010. 'Human remains from Zhi.rendong, South China, and modern human emergence in East Asia'. *PNAS*.

Lombardi, Alessandra. 2105. 'From Magan to Qade'. In *In the heart of Oman the castle of Salut*. Alessandra Avanzini, ed. L'ERMA di BRETSCHNEIDER, Via Cassiodoro, 11 - 00193 Roma.

Lommel, H. 1954. 'Anahita-Sarasvati'. *Asiatica*, Festschrift F. Weller, Leipzig.

Lopez, Saioa et al. 2017. 'The Genetic Legacy of Zoroastrianism in Iran and India: Insights into Population Structure, Gene Flow, and Selection'. *The American Journal of Human Genetics*.

Lubotsky, Alexander. 2001. 'The Indo-Iranian substratum'. In *Early Contacts between Uralic and Indo-European: Linguistic and Archaeological Considerations*. Papers presented at an international symposium held at the Tvärminne Research Station of the University of Helsinki 8–10 January 1999. (Mémoires de la Société Finno-ougrienne 242.) Chr. Carpelan, A. Parpola, P. Koskikallio (eds.), 301–17. Helsinki.

Lucotte, G. 2015. 'The Major Y-Chromosome Haplotype XI – Haplogroup R1a in Eurasia'. *Hereditary Genetics*.

Luneau, Elise. 2019. 'Climate Change and the Rise and Fall of the Oxus Civilization in Southern Central Asia'. German Archaeological Institute, Berlin.

McAlpin, David. 1975. 'Elamite and Dravidian: Further Evidence of Relationship'. *Current Anthropology*.

———. 1981. *Proto-Elamo-Dravidian: The Evidence and its Implications*. Philadelphia: The American Philosophical Society.

McElreavey, K. et al. 2005. 'A population genetics perspective of the Indus Valley through uniparentally-inherited markers'. *Annals of Human Biology*. March–April 2005; 32(2): 154–62.

McIntosh, Jane. 2005. *Ancient Mesopotamia: New Perspectives*. ABC-CLIO.

———. 2008. *The Ancient Indus Valley: New Perspectives*. ABC-CLIO.

Macaulay, Vincent. 2005. 'Single, Rapid Coastal Settlement of Asia Revealed by Analysis of Complete Mitochondrial Genomes'. *Science*.

Macdonell, A. 1912. *Vedic Index of Names and Subjects*. Vol I. London. John Murray, Albemarle Street, W.

———. 1912. *Vedic Index of Names and Subjects*. Vol II. London. John Murray, Albemarle Street, W. Govt. of India.

Macedo, Stephen. 2015. 'Introduction: Farmers'. In *Foragers, Farmers, and Fossil Fuels*, by Ian Morris. Princeton University Press.

Madella, Marco et al. 2006. 'Palaeoecology and the Harappan Civilisation of South Asia: a reconsideration'. *Quaternary Science Reviews*.

Mahabharata. Kisari Ganguli tr. 1883–96. https://sacred-texts.com/hin/maha/index.htm.

Maemoku, H. et al. 2012. 'Geomorphological Constraints on the Ghaggar River Regime During the Mature Harappan Period'. *Geophysical Monograph Series*.

Mahal, D. et al. 2018. 'The Geographic Origins of Ethnic Groups in the Indian Subcontinent: Exploring Ancient Footprints with Y-DNA Haplogroups'. *Frontiers in Genetics.*

Maine, H. 1875. *The Effects of Observation of India on Modern European Thought.* London.

Maisels, Charles Kieth. 2001. *Early Civilizations of the Old World*, Routledge.

Malla, Bansi Lal. n.d. 'Early Man at Bhimbetka'. https://ignca.gov.in/rockart.

Mallory, J. 2007. 'Indo-European Warfare'. In *War and Sacrifice, Studies in the Archaeology of Conflict.* Tony Pollard and Ian Banks, eds. Leiden, Boston: Brill.

Mark, Darren et al. 2013. 'A high-precision 40Ar/39Ar age for the Young Toba Tuff and dating of ultra-distal tephra: Forcing of Quaternary climate and implications for hominin occupation of India'. *Quaternary Geochronology.*

Masica, Colin. 1991. *The Indo-Aryan Languages.* Cambridge University Press.

Maslin, Mark et al. 2014. 'East African climate pulses and early human evolution'. *Quaternary Science Reviews.*

———. n.d. 'Changing trends in the study of a Paleolithic site in India: A century of research at Attirampakkam'. In *The Evolution and History of Human Populations in South Asia.* Springer.

———. n.d. 'Hominids, humans and hunter-gatherers: An evolutionary perspective'. In *Hunters and Gatherers: History, evolution and social change.* T. Ingold et al., eds. Oxford.

Mason, Philip. 1985. *The Men Who Ruled India.* Rupa & Co.

Masson, C. 1844. *Narrative of Various Journeys in Balochistan, Afghanistan, the Panjab, & Kalat.* Vol. 4. London. Richard Bentley.

MehrAfarin, Reza et al. 2010. 'The Zoroastrian Holyland of Haetumant'. In *An Academic and Religious Journal of Greek, Roman and Persian Studies.* Payam Nabarz, ed. Web of Wyrd Press.

Meier-Brugger, M. 2003. 'Indo-European Linguistics'. Berlin-New York: Walter de Gruyter.

Mejia, Vincent. 2009. 'The Tripartite Ideology: Functions, Methods and Applications'. Honors Thesis, Rutgers, The State University of New Jersey.

Menzel, Philip et al. 2014. 'Reconstruction of the Holocene Indian monsoon climate variability based on biogeochemical analyses of lake sediments'. Doctoral thesis. University of Hamburg. Dissertationes Biologicae Universitatis Tartuensis 114.

The Metropolitan Museum of Art. 1992. *The Royal City of Susa*. New York.

Metspalu, Mait et al. 2004. 'Most of the extant mtDNA boundaries in South and Southwest Asia were likely shaped during the initial settlement of Eurasia by
anatomically modern humans'. *BMC Genetics*.

———. 2005. 'Through the Course of Prehistory in India: Tracing the mtDNA Trail'. Tartu University Press. Dissertationes Biologicae Universitatis Tartuensis 114. http://hdl.handle.net/10062/853.

Michalowski, Piotr. 1993. 'Memory and Deed: The Historiography of the Political Expansion of the Akkad State'. In M. *Liverani, ed. Akkad: The First World Empire*. Cambridge University Press.

Mondal, Mayukh et al. 2016. 'Genomic analysis of Andamanese provides insights into ancient human migration into Asia and adaptation'. *Nature Genetics*.

Moorjani, Priya et al. 2013. 'Genetic Evidence for Recent Population Mixture in India'. *The American Journal of Human Genetics*.

Moreno, E. 2011. 'The society of our "out of Africa" ancestors (I) The migrant warriors that colonized the world'. *Communicative & Integrative Biology*.

———. 2013. 'The "Out of Africa Tribe" (II). *Communicative & Integrative Biology*.

Mountjoy, S. 2005. *The Indus River*. Chelsea House Publishers.

Muller, Max. 1847. *On the relation of the Bengali to the Arian and aboriginal languages of India*. John Murray, London.

———. 1885. *Lectures on the Science of Language*. Vol. I. London. The Project Gutenberg EBook of Lectures on The Science of Language by Max Müller.

Murty, M. 1993. 'Ethnohistory of Pastoralism: A study of Kuruvas and Gollas'. In *Studies in History, 9, 1, n.s.* Sage Publications. New Delhi, London.

Mutin, Benjamin. 2012. 'Cultural Dynamics in Southern Middle Asia in the fifth and fourth millennia BC: A reconstruction based on ceramic tradition'. *Paleorient*.

Narasimhan, Vagheesh et al. 2018. 'The Genomic Formation of South and Central Asia'. *bioRxiv*.

Narasimhan, Vagheesh et al. 2019. 'The Formation of Human Populations in South and Central Asia'. *Science* 365(6457). doi:10.1126/science.aat7487 (accessed April 2024).

National Archives UK Government. https://www.nationalarchives.gov.uk/education /empire/g1/cs3/default.htm (accessed April 2024).

Newman, Robert. 2019. *Goan Anthropology: Mothers, Miracles and Mythology*. Goa 1556.

Nieuwenhuyse, Olivier et al. 1994. 'The 8.2 Event in Upper Mesopotamia: Climate and Cultural Change'. In *Climate and Cultural Change in Prehistoric Europe and the Near East*. IEMA Proceedings, Volume 6. Peter Biehl and Olivier Nieuwenhuyse, eds.

Novak, M. 2007. 'Mittani Empire and the Question of Absolute Chronology: Some Archaeological Considerations'. Originalveröffentlichung in M. Bietak – E. Czerny (Hg.), 'The Synchronisation of Civilisations in the Eastern Mediterranean in the Second Millennium B.C. III.' Proceedings of the SCIEM 2000 – 2nd Euro Conference (Wien 2007), S. 389–401.

Nyberg, Harri. 1995. 'The problem of the Aryans and the Soma: The botanical evidence'. In *The Indo-Aryans of Ancient South Asia: Language, Material Culture and Ethnicity*, ed., George Erdosy. Walter de Gruyter.

Oldham, C. F. 1874. *Notes on the Lost River of the Indian Desert*. The Calcutta Review, Volume LIX.

Olijdam, Eric. 1995. 'Babylonian Quest for Lapis Lazuli and Dilmun during the City III Period'. *South Asian Archaeology*.

Oppenheimer, S. n.d. '*Mt Toba genetic evidence*'. Bradshaw Foundation.

Orengo, H. et al. 2017. 'Large-scale, multi-temporal remote sensing of palaeo-river networks: A case study from northwest India and its implications for the Indus Civilisation'. *Remote Sensing* 9(7): 735; https://doi.org/10.3390/rs9070735.

Pagel, Mark et al. 2013. 'Ultraconserved words point to deep language ancestry across Eurasia'. *PNAS*.

Palanichamy, Malliya, et al. 2014. 'Tamil Merchant in Ancient Mesopotamia'. *PLOS ONE*.

———. 2015, 'West Eurasian mtDNA lineages in India: an insight into the spread of the Dravidian language and the origins of the caste system'. Berlin: Springer-Verlag.

Pappu, Shanti et al. 2011. 'Early Pleistocene Presence of Acheulian Hominins in South India'. *Science*. 331, 1596; DOI: 10.1126/

science.1200183. In M.D. Petraglia and B. Allchin (eds.), *The Evolution and History of Human Populations in South Asia*, 121–35. Springer.

Pargiter, F, tr. 1904. *The Markandeya Purana*. Calcutta.

Parpola, Asko. n.d. 'Is there any connection between Elam of Mesopotamia and the Indus Valley civilization'. *Harappa.com*.

———. 1988. 'The Coming of the Aryans to Iran and India and the Cultural and Ethnic Identity of the Dasas.' Studia Orientalia Electronica, https://journal.fi/store/article/view/49745.

———. 1994. *Deciphering the Indus Script*. Cambridge University Press.

———. 2005. 'Study of the Indus Script'. *Paper, 50th ICES Tokyo Session*.

———. 2010. 'A Dravidian solution to the Indus script problem'. Kalaignar M. Karunanidhi Classical Tamil Research Endowment Lecture World Classical Tamil Conference, Coimbatore.

———. 2015. *The Roots of Hinduism*. Oxford University Press.

Pathak, Ajai et al. 2018. 'The Genetic Ancestry of Modern Indus Valley Populations from Northwest India'. *The American Journal of Human Genetics*.

Perera, Nimal et al. 2011. 'People of the ancient rainforest: Late Pleistocene foragers at the Batadomba-lena rockshelter, Sri Lanka'. *Journal of Human Evolution*.

The Periplus of the Erythrean Sea. Schoff, W. tr. 1912. New York City. Longmans, Green, and Co.

Petersen, M. 2012. 'Aggressive architecture: Fortifications of the Indus valley in the Mature Harappan phase'. MA thesis, University of Leiden.

Petraglia, Michael et al. 2009. 'Population increase and environmental deterioration correspond with microlithic innovations in South Asia ca. 35,000 years ago'. *PNAS Early Edition*.

———. 2010. 'Out of Africa: New hypotheses and evidence for the dispersal of Homo sapiens along the Indian Ocean rim'. *Annals of Human Biology*.

———. 2011. 'The Toba volcanic super-eruption, environmental change, and hominin occupation history in India over the last 140,000 years', *Quaternary International*.

———. 2012. 'The Toba Volcanic Super-eruption of 74,000 Years Ago: Climate Change, Environments, and Evolving Humans'. *Quaternary International*.

Petraglia, Michael. 2015. 'Green Arabia: Human prehistory at the Crossroads of Continents', *Quaternary International*

Petrie, C. A. et al. 2016. 'Feeding ancient cities in South Asia: Dating the adoption of rice, millet and tropical pulses in the Indus civilisation.' *Antiquity*. December 2016.

Pinheiro, E. 2010. 'The Origin and Spread of the War Chariot'. Dissertation, University of Lisbon.

———. 2011. 'The Sintashta cultural particulars and the origin of the war chariot.' *ResAntQ* Vol. 2.

Pluciennik, Mark. 2004. 'The Meaning of 'Hunter-Gatherers' and Modes of Subsistence: A Comparative Historical Perspective'. In *Hunter-Gatherers in History, Archaeology and Anthropology*, ed., Alan Barnard. Berg

Ponton, Camilo. 2012a. 'Aridification of the Indian subcontinent during the Holocene: Implications for landscape evolution, sedimentation, carbon cycle, and human civilizations'. *Geophysical Research Letters* 39(3), doi:10.1029/2011GL050722, 2012.

Ponton et al. 2012b. 'Holocene aridification of India'. *Geophysical Research Letters*.

Possehl, Gregory L. et al. 1979. 'Hunter-Gatherer/Agriculturalist Exchange in Prehistory: An Indian Example'. *Current Anthropology*.

———. 1990. 'Revolution in the Urban Revolution: The Emergence of Indus Urbanization'. *Annu. Rev. Anthropol.*

———. 1997a. 'The Transformation of the Indus Civilization.' *Journal of World Prehistory* II (4).

———. 1997b. 'Climate and the Eclipse of the Ancient Cities of the Indus'. In *Third Millennium* BC *Climate Change and Old World Collapse*. NATO ASI Series, Springer.

———. 2008. 'Indus Folklore: An Unknown Story on Some Harappan Objects'. *BAR International Series*

Potts, David. 1981.'The Potter's Marks of Tepe Yahya'. *Paléorient*,

———. 2004. *The Archaeology of Elam*. Cambridge University Press.

Prasad, M. 2011. *India's foreign trade from antiquity to date*. Delhi. Kalpaz publications.

Prasad, Vandana et al. 2014. 'Mid–late Holocene monsoonal variations from mainland Gujarat, India: A multi-proxy study for evaluating climate culture relationship'. *Palaeogeography, Palaeoclimatology, Palaeoecology*.

Pugach, Irina et al. 2012. 'Genome-wide data substantiate Holocene gene flow from India to Australia'. *PNAS Early Edition.*

Pusalkar, A. D. 1951. 'Aryan Settlements in India' In *The History and Culture of the Indian People*, Vol. 1: *The Vedic Age*, edited by R. C. Majumdar. Bharatiya Vidya Bhavan.

Qamar, R. et al. 2002. 'Y-Chromosomal DNA Variation in Pakistan'. *Am J Hum Genet.* 70:1107–1124.

Quintana-Murci, Luis et al. 2001. 'Y-Chromosome Lineages Trace Diffusion of People and Languages in Southwestern Asia'. *Am. J. Hum. Genet.*

———. 2004. 'Where West Meets East: The Complex mtDNA Landscape of the Southwest and Central Asian Corridor' *Am. J. Hum. Genet.*

Rahmstorf, Lorenz. 2012. 'Control Mechanisms in Mesopotamia, the Indus Valley, the Aegean and Central Europe, c2600–2000 BC, and the Question of Social Power in Early Complex Societies'. *Beyond Elites, Alternatives to Hierarchical Systems in Modelling Social Formations.* International Conference at the Ruhr-Universitat, Bochum, Germany, October 22–24, 2009 Teil [part] 2. Dr. Rudolf Habelt GmbH. Bonn.

Rao, Rajesh. 2010. 'Probabilistic Analysis of an Ancient Undeciphered Script'. *IEEE Computer Society.*

Rasmussen, M. et al. 2011. 'An Aboriginal Australian Genome Reveals Separate Human Dispersals into Asia'. *Science.*

Raulwing, P. n.d. *The Kikkuli Text (CTH 284) – Some Interdisciplinary Remarks on Hittite Training Texts for Chariot Horses in the Second Half of the 2nd Millennium B.C.* In Armelle Gardeisen (ed.), 'Les Équidés dans le monde méditerranéen antique. Actes du colloque organisé par l'École française d'Athènes,' le Centre Camille Jullian, et l'UMR 5140 du CNRS, Athènes, 26–28 Novembre 2003. Lattes: Éd. de l'Association pour le développement de l'archéologie en Languedoc-Rousillon, 2005 [2006]. (Monographies d'archéologie méditerranéenne, ISSN 1286-8868, 1 vol., 324 p.: iii; 27 cm. ISBN: 2-912369-09-6), 61–75.

———. 2009. *The Kikkuli Text: Hittite Training Instructions for Chariot Horses in the Second Half of the 2nd Millennium B.C. and Their Interdisciplinary Context.*

Rawlinson, H. 1938. *A Concise History of the Indian People.* Madras: Oxford University Press.

Reade, Julian. n.d. 'Magan and Meluhhan merchants at Ur?' In *Beitrage zur Kulturgeschichte Vorderasiens*, 597–99. Philipp von Zabern. Mainz.

Redd, Alan et al. 2002. 'Gene Flow from the Indian Subcontinent to Australia: Evidence from the Y Chromosome'. *Current Biology*.

Reich, David et al. 2009. 'Reconstructing Indian Population History'. *Nature*.

———. 2011. 'Denisova Admixture and the First Modern Human Dispersals into Southeast Asia and Oceania'. *The American Journal of Human Genetics*.

———. 2018. *Who we are and how we got here: ancient DNA and the new science of the human past*. New York: Pantheon Books.

Review and Assessment Report of the Expert Committee to Review Available Information on Palaeochannels. 2016. *Palaeochannels of North West India*. New Delhi.

Reyes-Centeno, Hugo et al. 2014. 'Genomic and cranial phenotype data support multiple modern human dispersals from Africa and a southern route into Asia'. *PNAS*.

———. 2015. 'Testing modern human out-of-Africa dispersal models and implications for modern human origins'. *Journal of Human Evolution*.

Richards, Martin et al. 2000. 'Tracing European Founder Lineages in the Near Eastern mtDNA Pool'. *Am J Hum Genet*.

Ringe, D. 2015. 'The Indo-European Homeland from Linguistic and Archaeological Perspectives'. *Annual Review of Linguistics*.

Roach, K. 2008. *The Elamite Cylinder Seal Corpus, c3500–1000 BC*. The University of Sydney.

Romero, Irene et al. 2012. 'Herders of Indian and European Cattle Share Their Predominant Allele for Lactase Persistence'. *Mol. Biol. Evol.*

Rose, J. 2007. 'The Arabian Corridor Migration Model: archaeological evidence for hominin dispersals into Oman during the Middle and Upper Pleistocene'. Proceedings of the Seminar for Arabian Studies.

Rouse, Lynne et al. 2017. 'Micro-dynamics and macro-patterns: Exploring new archaeological data for the late Holocene human-water relationship in the Murghab alluvial fan, Turkmenistan'. *Quaternary International*, xxx (2015), 1–15. http://dx.doi.org/10.1016/ j.quaint.2015.12.021.

Rowney, H. 1882. *The Wild Tribes of India*. London.

Roy, B. 2016. 'Friedrich Max Muller and the Emergence of Identity Politics in India and Germany'. The English Goethe Society.

Sadovski, Velizar. 2018. 'Vedic and Avestan Parallels from Ritual Litanies and Liturgical Practices I'. In *Farnah, Indo-Iranian and Indo-European Studies*. Ann Arbor: Beech Stave Press.

Sahoo, Sanghamitra et al. 2006. 'A prehistory of Indian Y chromosomes: Evaluating demic diffusion scenarios'. *PNAS*.

Saini, H et al. 2010. 'Luminescence dating of the sediments from a buried channel loop in Fatehabad area, Haryana: Insight into Vedic Saraswati River and its environment'. Geological Survey of India. versita.metapress.com and www.geochronometria.pl.

Salvatori, S. 2016. 'Bactria-Margiana Archaeological Complex: how terminology hides historical processes'. Centro Studi Sudanesi e SubSahariani, Treviso, Italy. 2016, Transactions of Margiana Archaeological Expedition – Vol. 6.

Sankararaman, Sriram et al. 2012. 'The Date of Interbreeding between Neandertals and Modern Humans'. *PLOS Genetics*.

———. 2016. 'The Combined Landscape of Denisovan and Neanderthal Ancestry in Present-Day Humans'. *Current Biology*.

Sankhyan, A. 1997. 'Fossil clavicle of a Middle Pleistocene hominid from the Central Narmada Valley, India'. *Journal of Human Evolution*.

———. 2013. 'The Emergence of Homo sapiens in South Asia: The Central Narmada Valley as Witness'. *Human Biology Review*.

Sarianidi, Victor. 2001. 'The Indo-Iranian Problem in the light of the Latest Excavations in Margiana'. Athens. https://journal.fi/store/article/view/43986 (accessed April 2024).

———. 2003. 'Margiana and Soma-Haoma'. *Electronic Journal of Vedic Studies*.

Sarkar, Anindya et al. 2016. 'Oxygen isotope in archaeological bioapatites from India: Implications to climate change and decline of Bronze Age Harappan civilization'. *Scientific Reports*.

Schleicher, A. 1868. *The Sheep and the Horses*, quoted from F. Kortlandt 2010, 'Studies in Germanic, Indo-European and Indo-Uralic'. Rodopi B.V. Amsterdam-New York, NY.

Schmidt, Klaus. 2010. 'Gobekli Tepe – the Stone Age Sanctuaries. New results of ongoing excavations with a special focus on sculptures and high reliefs'. *Documenta Praehistorica* XXXVII.

Schug, Gwen et al. 2012. 'A peaceful realm? Trauma and social differentiation at Harappa'. *International Journal of Paleopathology*.

———. 2013. 'Infection, Disease, and Biosocial Processes at the End of the Indus Civilization'. *PLOS ONE*.

———. 2016. 'Begotten of Corruption? Bioarchaeology and "othering" of leprosy in South Asia'. *International Journal of Paleopathology*.

Scott, Jonathan. 1794. *Ferishta's History of Dekkan Vol. II*. (Translation). London: John Stocksdale.

Sengupta, S. et al. 2006. 'Polarity and temporality of high-resolution Y-Chromosome distributions in India identify both indigenous and exogenous expansions and reveal minor genetic influence of central Asian pastoralists'. *The American Journal of Human Genetics*.

Shah, Anish et al. 2011. 'Indian Siddis: African Descendants with Indian Admixture'. *The American Journal of Human Genetics*.

Shi, Hong et al. 2008. 'Y chromosome evidence of earliest modern human settlement in East Asia and multiple origins of Tibetan and Japanese populations'. *BMC Biology*.

Shinde, V. et al. 2019. 'An Ancient Harappan Genome Lacks Ancestry from Steppe Pastoralists or Iranian Farmers'. https://doi.org/10.1016/j.cell.2019.08.048.

Shishlina, N. 2004. 'North-West Caspian Sea Steppe: Environment and Migration Crossroads of Pastoral Culture Population during the Third Millenium BC'. In E. M. Scott et al. (eds.) *Impact of the Environment on Human Migration in Eurasia*, 91–106. Netherlands: Kluwer Academic Publishers.

Silva, Marina et al. 2017. 'A genetic chronology for the Indian Subcontinent points to heavily sex-biased dispersals'. *BMC Evolutionary Biology*.

Simons, G., and C. Fennig, eds. 2018. *Ethnologue: Languages of the World*, 21st edition. (Dallas: SIL International). http://www.ethnologue.com (accessed April 2024).

Singh, Ajay et al. 2017. 'Counter-intuitive influence of Himalayan river morphodynamics on Indus Civilisation urban settlements'. *Nature Communications*.

Singh, Sakshi et al. 2016. 'Dissecting the influence of Neolithic demic diffusion on Indian Y-chromosome pool through J2-M172 haplogroup'. *Scientific Reports*.

Sinha, R. et al. 2012. 'Geo-electric resistivity evidence for subsurface palaeochannel systems adjacent to Harappan sites in northwest India'. *Quaternary International.*

Sirajuddin, S. et al. 1994. 'Population Structure of the Chenchu and Other South Indian Tribal Groups: Relationships between Genetic, Anthropometric, Dermatoglyphic, Geographic, and Linguistic Distances'. *Human Biology.*

Sjogren, Karl-Göran. 2016. 'Diet and Mobility in the Corded Ware of Central Europe'. *PLOS ONE.*

Skjaervo, Prods. 2015. 'Early India and Iran'. In *The Wiley Blackwell Companion to Zoroastrianism,* edited by Michael Stausberg et al. Wiley Blackwell, UK. SPi Publisher Services, Pondicherry, India.

Southworth, Franklin. n.d.a. 'Prehistoric Implications of the Dravidian element in the NIA lexicon, with special attention to Marathi'. University of Pennsylvania. http://ccat.sas.upenn.edu/~fsouth/DravidianElement.pdf

———. n.d.b. 'Proto-Dravidian Agriculture'. University of Pennsylvania. http://ccat.sas.upenn.edu/~fsouth/Proto-DravidianAgriculture.pdf

———. 2005. *Linguistic Archaeology of South Asia.* Routledge.

Sparavigna, Amelia. n.d. 'Icons and Signs from Ancient Harappa'. Torino. https://web-archive.southampton.ac.uk/cogprints.org/6179/1/icons-and-signs-harappa.pdf (accessed May 2024).

Staubwasser, M. 2003. 'Climate change at the 4.2 ka BP termination of the Indus valley civilization and Holocene south Asian monsoon variability'. *American Geophysical Union.*

Stein, A. 1942. 'A Survey of Ancient Sites along the "Lost" Sarasvati River'. *The Geographical Journal.* Vol. 99, No. 4 (Apr. 1942), 173–82. Published by The Royal Geographical Society (with the Institute of British Geographers)

Steinkeller, Piotr. 1993. 'Early Political Development in Mesopotamia and the Origins of the Sargonic Empire'. In *Akkad, the First World Empire: Structure, Ideology, Traditions,* edited by Mario Liverno. Padova, 107–29.

Stringer, Chris. 2000. 'Coasting out of Africa'. *Nature.*

Studevent-Hickman, Benjamin et al. n.d. *Old Akkadian Period Texts.* The ancient Near East: historical sources in translation; edited by Mark W. Chavalas. Malden, MA: Blackwell Pub., 2006.

Stuhrmann, Rainer. 2016. 'Die Zehnkonigsschlacht am Ravifluss.' *Electronic Journal of Vedic Studies* 23(1). Translated by Michael Witzel.

Su, B. et al. 2000. 'Y chromosome haplotypes reveal prehistorical migrations to the Himalayas'. *Hum Genet* 107: 582–590.

Sumer: Cities of Eden. 1993. Time-Life Books.

Tamang, Rakesh et al. 2012. 'Genomic view on the peopling of India'. *Investigative Genetics*.

Tacon, Paul et al. 2010. 'New rock art discoveries in the Kurnool District, Andhra Pradesh, India'. *Antiquity*.

Tassi, Francesca et al. 2015, 'Early modern human dispersal from Africa: genomic evidence for multiple waves of migration'. *Investigative Genetics*.

Tewari, Rakesh et al. 2006. 'Early Farming at Lahuradewa'. International Seminar on *First Farmers in Global Perspective*, Lucknow.

Tews, Sophie. 2011. 'Seals in Dilmun Society'. Leiden. Thesis Universiteit Leiden, Faculteit der Archeologie, December.

Thangaraj, Kumarasamy et al. 2005a. 'Reconstructing the Origin of Andaman Islanders'. *Science*.

———. 2005b. 'Different population histories of the Mundari- and Mon-Khmer-speaking Austro-Asiatic tribes inferred from the mtDNA 9-bp deletion/insertion polymorphism in Indian populations'. *Springer-Verlag*.

———. 2006. 'Unique origin of Andaman Islanders: insight from autosomal loci'. *Journal of Human Genetics*.

Thapar, Romila. 1996. 'The Theory of Aryan Race and India: History and Politics.' *Social Scientist*, Vol. 24, No. 1/3. (Jan.–Mar., 1996), 3–29.

———. n.d. *The Aryan Recasting Constructs*.

Thesiger, Wilfred. 1959. *Arabian Sands*. Penguin Books.

Thieme, Paul. "The 'Aryan' Gods of the Mitanni Treaties." *Journal of the American Oriental Society*, vol. 80, no. 4, American Oriental Society, 1960, 301–17, https://www.jstor.org/stable/595878.

Thompson, Thomas. 2005. 'Ancient Stateless Civilization: Bronze Age India and the State in History'. *The Independent Review*.

Thurgood, Graham, and Randy LaPolla, eds. 2003. *The Sino-Tibetan Languages*. Routledge, London.

Thurston, E. 1909. *Castes and Tribes of Southern India*. Vol. I – A and B, Vol. III. Madras: Government Press.

Trautmann, T. 1997. *Aryans and British India*. University of California Press, Berkeley & LA, USA.

Tripathi, J, et al. 2004. 'Is River Ghaggar, Saraswati? Geochemical constraints'. *Current Science*.

Tumonggor, Meryanne et al. 2013. 'The Indonesian archipelago: an ancient genetic highway linking Asia and the Pacific'. *Journal of Human Genetics*.

Tyler, Stephen. 1968. 'Dravidian and Uralian: The lexical evidence'. *Language*, Vol. 44, No. 4 (Dec. 1968), 798–812. Linguistic Society of America.

Underhill, Peter et al. 2014. 'The phylogenetic and geographic structure of Y-chromosome haplogroup R1a'. *European Journal of Human Genetics*.

Vahia, Mayank. et al. 2017. 'A diffusion based study of population dynamics: Prehistoric migrations into South Asia'. *PLOS ONE*.

van Buitenen, J. tr. 1973. *The Mahabharata* Book 1 *The Book of the Beginning*. The University of Chicago.

van Dijk, W. 2016. 'Linking themorphology of fluvial fan systems to aquifer stratigraphy in the Sutlej-Yamuna plain of northwest India.' *Journal of Geophysical Research: Earth Surface*.

Vendidad (Videvdad) or Laws against the Demons: Avesta – The Sacred Books of Zoroastrianism, Book 3. Darmesteter, J. tr. 1898. *Sacred Books of the East*.

Vermaak, Petrus. 2008. 'Guabba, the Meluhhan Village in Mesopotamia'. *Journal for Semitics*.

Vidale, Massimo. 2004. 'Growing in a Foreign World: For a History of the "Meluhha Villages" in Mesopotamia in the 3rd Millennium BC'. *The Melammu Project*.

Walter, Robert et al. 2000. 'Early human occupation of the Red Sea coast of Eritrea during the last interglacial'. *Nature*.

Wang, Chuan-Chao et al. 2013. 'Inferring human history in East Asia from Y chromosomes'. *Investigative Genetics*.

———. 2016. 'Agriculture driving male expansion in Neolithic Time'. *Science China Life Sciences*. June. 59(6): 643–46. doi: 10.1007/s11427-016-5057-y (accessed April 2024).

Warmuth, V. 2012. 'Reconstructing the origin and spread of horse domestication in the Eurasian steppe'. *PNAS*.

Watkins, W. et al. 2008. 'Genetic variation in South Indian castes: evidence from Y-chromosome, mitochondrial, and autosomal polymorphisms'. *BMC Genetics*.

Weiss, Harvey et al. 1993a. 'The Genesis and Collapse of Third Millennium North Mesopotamian Civilization'. *Science*.

———. 1993b. 'The Genesis and Collapse of the Akkadian Empire: The Accidental Refraction of Historical Law'. In *Akkad, the First World Empire: Structure, Ideology, Traditions*. Mario Liverani, ed. Padova, 131–55.

———. 2015. 'Megadrought, collapse, and resilience in late 3rd millennium BC Mesopotamia'. 2200 BC – A climatic breakdown as a cause for the collapse of the old world? 7th Archaeological Conference of Central Germany. October 23–26, 2014 Halle (Saale).

———. 2017. '4.2 ka BP Megadrought and the Akkadian Collapse'. In *Megadrought and Collapse from Early Agriculture to Angkor*. Harvey Weiss, ed. Oxford University Press, USA.

Wells, Spencer. 2002. *The Journey of Man: A Genetic Odyssey*. New York: Random House.

———. 2007. *Deep Ancestry: Inside the Genographic Project*. Washington D.C.: National Geographic Society.

Wen, Chenghao. 2018. 'Bronze Age Economic and Social Practices in the Central Eurasian Borderlands of China (3000–1500 BC): An Archaeological Investigation'. Doctoral thesis, University of California.

White, David. 1991. *Myths of the Dog-Man*. The University of Chicago Press.

Wilks, Mark. 1817. *Historical Sketches of the South of India*. Vol. 2. Longman, Hurst, Rees, Orme and Brown. London.

Witas, Henryk et al. 2013. 'mtDNA from the Early Bronze Age to the Roman Period Suggests a Genetic Link between the Indian Subcontinent and Mesopotamian Cradle of Civilization'. *PLOS ONE*.

Witzel, Michael. n.d. 'Aryan and non-Aryan Names in Vedic India. Data for the linguistic situation, c1900–500 B.C.' http://michaelwitzel.org/wp-content/uploads/2014/06/Lingsit.pdf

———. 1995. 'Early Sanskritization. Origins and Development of the Kuru State'. *Electronic Journal of Vedic Studies* (EJVS); 1–4; 1–26.

Witzel, Michael. 1999a. 'Substrate Languages in Old Indo-Aryan (Rgvedic, Middle and Late Vedic)'. *Electronic Journal of Vedic Studies* (EJVS); 5–1; 1–67.

———. 1999b. 'Early Sources for South Asian Substrate Languages'. *Mother Tongue.*

———. 2000. 'The Languages of Harappa'. In Kenoyer, J. (ed.) *Proceedings of the conference on the Indus civilization* (2000-02-17). *Madison, WI.*

———. 2001. 'Autochthonous Aryans? The Evidence from Old Indian and Iranian Texts'. *Electronic Journal of Vedic Studies* (EJVS); 7–3; 1–115.

Woodard, Roger. 2006. *Indo-European sacred space: Vedic and Roman cult.* University of Illinois Press, Urbana and Chicago.

Yadav, Nisha et al. 2011. 'Indus Script: A Study of its Sign Design'. *SCRIPTA.*

Zand-i Vohuman Yasht. West, E. tr. *The Zend-Avesta, Part I, The Vendidad.* 1880. Translated by James Darmesteter. Oxford University Press.

Zhang, Feng et al. 2007. 'Genetic studies of human diversity in East Asia'. *Philosophical Transactions of the Royal Society. B.*

Zhang, Xiaoming et al. 2015. 'Y-chromosome diversity suggests southern origin and Paleolithic backwave migration of Austro-Asiatic speakers from eastern Asia to the Indian subcontinent'. *Scientific Reports.*

Zhong, Hua et al. 2010. 'Global distribution of Y-chromosome haplogroup C reveals the prehistoric migration routes of African exodus and early settlement in East Asia'. *Journal of Human Genetics.*

Index

Afanasievo culture 195, 211
Africa xv, 12
  dispersals 2, 7, 9, 19, 22–23, 26, 30
  genetic diversity 28
  human origins 13–16
  lithic technology 2, 3, 6, 18–19, 22
  routes out of 2, 23, 24, 26
Agni 103–104, 139, 215, 227, 244, 247
Airyanem Vaejah 218, 224, 271, 285
Akkad 110, 112–114, 118
  The Curse of Akkad 119
Amri 127, 134, 144, 147, 175, 187
  burning 148
Anatolia 64, 81, 111, 122, 194, 216
Andronovo culture 37, 192, 204, 216, 218, 220, 223, 228
  Indo-Iranian cultural traits 201, 220
  innovations 221
Aradvi Sura Anahita 285–287
Arkaim 201–204
arya 101–102, 225, 232,
  admixture 266
  Finno-Ugric loanword 219
  gods 214–215, 263
  mythology 268
  patriarchal society 260–261
  tri-functional ideology 265
  Vedic 235–236
'Aryan' xvi-xvii,
  Darius 231
  identity 270–273, 275
  race 273
aryavarta 243–244, 249–250
  in Vendidad 249, 256
  eastward migration 238, 249, 258
ashmounds 89–90
Attirampakkam 1–2, 15
Avesta 213, 217, 220, 221, 229

Bab al-Mandab 16, 22, 24, 30–32
Bactria–Margiana Archaeological Complex (BMAC) 217–218, 230
Baluchistan 55, 66, 72, 105, 116, 123, 126, 131, 143, 148, 157, 179
Banawali 159, 161, 171–172
Beas (Vipas) 72, 156, 225, 238, 275, 281–282
Bharatas 236, 238, 244
Bhimbetka 98–101
Black Sea 196, 210
Bolan Pass 138, 143, 155, 230, 256
Brahui 74, 83, 167
Bronze Age 42, 191, 206, 220
buffalo 59, 83, 87, 89, 152, 175–176, 179
Burushaski 68–69, 72

Caspian Sea 147, 155, 217
caste 45–46, 56, 178, 258, 271, 273
  Hg R1a1 94
  admixture asymmetry 108–109

cattle
  domestication 52, 59, 83
  economy 74, 83, 88–90, 132, 144–145, 151, 191–193
  gifts 198
  Indo-Iranian 220–221, 224, 261
  sacrifice 202
  slaughter 164, 202
  theft 102, 192, 245
  Yamnaya 212
  wealth 234, 236, 238, 248
Central Asia
  genetic source/ diversity 37, 41, 44, 49, 58, 61, 94, 140,
  Indo-Iranian diaspora 232
  language substrates 69, 226
  trade 121, 133, 136, 147–148, 203
ceramics 90, 115, 122–123, 134, 161, 189
Chalcolithic (Copper) Age 72–74
chariot 201–204, 210, 215, 233, 238, 247–248, 258, 285
Chenchus 56, 94–95, 108
Chogha Mish, burning of 121, 127, 148
Cholistan 133, 149, 156, 182, 185, 277, 282
climate change 11–12, 23, 51, 57, 66, 80, 90, 118, 184, 193–194, 197, 202, 210, 220, 256
  Milankovitch Cycles 12
  Toba effect 6, 8, 18
Corded Ware Culture 197, 212
cupule 100

Daoxian 3, 18
dasas 70, 101–102, 155, 236
  Balbutha Taruska 102, 258
dasyus xvi, 70, 101–102, 236, 271
Dasarajna 236–237
Denisovans 26
Dhofar 3, 25
Dholavira 126, 136, 154, 159–160, 162, 164, 171–175, 184
Dilmun 111, 113–114, 117, 122, 171
  stamp seals 114
DNA *see* genetics
dog/wolf sacrifice 200, 203
domestication plants/animals 81–83
Dravidian place names 73
Drishadvati 72, 164, 235, 279

Elam 54, 112, 116, 120–122, 171
  eelam 66
  seals 125, 167
  trade 127
Elamite
  culture 122
  iconography 125–126, 176, 179–180
  language/script 54, 66, 123–124
endogamy 45, 109, 259–260
Eurasian steppes 191, 197, 200, 219–220, 222, 239, 261, 263, 265
Eurasiatic super-family language 66

food-producers 80
food-gatherers 80
Fertile Crescent 81
  diffusion of wheat 83
  diffusion of herders/farmers 86, 138, 146

domestication of wheat/ barley 51, 132
foragers 77, 79, 86, 88, 92–93, 143, 192
demonisation of 95, 102–103, 106–109
languages 78
traits 77–78, 97

Ganweriwala 135, 162, 164, 172, 182, 184, 277
Gathas 65, 213, 218
genetics
genome 32, 140, 259
definition 291
mutation 28
genetic profiles
Andamans 34, 35–36, 48
Arabia 33–34
Asia 35–36
Australia 36–37
Eurasia 37–38
South Asia *see* South Asia
Ghaggar-Hakra River 131, 133, 143–144, 152, 157–158, 162, 164, 173, 275–283, 288
Gobekli Tepe, xviii, 80–81
Gonds 77, 99, 107
Gonur 140, 217, 222, 229

Haetumant River 224, 285
Hakra Ware 144, 147
Haplogroup (Hg) 28, 291
Haplotype 28, 291
Hapta Hendu 218, 224–225
Harappa city 163–164
Harappa megadrought
8.2 ka event 132, 137, 146
4.2 ka event 118, 137–138, 182–183, 225, 283
Harappa-Mesopotamia-Elam timeline, 128–130
Harappan Civilisation
agriculture 136, 152
bangles 115, 141, 155, 179–181, 188
bricks 86, 149, 159–161, 184–187
citadel 159–160, 162–165, 172
definition 131
discovery 131
extent 132, 150
jewellery 111, 134, 136, 144, 178, 181
mounds 131, 150, 159, 163–164, 170–172, 237, 279–280
phallus worship 126, 263, 266, 270
population 150
sanitation 136, 160
seals *see* seals
shell ornaments 184
shipping 154
sites and areas 168
standardisation 135, 201
time span 150
town planning 121, 149, 153, 158–161
trade 153–155
traits 153, 190
urban traits 158–161
urbanisation 150, 156–158
uniform cultural pattern 158, 170
water transport 156

wheel 154
Zagros influence 145–146
Harappan Eras 132–137
Foraging 132, 143
Early Food Producing 132, 143
Early Harappan 143–148
Transition 149, 152
Mature Harappan *see* Mature Harappan
Late Harappan *see* Late Harappan
Harappan languages 166–168
Harappan mega-urban sites 162–165
Harappans
identity 141–142
literary sources 139
genetic sources 140
Haraxvaiti 218–219, 224, 285–287
Hathnora 8, 100
Helmand 151, 155, 218, 234, 286
Herto 16
Holocene 11, 51, 80, 282
hominid 1, 19–20, 77
definition 291
evolution 13
hominin 1, 2, 5, 8,
brain size 14
definition 291
diet-induced behavioral adaptations 20
earliest Indian fossil 100
genus 14
horse 195, 247, 256
burial 203, 233
domestication 191, 193, 195
earliest evidence in South Asia 233
hunter-gatherers xv, 42, 265
birth rate 92
conflict with farmers 92, 96, 106, 108
economy 52, 63, 77
genetic admixture 56
multiple languages 75, 78

ice age 31, 34, 51, 66
Indo-Aryan speakers 45, 58, 70–71, 73, 76, 102, 109
archaeological evidence 233–234
genetics 94–95
gods *see* Mitanni
horse training *see* Kikkuli
migration 226
Old Indo-Aryan 69, 230
parallels with British colonisation 256–259
Proto-Indo-Aryan 65, 231–232,
Uralic 219
Indo-European languages 38, 66, 83, 205 208
centum-satem classification 208
reconstructing the lexicon 209
vocabulary 64, 199
Indo-European speakers
cow 193–194, 221
lactose tolerance 59, 64
male-dominated society 193, 214, 242
male-dominated migrations 42, 54, 197, 206, 267
war-influenced mythology 199–200, 239

religion 198, 265
Indo-Iranian speakers
Andronovo 201, 204, 218, 220
BMAC 218, 229
borderlands 120–121, 124, 131
cattle economy 220–221
chariot 247
diaspora 232, 239
gods 215
homeland 218–220
language 64, 71, 140, 208, 213, 226
shared rituals 227
split with Indo-Aryan 65, 229–230
Indra 101, 103, 199, 214, 228, 237–240, 243, 256, 258, 264
Indus River 4, 115, 131, 144, 147–148, 152, 154–158
Indus–Sarasvati Civilisation *see* Harappan Civilisation
Indus Valley Civilisation *see* Harappan Civilisation

Jebel Faya 3, 16, 25, 27, 34
Jurreru Valley 1, 4–7, 10, 50

Kachi Plain 143, 147, 172
Kalibangan 159–161, 171–173, 277, 279, 281
*kalpavriksha*s 106
Kansaoya (Hamun) Lake 225
Katoati 3
Kazakhstan 57, 191,
horse domestication 195
Khandava Forest 103, 268
Khasian 68
Kikkuli Text 216–217
Kili Ghul Mohammad 143, 145
Korku 69
Kot Diji 134, 144, 167, 187
burning 127, 175
Krasnosamarskoe 200
kurgans (burial mounds) 196, 208, 211–212
Kurukh 69, 74
Kuruvas 96
Kuru 236, 241, 244–246, 249
Kurukshetra 235, 241, 244, 249, 288–289

lactose tolerance 58–59, 64,
in Yamnaya 194
in Ror community 58
Lahuradewan 87
Last Glacial Maximum 51
Late Harappan
bricks 187
cemeteries 188–190
climatic causes 182
date 182
economic causes 183
population shift 182, 184–185
urban breakdown 184
Levant 10, 16–18, 22–23, 25, 27, 31, 33, 81
Lothal 93, 111, 136, 151, 154, 159, 161, 171, 175, 178, 187
Lucy 13–14

Magan 111, 113–115, 117, 127
Mahabharata 103, 107, 242, 244, 270, 284, 287,
Maharashtra
Dravidian place names 73, 76
Munda speakers 68
isolate languages 69, 107
mahavedi 246–248

Maikop 196
Makran 72, 115–116, 122–123, 126, 133, 136, 148, 151
mannerbunde 199–200, 242
Marine Isotope Stage 3–4
Maruts 101, 199, 237, 239–241, 248, 256, 258, 264, 268
Mature Harappan
  economy in elite dominance 170–171
  fortifications 172
  iconography 180
  ideology in elite dominance 173
  integration 150, 156
  mounds 172
  script 165–169, 177
  seals 167, 174–176, 179–180
  rebuilding of cities 171, 175
  timing 151
  weights and measures 178
Mawmluh Cave 283
Max Muller 271, 273
Mehrgarh 86, 123, 143
  agriculture 82–84, 86, 126, 137, 144
  immigration 44, 126, 132, 138, 147, 233
population ancestry 147
west Asian influence 86, 145
Meluhha 110–111, 115–116
  colony in Mesopotamia 117–118, 154, 167
  in *Enki and the World Order* 117
  language 69, 71, 167
  Meluhhans in Mesopotamia 118
  mercenaries 112–113, 171
  trade 183
Mesopotamia 81, 110–112, 132, 137, 153–154, 196
  mega drought 119, 137, 182
  gods 112–113, 117, 176
  political/socio-economic systems 112
  weights and measures
  Harappan cultural/ trade relations 71, 115, 117, 122, 136, 149, 155, 174
Middle Son Valley 7–9
Mihr Yasht 214
Mitanni 214–216, 229, 232, 235
  Indo-Aryan gods 214–216
  language 216, 226
  Hittite treaty 64, 214
  texts 219
mleccha 71, 73, 155
Mohenjo-daro 131, 162–163, 172–173, 176
  area 184
  broken sculptures 126, 184
  citadel 159
  dancing girl 141
  flood protection 187, 276
  fortifications 171
  Great Bath 159, 162
  pillared hall 160
  priest-king 141
  seals 175
  wells 163
Mount Hara/Meru 219
mtDNA *see* genetic definition
Mundafan 25
Mundigak 144, 151, 155
myth/ mythology xv, xvii, 117, 193–194, 199–200, 219, 242, 245, 251, 265, 267, 274, 285

Narmada 4, 7–8, 72, 105, 151
Neanderthals 18, 20, 27

Neolithic 1, 19, 22, 41–42, 44, 49, 54, 63, 75, 143, 146, 274
nisada 107, 141–142, 265, 289

Oman 83, 111, 136
Omo Kibish 16, 22, 31
Onge 48, 78
Oraons (Kurukhs) 105
Orsang River 8, 19

Palaeolithic 1, 3, 6, 8, 9, 19, 22, 47, 49, 50, 79
pancajanah 106
Papuans 23, 274
pastoralism 54, 59, 74, 86, 88, 86, 119, 146, 152, 191, 210, 217
Pirak 88, 233, 256
polygamy 245
Pontic-Caspian steppe 57–58, 191–193, 195–196, 198, 205, 208, 210, 251, 267
pottery 86, 111, 114–115, 122–123, 132, 138, 143–144, 202–203, 256, 281
  ceramic traditions 122–123, 135, 147, 153, 169, 190
  potter's marks 121, 123–124, 139, 167–168
Pramaganda 236, 289
Punjab 44, 54, 70–71, 76, 84, 95, 184, 207, 214, 218, 225, 230, 238, 277, 283
Purana-Gondwana basins 5

Rajasthan 3, 48, 90, 164, 280
Rakhigarhi 164
Ravi River 156, 162, 225, 236, 237, 275
Rawlinson xv, 267
Red Sea 12, 16, 25, 32
relict population 23, 34–35, 291
Rgveda
  cultural traits 220, 222
  date 214, 230, 235, 289
  Gathas 213
  gods 215–216, 221, 238
  language 64, 71–72, 76, 215, 258
  narratives 101–102
  rivers 238, 283–284, 289
  social mobility 45, 109
  soma 228
rice 76, 87, 220
  cultivation 74, 87, 90, 105, 183
  domestication 87, 136
  spread 87–88
Rift Valley 12–13
river names, pre-Vedic 72
rock art 89, 98–100
Rudra 240–242, 256, 264, 265–266

Sanskrit 63, 66, 127, 204–205, 213, 219–220, 270–271
Sarasvati River 72, 232, 235, 275, 279, 282, 289
  goddess 227, 245, 248
  Haraxvaiti parallels 224, 226, 285–288
  in Rgveda 276, 283–284, 288–290
  pre-vedic name 288
Sargon 110, 112, 116
Satapatha Brahmana 71, 103, 245, 248
seals 167–168, 174
  administrative function 116, 125, 133, 150, 177
  cylinder 111, 114, 123–124

design 116
horned headdress 125
iconography 125–126, 142, 154, 181
master of animals motif 125, 179
number 175
Proto-Dravidian 74
stamp 113–115, 148
symbolic function 125, 176
seashells 24, 144
sesame 83, 114
Shiva 96, 264–266
Sindh 70 74, 76, 162, 167, 184, 187, 230–231, 233
Sintashta 38, 191, 201–204, 206, 213, 247
Skhul-Qafzeh 3, 16, 18, 22–23
soma 101, 227–229, 238, 246–247, 258, 263, 284
South Asian agriculture
Africa 83, 85, 90, 136
China 83, 85, 87, 88, 136, 152
primary domestication 84–91
Southeast Asia 83
west Asia 82–83, 85, 86, 126, 132
South Asian colonisation 40
South Asian gene pool
ancestral groups 43–46
Austro-Asiatics, Tibeto-Burmans 52–53
CE immigrants 59–61
colonisation 40
farmer-herder heritage 41, 51–52
genetic diversity 39
hunter-gatherer heritage 41, 46–52
Iranian farmers, Steppe pastoralists 54–58
mtDNA profile, 40–41, 260–261
Y-chromosome profile 41–43
South Asian languages
Austro-Asiatic 67–68
classification 39, 63
Dardic 65
Dravidian 65–66
Indo-Aryan 64–65
isolates 39, 68–70, 76
Kannada 74, 76
Munda 52. 67–69, 71–72
prefixes 72
Mon-Khmer 52, 68
Malayalam 74
Marathi 69, 73
Nuristani 65, 71, 230, 232, 234
Tamil 66,74
Telugu 74
Tibeto-Burman 68, 72, 75, 78, 83
Southern Coastal Route 25, 31, 34–35, 47
Southern Neolithic Archaeological Complex (SNAC) 66
Srubnaya 200–201, 206
Stone tools 1, 3, 16, 19, 24, 25–26, 89, 202
evolutionary stages 2, 15, 22, 52
tool technology 23, 100
Attirampakkam *see* Attirampakkam
Jurreru Valley 4–6,
Thar 3
microliths 3, 22, 79, 143–144
Middle Son Valley 9
Sudas 70, 235–237

Sumer 110–111, 116, 118, 121–122
Susa 120–122, 124
Sutlej (Sutudri) 72, 156, 275, 278–282
swastika 126, 202
Swat 234, 275

Tajikistan 196, 217
tanks 91
Tell Leilan 138–139
Thar 2, 3, 9, 39 73, 131, 279, 283
  Thar-Deccan corridor 91
Tibetans 36
Tiger 99, 142
  iconography 126, 175–176, 179–180
Toba 1, 3, 5–10, 18, 22–23, 61
Tocharian 208, 211

Ukraine 57, 191, 195, 206–207
unicorn 175–176
Upanishads 242, 284
Ur 110–111, 127, 154, 189
Urals 201, 208, 212–213, 220, 247
Uruk 110–111

vajra 101, 199, 237–239, 246
varnas 106
Varuna 205, 214–216, 248, 265, 284
Vasistha 236, 243, 289
Vendidad 218, 224–225, 249, 256, 285, 288
Videgha Mathava 104, 245
Visvamitra 238, 240, 242–243, 289
Vratyas 199, 239, 241–243, 256

wagon 59, 191, 193, 196–197, 222, 232
west Asia 44–45, 54, 59, 119, 132, 136–138, 145, 175
wheel 64, 209–210, 219
William Jones 270
writing 177, 184, 124–125, 136, 148, 167–168, 173

Y-chromosome *see* genetic definition
Yamnaya 192–194
  Afanasievo 195
  burning of forests 197
  genetics 204, 206–208, 211
  horse 195
  mechanism of spread 197–199, 212
  migrations 38, 54, 57, 212
Yamuna 235–236, 249, 275, 278, 280–282, 288
yattsatra 258
Younger Dryas 146
yupa 139, 246

Zagros 120, 140
  burial traits 86
  drought 138
  genetic admixture 44
  goats 52
  migrations 126, 137
  proto-Dravidian 55
  trade routes 116, 155
Zebu (Bos Indicus) 59, 83, 89, 115, 132, 175
Zend-Avesta 271
Zhirendong 3, 16, 18
Zoroastrianism 61